HISTORY OF TH
YORKSHIRE LIG... INFANTRY

Photo by Catcheside, York

K.O.Y.L.I. MEMORIAL CHAPEL IN YORK MINSTER

Frontispiece

History of The King's Own Yorkshire Light Infantry in the Great War
1914-1918

By

Lt.-Col. Reginald C. Bond, D.S.O.

" *Infandum, regina, jubes renovare dolorem* "
Virgil, Aen. Bk. 2, line 3.

With 13 Illustrations & 14 Maps

VOLUME III

London
Percy Lund, Humphries & Co. Ltd.
Three Amen Corner, E.C.4

Printed by PERCY LUND, HUMPHRIES & CO. LTD.
THE COUNTRY PRESS
BRADFORD

This volume is dedicated
by gracious permission
to

H.R.H. THE DUCHESS OF YORK, G.B.E.
Colonel-in-Chief
The King's Own Yorkshire Light Infantry

FOREWORD

IN our Army the compilation of a Regimental History in suitable form is always a matter of difficulty, owing to the fact that the record of the services of the different battalions in different parts of the world makes a consecutive narrative impossible. This difficulty becomes all the greater when, as was the case in the Great War, the number of battalions is vastly increased. Colonel Bond has successfully overcome this obstacle. He has written a story of absorbing interest which is easy to follow from the point of view of a particular battalion or of the Regiment as a whole. This interest is increased by the delightful English in which the story is presented. The thanks of the Regiment for the time and labour which he has devoted to this successful achievement are gratefully accorded him.

C. P. DEEDES, MAJOR-GENERAL,
COLONEL,
THE KING'S OWN
YORKSHIRE LIGHT INFANTRY.

September, 1929.

PREFACE

THERE are certain outstanding events which have happened in the history of the King's Own Yorkshire Light Infantry since the war, which may rightly be claimed as correlative to the war period and should therefore be alluded to in the preface to this volume. By introducing them now there is no intention to prejudice the interest of any further volume of the history which may be written hereafter.

I refer first of all to the appointment of Her Royal Highness the Duchess of York in 1927 as Colonel-in-Chief of the Regiment, surely the most graceful and touching compliment that any war-scarred regiment could receive, to remind it of the royal promise to his troops made in the address of His Majesty King George V on August 9th, 1914 (which is quoted in full in the volume). The appointment has been loyally acclaimed by the Regiment with genuine feelings of pride and delight.

Next there is the grant by the Dean and Chapter of York Minster of the space in the north transept of the Minster which has been enclosed for use as a memorial chapel by the Regiment. This is the visible recognition by the Church of the sanctity of the aspirations of the soldiers of the Regiment whose lives were given in the war to the service of their country.

A third event to which I make allusion is the approval by His Majesty the King of an alliance between the 51st Battalion Australian Infantry, Australian Military Forces, and the King's Own Yorkshire Light Infantry. This alliance has been effected at the suggestion of the Australian Infantry battalion. The home regiment, indeed, is honoured in its association with the battalion having the magnificent record of the 51st Australian Infantry. The references made to the Australians in this volume will indicate something of the pride and reliance which other troops experienced in association with the Australian troops in the days of the war. The King's Own Yorkshire Light Infantry was already in alliance with the Canadian Militia regiment, the Saskatoon Light Infantry, before the war (then known as the 105th Regiment Saskatoon Fusiliers); so the triangle of its honourable comradeship is now complete.

This third volume of the regimental history is written to repay in some small measure the debt I owe to the Regiment, which was my home for thirty years; it is written with an earnest desire to do honour to the men of all ranks who were impelled, by forces human and divine, to risk death for their country in the Regiment during the Great War.

The majority of the soldiers of the Regiment are miners. Though previously little acquainted with the practice of discipline in any aspect of life, a lad from the pits has an innate sense of loyalty, primitive in its application as by a lad to his mate, but sensitive to leadership and capable of expansion with wider knowledge and higher training. He has, too, a natural fund of good humour and optimism, which induces him to sing his loudest at times when the discomforts of life are most dire and distressing, an unconquerable conviction that a Yorkshireman was not born to be beaten, and a toughness of fibre unsurpassed.

I regret that the generic term "Other ranks" has so frequently to be brought into use; though the names of officers have been given where obtainable, it has often been found impossible to particularise in the case of any but special members of the non-commissioned officer and private soldier ranks. The 9,447 names of those who died in the Great War are included in the regimental Book of Remembrance, laid up in York Minster, where all may read.

The necessity for economising space has compelled the employment of many abbreviations; the abbreviated forms generally used in the case of names of regiments are those in official use at the time of writing; an apology is tendered to regiments who were best known in the days of the war by other familiar names; for the sake of uniformity all have been treated alike.

I take this opportunity to render my sincere thanks to many members of the Regiment, past and present, of all battalions, who have assisted in the work by providing me with material and maps, with criticism and correction of detail, without which the stories of the battles would have been even less complete.

I especially thank General Sir Arthur Wynne for his criticism and encouragement; Major-General C. P. Deedes, who has corrected inaccuracies and supplemented my want of personal knowledge; Colonel H. C. B. Wilson, whose story of the early days of the war I have had the advantage of reading; Major H. E. Yeo, for valuable help connected with the early days of some of the Service battalions; and Colonel H. W. B. Thorp, who has readily assisted from his fund of knowledge.

Also I gratefully acknowledge the advantages I have experienced in having had many fine regimental diaries from which to collect the substance of this record. Outside the official diaries, private diaries, dispatches and official "Military Operations, France and Belgium (1914 and 1915)," the chief wells of information from which I have drawn have been the Encyclopædia Britannica, The British Campaign in France and Flanders (Conan Doyle), My War Memories (Ludendorff), The Fifth Division (Hussey and Inman), and The History of the 62nd W.R. Division (Wyrall).

The chapter on Memorials has been contributed by an officer of the Regiment.

Finally, I think this is the most suitable place in which to record the activities of the association of friends of the Regiment who organised and administered the King's Own Yorkshire Light Infantry War Fund. With a deep sense of gratitude all soldiers of the Regiment, including prisoners-of-war, acknowledged the devoted and unremitting care and solicitude of their friends at home who contributed their time, their energy and their resources to the supply of extra food and comforts to the troops. General Sir Arthur Wynne, G.C.B., Colonel of the Regiment, was Chairman and Hon. Treasurer of the fund; the Committee consisted of Mrs. J. G. Adamson, Mrs. B. Butt and Mrs. R. W. S. Stanton; Miss A. Donaldson was the Hon. Secretary. Out of the surplus funds at the end of the war the sum of £187 12s. 5d. was spent in the issue of 25,155 Commemoration Cards, £500 was granted to the funds of the Regimental Association, while £230 7s. 10d. was added to the Memorial Fund.

R.C.B.

Clare, Suffolk, July 1929.

CONTENTS

LIST OF ILLUSTRATIONS

LIST OF MAPS

The Coloured Maps In This Reprint Are Placed At The End

ABBREVIATIONS

Used in the Volume

Regiments and Corps:

Bays	The Queen's Bays (2nd Dragoon Guards).
Carabiniers	6th Dragoon Guards.
R.A.	Royal Regiment of Artillery.
R.E.	Corps of Royal Engineers.
Gren. Gds.	Grenadier Guards.
Coldm. Gds.	Coldstream Guards.
S. G.	Scots Guards.
I. G.	Irish Guards.
R. S.	The Royal Scots (The Royal Regiment).
Queen's	The Queen's Royal Regiment (West Surrey).
Buffs	The Buffs (East Kent Regiment).
King's Own	The King's Own Royal Regiment (Lancaster).
N. F.	The Northumberland Fusiliers.
Warwick	The Royal Warwickshire Regiment.
R. F.	The Royal Fusiliers (City of London Regiment).
Kings	The King's Regiment (Liverpool).
Lincolns	The Lincolnshire Regiment.
Devon	The Devonshire Regiment.
Suffolk	The Suffolk Regiment.
Som. L.I.	The Somerset Light Infantry (Prince Albert's).
W. Yorks.	The West Yorkshire Regiment (The Prince of Wales' Own).
E. Yorks.	The East Yorkshire Regiment.
Bedfs. Herts.	The Bedfordshire and Hertfordshire Regiment.
Leicesters	The Leicestershire Regiment.
Green Howards	The Green Howards (Alexandra, Princess of Wales' Own Yorkshire Regiment).
L. F.	The Lancashire Fusiliers.
R. S. F.	The Royal Scots Fusiliers.
Cheshire	The Cheshire Regiment.
R. W. F.	The Royal Welsh Fusiliers.
S. W. B.	The South Wales Borderers.
K. O. S. B.	The King's Own Scottish Borderers.
Inniskg.	The Royal Inniskilling Fusiliers.
Glosters	The Gloucestershire Regiment.
Worc. R.	The Worcestershire Regiment.
E. Lan. R.	The East Lancashire Regiment.
Surreys	The East Surrey Regiment.
D. C. L. I.	The Duke of Cornwall's Light Infantry.
D. W. R.	The Duke of Wellington's Regiment (West Riding).
Border	The Border Regiment.
R. Sussex	The Royal Sussex Regiment.

ABBREVIATIONS—*cont.*

Regiments and Corps:

Hamps.	The Hampshire Regiment.
S. Staffords	The South Staffordshire Regiment.
Dorset	The Dorsetshire Regiment.
P. W. V.	The Prince of Wales' Volunteers (South Lancashire).
Welch	The Welch Regiment.
Oxf. Bucks.	The Oxfordshire and Buckinghamshire Light Infantry.
Essex	The Essex Regiment.
Foresters	The Sherwood Foresters (Nottinghamshire and Derbyshire Regiment).
Loyals	The Loyal Regiment (North Lancashire).
R. W. K.	The Queen's Own Royal West Kent Regiment.
K.O.Y.L.I.	The King's Own Yorkshire Light Infantry.
K.S.L.I.	The King's Shropshire Light Infantry.
Mx.	The Middlesex Regiment (Duke of Cambridge's Own).
K.R.R.C.	The King's Royal Rifle Corps.
Wilts.	The Wiltshire Regiment (Duke of Edinburgh's).
Manch.	The Manchester Regiment.
N. Staffs.	The North Staffordshire Regiment (The Prince of Wales').
Y. & L.	The York and Lancaster Regiment.
D.L.I.	The Durham Light Infantry.
H.L.I.	The Highland Light Infantry (City of Glasgow Regiment).
Gordons	The Gordon Highlanders.
Camerons	The Queen's Own Cameron Highlanders.
R.U.R.	The Royal Ulster Rifles.
R. Ir. F.	The Royal Irish Fusiliers (Princess Victoria's).
A. & S. H.	The Argyll and Sutherland Highlanders (Princess Louise's).
R. B.	The Rifle Brigade.
R. Tanks	Royal Tank Corps.
R.A.S.C.	Royal Army Service Corps.
R.A.M.C.	Royal Army Medical Corps.
R.A.O.C.	Royal Army Ordnance Corps.
Yorks. D.	The Yorkshire Dragoons (Queen's Own).
9 London	9th London Regiment (Queen Victoria's Rifles).
12 London	12th London Regiment (Rangers).
14 London	14th London Regiment (London Scottish).
Hallams	The Hallamshire Battalions, York and Lancaster Regiment, *i.e.*, the 4/Y. & L. and the 2/4th Y. & L.

INTRODUCTION

THE order of the 4th August, 1914, to "Mobilise," issued from the War Office to the British Army in all parts of the Empire, was the signal that preceded the Army's entrance upon the world's stage in the Great War of 1914-1918.

The signal discovered each of the five battalions of the K.O.Y.L.I. intent on rehearsals of its part.

The command of the 1st Bn. at Singapore was temporarily vested in Maj. W. M. Withycombe, for Lt.-Col. A. G. Marrable was in England on leave. For two months the senior battalion was destined to stand fast, hardly content with the responsibilities connected with its duties in guarding the Straits, and supporting existence on the meagre telegrams which reached it from the far west.

The 2nd Bn. was in Dublin, bound, owing to its place in the Expeditionary Force, to be the first unit to represent the Regiment in the field of action.

The 3rd Bn., undergoing training at Strensall Camp, was moved into Pontefract at the precautionary signal. Actually in harness as it was at the time, it was to remain in close and inseparable connection with the regimental depot throughout the war, and so to continue as a unit while training and supplying new and renewed material for the battalions at the front.

The 4th and 5th Bns. were in camp at Whitby with their Territorial Infantry Brigade at annual training. The order to them to "Mobilise" was conveyed at the same time and in precisely the same characters as the order to the regular battalions of the line, nor were they kept in suspense as to the reality of the call for sacrifice and devotion, to which they were so eagerly prepared to respond.

In order to preserve the chronological sequence of events in this history of the Regiment in the war, it will be necessary to present the 2nd Bn. in the first scene.

The ten months spent in Portobello Barracks at Dublin had been as trying and unsatisfactory a period as any that that battalion had hitherto experienced in its history. Throughout the time every available man had been employed on picket duty, chiefly in guarding the tram termini. Dublin was seething with unrest. It was unsafe for soldiers to walk alone in many parts of the city. Political rancour was at its height. One sensational incident followed another. Gunrunning, seditious meetings, mobbing of soldiers, were everyday occurrences. Ulster was an armed camp; the other provinces were in a frenzy of excitement. Picket duty near some improvised guardroom, a monotonous service only enlivened as a rule by the routine of daily inspections, was varied by detachment duty to Ulster or elsewhere. Thus Carrickfergus Castle was occupied by "D" Company under Maj. J. B. G. Tulloch, having been secretly transported thither one night in March in one of H.M.'s ships of war; it remained there until the date of mobilisation. There was not even the relief which battalion or brigade training might have afforded. Orders for training were no sooner issued than they had to be cancelled; all was uncertainty and discomfort. Had it been in an enemy country the trials would have been considered to be all in the day's run, and no one would have thought of repining, but of all uncongenial duties that of policing Ireland during one of her periodical fits of political unrest and agitation, and of actively participating, to the possible point of having to shoot down civilians, is the most repugnant to the English soldier's mind.

Lt.-Col. Wells-Cole's last illness had been not a little aggravated by the mental anxiety of those days of March; they had been days of distracting difficulties. The Government appeared to be obsessed with the Irish question, and were suspected in some quarters of being blind to the urgency of affairs on the continent of Europe. Be that as it may, it was exactly such blindness that Germany was counting on to keep Great Britain out of the war. But Germany's calculations, so carefully based on material facts, had happily a habit of failing through misjudgment of the human factor. So the shock that the Central Powers gave to the world, so far from intensifying the preoccupation of British statesmen, and confirming them in their absorption in domestic politics, rather opened men's eyes and shook them rudely into action.

The Irish question took second place. It was with a sigh of relief that soldiers in Ireland turned from the sorry spectacle of Irish disunion to take part in the unfathomed horrors of a world-wide war.

The order for mobilisation was followed on the morning of the 5th August by the official notification that war had broken out with Germany.

The 2nd Bn. required 7 officers, 19 sergeants and 596 rank and file to complete establishment for war service.

Photo by Chancellor & Son, Dublin

The 2nd Battalion returning to barracks from a route march the day of the Declaration of War

To face page 715.

MONS AND LE CATEAU. 1914

I

THE mobilisation of the 2/K.O.Y.L.I. was carried through with one slight hitch only: six sets of heavy draught harness went astray; Guinness' Brewery at once undertook to supply the deficiency. The reservists answered their call to the colours like one man, and the drafts to make up the fighting strength of the battalion were received from the depot at Pontefract in accordance with the time-table.

Meanwhile at Pontefract the organisation of a new Service battalion was proceeded with at once, and on the 7th August Capt. J. E. Munby, Lt. T. E. F. Penny, and 2/Lt. W. N. Tempest, with six N.C.O.s, left Dublin for the depot for duty with the new unit, and a further party of twenty N.C.O.s, including seven for the new unit, left on the following day for the same destination. These formed the nucleus of the new 6th Bn.

The 2nd Bn. required several officers to complete the establishment. Maj. C. A. L. Yate, recently summoned to the War Office to take up a staff appointment, was permitted to rejoin the battalion as senior major a few days before embarkation. Lt. B. N. Denison also, who had just completed his course at the Staff College, applied, and was permitted, to join. Other vacancies were made good by the arrival for attachment of Capt. R. S. Ledgard, 1/Green Howards on the 12th, and of Lt. J. B. L. Noel and 2/Lt. H. J. Hardiman, both of the 2/E. York., on the 13th.

The list of the officers who sailed with the 2nd Bn. to France in the original Expeditionary Force was as follows: Lt.-Col. R. C. Bond. Majs. C. A. L. Yate; H. E. Trevor; C. E. Heathcote. Capts. L. Simpson; C. H. Ackroyd (Adjutant); A. C. G. Luther; A. R. Keppel; J. E. Simpson; W. E. Gatacre. Lts. B. N. Denison; C. H. Rawdon; W. H. de W. Unett; W. d' E. Williams; T. Reynolds; G. C. Wynne; C. E. D. King; C. Helm, R.A.M.C. (attached); H. L. Slingsby (attd. from 3rd Bn.). 2/Lts. J. Pepys; J. B. Noel; T. B. Butt; H. B. Hibbert; and A. F. Ritchie. Lt. and Qr.-Mr. A. E. Bentham, and the three attached officers named above in the preceding paragraph.

The 13th Inf. Bde. (Brig.-Gen. G. J. Cuthbert, Commanding) formed part of the 5th Div. (Maj.-Gen. Sir Charles Fergusson) and of the II Corps (Gen. Sir Horace Smith-Dorrien[1]). It consisted of the 2nd Bn. King's Own Scottish Borderers, the 2nd Bn. Duke of

[1] *After the death of General Sir J. Grierson.*

Wellington's (West Riding), 1st Bn. Queen's Own Royal West Kent Regiment, and 2nd Bn. King's Own Yorkshire Light Infantry.

On the 12th August all posts held by the 2/K.O.Y.L.I. in area 3, Dublin Defence Scheme, were relieved by the unfits and by Dublin cadets.

After a slight delay caused by the refitting of the necessary transports for their new duties, the battalion embarked in the *S.S. Buteshire* at the North Wall, Dublin, at 5 p.m. on the 14th, and the ship was under way at 7 p.m. The remainder of the 13th Inf. Bde. with the Bde. Headquarters had preceded the battalion. The 2/Manch., of the 14th Inf. Bde., also sailed in the *S.S. Buteshire*.

Quite an unexpectedly hearty send-off was accorded to the men in the streets of the city on the march down to the ship, and when the vessel left her moorings it was the signal for a true riverside chorus of sirens and hooters.

The passage was a slow one, especially after joining a stately procession of transports off Land's End, in which the pace was set by the slowest ship of the convoy. The destination, Le Havre, was only disclosed on arrival off the French coast on the evening of Sunday the 16th.

The historic messages of His Majesty The King and of Lord Kitchener[1] were read to the troops on board. Off the Channel Islands six French submarines and a dreadnought were sighted. Shortly afterwards the transport was forced to lie to while it was overtaken by a French torpedo-boat, whose crew, after an interchange of messages, parted with a hearty cheer. These visible signs of protection brought the reality of the business in hand home to the voyagers. The sight of Land's End, standing out rugged in an angry sky, was the last bit of England that many on board were destined ever to see. It was a sight that kindled in the heart the sense of romantic enterprise which the secrecy of the departure and the pride of participation in a great adventure had already engendered. It was well understood that the censorship would see to it that no account of the sailing of the troops from Ireland would be broadcast in the English homes.

The disembarkation commenced on Sunday night at 11 p.m. and proceeded for some time into the night owing to certain structural difficulties having to be overcome, which interfered with the proper working of the cranes. Those not on duty meantime got all the sleep they could in a huge shed by the quay. One quayside is very like another. But for the fact that the few dock workers on the wharf spoke in a foreign tongue there was not much to strike the imagination of soldiers who were setting foot in France for the first time in their lives. Conversation with the strangers was fitful, if hearty, and apparently consisted mainly of tender enquiries after the health of the popular champion, Georges Carpentier (the name being quite

[1] *Vide end of Chapter I.*

unrecognisable in its Anglicised version) on the one hand, and the courteous reply "*Vivent les Anglais*" on the other. The following day the train that was to carry the battalion to the front, left the railway station at 6.30 p.m. Col. R. C. Money, late commanding the 1st Bn., now Camp Commandant at Le Havre, came to the train to see the battalion off.

The journey *via* Rouen, Amiens and Busigny was slow. Every bridge and culvert had its picket of *gardes civiles*; every cottage its waving flags of friendly greeting. So the train moved steadily forward through the battlefields of the near future.

On arrival at Landrécies at midday on the 18th, Capt. Hon. E. P. J. Stourton, who had recently left the battalion for the Staff College, was on the platform to receive the train and to direct the battalion to Maroilles, where it joined up with the 13th Inf. Bde. the same evening. In the absence of the band instruments, which were not taken on active service, the place of the regimental band was taken by the buglers. Since the South African War the buglers had carried key-bugles of the Italian Bersaglieri pattern in addition to the ordinary bugle of the government issue. Some of these bugles had been presented by Count Roberto Zileri dal Verme, who had been attached to the battalion during the South African War and had won an honorary D.S.O. in the early fighting. Both sets of bugles were taken to France and were placed at the head of the column, drawing many of the inhabitants to the roadside. The buglers were the objects of many flattering attentions, and received presents and garlands of flowers.

Billets were in the village, and the section of the outpost line taken over lay north and north-east of Maroilles overlooking the river Sambre, and had the great forest of Mormal stretching across its front.

On the 20th August Maj.-Gen. Sir Charles Fergusson addressed each of the battalions in his division in turn in stirring words. He made use of this expression: "*There must be no surrender, men must fight to the last, with their fists if their rifles are useless; this will be a war of self-sacrifice; possibly whole battalions, even brigades, may have to be sacrificed in order to make it good for others.*"

On the 21st a forward move was made and the first day's march was through Bavai to the outpost line Houdain-Taisnières. The latter place overlooked the old battlefield of Malplaquet, the historic associations of the place appealing strongly to at least one subaltern whose platoon was on outpost duty there that night.

Next morning the Belgian frontier was crossed at 9 a.m., and the battalion, after marching through the densely crowded streets of the mining villages, reached Boussu, where they occupied the buildings of a large brewery close to the station.

The 13th Inf. Bde. was ordered to hold the line of the Mons-Condé Canal from Les Herbières to Mariette on the right, with two battalions on outpost duty on a three-mile front. Reports from cavalry patrols and air observation indicated the presence of considerable bodies of the enemy of all arms, and in the evening news arrived that the French line had been forced to retire a considerable distance, except their left, which was separated from our right by a gap of about 9 miles. The 2/R.W.K. was on the right with the 2/D.W.R. in immediate support; the 2/K.O.S.B. on the left with the K.O.Y.L.I. in support. The K.O.Y.L.I., however, were represented in the front line by their Machine-Gun Detachment under Lt. J. Pepys in a position between the two forward battalions. East of Mariette came the 9th Inf. Bde. of the 3rd Div.

In the course of the morning of Sunday the 23rd August covering parties of infantry who had been pushed across the canal to the north were in contact with German infantry, and about 9 a.m. the attack opened on that part of the line held by the 8th Inf. Bde. of the 3rd Div., about 6 miles to the east, where they were well held. The attack gradually extended westward. Beyond the 13th Inf. Bde. to the westward the 14th Inf. Bde. held the left of the British line on the canal bank.

As the K.O.Y.L.I. men were about to eat their dinners at midday, shells from a German field battery commenced to fall round the brewery. One man was hit; dinners were hurried through and the battalion took up its position in close support of the 2/K.O.S.B.

About 1 p.m. the German attack developed along the whole front, the German infantry working forward to occupy positions closer to the canal by wading up the wet ditches which branched from the canal. The defenders were soon heavily engaged throughout the length of the position. The K.O.Y.L.I. Machine-Gun Detachment withheld their fire from their concealed position in the bank of the canal until German infantry in force attempted to rush the crossing of a bridge by St. Ghislain. By the deadly accuracy of their fire the machine-gunners supported the defenders of the bridge, and the attempt was frustrated. The attack was made by the Brandenberg Grenadier Regiment, covered by strong artillery fire, whose losses were so great, according to a German account, that the regiment was reduced to a mere wreck. Unfortunately, while taking observations of the enemy immediately after the attack rolled back, Lt. Pepys, the commander of the detachment, was killed by a rifle bullet from the trees near the opposite bank. Lt. Denison was sent forward to take his place.

About 2.30 p.m. one platoon of "C" Company reinforced the firing line of the 2/K.O.S.B., taking position near the machine-guns. At about the same time written instructions were received from

Brig-Gen. Cuthbert for the occupation of a position in rear by Wasmes in the event of a general retirement.

German infantry attacks were succeeded once more by heavy shell-fire. The 2/K.O.S.B. sustained many casualties and at about 6 p.m. were forced to abandon their bridge-head on the north bank of the canal, doing as much damage as they could to the Herbières railway bridge in their withdrawal.

Between 6 and 7 p.m. the positions along the bank held by the 2/K.O.S.B. were taken over altogether by the 2/K.O.Y.L.I., while the K.O.S.B. Bn. retired to the railway crossing previously occupied by the K.O.Y.L.I. in support. Owing to the withdrawal of the 14th Inf. Bde. too, in accordance with their orders, the left of the 2/K.O.Y.L.I. was in the air, so that the supporting companies "B" and "A" had to extend across the railway embankment and watch the exposed flank. From right to left the position was accordingly held by the machine-guns, "C", "D," "B" and "A" Companies in that order. Pending the arrival of "A" and "B" Companies to defend the railway bridge the O.C. the East Surrey Bn. left his machine-gun detachment in position to support the flank of the 13th Inf. Bde.

Attempts had already been made to destroy both this bridge and the lock gates which were within the position by Les Herbières, but the destruction had been only partial, and the troops defending this part of the line received a heavy pounding at the hands of the enemy artillery while daylight lasted.

It seemed certain that the Germans would attempt to rush the crossings under cover of darkness or that they would cross further west to turn the flank of the division. The actual order to the K.O.Y.L.I. to retire to the prearranged position by Wasmes was not received till after 10 p.m. Meanwhile the small woods on the northern bank of the canal, in which the enemy could collect before rushing the bridges, were carefully searched from time to time with bursts of rifle-fire along the bank. The effect of this firing was made known to the prisoners-of-war in Torgau later in the year when they were visited by the Lt.-Col. of a German infantry regiment who had been wounded; when visiting them he spoke of the great losses sustained by his regiment in the fight for the Mons canal on the 23rd August, particularly after dark. He said that some battalions were concentrating in a little wood prior to a rush to cross the bridge at Herbières; that the British troops had apparently discovered the concentration and poured such a deadly fire into the wood that the place was turned into a shambles and the battalions had to be withdrawn.

A number of Belgian refugees came over the half-broken bridge, among them a voluble young priest with a tale of the retirement of the Germans away to the north. There was a suspicious calm in the enemy's position, and German bugles had been sounding further and further away. The priest's story was not believed; fire was still opened at intervals into the belt of trees. Suddenly the position held by the defenders became lit up by the white light from enemy rockets and the suspicion that the enemy was lying low on the far side was confirmed. When the time came for the 2/K.O.Y.L.I. to withdraw, the movement had to be carried out with the utmost caution. The front was a long one and the section farthest on the right could only be approached after crossing several wet dykes behind the line. Capt. Luther with "C" Company remained almost till midnight as rearguard until he was satisfied that the retirement was completed.

The machine-gun detachment was the last to be withdrawn; the men brought back the body of their officer, Lt. Pepys, and buried him at dawn on the outskirts of Wasmes. The battalion concentrated at the level crossing and then marched on towards the new position, resting for 2½ hours in the pitch-dark night in a cornfield. The march into Wasmes was resumed before daylight.

All through the night the countryside to the east and north-east was a blaze of light where villages were in flames, and before the battalion could discover the new position in the line (for the officer sent on ahead to be their guide had lost his way) the German guns were again in action and our batteries were hastening to take up positions from which to reply.

No Germans crossed the canal in this section of the front during the night, although they were in great numbers on the northern bank. Owing to the darkness one small party of "D" Company under Sgts. Mullins and Walker, was left behind asleep in the village of Les Herbières. At dawn, in total ignorance of the retirement of the battalion, this party observed German patrols crossing the canal by the bridge and canal lock, followed by columns of infantry. With all speed they took to the road and eventually made good their junction with the battalion. Other German columns during the night had crossed the canal to the east and west.

By 6 a.m. on the 24th the K.O.Y.L.I., whose position was shown to them by the Brigadier's Staff Officer, were holding a section of the new front; "A" and "B" Companies were in the front line, the other two companies in support. Away to their right, but separated from view by a huge group of railway buildings, were the D.W.R. The gap which existed was filled later by the arrival of part of the R.W.K. Bn. The position for occupation had been partially prepared with trenches by the 15th Inf. Bde., who handed them over to the 2/K.O.Y.L.I. on their approach. The fight was still in the artillery stage on this portion of the front when orders were received to prepare for retirement to Bavai, but opposite to the D.W.R., who held a salient rather in advance, German infantry, after a very heavy shelling, deployed to the attack and that battalion suffered very heavily. The 14th Inf. Bde., too, to the left of the 13th was violently attacked.

German infantry were extending to attack the position held by "A" and "B" Companies at this time when the order came to put into operation the withdrawal towards the road to Bavai. The withdrawal was conducted with the greatest care (and most reluctantly) and the companies came away unperceived, while the position of the supporting companies received a severe shelling. At about 1 p.m. the 2/K.O.Y.L.I. was extended to cover the approaches to the Bavai road close to the guns of Maj. Ballard's field battery. Here, orders for a renewal of the retirement were received and the 13th Inf. Bde. withdrew down the road, covered for some distance by the remnants of the D.W.R. on the right and by the K.O.Y.L.I. on the left. A long and tedious march ensued, after other troops had taken up the duty of rearguard, for the heat of the sun was distressing and the road was often blocked with vehicles, while the enemy was pressing hotly; the fighting on the northern side was close to the line of march and very concentrated. It was in the rearguard fighting this day that the battalion witnessed the splendid stand of some of the batteries of the 5th Div., especially of the 121st Field Battery, commanded by Maj. C. N. B. Ballard and of the 37th Howitzer Battery under Maj. Eustace Jones. There were thrilling episodes when the time came for the retirement of some of the guns.

During one of the checks on the road the K.O.Y.L.I. column was waiting for some field ambulances to move on. In one of these there was a wounded German cavalry officer. An officer at the head of the infantry column spoke to this German officer and expressed a hope that he was being well attended to. "*Too well,*" was the answer in English, "*My fear is that your people won't be so well treated in similar case.*"

That night the 13th Inf. Bde. bivouacked in a field 1½ miles west of Bavai. A roll of the 2/K.O.Y.L.I. was called and it was found that up to that time one officer had been killed, while twenty-seven other ranks failed to answer their names.

Next morning, the 25th August, at 3.15 a.m. the battalion continued the retreat, moving down the Roman road and arrived at Le Cateau, the destination, in the middle of the afternoon. It had been a trying march under a blazing sun. There had been a check on the road outside the town while six French cavalry regiments and a cycle corps of Gen. Sordet's command filed across the road in front of them. This was a welcome sight to troops who were weary from the severe marching and constant excitement of the last few days. The news of the arrival of the 4th Div. from England and of its position on the left of the line was welcome also and men looked forward eagerly to a night's rest and food. It was the hope that they were now in the chosen position and that the miserable retirements were at an end.

It rained in the evening and during the night. The battalion train transport, which had been separated since the 23rd, had joined up on the march and the men got a meal in the evening; the iron (emergency) rations had been eaten the night before at Bavai.

Maj. Heathcote's company ("A") was sent out during the night on outpost duty. At 2.35 a.m. came orders for a renewed retirement. The K.O.S.B. and K.O.Y.L.I. were to be rearguard. It was calculated that the divisional transport would not be clear before 11 a.m., until which hour the rearguard troops must hold their positions. It was dark when the battalion moved forward to find their ground. The front allotted stretched to north and south of the Bavai-Reumont road. "C" Company under Capt. Luther was at first destined for the southern portion, while the northern half was given to "D" Company under Maj. Trevor. That to the south consisted of a ridge with the little town of Le Cateau lying under its further slope; the top of the church spire could be seen beyond the ridge from many parts of the battlefield. The town lies in a valley, the slope into the valley being convex in places, very favourable to troops advancing to attack the ridge.

No trenches had been dug on this side of the road. The little entrenching tools, carried in his field equipment by each man, were the only tools available.

The road leading from Le Cateau to Cambrai, edged with poplar trees, cuts the main road from Bavai at right angles. It ran parallel to the general front of the division from 400 to 600 yards from the front trenches. Owing to undulations the road disappears into cuttings, and the enemy had natural infantry positions within short range to which he could approach under cover when once the town was in his hands.

The holding of the ridge was a task far beyond the powers of a single company of infantry, and it was not surprising that with the light of day two battalions of the 14th Inf. Bde., the 2/Suffolk and the 2/Manch. were assigned to the position, while "C" Company was withdrawn and sent across to support the left of the line of the 2/K.O.Y.L.I.

The position to be held by "D" Company was marked by half-dug trenches, not continuous but sited in parallel straight lengths at intervals, some 400 yards from the line of poplars that marked the Cambrai road. To the left of "D" Company came "A," who had been on outpost and were now concentrated to prolong the line towards the right of the K.O.S.B. The ground fell away on the left of "A" Company and rose again where the K.O.S.B. were entrenched. Beyond the K.O.S.B. came the 3rd Div.; further still to the north-west was the newly-arrived 4th Div.

The 14th Inf. Bde. held the extreme right of the battle line, for the British I Corps, centred on St. Quentin, was out of touch and out of reach.

At the same time that "C" Company was being withdrawn from the ridge, Brig.-Gen. Cuthbert directed that a company should entrench itself alongside the Bavai-Reumont road, facing south-east, in order to defilade the front now held by the battalion of the Manchester Regiment, for there was hollow ground to their front which was covered from their view. Maj. Yate with "B" Company took over this duty; they had just commenced to prepare some form of cover on the crest of the rise behind "D" Company as battalion reserve. Thus "B" Company was now at right angles to the line held by "D" and it linked up the right of "D," where Lt. G. C. Wynne's platoon was in position, with the left of the 14th Inf. Bde. which was echeloned back on the right of the 2/K.O.Y.L.I.

The arrival of the field batteries of the 5th Div. complicated matters for the infantry, for the batteries took up positions within the line of the infantry supports; the teams and limbers of the 28th Bde. R.F.A., packed in a sunken road which ran diagonally from Le Cateau to Troisvilles, severed communication between portions of the K.O.Y.L.I. battalion.

The battalion machine-gun detachment was commanded for the day by Lt. Unett, who was really brigade machine-gun officer, but he asked for, and was accorded, permission to fight his battalion guns in the rearguard battle. He found a most useful position south of the right flank of "B" Company. Lce.-Cpl. King and Pte. H. Mitchell distinguished themselves by digging the pits for the guns under shrapnel fire. Lt. C. H. Rawdon, who was acting transport officer, having seen his charges safely away, volunteered and served in the trenches also.

The Bn. Headquarters had been established by the side of the Bavai-Reumont road to the right of the cover originally made by "B" Company, whose position was now occupied by one platoon of "C" Company under Lt. W. d'E. Williams. Here the battalion travelling cooker issued tea for all ranks in the early morning, the provision of a devoted Quartermaster, Lt. A. E. Bentham, who never neglected an opportunity, when it was possible, to feed the men.

The whole position of the battalion had a front of three companies; the supports of "B" Company were entrenched immediately behind their firing line, the latter being in front of the south bank of the road, the former in the ditch on the north side; they thus formed two tiers of fire. A culvert under the road was used as a channel of communication between the two firing lines; the supports of "D" Company were 200 yards behind their firing line, with a turnip field separating them; those of "A" Company were relatively in the same position, while three platoons of "C" Company were behind the left flank of "A," disposed in the open but in sunken ground, between the guns of the 122nd and 123rd Batteries. There was no opportunity to dig trenches for these supports. A hundred yards or so in rear of the 2/K.O.Y.L.I. reserve the R.W.K. Bn. was entrenched as brigade reserve.

About 6 a.m. the Brig.-Gen., whose headquarters were established in the sunken road leading to Troisvilles sent the following message to the O.C., 2/K.O.Y.L.I.:

"*Orders have been changed. There will now be NO retirement for the fighting troops; fill up your trenches with water, food and ammunition, as far as you can.*" Messengers were sent with copies of this order to the companies and the order was personally communicated by the O.C. Bn. to Maj. Yate in the trenches; further action was taken on it by sending back for the battalion ammunition reserve, which was dumped from the carts on the ground alongside the Bn. Headquarters, the teams being brought up at a canter and the carts offloaded in the shortest possible time, for the German batteries were already beginning to find their ranges on all visible objects. The boxes of ammunition were distributed by the buglers to the companies within reach. The ground was rapidly cleared for action before the oncoming storm of shell.

The order for "*No retirement*" was confirmed by Colonel Romer[1] of the II Corps Headquarters Staff, who rode up to 2/K.O.Y.L.I. Headquarters and repeated it.

The Adjutant, Capt. C. H. Ackroyd, riding back from the left flank, drew the enemy's rifle-fire, a fact that showed that his patrols at any rate were already in a position to overlook the nearer portions of our field of defence. This was as a puff of wind that precedes a storm. Within a few minutes the air was being torn and ripped by the whistling shells; inter-communication had become impossible; telephone wires were rent and scattered; a tornado of shrapnel and high-explosives burst over and around our guns. The weak spots of a position taken up in a half-light, and only half prepared, were soon only too apparent.

The little town of Le Cateau had been in the enemy's hands since the small hours. He had command of all the covered ways to our position; there was dead ground everywhere to cover his infantry in their approach, and there were commanding positions for his guns. The ridge held by the 2/Suffolk was raked by fire. Men lying

[1] *Now Lt.-Gen. Sir C. F. Romer, K.B.E., C.B., C.M.G.*

in their shallow trenches, which faced generally south-east, were caught in enfilade by rifle-fire from the north-east, where German machine-gunners soon established themselves in the crest of the cutting where the road to Cambrai ran. Batteries plastered the ground with shrapnel where the 2/Suffolk, the 15th Bde. R.F.A., and the 37th Howitzer Battery were in position, and the shelling came from south-east, east and north-east. It was soon obvious that the first concentration for attack was being made on this section of the defence.

Two battalions of the 14th Inf. Bde., cut off from the division the far side of Le Cateau, after maintaining for a time a fight against odds, gave ground and passed round the right flank of the position. They were followed up by German infantry, whose close formations had been viewed as they issued from the cover of woods some miles to the east of Le Cateau, and these formations were then lost to view in the valley by the town. Their presence was later felt when the ridge was attacked. Some of these troops moved on past the flank till they came into contact with the 2nd Bn. Argyll and Sutherland Highlanders, who, with other battalions of the 19th Inf. Bde., were posted in rear of the 14th Inf. Bde. to support the right flank. It was about 11 a.m. when the 2/A. and S.H. moved forward into closer support and into the trenches of the Suffolks. The Suffolks were attacked from front and right flank, but were not finally overwhelmed in their trenches till late in the battle. The fight for the ridge was watched anxiously by the K.O.Y.L.I., who saw it in the hands of the Germans and again in the hands of the Suffolks. The 2/Manch. made a counter-attack past the left of the Suffolks down into the low ground towards Le Cateau in order to relieve the pressure; they could not penetrate far, for the low ground was strongly held and wooded in places; the ground was strewn with their dead and wounded.

"B" Company K.O.Y.L.I. had not been called upon hitherto to fire a shot, and their commander was careful not to disclose his position in the roadside prematurely, but about 11 a.m. Maj. Yate had the target he had waited for, and opened fire. From that time forward the company were constantly engaged.

"D" Company had been engaged from a much earlier hour in holding off frontal attacks, and in bringing a diagonal fire to bear on the place where the Germans were holding the top of the cutting through which ran the road to Cambrai. Lt. Wynne with his platoon was at the most exposed salient, his right thrown back towards "B" Company, from which he was distant some 250 yards.

The remainder of the battalion was heavily engaged along its front. The enemy in front of the K.O.S.B. position shortly after 11 a.m. established themselves on the rise in the ground on the near side of the Cambrai road, and thus were able to enfilade some of the trenches of the K.O.Y.L.I. The extreme left section of "A" Company, under Sgt. Marchant, time after time by its fire threw back a German machine-gun detachment which was attempting to bring forward its guns to enfilade the line, but it could not prevent the occupation of the ground by the enemy infantry.

Until shortly after midday the enemy's main bombardment was directed against our field artillery batteries, whom they far outnumbered, while the number of our guns that were able to reply steadily diminished. It was a day of self-sacrifice; as long as there were men left and guns to be fired some reply was made. The occupation by the enemy of the eastern portion of the ridge that was still held by the Suffolks occasioned further heavy losses to our artillery, who were taken in enfilade.

About 12.45, an order, apparently, was given to retire any gun that could be moved of the batteries in the centre sector of the 5th Div. front. The movement of the gun-teams, or of what remained of them, was the signal for a perfect hailstorm of projectiles. Two guns only of the three batteries in the K.O.Y.L.I. sector were seen to be brought out; the rest remained on their ground silent, with their detachments lying round them. Then there was a lull for nearly half-an-hour; the rattle of musketry was still incessant, but the sudden silence on the part of the enemy guns, with the absence of shell-bursts, was most impressive. The bombardment was renewed. The shelling and rifle-fire were now directed exclusively on the infantry trenches, the enemy infantry gradually working forward and gaining ground on the ridge by Le Cateau.

The K.O.Y.L.I. machine-guns had opened fire about 8.30 a.m. and remained in action till about 2.30 p.m. By this time one of the two guns had been knocked out and Sgt. Nunn and several men had been wounded. With difficulty the remaining gun was carried into one of the trenches of "B" Company, where it was finally broken up. Lt. Unett joined Bn. Headquarters in the trench hard by.

Following the artillery preparation in the afternoon there advanced over the ridge to the east of the position held by the Suffolks, two battalions of Germans in close formation. The range to the ridge was 600 yards. The fire from "B" Company was withheld until the masses were well down the forward slope, then 'rapid' was opened from both tiers of fire. There was a moment of confusion, hesitation, and the masses rolled back and disappeared from view, leaving the ground strewn with men.

At a time when the casualties in "D" Company were known to be heavy and the forward platoons were running short of ammunition, Capt. L. Simpson led a reinforcement from the company supports into the trenches under a heavy fire; he was wounded in getting there.

Further to the left at about 1.30 p.m. Lt. T. B. Butt, with half No. 11 Platoon of "C" Company, had reinforced the firing line, and

Sgt. A. W. Patterson (whose promotion to a commission dated from this day) brought up the second half of the platoon. They continued to occupy their trenches until badly enfiladed from higher ground north of them, but about 3.30 p.m., finding their position untenable, they attempted to retire to their former place. Lt. Butt was wounded and Sgt. Patterson was killed.

At 3.25 Capt. Luther, conforming to an advance made by Maj. Heathcote, attempted to reinforce the "A" Company trenches held by Capt. Gatacre. With him went 2/Lts. Slingsby and Ritchie with their platoons. The intervening ground was swept by fire; only about a dozen men reached Capt. Gatacre. Capt. Luther was wounded in this rush, 2/Lt. Ritchie was killed.

Lt. Denison held a portion of the trench line here; he was wounded by a rifle bullet through the temple, but his men bandaged him, and he continued to cheer and encourage them, propped up against the side of the trench. His sight had failed and he was unconscious when the end of the day came, but the Germans picked him up and he died in hospital some weeks later at Mons.

Lt. J. B. Noel was also wounded in the trenches, a rifle bullet striking the glasses through which he was looking at the time.

Meanwhile, the divisional baggage trains having been successfully got away, the covering troops were withdrawn as far as possible. At about 3 p.m. the brigade reserve battalion was seen to be retiring to a position in rear, covering the retirement of the other troops. There was no question of retirement for the companies in the firing line. Even if it had been possible to communicate an order to retire, had such an order been intended, very few men could have got away owing to the proximity of the enemy and the nature of the ground. Some of the occupants of the lines of supports, however, did receive the signal to retire direct from the Bde. Headquarters, and thus a portion of the battalion was saved and conformed to the movements of the brigade.

Some of the trenches were without ammunition, and in the last stage of the fight, when a determined advance by the enemy must at any moment have settled the business, some officers told their men they could take their chance of getting back to the column. Many men who made the attempt must have lost their lives, but a few managed to win through, for there were men who later in the week were able to give evidence of what had taken place in the trenches in the last phases of the action. Such evidence was impressionistic, as evidence gathered under the conditions was bound to be.

For the last hour of the fight, so far as they could see, the K.O.Y.L.I. were alone in the line to stem the German advance; it was conceived that their duty lay in blocking the great high road and in denying it till the last possible minute to the enemy. Though their troops surrounded the 2/K.O.Y.L.I. on three sides, completely dominating their flanks, and were supported by field-guns brought up to within 900 yards of the trenches, the Germans still hesitated to rush in. Time after time their bugles sounded the British 'Cease Fire,' and attempts were made to send forward a flag of truce. Each overture was answered with bursts of fire and the remnants of the companies made it evident to the enemy that the resistance was being maintained.

Maj. Yate had with him in his trench Capt. Keppel (who had commanded and trained "B" Company in Dublin) and Lt. Reynolds. 2/Lt. Hibbert was wounded in an attempt to cross the road to warn him of a newly-discovered point of danger. The left companies' trenches were already overrun; the fire of the attack was closer and even more intense; when suddenly the whole countryside, as far as the eye could reach to right and left, seemed alive with advancing Germans. Maj. Yate shouted to his men to charge, but was instantly afterwards struggling in the hands of Germans who had approached the trench from behind. Some few of the survivors were bayonetted, but to the credit of the German soldiers, be it mentioned, most of the unwounded were made prisoners and the wounded in the trench were respected. Sgt. J. W. Clarke, who would also have been a commissioned officer from this day, was killed in the act of firing on the enemy in this final rush.

There was no surrender. The occupants of the trenches were mobbed and swamped by the rising tide of grey-coated Germans. The Bn. Headquarters' trench from its position was naturally the last to be overrun. The amount of resistance any company was capable of offering at the last moment may be gauged from the fact that on the day following the battle a British officer prisoner-of-war, on his way down the road under escort, counted sixty-two dead in the trenches by the side of the road alone, *i.e.*, in "B" Company's trenches. And this was after all the wounded had been accounted for. The other companies had suffered no less severely.

Resistance ended about 4.30 p.m. (Note—"The Official History of the War" gives the time as 3.30 p.m. when the battle was over, not taking into account the action of so small a unit).

The 5th Div. had made good its retirement; a new rearguard lingered near the battlefield, including the K.O.Y.L.I. reserve under Lt. Williams, which had received a direct order to retire from Bde. Headquarters. The work of this and similar detachments, many of whom were acting independently in the rôle of covering troops, proved invaluable in checking the enemy. This view is supported by a quotation from a German writer present on the occasion:

"*In front of us there still swarmed a number of scattered English troops, who . . . again and again forced us to waste time in deployments, as we could not tell what their strength might be.*"

THE BATTLEFIELD BY LE CATEAU, 26TH AUGUST, 1914

Looking N.E. up the road towards BAVAI. Bn. H.Q., 2/K.O.Y.L.I., by the side of the main road. German formations in the distance advancing to the attack, while their guns are shelling the artillery positions of the 5th Division. The spire of Le Cateau Church is seen over the ridge, which was the right of the British position

The retirement of the 13th Inf. Bde. from the field was effected under the circumstances in remarkably good order. The 5th Div. fell back during the night along the Reumont-Estrées road. Rain had set in at dusk, and the night was dark, cold and wet. At the Estrées cross roads a halt was made, and the intermixed parties of different units were sorted out. The remains of the 2/K.O.Y.L.I. were collected in an adjoining field, and marched off with the rest of the brigade, passing through St. Quentin, into billets at Ollezy on the night of the 27th.

Maj. Trevor, with 2/Lt. Hardiman (E.York., attached), joined up at Ollezy with a party; the other officers now present with what remained of the battalion were Maj. Heathcote, Capt. J. E. Simpson, Lt. Williams and 2/Lt. Slingsby, besides the Quartermaster and the Medical Officer. The 2/K.O.Y.L.I. was reorganised in two companies with two officers each, Maj. Trevor taking command, with Lt. Williams as Adjutant. Lt. Bentham, in addition to his duties as Quartermaster, did the work of Transport Officer, and continued to act in the dual capacity for some months to come.

The total losses of the battalion at Le Cateau were returned as: officers 18, sergeants 21, corporals 22, buglers 7, privates 532, making a total of 600. Out of this number a total of 310 were later reported to be prisoners in Germany, 170 of whom were wounded. The proportion of killed to the number of the wounded who were left on the field is very high, but it must be remembered that the ground over which attempts to reinforce or to change position in the late stages of the battle were made, was open, and was swept by shot and shell; where men fell wounded they continued to suffer from a rain of bullets till they died.

The finest tribute to the work performed by the 2/K.O.Y.L.I. that day, is contained in a letter written by their Div.-Gen., Sir Charles Fergusson, who, in referring (after the war) to the 2/K.O.Y.L.I. wrote:

"...... *I am only too pleased to do anything in my power to recognise the behaviour of that Battalion. It was mainly thanks to them that the 2nd Corps was extricated that day, and their stand is historic*......"

The following day, the 28th August, the brigade continued the march towards Paris and passed through Noyon. That night it bivouacked in a field near Pontoise and rested the next day. On the 30th the river Aisne was reached and crossed at Attichy, and at Faulzy a halt was made for the night. Here Maj. Heathcote was admitted to hospital.

On the 31st the march was resumed to Crépy-en-Valois. This was a long march, 23 miles, and very trying owing to the great heat; however, the K.O.Y.L.I. marched conspicuously well and with unflagging spirit.

It was not till the morning of the 1st September that the 5th Div. came into touch with the enemy who were following them. The 13th Inf. Bde. held the outpost line covering Crépy-en-Valois during the night. The D.W.R. and the R.W.K. were in the first line, the K.O.S.B. and K.O.Y.L.I. in support. German cavalry patrols had been following the rearguard the day before, but had made no attempt to delay the march, and in the evening their cavalry were known to be in force at Compiègne, having crossed the Aisne. At 6 a.m. they began to be seen; the two supporting battalions were moved up into the front line, the K.O.Y.L.I. reinforcing the right of the line, under Maj. Trevor. An attack, however, was delivered on the left and firing became fairly brisk on this flank. The enemy brought up no guns to support the attack, which was obviously of the nature of a reconnaissance, and when some British guns opened on the advancing lines the action was at an end.

The retirement of the brigade, following that of the rest of the division, was then resumed. The K.O.Y.L.I. were in rearguard, considerably enlivened by the experiences of the morning, which had come as a relief to the eternal 'foot-slogging.' Their march was through Nanteuil into billets at Silly.

On the 2nd September they moved on to Cuisy, and on the 3rd the Marne was crossed at Isles-les-Villenoy and billets were found for the K.O.Y.L.I. at Couilly. The division marched again at 9 p.m. the night of the 4th, a trying march by night with many delays. Tournan, only 15 miles from Paris, was reached at 10.30 a.m. and the great retreat from Mons came to an end.

While in bivouac here south of the town, the K.O.Y.L.I. welcomed their first reinforcement, being joined by 2/Lt. W. Carrington and eighty rank and file. This brought the strength of the battalion up to eight officers and 512 other ranks.

Two V.C.s were a little later on bestowed in the 2/K.O.Y.L.I. for exceptionally gallant services rendered on the 26th August at Le Cateau. The following is the official account of the deeds for which the crosses were awarded:—

(1) Maj. C. A. L. Yate, for conspicuous gallantry and devotion to duty at Le Cateau on August 26th, 1914, in maintaining a vigorous resistance to the last possible moment, refusing all demands to surrender, and attempting to charge the enemy when the trenches were being overrun.

(2) No. 9376 Lce.-Cpl. F. W. Holmes, carried a wounded comrade on his back out of the firing line at Le Cateau under desperate circumstances, and then proceeded to bring a gun team with its gun, which he found limbered up, with all its detachment killed, out of the battle, first with the aid of a trumpeter, and finally single-handed.

The inspiring messages by H.M. The King and Lord Kitchener to the original four divisions are truly expressive of the spirit and atmosphere of early August, 1914. They were as follows:—

The King's message:

Buckingham Palace,
August 9th, 1914.

You are leaving home to fight for the safety and honour of my Empire.

Belgium, whose country we are pledged to defend, has been attacked, and France is about to be invaded by the same powerful foe.

I have implicit confidence in you, my soldiers. Duty is your watchword, and I know your duty will be nobly done.

I shall follow your every movement with deepest interest and mark with eager satisfaction your daily progress; indeed your welfare will never be absent from my thoughts.

I pray GOD to bless you and guard you and bring you back victorious.

(sd.) GEORGE, R.I.

Lord Kitchener's message:

You are ordered abroad as a soldier of the King to help our French comrades against the invasion of a common enemy.

You have to perform a task which will need your courage, your energy, your patience. Remember that the honour of the British Army depends on your individual conduct. It will be your duty not only to set an example of discipline and perfect steadiness under fire, but also to maintain the most friendly relations with those whom you are helping in this struggle.

The operations in which you are engaged will, for the most part, take place in a friendly country, and you can do your own country no better service than in showing yourself in France and Belgium in the true character of a British soldier.

Be invariably courteous, considerate and kind. Never do anything likely to injure or destroy property, and always look upon looting as a disgraceful act. You are sure to meet with a welcome and to be trusted; your conduct must justify that welcome and that trust. Your duty can not be done unless your health be sound. So keep constantly on your guard against any excesses. In this new experience you may find temptations both in wine and women. You must entirely resist both temptations, and, while treating all women with perfect courtesy, you should avoid any intimacy.

Do your duty bravely.

Fear GOD.

Honour the King.

(sd.) KITCHENER, Field-Marshal.

THE MARNE AND THE AISNE. 1914

II

THE great retirement was indeed ended at last; the nearest point to Paris was reached. In addition to the reinforcement of personnel there came fresh supplies of equipment and material. In a few hours a transformation was effected. The battalion, which had marched into bivouac at 10.30 a.m. at the end of a rapid and exhausting retirement under all the most arduous and disintegrating conditions, was by 5 a.m. the following morning (6th September) rehabilitated and transformed into an advancing force of potential victors. The brigade moved at 5.10 a.m. on Villeneuve in high spirits in order to take up its assigned place in a change of front; thence it moved eastwards to outposts covering Mortcerf, meeting on the way in the forest of Crécy a few stray Uhlan scouts, whom it captured. In the two next marches Coulommiers and Boissy-le-Chatel were reached.

Throughout those three days, the 6th-8th September, although the British line met with comparatively little opposition, a great battle, to be known as the Battle of the Marne, was raging on either flank; in it the French Sixth Army on the line of the river Ourcq and the French Fifth Army in the crossings of the two rivers, the Grand Morin and the Petit Morin, were heavily engaged with the enemy. The battle lasted till the evening of the 10th, on which day the British army was fighting its way to the crossing of the river Aisne.

The information vouchsafed to the fighting troops by the British General Headquarters Staff in a brief message (none the less heartening because messages had hitherto been so rare and unilluminating) was to the effect that a great *coup* might be expected to be made within the next few days.

What had happened to change the face of affairs was this. Gen. Joffre, the French Commander-in-Chief, had assembled his Sixth French Army (under Gen. Manoury) between Betz and Meaux, in such a manner that this army now threatened the flank of the German advance. Gen. Manoury was ready to strike, and Gen. Joffre called on Sir John French to support this attack by changing his position a little to the east and then coming up into the line of attack on the left of the French Fifth Army.

On the 8th September, accordingly, the 13th Inf. Bde. advanced in attack formation, clearing the enemy out before it, through St. Cyr, the 14th Inf. Bde. being on its right in the direction of St. Ouen. Maj. Heathcote was in command of the firing line, having just got back to duty. The night of the 8th was spent by the 2/K.O.Y.L.I. in bivouac near Rougeville, south of the Marne. The advance was continued on the morning of the 9th, and the Marne was crossed at Saucy, east of La Ferté, in the face of slight opposition; the advanced guard being enfiladed and held up for a time by an enemy battery.

Thanks to the heavy pressure of the French on either side, Manoury with the Sixth Army on the left, and d'Esperey with the Fifth Army on the right, the advance of the British was still fairly simple at this stage, for the Germans were continually falling back to straighten their line and were not inclined to risk their rearguards except when it became of vital importance to do so.

After crossing the Marne the direction was north. When some advance had been made towards Montreuil the 14th Inf. Bde., which was leading, came under heavy shell-fire, and later encountered enemy infantry in position. A delay was caused in forcing them back. When the 2/K.O.Y.L.I. was passing through Chaumont numbers of wounded were being brought back, chiefly men of the E. Surrey and D.C.L.I., whose battalions had suffered heavily from the opposition ahead. The pursuit was continued northwards through Montreuil, thence through Goulombs and Brumetz to Chézy on the 10th.

On the 11th the advance was through Billy in a north-easterly direction to Hartennes. Next day it was through Droizy to the neighbourhood of Serches, where the Germans were discovered in strong positions covering the crossings of the Aisne. A battle was in progress all along the river valley, being especially heavy on the left about Soissons. The enemy was forced out of Serches and the 13th Inf. Bde. went into close billets there.

On the 13th September the 13th Inf. Bde. was allotted the task of seizing the bridge over the Aisne at Missy. The 2/R.W.K. and the 2/K.O.S.B. were in the first line, the other two battalions in support. It was soon discovered that the northern bank was to be strongly defended by the enemy. Missy is overlooked by the Chivres ridge: the Germans evidently intended to make the crossing of the river a costly one and were entrenched in strong positions on the ridge. Their guns were searching the approaches, and Ciry, which was occupied by the supporting battalions, suddenly became the object of their attentions. Ciry lies in the valley just at the foot of the slope down which the valley is approached from the south. The regimental transport was on the road descending the slope when a heavy artillery fire was opened which took this column in flank. The infantry who were ahead were hastily withdrawn behind Ciry to a sunken road by Les Carrières: thanks to the prompt action of Lt. and Qr.-Mr. Bentham the transport was turned and withdrawn behind the crest with the loss of one S.A.A. cart only: the vehicles were subsequently brought forward to Les Carrières when night fell. Missy bridge had been destroyed, but the two leading battalions managed to cross after dark, being ferried over the Aisne, a sluggish stream some 70 yards in width, using five rafts improvised by the R.E. on the spot (14th Sept.).

The 5th Div. pushed on and attacked the enemy position on the southern edge of the Chivres plateau, but Sir Charles Fergusson found it impossible to maintain the position he had won owing to the devastating fire which caught the lines in enfilade from the village of Vregny. He therefore withdrew a little to a line which ran through the north edge of Missy on the 15th.

The 2/K.O.Y.L.I. advanced at 1.45 a.m. this day with the intention of crossing by Missy in order to join the remainder of the 13th Inf. Bde. on the northern bank, but owing to the absence of the necessary pontoons the crossing could not be carried out, and, the battalion being left in a very exposed position, within one hour of dawn Maj. H. E. Trevor withdrew it to find some sort of cover in a belt of trees 400 yards from the river. The cover from view, however, was not sufficient protection, for the enemy's guns opened a destructive fire on the ranks, causing heavy losses. The horses and mules of the battalion transport stampeded and it was under these difficult conditions that the battalion had hastily to entrench itself along the front and rear edges of the little wood. There were three separate storms of fire and there was no possibility of crossing the river to escape from the exposed position. The casualties (killed and wounded) numbered fifty-three. It rained heavily and the trenches were very wet. A message was received from Sir Charles Fergusson, whose headquarters were now at Serches, to the following effect: "*Serches,* 15.9.14. *My dear Trevor, I am so dreadfully sorry that the Regiment has suffered again. It is really a grief to me. I have been hoping to come and say a word to the Regiment for a long time, but, as you know, it has been hard to get an opportunity to do anything of the sort, but I shall do so at the first chance. Will you tell all ranks how very much their devotion and gallantry has been appreciated by me and by all who have watched them, and tell them that I know they will not begrudge the sacrifice if they remember it has helped the side.*"

The bombardment was continued at dawn with further casualties. At night (16th September) the battalion was withdrawn to La Corbinne Wood immediately in rear. Here nine fresh officers were able to join up, *viz.*, Maj. G. M. Renny, Capt. R. W. S. Stanton, Lt. T. H. Richmond and 2/Lt. C. E. L. Watkins (all K.O.Y.L.I.) with Lts. E. G. Lamb, B. E. Hervey-Bathurst and C. F. Nunnely (N.F.), and Lts. T. H. Clemson and E. M. Bishop (Dorset).

The 2/K.O.Y.L.I. remained at La Corbinne for a week, the battle of the Aisne raging fiercely throughout the time. The Aisne had been crossed by the I Corps with its right on Bourg, and by the II Corps at Vailly and Missy, where strong bridgeheads were maintained to cover the crossings over the river by these towns. Condé, between the two, was, however, still in the hands of the enemy. The armies of Von Kluck and Bülow were concentrated to resist any further advance on the part of the allies and were entrenched on the line of dominating heights on the northern side of the Aisne. The British army could not force the position, but it held on with the utmost tenacity to the ground immediately north of the river. The attacks continued from the 14th to the 18th, after which date there was no definite attempt to better our position, and the strenuous attempts of the enemy to dislodge the Allied armies continued. The day of the big gun was at hand: trenches were steadily being improved and the thunder of the guns, which was now becoming continuous, was the prelude to the ceaseless battle which was to be waged between two opposing forces in position for four long years to come.

On the 24th September the 2/K.O.Y.L.I. relieved the D.W.R. Batt. north of the river in the trenches by Missy. Companies crossed the river by ferry after dark at intervals of two hours. Maj. J. B. G. Tulloch arrived on the 26th and took over the command of the battalion from Maj. H. E. Trevor. With the arrival of fresh drafts the strength was now brought up to 21 officers and 780 other ranks. Lt. W. d'E. Williams was now Adjutant.

The trenches occupied near Missy were about 400 yards from those of the enemy. Constant and unremitting vigilance was enjoined to guard against surprise. The value of improved trenches was soon felt, for on the 27th the enemy shelled the line of trenches heavily all day, and the shelling culminated about 5 p.m. in terrific bursts of shrapnel fire, with no resulting casualties in the K.O.Y.L.I. or the Dorset Bn. which was alongside.

On the 30th September Brig.-Gen. Cuthbert bade farewell to his brigade. All ranks felt that in losing him they were losing a personal friend as well as a fine Commander. His farewell order to the battalion is worth recording in the annals of the regiment, and runs as follows:—"*In relinquishing command of the brigade I am so proud of, I want to bid you one short word of goodbye, as owing to your being in the trenches I am unable to parade the battalion and speak to you personally as I should have liked to have done. I have known you now for eight months, nearly two of which have been passed in the most severe campaign of modern times, and I have lived with you under all conditions, both of peace and war. Never has a Brigadier been better or more loyally served by all ranks than I have been by you: my orders fully and thoroughly carried out, my least wish anticipated and fulfilled. Your steadfastness under hardships, your gallantry and high courage under fire, and your unhesitating obedience and discipline, have been my constant delight and admiration, and your intense spirit, both regimental and brigade, could be excelled by none. I have indeed been most proud to command you, and in bidding you goodbye I wish you all health and success, added laurels, and a happy and speedy return home."*

THE FLANDERS FRONT. 1914
LA BASSÉE AND MESSINES
III

AS soon as the situation on the Aisne had arrived at a deadlock, each side made strenuous endeavours to turn the northern flank of its adversary. The so-called "Race for the Sea" had begun. Corps and divisions made progress until they were stopped by similar formations of the enemy engaged on the same task. On the Allied side these turning movements were first carried out by French troops, but later in September—at the request of Sir John French—the British Expeditionary Force began quietly to withdraw from the Aisne in order to take part in an offensive through Flanders, where they would be in a more convenient situation for receiving reinforcements and supplies from England.

At this time the Belgian army had evacuated Antwerp and was retreating towards the Yser pursued by German troops released from their operations against the city.

There is not space in this record to do more than mention briefly the larger issues, but the part which the 2/K.O.Y.L.I. was to play in the forthcoming struggle can be realised properly only if the general trend of the operations is understood.

Incidentally the following story, which is authentic, may be of interest as throwing a sidelight, if light were needed, on the German objective at this time.

The Kaiser, during a visit to a German war hospital at Cambrai in September, hesitated as he entered one of the wards, when a member of his Staff told him that there were 'only English in this ward.' He was turning to leave, but apparently struck by a sudden thought, turned again and walked into the centre of the room. "*Englishmen,*" he said, "*I am about to do what Napoleon failed to do!*" When he had left, the wounded prisoners put their heads together and guessed the intention of the Kaiser to be to possess himself of the Channel ports and to attack England from the northern coast of France. Among the wounded in the ward was No. 10240, Pte. A. Trotter, 2/K.O.Y.L.I., who told the story to an officer of his own battalion shortly after, when they met in Germany.

The situation in Flanders at this time was as follows:

Sir Henry Rawlinson, commanding the IV Corps, with the 3rd Cavalry Div. (Byng) and the 7th Div. (Capper), had been on detached duty and was covering the retirement of the Belgians: he was now placed under Sir John French's orders and continued to fall back on the right of the Belgians, who were between him and the sea, being heavily pressed by the advancing Germans.

The French had extended their line northwards from Compiègne by putting in fresh troops, till they now stood in unbroken line with the new French X Corps under Gen. Foch, with its left resting on La Bassée. To fill the gap between La Bassée and the British 7th Div. Sir John French brought in the British corps in succession to the north or left of Foch's army.

The British II Corps was the first to be withdrawn and the first consequently to take up the line, thus becoming the right of the British line.

The III Corps prolonged the line northwards, fighting its way into line from the 13th to the 19th October simultaneously with the II Corps, for the III Corps was brought by train as far as Hazebrouck.

A French cavalry division under Gen. Conneau occupied the space between the two British corps and preserved touch.

The I Corps on arrival from the Aisne detrained north of the III Corps.

The 5th Div. occupied the right of the II Corps in the new line. On the promotion of Sir Charles Fergusson to command a corps, Gen. Morland was appointed to the command of the 5th Div. (16th October).

The fighting was incessant from the 13th October. Indeed the battle may be said to have commenced on the 11th (*vide* Sir John French's Dispatches), for on that day the 2nd Cav. Div. under Gen. Hubert Gough first came into contact with the enemy's cavalry north of the Béthune-Aire canal.

By the 19th of the month it was clearly seen that the Germans had been able to keep pace with the Allies in prolonging their line, and there was now no flank to be turned, so that the projected turning movement was materialising into a continuous chain of resistance to meet the massive attack of new German armies.

The German Sixth Army opposed the British Corps from Armentières to the neighbourhood of Ypres, while their new Fourth Army, which included the XXVII, XXVI, XXIII, XXII and III (Reserve) Corps, opposed the Allied front from Ypres to the sea in that order.

At no time during the war was the fighting more desperate than it was during this period; the losses were often terrific; on both sides soldiers were becoming imbued with the spirit of absolute self-sacrifice and selflessness which characterised the fighting. A task would be entrusted to a battalion to carry out and that battalion would be effaced rather than betray its trust. The Yorkshiremen of the K.O.Y.L.I. were no exception to the rule, for your Yorkshireman never 'gives best' to any man, and so when their turn came in the latter days of October in the terrific fighting for Messines and Neuve Chapelle, at the point where the Germans looked like breaking our line, after many desperate efforts on the part of the enemy, each night found the battalion still holding on, but at last in such reduced numbers that when orders finally came to withdraw, it had not the strength of a single company.

According to the German official monograph entitled 'Ypres, 1914,' the heaviest fighting was experienced in the four following periods:—

(*a*) The operations of their Fourth Army, 20th-31st October, 1914.

(*b*) The attempt to break through south of Ypres.

(*c*) The operations of the same Fourth Army from the end of October to the 9th November, 1914.

(*d*) The last phase.

Our 5th Div. was concerned in (*b*) and (*d*). The period (*b*) in the German account covers only that between the 30th October and the 10th November, but during the period 20th to 29th October the British II and III Corps had a hard defensive battle to fight, and the only assistance they received was on the arrival of the Jullundur Bde. and part of the Lahore Div. which replaced Gen. Conneau's cavalry between the two Corps.

It was on the morning of the 30th October in pouring rain that the XXIII, XXVI and XXVII German Reserve Corps advanced to the attack to 'force a break through.' A final combined attempt, constituting an attack of sheer desperation, ensued during the period 11th-17th November all along the line of the German Fourth and Sixth Armies. On the latter date the final decision was come to, to discontinue the attacks and resort to trench warfare. So ended the great combined offensive of the German Fourth and Sixth Armies with the army groups of Linsingen and Fabeck, to force a passage by way of Ypres to Calais and the coast. No wonder that among German soldiers in Germany in the drafts awaiting orders for the front it was whispered that the Ypres sector was a veritable hell; or that a prince on the Kaiser's staff, when visiting the British officers prisoners-of-war at Torgau in Saxony in November, told these officers that it was thanks to their countrymen that the first German objectives had not been attained, and that the Germans could now see no end to the war, for "*Germans could be obstinate as well as the British!*"

The story of the withdrawal of the 2/K.O.Y.L.I. from the Aisne may now be given, with an account of its actions on the Flanders front.

In accordance with the general scheme the battalion was relieved near midnight on the 1st October by the 1/Essex in the trenches by the Aisne, and it marched to billets near Vassemy. On the 6th October under cover of the night it marched with the rest of the 13th Inf. Bde. *via* Villers Cotteret to Fresnoy. Next day trains were found awaiting the battalion at Verberie on the Oise; it left the trains on arrival at Abbeville at 9 a.m. on the 8th. The battalion was billeted for the day at Drulat, a suburb north-east of the town, and moved in the evening to Gueschart. Marching always by night Haravesnes was reached in the morning of the 10th October. The march was continued towards Villièvres, but at a point just short of that village motor-'buses took the men up and transported them to Valhuon.

The British Second Army was now concentrating west of the gap which existed north of the French (whose left was about to attack Vermelles), and, pivoting on its right, it swung round and proceeded eastwards to come up into line with the French.

The French failed to retake Vermelles in spite of repeated attempts, and on the 12th October the 13th Inf. Bde. was pushed in to fill a gap south of the Béthune-La Bassée canal between Vermelles and the railway. Brig.-Gen. Hickie had succeeded Maj.-Gen. Cuthbert (promoted) in command of the 13th Inf. Bde. The 2/K.O.Y.L.I. remained in reserve at Annequin, while Gen. Hickie sent the other three battalions into the line to co-operate with the French.

On the 13th October the 5th Div. attacked, but the enemy put up a strong resistance. The 13th Inf. Bde. was on the right, and a portion of the 2/K.O.Y.L.I., who had been reserve battalion of the brigade, was sent up to reinforce the firing line. The 14th was spent in resisting German counter-attacks, but in the evening the trenches occupied by the 13th Inf. Bde. were taken over by French Territorial battalions, and the 13th Inf. Bde. was withdrawn to billets in Le Hamel, where it became Corps reserve.

The casualties in the 2/K.O.Y.L.I. on the 14th October amounted to eighteen.

At Le Hamel the fifth reinforcement of 94 men under 2/Lt. A. H. P. Errington joined the battalion. There had been a few cases of sickness and some transfers of attached officers, which left the strength of the battalion at 16 officers and 839 rank and file. Maj. Renny was admitted to hospital on the 15th; Maj. Trevor and Lt. Carrington on the 16th. Capt. Lamb and Lt. Nunnely left to join the Northumberland Fusiliers.

On the 18th October the battalion, which was now acting as reserve to the 3rd Div., was sent up in the early morning to relieve the Royal Ulster Rifles (7th Inf. Bde.) in the trenches in front of Lannoy. In an advance which was ordered on Château Wood, which commenced at 6.30 a.m., the battalion fought its way to a position 350 yards from the edge of the wood, where it dug itself in, being in advance of the attacking battalions on either flank. They came under a very heavy fire from front and flanks; their supporting companies were moved up into close support in an old trench. Here they held on for many hours. Some splendid work was done in getting the wounded away from the firing line, in which Sgt. A. Macdonald[1] distinguished himself, repeatedly going back from the firing line with wounded men and returning with ammunition.

Some seventy wounded passed through the hands of Lt. C. Helm, R.A.M.C., this day, the total casualties being seventeen killed and eighty-two wounded. The night and the whole of the following day were spent in this position.

On the 20th the R.U.R. again relieved the battalion, which was passed back to the 13th Inf. Bde., rejoining it at Festubert after a night in billets near the Bois du Biez. But the same afternoon they were sent on to the 14th Inf. Bde. at the cross-roads south-west of Neuve Chapelle, and again on to relieve the D.C.L.I. at Lorgies in the trenches by Richebourg l'Avoué at 5 a.m. the 22nd.

The enemy was attacking all along the line. At dawn the firing became general and the 2/K.O.S.B. on the right made a vigorous counter-attack, which was pushed home with the bayonet. However, further to the right, part of the line had to fall back, and this portion of the line was later withdrawn to a new position running from La Bassée canal through La Quinque Rue and east of Neuve Chapelle to Fauquissart.

On the 24th Maj. Heathcote temporarily took over the command of the battalion, replacing Maj. Tulloch who was in hospital. Determined attacks were repulsed on the 24th and 25th October, preceded by heavy gun-fire preparation. The trenches had a rough handling and were broken up badly by the heavy shells. Capt. Stanton was wounded in the thigh by a fragment of a shell: three men were buried alive, others were only just dug out in time to save their lives, but the defenders were undaunted and repelled the attack which followed the bombardment most gallantly. Sgt. R. Willington and Cpl. Copley on bicycles managed to get through to Bde. Headquarters under the shell-fire with messages which resulted in the arrival during the night of reinforcing companies of the D.C.L.I. The casualties were seventeen killed (including three sergeants), one officer and twenty-five men wounded. It was noted that the shelling which had

[1] *No.* 6923, *Sergt. Archibald Macdonald, D.C.M.,* 2/*K.O.Y.L.I., had won the D.C.M. in S. Africa in* 1899 (*when serving with the Hampshire Regt.*) *He was awarded the French Médaille Militaire for gallantry, August* 21*st to* 30*th,* 1914, *by special A.O. dated December* 21*st,* 1914 (*A.O.* 23 *of* 1915), *and was awarded Clasp to D.C.M. for conspicuous gallantry at Illies on October* 19*th,* 1914, *in "London Gazette," December* 17*th,* 1914 (*A.O.* 22 *of January,* 1915). *He was killed on* 28*th October,* 1914. *His brother, Edmund Maxwell Macdonald, did good service as a stretcher-bearer in the* 2/*K.O.Y.L.I. at Shinkamar, January* 29*th,* 1898, *and in S. Africa,* 1899–1902. *He was appointed Bandmaster* 1/*A and S.H. in* 1909. *He resigned his Bandmastership in the Great War and took a permanent commission in the A. and S.H., serving in France, where he was wounded.*

so grievously damaged the trenches was by the so-called 'Jack Johnsons' throwing 738-lb. shells.

Capt. H. F. G. Carter with 2/Lt. R. N. Carswell and a draft of 149 men had arrived and went straight up into the trenches at night. The following day, the 26th October, the Germans again attacked. They broke through on the left flank of the 2/K.O.Y.L.I. but were checked and driven back in front of the draft. 2/Lt. Carswell's brief career at the front was ended in his death, and Lt. C. E. L. Watkins was wounded.

On the 27th, 28th and 29th the attacks were no less severe; Capt. T. N. Richmond was killed. All companies suffered severely; "A" Company came in for the worst of the shelling, but was prominent in resisting the attack of which the shelling was a prelude. The enemy retired to his trenches 500 yards distant. The battalion was replaced at 3 a.m. the 30th, by the 2/39th Gwalior Rifles. After spending some hours at Le Touret it arrived at Merville at 6 p.m. There was, however, to be no rest for the men.

In these nine days' fighting in the trenches by Richebourg l'Avoué the losses to the battalion had been roughly 300. Besides the casualties among officers mentioned above, 2/Lt. B. E. Hervey-Bathurst (N.F., attd.) was wounded and Lt. T. H. Clemson (Dorset, attd.) was missing. Also 2/Lt. G. S. Shannon (Dorset, attd.) was admitted to hospital.

At 3 a.m. the 31st October orders reached the battalion to proceed at 6.30 a.m. to Neuve Eglise with the 2/K.O.S.B.; the troops were conveyed in motor-'buses to reinforce the 2/Cav. Div. at Messines. Trenches east of Messines had to be retaken, our cavalry patrols were said to be still in the village itself; shortly after 10 a.m. the K.O.S.B. and K.O.Y.L.I. were sent to the attack. However, it was found that the western portion of the village was still in the enemy's hands, and that he had collected machine-guns there; the reception that the attacking companies met with rendered a further advance impracticable until our artillery should have had time to destroy the houses in which these machine-guns were mounted. The trenches were therefore not retaken, but the battalion dug itself in under a devastating fire. By 2 p.m. the supporting companies and the remnants of "B" and "C" Companies had entrenched themselves and were prepared to hold the line of the road running north and south through Messines. Casualties were very heavy, approximating five officers and 150 other ranks. Capt. J. E. Simpson was killed, Lt. A. H. P. Errington was 'wounded and missing,' Maj. Heathcote, Capt. Stourton and 2/Lt. Chalker were wounded. Thus by 6 p.m. Capt. Carter was left in command of the battalion and 2/Lt. B. J. Corballis (Som. L.I., attached) was the only other officer left with it. At that hour Capt. Carter requested the O.C. the London Scottish to fill a gap between his men and the Carabiniers; when this was done the line, though much attenuated, was made continuous, if scarcely to be called solid. The attacking Germans had been unable to make any impression on this section, as their accounts admit, and they suffered heavy losses.

The 1st November was an anxious day; it was difficult to arrive at orders. Capt. M. R. K. Hodgson of the R.F. had come in during the night with two other officers (Capt. A. B. Smyth, K.O.Y.L.I, and 2/Lt. Snape, Som.L.I.) and 30 men to reinforce, and had assumed command, Capt. Carter taking on the duties of Adjutant. Throughout the night, by the light of the blazing houses, under heavy fire and repeated attacks, the remnant of the 2/K.O.Y.L.I. stood firm in their position. During the early morning the Carabiniers on the right, then (at 6.30 a.m.) the London Scottish firing line, and finally at 7 p.m. the 2/K.O.Y.L.I., all of them in the face of crushing superior numbers, were forced to retire into their supporting line of trenches; and again an order came from the Major commanding the 18th Hussars on the left to withdraw further. At 7.45 they were ordered back by the headquarters 2nd Cav. Div. Accordingly a retirement was made to the north side of the Wulverghem-Messines road. The 2/K.O.Y.L.I. were then relieved in its new position by the 18th Hussars and was withdrawn to billets.

A private letter written by Capt. Carter[1] on the 3rd November immediately after these events, gives such a vivid picture of these strenuous days and reflects so clearly the spirit which animated this gallant leader and the men under him, that it must be inserted here; it runs:

"*After a tiring fortnight at the base I took a draft up to join the battalion, where they were plumped into a ditch and made to dig themselves in in the rain on arrival at* 10.30 *p.m. They had a bayonet charge next day. Heavy lyddite* (738-*lb. shell, Jack Johnson*) 500 *a day and shrapnel for nine days in one trench without leaving it. The draft lost forty-five out of* 150 *and the Regiment some* 300 *and about eight officers in the nine days. Poor Carswell was killed the first night .... Williams, who has been splendid, got wounded taking a message to the French gunners, who had plumped twenty shells into my trench, killing eight men and wounding nine more. Young Sgt. Macdonald was killed by a sniper: unfortunately the elder brother was killed the same day. I got hit four times, but being too fat I was not hurt; a time fuse even struck me on the leg. After this terrible nine days we were relieved for a rest by the Indian Div., but had hardly got into billets when we were hauled off to help the Cavalry Div. and carried thither by motor-'buses. We attacked a difficult position. Poor J. E.* (*Simpson*) *died gallantly leading*

[1] *Bt. Maj.* (*temp. Lt.-Col.*) *H. F. G. Carter, M.C., died in Vladivostok* 28 *Feb.,* 1919, *from pneumonia following influenza.*

a charge, but one which failed owing to concealed German machine-guns. Heathcote was wounded, as were Stourton, Errington and Chalker. Errington is still missing. The next day we were forced to retire .... A very strenuous day. The night before I found myself O.C. 2/K.O.Y.L.I. with one Som.L.I. officer of three months' service, the only other officer left. Late that evening Hodgson of the Royal Fusiliers, Smyth and Snape, Som.L.I., and thirty men arrived. The retirement finished, we were relieved by the 18th Hussars and returned to billets 200 strong. The men fought gallantly and stood fighting and shell-fire for eleven days. Their spirit is fine and I must say it is damnably frightening, but the excitement and comradeship is wonderful and I feel proud of belonging to our Regiment whose name is on the roll of those who know what 'fighting and sticking it' means. My salaams to all and DO TRAIN SOME MORE MACHINE-GUNNERS."

The two brothers Sgts. W. G. and A. Macdonald referred to in this letter were the worthy representatives of a gallant family whose father had served in the Regiment before them. Clever musicians and devoted soldiers, their charming personality had won them many friends in and outside the Regiment, while their wonderful coolness at critical moments and their courage and resource had earned them many honours on the Indian frontier, in S. Africa, and now in France.

The following is an extract from a letter received from the G.O.C. II Corps: it is a quotation from one written to that officer by the G.O.C. Cavalry Corps and published in the Corps Orders:—"*Headquarters, Cavalry Corps, 1st November. I must thank you for the help given to me during the last forty-eight hours by the battalions you so kindly sent to our aid, the K.O.S.B., K.O.Y.L.I., the Northumberland Fusiliers and the Lincolns. They arrived at a very critical time, and their arrival saved the situation. I fear that they have suffered some loss, but they fought brilliantly. I am deeply indebted to them and to Brig.-Gen. Shaw. (Signed) E. H. H. Allenby.*"

A further letter was received by the O.C. 2/K.O.Y.L.I. from Maj. A. Mathew-Lannowe, Commanding the Bays: "*7th November. On the 31st October in the action just north side of Messines your regiment, or part of it, advanced with us to re-occupy the ridge marked by the Ypres-Messines road, and together we held on to it up to and after the enemy's attack that evening. In my report as O.C. Bays, I took the opportunity of bringing forward the names of Capt. Carter, who had been O.C. the battalion owing to casualties, and also that of C.S.M. C. T. Marchant. The line was broken at a point where there was rather a mix-up of units, and Sgt. Marchant on his own initiative hurried back and brought back his men to re-establish the line. I take the liberty of bringing to your notice the excellent work (at a critical time) of Capt. Carter and Sgt. Marchant. (Signed) A. Mathew-Lannowe, O.C. Bays.*"

On the 4th November a message from F.M. Sir John French was received in which he told the II Corps that he had watched "*with deepest admiration and solicitude*" the splendid stand made by the men, and calling on them for yet another effort.

Capt. Carter was awarded the M.C. C.S.M. C. J. Marchant received the D.C.M. (*Gazette* 11 Nov., 1914) for his gallantry at Illies on the 18th Oct., 1914. For the part that he played when in command of two companies on the 31st Oct., in the action just north of Messines, he received no reward: he was wounded and taken prisoner that night by the Germans.

So by its courage and tenacity in the face of overwhelming odds the 2/K.O.Y.L.I. had contributed to the achievement of saving the situation at a most critical moment. The spirit of the battalion communicated itself to the new drafts, who maintained it honourably on every subsequent occasion when a critical situation subjected the battalion to the severest tests.

The following is a letter dated "In France with 2/K.O.Y.L.I., 16th October, 1914," from 5216 Sgt. E. T. Richards, 2/K.O.Y.L.I., to Capt. H. W. B. Thorp, K.O.Y.L.I. It throws some interesting light on the life at this period at the front.

Friday, 16th *October*, 1914.

Dear Sir,

The battalion is still going strong in spite of casualties. More reinforcements joined yesterday which included several of our old company at CRETE, 1904, *Section D men. Young Richards came up with the second lot of reinforcements and was in time to go with the battalion up to the Aisne. Our brigade was the thin edge of the wedge between the Aisne river and the enemy. The battalion was in support and had twelve killed the first morning we were there. I was scratched with a piece of brass on the ribs just below the right breast, nothing serious. I had a charmed life at Le Cateau, but had to leave everything except my rifle; only ten of the company ("B") from the trenches got back except a few who were wounded very early. I expect several of them are in German camps, as I have seen a photograph with a "B" Company Corporal on it. I am told that Maj. C. A. L. Yate has been shot while trying to escape.*

We had thirty-eight hours in the trenches 12, 13 *and* 14*th October,* 1914, *and had a purely rifle and maxim fight from* 6.30 *p.m.,* 13*th, to about* 3.30 *a.m.,* 14*th. We had three killed and four wounded. One German was acting the wounded Tommy and shouting out "Oh Sergeant-Major, I can not go any further." They also gave a poor imitation of our bugles on their trumpet, sounding the cease fire.*

We did not see the result of the night fight as we were relieved by the Frenchmen at 4.0 *a.m. and I occupied a feather bed at* 9.0 *a.m., the first since Dublin.*

At present we are living in the Post-Master's house at X, and have been for the last three hours, and as it is getting dark we look like staying; if so, it means another feather bed to-night as the Germans have not had time to burn everything.

Capt. E. P. J. Stourton and Col. R. C. Money are the only officers not with the Regiment that I have seen, though I have been very close to Capt. C. P. Deedes on two occasions.

Maj. J. B. G. Tulloch commands the Regiment at present, and Capt. Richmond, 3/K.O.Y.L.I., commands "B" Company. Maj. G. M. Renny was in command of "B" but reported sick yesterday.

Portobello Barracks, Dublin, has been cleared of all married families and Mrs. Richards and daughters have gone to Hull.

We are getting excellent supplies of tobacco and cigarettes, thanks to the people at home, and our rations are A.1. I could not feel sick if I tried since we arrived in France and I have no doubt you are the same.

I expect I shall figure in Army Orders for the Good Conduct Medal shortly; will you please let me know if you see it, Sir. A list of casualties to some you know. Pte. F. W. Cox (Crete) killed. Sgt. A. W. Patterson killed almost certain. Pte. J. W. Christopher killed, I think he used to be your servant 1898-1899. Wounded C.Q.M.S. Whitworth, Sgt. Patten (formerly Bugler), C.Q.M.S. Heslop, Sgt. Barnes (1/K.O.Y.L.I.), Sgt. C. Healey. I am the only Sergeant or Corporal left in the company that marched out of Dublin with it.

Trusting you are well, I remain, Sir,
Your obedient Servant,
E. T. RICHARDS, Sergeant,
2/K.O.Y.L.I.

Sgt. E. T. Richards was awarded the Silver Medal for Long Service and Good Conduct by Army Order 412, October 1914. He was killed in the fighting by Messines at the end of the month. "Young Richards" is his younger brother, who transferred from the Lincolns to "F" Company 2/K.O.Y.L.I. at Hillsborough Barracks, Sheffield, in 1906.

The 2/K.O.Y.L.I. were billeted for some days in Neuve Eglise. Lt.-Col. W. M. Withycombe, who had arrived from Singapore on appointment to command the battalion, found a rugged and war-scarred remnant of his new command, but with fresh reinforcements arriving the battalion was quickly organised for further action. Some idea of the change which 2½ months of modern warfare make in a battalion may be gained from the fact that at this period there was only one officer in the fighting line (2/Lt. Slingsby) who went to France with the battalion in August. Nor were there any of the sergeants or corporals remaining.

On the 7th November the 13th Inf. Bde. was sent to support an attack made by the French on Spanbrooke Molen. The attack did not progress far, and the brigade returned to Neuve Eglise without being seriously engaged. There were few casualties in the brigade, but Lt.-Col. Martin of the 1/R.W.K., who commanded the brigade, was wounded.

On the night of the 11th-12th November the 2/K.O.Y.L.I. relieved a French formation in trenches south of the Douve. This was a very complicated relief, as the battalion had so few men compared to the numbers the French had in the line. The night was very dark and it was raining hard. The French Commandant fell into the river up to his neck in the water, when showing Col. Withycombe round the line.

The battalion was relieved on the night of the 12th November and marched through Ypres to some open trenches north of the Menin Road on the 13th, where it remained all night in the rain. On the 14th the battalion was placed under the orders of the G.O.C. 9th Inf. Bde., and was sent to Hooge Wood, where the situation was obscure. The line was held by various battalions of the 9th Inf Bde., which had been having a bad time and had lost most of its officers. A reconnaissance was made and it was found that the line was intact, although weakly held, except that the stables of the Harenthage Château had been captured by the enemy. The Château itself was still in our possession. The orders to the 2/K.O.Y.L.I. were to take over some of the trenches and to retake the stables as soon as it was dark.

Fifty men under Capt. A. B. Smythe, with 2/Lts. J. H. Boardman and L. E. P. Grubb, were picked for the attack. The enemy were expecting the attack and opened a merciless fire, which prevented our men from reaching the stables. Capt. Smythe was lost, and doubtless killed: 2/Lt. Grubb was killed, and 2/Lt. Boardman was wounded. The Château was temporarily evacuated, re-occupied by the enemy, and again assaulted and taken by a platoon of "D" Company under 2/Lt. Corballis. During the night a field-gun was brought up a ride in the wood to within about 50 yards of the stables, and as soon as it was light enough to see the outline of the stables four rounds were fired from it into the building. A party of the N'd Fusiliers under Capt. Gordon then charged, taking the position with the loss of only one man: the enemy had bolted after the first shell was fired. The gun was at once limbered up and it disappeared as rapidly as possible. This was a rare example of the use of a single field-gun to which it might be difficult to find a parallel in the war.

Capt. H. F. G. Carter, who had been appointed Adjutant of the 2/K.O.Y.L.I. on the 3rd November, was wounded in Hooge on the 17th, and Capt. M. F. Day on his arrival to join found himself appointed in Capt. Carter's place.

In a letter dated "Headquarters, 2nd Inf. Bde., 1st Div., Monday, 16th November, 1914," from Lt. C. R. T. Thorp, K.O.Y.L.I. Bde. Signalling Officer, 2nd Inf. Bde., addressed to his brother he says:

"*The 2nd Battalion K.O.Y.L.I. were brought up into our line on the 14th; they did well as usual, but three officers, including A. B. Smyth, were missing when I went round near Harenthage at dawn yesterday* (*15th Nov.*). *Probably all killed. Withycombe is now in command of 105th with Carter as adjutant. Fernyhough*[1] *is our Divisional Ordnance Officer* (*1st Div.*). *I am fit but it is snowing and raining, trenches half-full of water.* . . ."

Fighting was now constant; bombardment by high-explosive shells and bombs forced portions of the line temporarily out of their trenches, which were immediately retaken; occasionally a particularly well-aimed shell would destroy a portion of a trench and men would be buried and lost. In this way Capt. J. Pyman lost his life on the 18th November.

On the 20th the battalion marched to billets at Locre, where they were met by a reinforcement of 193 N.C.O.s and men under Capt. Day. On the 26th there arrived a further draft of 100 rank and file with Capt. F. W. Yates and 2/Lt. W. Plumer.

Field Marshal Sir John French paraded the battalion and addressed it in most complimentary terms.

Their brief period of rest came to an end on the 28th, when the battalion went again into the trenches 1½ miles to the east of Wulverghem, with its right resting on the river Douve. The enemy trenches were 150 yards distant, and snipers were most active both day and night when the moon was bright.

On the 1st December, five officers (Capt. R. T. A. Ball-Acton and 2/Lt. T. Gash, K.O.Y.L.I., with Lt. E. W. Leather and 2/Lts. G. F. Hadow and N. E. Lee, Green Howards) and 190 rank and file joined the battalion, as did also another draft of sixty-six with three officers (2/Lts. R. A. W. Williams, C. G. R. Hunter and M. R. Singleton) on the 6th December. With a brief interval in billets at St. Jans Cappel in Corps reserve, trenches east of Lindenhoek on the slopes of Hill 75 were occupied. These trenches were in many places waist deep in water owing to recent heavy rains, and on one occasion it became a matter of hours to drag out four men by means of ropes who had got badly stuck in the mud, for the enemy's trenches were here only fifty yards away. On the 12th December a draft of ninety-five men arrived. From these trenches it was a relief to be withdrawn to

[1] *Now Brigadier H. C. Fernyhough, C.B., C.M.G., D.S.O., of the R.A.O.C. Formerly in the 2/K.O.Y.L.I.*

Dranoutre. During the next period in the same trenches the casualties from the enemy's fire numbered six killed and eleven wounded, all due to snipers: during the same period eighty-odd men were lost to the ranks from swollen feet and legs as a result of standing for forty-eight hours on end knee-deep in water and mud. Christmas Day, a clear frosty day, was spent in billets at St. Jans Cappel. A six-a-side inter-company football competition marked the day and was won by "A" Company, and a draft of ninety-two rank and file under Capt. E. C. de R. Martin joined up. Capt. C. S. Buckle and 2/Lt. G. J. Child joined shortly after on the 29th at Neuve Eglise, when the battalion was about to occupy trenches on the river Douve. New Year's Day, 1915, found it once more in billets at Neuve Eglise. It must not be imagined that Neuve Eglise was exactly a haven of rest, for one big shell alone on the 5th January, which dropped in the town, killed nine men of the Q.V. Rifles, three of the K.O.S.B., and one of the K.O.Y.L.I. and the Army Chaplain, besides wounding twenty-five others. On the 6th January a move was made to the trenches by way of Wulverghem, and Sir Charles Fergusson, now in command of the II Corps, inspected the battalion on its way and addressed it.

This period of the trench life was marked by the overflowing of the river Douve, which flooded some of the trenches and temporarily cut the headquarters of the battalion off from the companies.

The next period was in divisional reserve at Bailleul from the 11th to the 15th January. The occupation of fire trenches and withdrawal to positions in reserve were becoming matters of routine now; a certain number of casualties were constantly inflicted by the enemy snipers, and others by their shell-fire. It was an event affording great satisfaction and a happy break in the monotony of trench warfare when the news of the arrival in France of the 1/K.O.Y.L.I. with the 28th Div. was received, and when it became known that the two battalions were likely to meet. The first intimation was the arrival of Capts. H. Mallinson and G. H. Staveley and Lt. A. U. Collis-Browne, all of the 1st Bn., who were attached to the 2nd Bn. for instruction in trench work. During the next rest at Bailleul the C.O.s. of the two battalions were able to arrange their meeting near Outersteene. On the 29th January, accordingly, the battalions marched out of their billets and marched till they met; they were drawn up in a field facing one another: after piling arms the men were allowed to fall out and make one another's acquaintance or renew old friendships. After two hours they returned to their respective billets. It was a memorable day for both battalions. The 29th January is observed in the 2nd Bn. to commemorate the fight at Shinkamar on the north-west frontier in 1898, and is regarded as an annual holiday when circumstances permit.

Up to this day the history of the Regiment in the great war had been the story of one battalion alone; the second period of the war for the Regiment started with the arrival of the 1st Bn. on the field.

For nearly six months the whole brunt of the fighting had fallen on the shoulders of the 2nd Bn., and to them alone had been confided the task of upholding the high traditions of the King's Own Yorkshire Light Infantry bequeathed to the Regiment by the men of Minden, Corunna, and The Peninsula.

Once the stabilised warfare 1915 to 1918 set in, the individual actions of battalions become merged in the mighty mass of fighting humanity. One after another battalions arrive in the field until the representatives of a regiment have the strength of the infantry of a division. Their achievements are the achievements of the divisions to which they were allotted: it is often no simple matter to extract their personal history to make a more intimate record.

A break may well be made here to trace the movements of the 1st Bn. which led up to its appearance as a part of the reinforcements which were received with such a deep sense of relief by the hard-pressed and battered troops of the thin khaki line of resistance in northern France.

The following, which shows how history repeats itself, and reflects the hopes and anxieties at the front at this period, may fittingly be introduced to conclude this chapter: it is justly described as "*An interesting coincidence.*"

Maj. Samuel Rice, 51st Light Infantry, during the Peninsular War (in later days often referred to as The Great War), from Headquarters, 51st Light Infantry at Pena Macor dated 4th December, 1811, wrote:—

"*We have got papers down to 15th November, 1811. Grand news was expected such as 'Northern Coalition,' the old joke. I wish we could get those 'Russian Bears' on foot. Nothing can be done here but by something of the sort.*"

Lt. C. R. T. Thorp, K.O.Y.L.I., writes during the European War of 1914, subsequently called The Great War, from Headquarters, 2nd Inf. Bde., near Essars, north-east of Béthune, dated 27th December, 1914:—"*Good news from Russia to-day. I hope the 'Russian Steam Roller' will work. We want it.*"

THE ARRIVAL OF THE FIRST BATTALION. 1915

IV

THE 1/K.O.Y.L.I. was stationed in Tanglin Barracks, Singapore, in 1914, and was carrying out its usual routine when at 12.30 p.m. the 30th July a bombshell burst over it in the shape of a cable message ordering the precautionary stage of mobilisation. It must be remembered that mails took three weeks to make the journey from England, and except for some startling cables which appeared in the local Press, rumours of war had been very meagre. Lt.-Col. A. G. Marrable was in England on leave and had been instantly appropriated by the home authorities for important staff duties in France. Maj. W. M. Withycombe was left in command. The battalion moved to its mobilisation stations early the following morning.

The following is a list of the officers who were serving with the battalion at the time:—

Maj. W. M. Withycombe, O.C.; Capts. W. Gowans, K. E. Warden, F. J. G. Agg, H. Mallinson, H. K. Hughes (Adjutant), G. M. Bond; Lts. G. H. Staveley (Intelligence Officer), F. J. Wyley, K. Lambert, E. H. de W. Bradley (Bde. Signalling Officer), J. A. Jervois, Hon. H. A. Law (Cyclist Scout Officer); 2/Lts. A. U. Collis-Browne (Machine-Gun Officer), H. L. Bowen, W. P. Bradley-Williams; Lt. and Qr.-Mr. J. C. Brasier.

The strength of the battalion, exclusive of officers, was 882.

The battalion did not omit to commemorate Minden Day on the 1st August; a parade to troop the Colour was held at sundown on the barrack ground, companies returning afterwards to their mobilisation stations. His Excellency The Hon. R. J. Wilkinson, the officer administering the government, attended by the G.O.C., Maj.-Gen. R. N. R. Reade, was present, and addressed the battalion in a fine stirring speech, all the more impressive seeing how critical were the times in which they were all living.

At 9.30 a.m. the 4th August, news of the Declaration of War were received, and mobilisation was forthwith carried out. On the 7th the first active participation in the war occurred when a party of twenty-one men under an officer was sent to Tanjong Pagar Wharf to arrest thirty-three German reservists who were attempting to leave for Europe by a Dutch boat. The island was regularly patrolled and the first prisoners were secured.

The battalion was in a state of preparedness to embark at the shortest notice; a succession of orders and counter-orders was received. Hopes of active service were high and the situation became tense as week succeeded week without the arrival of the anticipated orders. Maj. W. M. Withycombe received orders to proceed home to take command of the 2nd Bn., that command now being vacant. As battalions always will, when serving in far-away stations abroad, the 1st Bn. began to fear it might be overlooked, until at last orders were received to embark in H.M. Transport *Carnarvonshire*. The embarkation actually took place on the 27th September, under the command of Capt. W. Gowans, the battalion numbering 887 all ranks, with twenty-five wives and forty-four children. The destination was said to be Mhow in India. The transport sailed in company with the *Arcadia*, having on board the 2/Glosters from Tientsin, and the *Nile*, with the 2/D.C.L.I. from Hongkong. The Russian cruiser *Askold* acted as escort with the armed merchant cruiser *H.M.S. Empress of Asia* (a Canadian-Pacific converted liner).

The convoy arrived at Colombo on the 4th October. An amusing scene occurred there when the Lascar crew assembled on the poop, and using mooring chains and ropes, deserted the ship. The regimental police in the ships' boats gave chase and recovered some of the crew who were swimming for shore. Rumours of the activities of the German cruiser *Emden* in eastern waters probably accounted for this unsettled state of the Lascars. Great secrecy was preserved as to the destination of the convoy and its movements, in order to escape the attentions of this most active enemy. In the end a crew was collected chiefly of men whose ships had been sunk by the *Emden*.

On the 6th the convoy sailed with sealed orders, the escort being joined by the French cruiser *Dupleix* which the men said looked like a resurrected ark with a couple of funnels stuck on bow and stern. They irreverently nicknamed the *Askold* the *Packet of Woodbines*, a brand of cigarettes made up in packets of five, the number of her funnels. The course was changed for Aden, which was made on the 14th of October and left behind again on the 17th. Whilst the *Carnarvonshire* was lying to at Ismailia, a large convoy of ships passed outward bound with British Territorial troops on board. Much chaff passed between those who were bound for Europe and those who were bound 'in the wrong direction.' The outward bound dubbed the homecomers 'Kitchener's Roses,' for Lord Kitchener had recently stated in a speech that the flower of the army was still to come from India. It was here that the first English papers were received which contained casualty lists, which were received with consternation, for the names of the greater part of the 2nd Bn. were included.

Port Said was left behind on the 26th October. Malta was reached three days later, and Gibraltar was sighted the 1st November, after two days of heavy weather during which the transport, a heavy cargo boat, behaved with commendable sobriety. Finally, Southampton was reached at 11 a.m. on the 9th November, the battalion being entrained for Winchester by 4.30 p.m. and marched straight for Hursley Park Camp.

Here the arrival was unexpected. Married families had been dropped at Southampton and heavy baggage forwarded to Dewsbury.

Hursley Park presented a dismal appearance. Imagine 900 men direct from the tropics, arriving at night in drizzling rain, in mud up to the knees, clad in khaki drill, in a camp of crazy tents mostly lying about on the ground, with no preparation made for their reception. The realities of wartime were brought instantly home to the men. Sleep was out of the question; most of the men tramped up and down throughout the night to keep warm, while the camp staff were doing what they could to mobilise oilsheets and blankets for them. There was no breakfast available, and the morning was fully spent before rations arrived. The days that followed were not so uncomfortable. On the 18th the battalion moved to Parkeston Quay, Harwich, where the men went into billets and were warmly welcomed by the inhabitants. Lt.-Col. C. R. Ingham Brooke joined on the 16th December to take command, and many new officers reported their arrival. The following day the period of refitment was completed and the battalion returned to Hursley Park to be incorporated with the 28th Div. (Maj.-Gen. Bulfin). The battalion became a unit of the 83rd Inf. Bde., under the command of Brig.-Gen. R. C. Boyle.

Owing to the continual bad weather and the state of the camp, the whole division was moved into billets in Winchester, the 1/K.O.Y.L.I. finding comfortable quarters in the Castle.

On the 12th January H.M. King George inspected the division. The following day the Colonel of the Regiment, Gen. Sir Arthur Wynne, arrived to inspect the battalion before its departure to the war.

On the 15th the 28th Div., with the 1/K.O.Y.L.I. as leading battalion, marched to Southampton. The battalion embarked in *H.M.T. City of Benares* for Le Havre, disembarking and entraining there next morning. It was carried to Hazebrouck and marched to billets in Outersteene (18th January). The weather was very severe. War training was at once in full swing. Parties were sent up to the trenches in the front to be initiated. Inspection visits were made, the most notable being that on the 28th when the G.O.C. in C., Lord French, accompanied by H.R.H. The Prince of Wales, inspected the 83rd Inf. Bde. As mentioned in a previous chapter, the 1st and 2nd Bns. met on the road to Bailleul on the 29th January.

With the opening of the year the British army in France underwent a reconstruction. The biggest unit hitherto had been the Army Corps; with the growth of the force a higher unit became necessary and the several corps were henceforward organised by 'Armies.' Two Armies were complete and were composed as follows:—
The First Army, under Sir Douglas Haig, comprised the I (Sir Hubert Gough), the IV (Sir Henry Rawlinson), and the Indian Corps (Sir James Willcocks).

The II Army, under Sir Horace Smith-Dorrien, consisted of the II Corps (Sir Charles Fergusson), the III (Gen. Pulteney), and the V Corps (Gen. Plumer).

A Third Army was also forming. Most brigades were strengthened by the addition of one or two Territorial battalions, as fast as the latter came upon the scene.

(The 4th and 5th Bns. K.O.Y.L.I. arrived in France on the 13th April, 1915, with the 49th Div., Maj.-Gen. Braithwaite being G.O.C.)

At the time of the arrival of the 1st Bn. in the field the First Army was holding the southern sector of the British front. The Second Army was responsible for the northern sector. The 28th Div. joined the II Army, being in Gen. Plumer's Corps. Thus the two old regular battalions were in the same army and belonged to two corps which were fighting side by side: in the constant interchange of positions, occasioned as the fighting waxed hottest in one or other section of the front, it will be seen that there were times when the battalions actually marched in relief one of the other.

Though the next massed fighting was not to be experienced till the middle of April in the second battle of Ypres, the rival armies were locked in one another's embrace like two men boxing who lean on one another to recover their wind, and are ever watchful for an opening and alert that they may not be taken unawares. The winter 1914-1915 had been a period of unmitigated hardship and unremitting toil for the soldiers in the field.

The initiative in the spring campaign could hardly fail to be with the German forces. That the links in the chain of resistance had been forged in the face of the colossal attempts to break through, and that the northern ports of France were saved, had been achievements of the Allied armies of northern France in 1914 which may well be called providential. Every man in England who could be sent out trained and equipped, and every gun that could be assembled, were being hurried across the Channel to help to withstand the shock of the inevitable storm to come, for the Germans could not have relinquished their designs on Calais.

The 1st Bn. went into the trenches at Verbrandenmolen for the first time on the 1st February, arriving there by means of buses which they parted from at Vlamertinghe. They relieved a French battalion.

Some miles of front of what is known as the Ypres Salient were thus occupied by the 27th and 28th Divs. in relief of the French. The reliefs were carried out in the night, French guides leading the companies to their trenches. The 1/K.O.Y.L.I. trenches lay on either side of the Ypres-Comines Canal, about 4,000 yards south-east of Ypres. It was an unpleasant experience for the newcomers, for the trenches were bad and isolated, many were waterlogged and filled with the bodies of dead Frenchmen, indeed some parapets appeared to be built of bodies. The battalion was relieved on the night of the 4th-5th February. It marched to Ouderdom. The casualties during the period had been four officers wounded, eleven other ranks killed and sixty-eight wounded.

The second period in the trenches was a repetition of the first; casualties, seven other ranks killed and twenty-nine wounded. Already 207 men had been evacuated sick with 'trench feet.' The recent transference from a tropical climate accounted for numerous cases of sickness.

Many of the trenches on this front had been mined, and the exploding of the mines shortly after the arrival of the new divisions caused heavy losses. Thus short lengths of trench were taken by the Germans temporarily, and a series of minor operations would be initiated in order to re-establish the line. The 1st Bn. gained some local successes of this nature, which were marked by the recognition and approbation of their Brigadier. There were a number of casualties. Four officers were wounded (Capts. H. Mallinson and G. H. Staveley, Lts. H. Briguier and J. A. S. Trydell): of other ranks eleven were killed and sixty-six wounded; twenty-four men were sent down with trench feet during the same period.

The next sector held by the battalion covered Verbrandenmolen. The famous Hill 60, destined to become the scene of desperate fighting later, was immediately to the front of the left company's trenches. Hill 60 was strongly held by the enemy with machine-guns. Our artillery at times gave its attention to the spot, a compliment which would be returned by the enemy guns with particular attention paid to the opposing battalion's headquarters.

On the 25th February the 1st Bn., being in relief of a battalion of the 13th Inf. Bde., temporarily established the headquarters of its transport in Ypres. This city at the time was recovering from the first bombardment of November, 1914, and the inhabitants were returning. Shops were being opened and stalls were being erected in the streets on market days.

On the 1st March relief came, and on the way to Ouderdom the 2nd Bn. was passed. Next day the 1st Bn. (with the 83rd. Inf. Bde.) was temporarily transferred for duty with the 5th Div., while the 13th Bde. went to the 28th Div. The 1st Bn. was in the trenches for 14 days in the Wulverghem sector. Three small drafts totalling four officers and 110 other ranks joined. A further draft of one officer and 45 other ranks came in on the 20th March. On the 7th April Gen. Smith-Dorrien inspected the 83rd Inf. Bde. on its rejoining the 28th Div. On the 12th April the 1st Bn. marched out of Ypres by the Menin Gate to relieve the 2/E.York., holding the right section of the 83rd Inf. Bde., south of Zonnebeke, 4½ miles east of Ypres. The trenches were in a wooded country, many in indifferent repair: the Germans who had sapped to within a few yards were able to fire down the communication trenches, so that reliefs had to be carried out at night with the greatest caution. Lt. A. U. Collis-Browne was killed in the trenches on the 13th April; he was machine-gun officer. The enemy's trench-guns were a nuisance which could only be temporarily stopped by our artillery shrapnel-fire. Lt. R. A. Houghton was wounded before the battalion returned to temporary quarters west of Ypres.

The two battalions had from the 19th February onwards been in close co-operation, for the 13th and 83rd Inf. Bdes. were interchanging positions, and the former relieved the latter in the trenches by Verbrandenmolen on the 19th February. The German trenches were only 25 yards distant, so close indeed that the German soldiers on one occasion attempted to draw the occupants of our trenches into communication by throwing letters and newspapers across. They shouted for cigarettes, but the men opposed to them were in no mood for such pleasantries and replied with hand-grenades.

The 13th was by this time a seasoned brigade. Though few of the original officers and men of the 2/K.O.Y.L.I. remained, the prestige of the battalion was firmly established. The wastage suffered under the enemy's fire was constant. On the 23rd February 2/Lt. H. L. Slingsby had been wounded, so leaving Lt. and Qr.-Mr. A. E. Bentham as the sole representative of the original officers who left Dublin. Capt. G. H. C. Palmer, with a draft of forty-three other ranks, joined the 2nd Bn. on the 24th February. The 1/R.W.K. and the 2/D.W.R. lost six officers and 100 men on the 25th from shell and minenwerfer fire in the trenches: to add to the discomforts there was a heavy fall of snow. The following day was quieter and the 2nd Bn. was this day relieved in its trenches at Blaauwepoort by the 1st Bn.

During a rest at Vlamertinghe about the 7th April, after the 13th Inf. Bde. had completed a period of duty with the 28th Div., a letter was received by Lt.-Col. Withycombe, written by Brig.-Gen. Wanless-O'Gowan, now in command of the 13th Inf. Bde., in which he wrote: "*Yesterday I received a letter from Sir Charles Fergusson saying that Sir Horace Smith-Dorrien had told him that Gen. Bulfin reported that he had never seen battalions with more go and spirit than those of the 13th Inf. Bde., or battalions that gave more complete confidence. Sir Charles wishes me to tell you how proud and delighted he is, and to congratulate you and all your officers, N.C.O.'s and men. Everyone says it is all right now that these two brigades have arrived, and every bit of work now put in will be for the safety of the army as there is little doubt that sooner or later a big struggle will take place in this area. I am writing to Sir Charles to assure him that his confidence will not be misplaced so far as the 13th Brigade is concerned."*

HILL 60. 1915

V

IT was obvious that the storm clouds were gathering round Ypres, for the activity of the enemy was incessant, snipers were constantly on the alert and casualties were numerous. The bombardment of the town of Ypres became more and more frequent. Neither 1st nor 2nd Bn. had participated in the battle of Neuve Chapelle of the 10th-12th March, which was notable as the first hard knock of the year in which British troops wrested a portion of the line from the Germans and established themselves in possession in the face of all counter-attacks. The operations of Neuve Chapelle had been entrusted to the IV Corps (Rawlinson) and the Indian Corps (Willcocks). The 2nd Cav. Div. had been held in reserve. Echoes of the thunder of the guns came down the line, but attention was so riveted on the immediate front that an operation of this magnitude at this period merely obtained passing reference. A second operation of the same nature as that of Neuve Eglise followed in the attack and capture of Hill 60. In this the 2nd Bn. took a prominent part, for the attack on the hill was originally entrusted to the 13th Inf. Bde. The attack formed the overture to the second great battle of Ypres, but as it formed a definite operation in itself and for the time being focussed the attention of a considerable portion of the troops on one little rising bit of ground, it is worthy of a short chapter to itself.

The attack was made on the 17th April and the hill remained in our hands only after a sanguinary battle lasting three days. For weeks after that the question of the retention of the hill was disputed intermittently, but the fight that we are now concerned in was the fight of those three days of April.

The importance of the hill lay in the fact that in its elevation of some 50 feet above the surrounding flat country it formed a most important post for the direction of artillery batteries. From its highest point the Germans could overlook our position and its approaches for some miles back to Ypres: occupied by us, movement for our troops in the area between the front line and Ypres would become comparatively safe in daylight.

The total length of the hill was only some 250 yards, so that when captured there was not room in the trenches on its heights for more than one strong company of infantry. It was very uncomfortable for the companies of the brigade who were immediately opposed to it to have this hillock dominating them, bristling with machine-guns as it was and harbouring snipers who were always on the lookout for a snap shot. The preparations for the attack had been carefully made; six mines had been driven underneath the hill and the explosion of the mines was timed for 7 p.m. on the 17th April. The storming party was drawn from the R.W.K. and the K.O.S.B., Maj. Joslin of the former regiment being in command the remainder of the 13th Inf. Bde. were in support.

On the morning of the 17th April the 2/K.O.Y.L.I., who had been in support resting in billets at Reninghelst since the 11th April, moved to Ypres in connection with the forthcoming attack. The six mines were duly exploded in three series at ten seconds interval, under Hill 60. The explosion was accompanied by a heavy bombardment of the hill, lasting about fifteen minutes. Immediately after this the hill was stormed and captured by the storming companies of the R.W.K., who were twice counter-attacked but who held on to the trenches in spite of bombs and guns, until the K.O.S.B. took their place in the forward positions. At dawn on the 18th a very strong counter-attack on the northern end of the hill compelled the K.O.S.B. to give way and the summit was retaken by the Germans.

At 7 a.m. the 2/K.O.Y.L.I. moved forward from Ypres and took the place of the 2/D.W.R. (who had moved forward to the hill) under the railway embankment short of the hill, where it remained until noon. In the meantime the D.W.R. relieved the K.O.S.B. under the hill. At 12.30 the K.O.Y.L.I. moved forward into a larch wood just short of Hill 60, where the men were under heavy shell-fire and were in support of the D.W.R. The R.W.K. and the K.O.S.B. retired behind the railway.

At 3 p.m. orders came that the hill must be retaken at all costs, and it fell to the D.W.R. and the K.O.Y.L.I. to make the assault. The situation and order of battle were as follows:—The D.W.R. were in position in dead ground at the foot of the hill and also held trenches numbered 39 and 40 (*vide* sketch): the K.O.Y.L.I. held ground just in rear. At 5 p.m. the D.W.R. filed up some communicating trenches leading to the base of the hill, where they massed. The K.O.Y.L.I. at the same time moved forward up the railway cutting and communicating trench into 39 and 40 trenches, about 80 yards from the foot of the hill, Bn. Headquarters moving at the same time from the little larch wood into 39 trench. At 6 p.m., the hour at which the assault was timed to take place, the D.W.R. advanced up the slope of the hill, and at the same moment "B" Company, K.O.Y.L.I., under Capt. G. E. Alt, and "C" Company under Capt. G. H. Kent, rushed forward from 39 and 40 trenches, dashed across the open space to the foot of the hill and up the slope, intermingling with the D.W.R. in the assault. "A" Company under Capt. F. W. Yates followed close, carrying spades and hand grenades, "D" Company under Capt. G. H. C. Palmer, which had been waiting behind in the communicating trench, moved up to occupy trenches 39 and 40. The whole advance was covered by our artillery fire, which heavily bombarded the hill and the ground in rear of it, to prevent reinforcements of Germans from coming up to the hill crest. Immediately they left the cover of the trenches and went over the top, "B" and "C" Companies were met by a hail of artillery, machine and rifle-fire, which caused very heavy casualties. However, they reached the base of the hill and dashed up the slopes, carrying forward the D.W.R., who were by that time being hard pressed, and after a momentary hesitation, which gave the appearance that the attack was doomed to failure, the line crossed the German parapet, and the crest of the hill was retaken. When once the stormers got to close quarters the German troops fled in panic down the communicating trenches, leaving rifles, equipment and ammunition behind them. They could not, however, get away, for their trenches became blocked with their own dead and wounded, and most of them were either captured or killed by our rifle-fire, bayonets or hand grenades.

After the capture of the hill, "A" Company, who had arrived with spades, transferred the parapet of the trench to the opposite side. It was one thing to take the hill; to hold it was another. Throughout the night the companies on the top were subjected to the concentrated fire of forty-four German batteries of field and heavy artillery (the number was given by a German officer captured on the hill, who had been observing for his artillery). The Germans also counter-attacked continuously, using hand grenades and bombs, and furious encounters took place in the craters made by the explosion of the mines. These soon became a shambles filled with the dead and the dying. There was one crater on the extreme left which could not be held, as the new trench cut by our men ran a few yards short of it; the position of occupation was continued to the right to include all the other craters. The German high-explosive shells gave off suffocating fumes which caused great distress among the men who continued to hold on. Rifles got jammed from the heat engendered by the rapid firing, and grenades and ammunition were difficult to bring up owing to the block of wounded in the communicating and fire trenches. If it had not been for the stacks of rifles and ammunition left behind by the enemy and used by our men in the place of their own, the position on the hill would have been maintained with even greater difficulty; however, the grip on the hill was never lost and the trenches passed to the Bedfs. (15th Inf. Bde.) at dawn on the 19th April. After the relief the 2/K.O.Y.L.I. retired to the wood in rear of 35 trench.

During the 19th the enemy again effected a footing on the left crest of the hill but a counter-attack by the 9/London (Q.V. Rifles), the last remaining battalion of the 13th Inf. Bde., dislodged him again and the hill was finally secured.

The 2/K.O.Y.L.I. rested and bivouacked in their little wood throughout the 19th April, and marched at 10.30 a.m. on the 20th to the huts at Ouderdom. Gen. Smith-Dorrien, Gen. Fergusson and Gen. Morland all called in the course of the day to congratulate Lt.-Col. Withycombe and the battalion on the recapture of Hill 60, and on the following day Brig.-Gen. Wanless-O'Gowan paraded the battalion and addressed it.

A draft of fifty-two other ranks joined, and Capt. C. E. D. King also rejoined for duty with the battalion, but the gaps made in the ranks during the three days' fighting were such as required many drafts of that size to refill.

Of the officers, Capt. G. E. Alt and Capt. G. W. Leather had been killed; also Lts. G. J. Child, R. A. W. Williams, H. B. Hodges, J. H. Oldham and F. J. M. Chubb. Capts. F. W. Yates and F. J. Wyley died from wounds.

The wounded officers were Capt. G. H. Kent and Lts. T. Wells, C. H. Dixon, T. F. J. Upton, R. H. Way and C. H. Webb.

Of the other ranks twenty-five were killed, 190 wounded, and ten were accounted for as missing.

A special Order of the Day contained a message from H.M. The King, congratulating the troops who took part in the capture of Hill 60.

The C.-in-C. addressed the 13th Inf. Bde. at Ouderdom on the 22nd April in these words:—

"*. . . . This is the first opportunity I have had of seeing you and saying how deeply and truly I appreciate your magnificent work, and the operation of bringing to a glorious conclusion a great and important plan with far-reaching results.*

"*The operation was planned by Lt.-Gen. Bulfin, who knew the ground so well, and it was ably planned and ably carried out. It fell to you to carry it through; on the 17th April at 7 p.m. six mines were exploded under the enemy's trenches on Hill 60. The hill had to be taken, and the West Kent and K.O.S.B. were chosen to take it. These two regiments gallantly and splendidly advanced and took the position. But they knew that the taking of it was only the smallest part of the work to be done. All through that long night they were subjected to the terrific fire of the enemy's artillery.*

"*That piece of ground was very important to either side. It is good as an artillery observation post. It is useful to us, but it was much more important to the enemy. From it he can observe all the surrounding country back to Ypres, and thus we knew that on account of its great importance he would put up a stubborn fight to regain it. Whatever we may say against the Germans, they are brave, courageous men and worthy of our steel. Early next morning found the West Kent and K.O.S.B. repelling attack after attack with the utmost gallantry and tenacity. At last it was necessary to relieve them, though they would have stayed to the last man, so the K.O.Y.L.I. and West Riding were sent up, and it was the same that awaited them; violent attack after attack was delivered against them; with the same gallantry and tenacity as the other two battalions showed they held the position for thirty-six hours and threw the enemy back time after time with heavy loss. Then came the time to relieve them, and the Bedford and East Surrey Regiments took their place; and again the same attacks, and again the same loss to the enemy. Yet this does not tell one-hundredth or one-thousandth part of all that you did.*

"I can only thank you with all my heart, men. I thank Gen. Smith-Dorrien, I thank Gen. Sir Charles Fergusson, Gen. Morland and Brig.-Gen. Wanless-O'Gowan.

"Here again let me say, though your casualty lists have been heavy, your officers are in greater proportion than the N.C.O.s and men. They go forward like true British soldiers, knowing that you will follow them. That is the secret of the greatness of our success: it will live for ever.

"I have heard it said that education and temperance have lowered the standard of our army, and that unless you carry on as they did, you will not be so good campaigners as the men of the Crimea or Peninsula. You have lived to give the lie to that statement, and that is what this campaign has brought out—that the higher the moral tone of the men, the greater will be our success—so, I leave you something to think about . . . ."

Man of the K.O.Y.L.I. washing clothes in an officer's canvas bath. Ypres-Comines Canal

To face page 763.

THE SECOND BATTLE OF YPRES. 1915

VI

THE German preparations for the second great attack, made with the object of bursting through the defences of the Ypres salient, were complete. Their XXVI and XXVII Corps were those immediately opposed to the salient.

The salient, that is, the semi-circle of protecting lines established at an average radius of five miles east of the city of Ypres, was held as to the northern sector by troops of the French Eighth Army: they held the line from Bixschoote (in advance of the Yser canal) as far as the Ypres-Poelcapelle road, 2,000 yards east of Langemarck.

Gen. Plumer's V Corps came next, his line curving southwards by the Gravenstafel ridge, and passing about a mile east of Zonnebeke; then its trend was more directly southwards, outside the Polygon Wood, to the neighbourhood of Hill 60 where the 5th Div. (II Corps) were in position.

The divisions of the V Corps occupied sectors in the following order from left to right:—the Canadian Div. (Alderson), the 28th (Bulfin) and the 27th (Snow).

The second battle of Ypres, which was immediately preceded by the struggle for Hill 60, commenced on April 22nd with the gas attack on the northern sector,and lasted till the night of May 24th. It constituted the one great and serious effort on the part of the Germans to break the line at Ypres in 1915. Division after division was called upon to assist the heroic defenders in stemming the German onslaught. Besides the three divisions of the V Corps enumerated above, portions of the Indian Corps, of the 50th Territorial Div., and portions of the 4th and 5th Divs. were hurled into the fight to fill the gap.

The 13th Inf. Bde. had been badly mauled in the fight for Hill 60 and had withdrawn to the shelter of the dug-outs at Ouderdom to dress its wounds and refit. It was here that on the 22nd April Field Marshal Sir John French came to address the brigade, when he concluded by saying that he left his hearers something to think about, but he did not leave them overmuch time to assimilate the food for thought which he had brought them, for it had been 2.30 p.m. when the men were paraded to receive him, and at 7 p.m. the same afternoon the 2/K.O.Y.L.I. marched again with orders to relieve the Dorset battalion in sector C. However, as soon as the Ypres-Poperinghe road was reached the battalion was met by a continual stream of refugees coming from Ypres, followed by the

French Algerian troops and transport of all sorts, which completely blocked the road and the further march of the column. It soon became known that the Germans had used asphyxiating gases from cylinders on the French Algerian troops in their trenches between the Yser Canal and St. Julien, and that these troops had left their line of trenches, through which the Germans had broken and were advancing southwards on Ypres. It was known too that by this retirement the left of the British line had been left in the air.

This was on the 22nd April, and the attack on the Algerian troops, marked by the infamous use of poison gas, had opened at 5 p.m. that day and was the commencement of the German attack in what is known as the second battle of Ypres. Just how dastardly Germany as a nation considered the use of poison in warfare in order to effect that which could not be effected by legitimate means, was gleaned by those who read the German papers at this period. There was a howl of execration against the perpetrators and Germany expressed herself in unmeasured terms of horror. But as the German High Command had referred to the use of poison gas as the diabolical wickedness of the British and had pretended that it was German troops who had been asphyxiated, the German execration was directed the wrong way.

Though the Algerian troops suffered from the full force of the gas attack, the attack was by no means confined only to their sector. Their immediate neighbours of the Canadian Div. suffered severely from gas also, and the whole of the defence troops of the salient were involved in the German preparatory gun-fire.

There was no time to be lost in retrieving the position between St. Julien and the Canal. Among other troops, the 13th Inf. Bde. happened to be at hand. One battalion, the D.W.R., was temporarily withdrawn to repair the damages suffered on Hill 60. The other four battalions, weakened though they were, were still in a condition to uphold the reputation of the brigade, and these were promptly diverted to assist the Canadian Div. under Gen. Alderson, whose position, with German troops pouring round its left flank, was one of desperation. Thus the 2/K.O.Y.L.I. once again came under the orders of a General who had led them in S. Africa, in 1901, when as a unit of his column they served in what was then known as the Great Eastern Trek.

The 13th Inf. Bde. marched *via* Vlamertinghe to the neighbourhood of Brielen. The Germans were now occupying a line south of Pilken from the Yser Canal to St. Julien. The brigade advanced to the attack at 5 p.m. on the 23rd April. Other battalions under Col. Geddes of the Buffs were on the right. A considerable advance was made before nightfall and the line was consolidated during the night; the 2/K.O.Y.L.I., who had been in reserve, dug the trenches for the new position; they were relieved in the position at dawn on the 24th by the 4/R.B. At midday the 13th Inf. Bde. was called upon to assist the 10th Canadian Bde. in retaking the lost line north-east of Wieltje. The Canadian line was at the time being subjected to a heavy bombardment and the trenches preparatory to an advance were crowded with Canadian Highlanders. So the newcomers had to lie out in the open under the shell-fire, where they suffered heavily. Lt. C. G. R. Hunter was killed, and Capt. G. H. C. Palmer and Lt. Webb were wounded. Next morning early the attack was launched: the 2/K.O.Y.L.I. was at this time reduced to 250 bayonets and was in reserve to the Canadians. Fortuin was occupied. St. Julien was entered but could not be held. On the 26th the battalion was withdrawn to St. Jean, where it proceeded to dig itself in and came under a heavy shell-fire all that day and the next. A draft arrived, and Maj. C. E. Heathcote with six subaltern officers came in. Maj. W. Gowans, who had recently been transferred from the 1st Bn., was wounded on the 28th by shrapnel fire and died on the 2nd May. Fresh attacks were being delivered against the Germans by the French and by the Sirhind Div., so that the Germans were at least held for the time being, and by the 30th were forced to give ground. After a short experience in the firing line north of Wieltje the 2/K.O.Y.L.I. was withdrawn temporarily to Vlamertinghe and thence to Ouderdom on the 4th May. Here it had barely time to read the two very gratifying messages expressing the warm thanks of Gens. Plumer and Alderson in acknowledgment of the timely assistance rendered to the V Corps and 10th Canadian Div. respectively, when news came that Hill 60 had once again been lost after an attack preceded by poison gas. The 13th Inf. Bde. were advanced in order to retake the hill and the Zwartelleen salient.

An attack was made on the 5th May, but though the hill was occupied, the salient could not be taken, and so once again the hill had to be abandoned for the time being. The 2/K.O.Y.L.I. had been held in reserve during this attack.

A fresh attack was necessitated; orders came to carry this out, commencing at 2.30 a.m. on the 7th. The new attack on that portion which was known as the salient was entrusted to Lt.-Col. Withycombe and his men, supported by other battalions. The German line could be reconnoitred from 41 trench, which was only 100 yards distant from a new trench which the Germans had dug across the mouth of the salient. The plan of attack was formulated after a close reconnaissance by Lt.-Col. Withycombe and his company commanders.

A reference to the sketch map will explain the position. The enemy held Hill 60, the Zwartelleen salient, and all the line of trench marked (-------) on the map. The 2/Cheshire R. on the right was holding 38, 39 and 40 trenches. The position held by the Germans was therefore in prolongation of 40 trench, and between them and the Cheshire Bn. there was merely a barrier which both sides had been busy in erecting. On the left of the salient, as the 2/K.O.Y.L.I. stood facing it, the R.U.R. occupied a position similar to the Cheshire Bn. on the right. The plan was to blow in the barrier on the Cheshire side with gun-cotton at 2.30 a.m. which was to be the signal for the assault by the 2/K.O.Y.L.I. The assault would take place in any case even should the explosion not be successfully brought off. The explosion did not occur. At the appointed hour "B" and "A" Companies, the stormers, led by Capt. C. E. D. King and Lt. R. M. Roberts respectively, went over the top of 41 parapet and dashed for the German trenches which spanned the salient. Before ten yards were crossed they were met by a terrific fire from rifles and machine-guns, which mowed them down. They reached the enemy's trench, or at least some of them did, and captured it, and they crossed it into the salient. They were followed by "C" Company, and then by "D." The latter company, however, in the darkness lost direction and found itself in 40 trench. Meanwhile the looked-for explosion had taken place and the Cheshiremen advanced along 40 trench part way into the salient. The Germans were still holding the back trenches of the salient. The attackers were swallowed up in the darkness.

The first information as to the fate of the attackers was brought when Lt. R. M. Roberts came in wounded. All he knew was that the first trench had been crossed and that the survivors of "A" and "B" Companies were well up the salient. When dawn broke the postion was partially cleared up; it was obvious that the trenches of the salient itself were still occupied by the enemy. It was also obvious that if any of the attackers survived they could not communicate back or move before nightfall. The men of the Cheshire Bn. had been bombed back to their old position and had re-erected their barrier. The day that followed was a day of suspense all round. Darkness came at 7.45 p.m. and patrols were sent out to look for wounded men and to endeavour to ascertain what had become of the attack. Capt. C. E. D. King crawled in after dark. He had been wounded in the face and knocked over by a splinter during the dash across the open, but had carried on and crossed the first trench almost alone; inside the salient he tried to gather his men but, finding his party reduced to eight, had waited in a shell crater for reinforcements within twenty-five yards of the enemy's second line. The enemy discovered them and bombed them. The little party lay the whole of the next day in the shell-hole and crawled back at night. It was now evident that only a small number of men out of the three weak companies lived to enter the salient, and, as only a sprinkling from these companies ever returned, the remainder must have been killed or captured. Doubtless many wounded who were unable to get back died under the fire. As late as the 12th May three of the men crawled into 40 trench, two of whom died of exposure before they could speak. The third had a story to tell to the men of the P.W.V. Bn. whom he found in the trench; he said there was still a party consisting of an officer and about a dozen men in an old trench inside the salient quite close up to the enemy, and that they were living on raw potatoes and water. They refused to surrender and fired on the Germans whenever the latter attempted to advance on them. He gave it as his opinion that these men had no hope of getting back. The narrator died shortly after delivering his message. The truth of his story could not be verified.

The casualties suffered by the 2/K.O.Y.L.I. in this attack were as follows:—

Killed: Lt. F. W. Snape and twenty-one other ranks. Wounded: Capt. C. E. D. King, Lts. R. M. Roberts, M. Thom, A. D. Lumb, W. A. White, E. M. Gosschalk, J. R. Clarke and L. E. Roe; 116 other ranks. Missing: Lts. M. R. Singleton and G. B. Addenbrooke; forty other ranks. Total, eleven officers and 177 other ranks.

That night the battalion was relieved, and it returned once more to the railway embankment near Bde. Headquarters (7th May).

To return to the northern sector of the Ypres Salient, the net result of the strenuous fighting from the 22nd April to the end of the month was that the Germans were pushed back and held, but had advanced their line some two miles nearer to Ypres. The Germans then developed attacks further down the line and the 28th Div. was one of those that had to bear the brunt. The pressure throughout the end of April had been severe and the bombardment terrific. In order to conform to the new line and to prevent the salient protecting Ypres from becoming too pronounced, the line had to be modified and the semi-circular line from Zonnebeke southwards, which the 27th and 28th Divs. were holding, was drawn back, so that instead of having a radius of five miles from the city it now had a radius of three only. The 1/K.O.Y.L.I. were in the head of the salient about Friezenberg when the withdrawal took place on the 4th May, and the evacuation of the trenches was a matter that required skill and high discipline. The same night the battalion was taken out of the line for one of its periodical rests after a most strenuous week, during which it had lost in killed Lts. W. E. Boone and Swabey with forty-three other ranks, while Lt. A. Munro and 150 other ranks were wounded. However, the next day the full force of the German attack descended on the new line, and the battalion was ordered back into the trenches.

The gun-fire was tremendous. The 83rd Inf. Bde, suffered enormous casualties during this and the succeeding days. The battalion now showed that it could "stick it" just as the 2nd Bn. had been called upon to do before it. On the 8th it had a particularly heavy day: its trenches were heavily shelled by high-explosive, followed by infantry attacks. "A" and "B" Companies were shelled out of their trenches, but "C" and "D", after resisting three attacks, only withdrew at nightfall to a position slightly in rear. Among the casualties the battalion sustained, Capts. H. K. Hughes and K. Lambert were killed, while 2/Lt. T. Palmes was wounded, as was 2/Lt. J. A. P. Fergusson of the R. Sussex (attached). Lt. C. F. Wharton died of his wounds. Lt.-Col. C. R. Ingham Brooke and 2/Lt. A. H. Hutchinson were wounded; also 2/Lt. W. W. Owbridge, E. York (attached). 2/Lt. W. Bateman and Capt. P. G. M. Elvery, R.A.M.C., were missing. R.S.M. G. Lewis was killed. Casualties in other ranks from the 19th April to the 7th May included thirty-four killed, three who died of wounds, and 112 wounded. Casualties on the 8th included fifty-three killed, ninety-two wounded, and 272 missing. The four machine-guns were either destroyed by shell-fire or buried. Capt. H. Mallinson was left in command. He had well earned the D.S.O. which was shortly afterwards awarded "for his conspicuous gallantry and ability" displayed in the resistance at Frezenberg.

The remnants of the battalion returned to Ypres, but only in order to be included temporarily in a newly-formed composite battalion under Lt.-Col. Worsley Gough, in which transport men, cooks and every available man were taken and hurled into the line to assist to stem the attacks.

On the 12th May the 83rd Inf. Bde. was relieved in order to refit. Drafts came in one after another: Lt. J. A. Jervois rejoined from the Cycle Corps and took over the Adjutancy; Lts. J. L. Heath, R. O. Ackerley and A. E. Kemble joined, also Lts. Wells (R.A.M.C.), A. F. Alderson and O. F. P. Marshall; Maj. C. E. Heathcote came in on the 17th May to take command till Lt.-Col. C. R. Ingham Brooke's return. The 1st Bn., which had been withdrawn by 'bus to Winnezeele, was paraded by Brig.-Gen. Marden on the 17th and was inspected on the 20th by Sir John French, a précis of whose address will be found at the end of this chapter. Only five days later the 2nd Bn. was being addressed in a similar manner by Lt.-Gen. Plumer on behalf of the C.-in-C. These two addresses mark the close of the second battle of Ypres.

On the 22nd May the 1st Bn. again marched up to the front through Ypres, and it occupied trenches south-east of the town in the Sanctuary Wood, where it resumed the normal life of the trenches, including warnings of approaching gas, with the necessary damping of respirators, local attacks and temporary rests, during the remainder of May.

Hitherto in this record only a brief reference has been made to the use by the enemy of asphyxiating gas. The following account, written by Lt. F. K. Lambert, who was at the time serving as a N.C.O. with the 1st Bn., gives a picture which vividly illustrates the sufferings of the troops who were subjected to this fiendish device:—

"*In the early days of* 1915, *General Headquarters sent out a circular-letter stating reports had been received that the enemy was suspected of preparing to use asphyxiating gases as a weapon of attack, and signs of preparation for such an attack had been observed. Long metal cylinders were reported to have been dug in at various points along the Boche front line. As no preparations were made in the way of issuing some protective device against this new kind of warfare, it would appear that the Allied Command did not think that the enemy would resort to its use. On the other hand, until it was seen in what way this new weapon was to be used, and its effect, it was a perplexing question to find protection against it.*

"*On the* 22*nd April the enemy opened a very intense bombardment in the Ypres sector. The* 1*st Bn. were holding a portion of the line about St. Julien, the* 28*th Div. being on the left flank of the British Army,*[1] *and joining with a French Colonial Div. on the right of the French Army in Belgium.*

"*In the early afternoon a greenish-yellow cloud was seen to be approaching the French Colonial Div. line from the Boche trenches. Men looked at it in wonderment, such a phenomenon had never before been seen, and nobody realised what it was until the French Colonials were seen leaving their trenches.*

"*The enemy with his terrible ingenuity had selected a junction of two armies composed on the one hand of native troops of simple mind, and a worn-out British division on the other. There was no doubt that he meant the full force of his new and horrible weapon to fall on the simple-minded Africans, to whom witchcraft and magic were dreadful and fearsome things to be avoided. These poor fellows had suffered terrible bombardments and attacks, but in this new weapon there was something uncanny. Men gripped their throats as the terrible gas went to their lungs, and writhed in agony as they slowly succumbed to its effects. The rain of shells and machine-gun bullets poured unceasingly and pitilessly amongst them, but these did not account for the effects of the yellow-green cloud about them. It was some unseen hand, some new and terrible 'white man's magic' brought against them. It was too much for their simple minds to grasp, and they fled terrified from it. The whole of the French Colonial Div. streamed off in panic back across the fields to Vlamertinghe and Poperinghe, leaving a tremendous gap in the line. The* 84*th Bde., which was holding the extreme left of the British line, was also caught by the gas cloud. They hung on to their trenches.*

[1] *This would appear to be not quite accurate.*—[ED.]

Men dipped handkerchiefs or socks in filthy water and put them over their mouths and nostrils, and stuck to their rifles until the deadly gas overpowered them.

"*It was not until about six days after the first gas cloud that any preventive measures were received. Then small respirators made of a strip of muslin enclosing a wad of tow soaked in chemicals began to arrive. Two came at first to the battalion with instructions that they were to be issued to the front line sentries, then half-a-dozen, each day bringing a larger number, until every man in the battalion had one. As the supply increased a second one per man was issued.*

"*These respirators were worn with the wad of tow over the mouth and packed round the nostrils and tied behind the head with the muslin strip. The taste and smell were horrible and at first many men were averse to using them. They soon learnt their value and took great care to protect them. These respirators were superseded by the flannel helmet with mica eyepieces about a month later, and these in their turn gave way to an improved pattern, which was eventually replaced by the small box respirator of the present day.*"

Précis of speeches delivered by Field Marshal Sir John French, G.C.B., O.M., etc., C.-in.C. of the British Forces in the Field, to Brigades of the 27th and 28th Divs. on the 21st and 22nd May, 1915. Also communicated to 13th Inf. Bde.

"*I came over to say a few words to you and to tell you how much I, as Commander-in-Chief of this Army, appreciate the splendid work that you have all done during the recent fighting. You have fought the second battle of Ypres, which will rank among the most desperate and hardest fights of the war. You may have thought because you were not attacking the enemy that you were not helping to shorten the war. On the contrary, by your splendid endurance and bravery, you have done a great deal to shorten it. In this, the second battle of Ypres, the Germans tried by every means in their power to get possession of that unfortunate town. They concentrated large forces of troops and artillery and further than that they had recourse to that mean and dastardly practice hitherto unheard of in civilised warfare, namely the use of asphyxiating gases. You have performed the most difficult, arduous and terrific task of withstanding a stupendous bombardment by heavy artillery, probably the fiercest artillery-fire ever directed against troops, and warded off the enemy's attacks with magnificent bravery. By your steadiness and devotion, both the German plans were frustrated. He was unable to get possession of Ypres—if he had done this he would probably have succeeded in preventing neutral powers from intervening—and he was also unable to distract us from delivering our attack in conjunction with the French in Arras-Armentières district. Had you failed to repulse his attacks, and made it necessary for more troops to be sent to your assistance, our operations in the South might not have been able to take place and would certainly not have been as successful as they have been. Your Colours have many famous names emblazoned on them, but none will be more famous or more well-deserved than that of the second battle of Ypres. I want you one and all to understand how thoroughly I realise and appreciate what you have done. I wish to thank you, each officer, non-commissioned officer and man for the services you have rendered by doing your duty so magnificently, and I am sure that your Country will thank you too.*"

THE TERRITORIAL AND SERVICE BATTALIONS. 1914-1915

VII

WE will now hark back to trace the history of the Territorial battalions from the day of mobilisation, and of the new battalions that were born into the family of the K.O.Y.L.I. for service in the war.

THE DEPÔT AND 3RD (RESERVE) BN.

The Regimental Depôt and the 3rd (Reserve) Bn. also have their story, but these units exist only to feed and reinforce the regular battalions: their separate history is a record of devoted effort and unremitting endeavour to supply the battalions in the field with all that was necessary in drafts of trained soldiers, their equipment and necessaries. The ingenuity and resources of the staff in both cases were constantly taxed to the utmost; depôt and reserve battalion gave their lifeblood cheerfully and unreservedly to maintain the fighting units at the front.

THE TERRITORAL AND SERVICE BNS.

The case of the Territorial and Service battalions is different. They went abroad as separate units and had their own organisation for maintenance of personnel, and became incorporated with their divisions. Side by side with the Regular battalions each carved out its own slice of the history of the war. In name, in uniform and badge, they were members of the K.O.Y.L.I., and both Territorial and Service battalions were, equally with the Regular battalions, the objects of interest and solicitude to the Colonel of the Regiment, Gen. Sir A. S. Wynne, G.C.B. Throughout the war he laboured, and not in vain, to focus the interests of all battalions and keep them in the mind of the public. Whenever possible he visited any battalion before it left the shores of England for the front, and maintained communication with its officers as far as active service conditions would permit.

The Territorial battalions were old friends, tried by the test of the war in South Africa and linked by mutual interests in peace: the Service battalions were assembled and trained to a great extent by officers and ex-officers of the 1st and 2nd Bns. But the ties of kinship among the men—Yorkshiremen raised within the regimental district—formed the strongest bond of all between the old battalions and the new.

The 4/K.O.Y.L.I. was formed in 1908, after the passing of the Territorial and Reserve Forces Act, 1907, out of the 1st Volunteer Bn. Of the ten companies of the old Volunteer battalion one, that of Goole, was transferred to the new 5th Bn., while a Wakefield company was broken up. Col. E. Hind, V.D., commanded the 4th Bn. from its re-formation till December, 1913, when he was appointed Honorary Colonel and was succeeded in the command by Lt.-Col. H. J. Haslegrave, T.D., who was in command at the outbreak of the war.

THE 4TH BN.

On Saturday, the 2nd August, 1914, the battalion went into camp at Whitby, this being a brigade camp under Col. Dawson (late The Queens) as Brigadier. On Sunday, the 3rd August, it became evident that war was imminent, and the activity at sea was very noticeable. On the 4th August orders were received for its return to Wakefield to be mobilised. Owing to the disorganisation of all traffic and the improvised arrangements for moving the troops, great difficulty and delay accompanied the return to Wakefield. Immediately after the mobilisation the 1st West Riding Bde., West Riding Div., of which it formed part, was assembled at Doncaster where it was encamped on the racecourse. Thence it moved in September to Sandbeck Park, the racecourse being required for the usual race meeting, and again to Gainsborough on the 18th November, where it remained in billets and had a spell of Coast Defence work. By an unfortunate accident, in practising with rafts, three men of the battalion were drowned while here. On the 26th February, 1915, the battalion moved to York and stayed there in billets in the Cocoa Works until it proceeded overseas *via* Southampton and Folkestone to join the Expeditionary Force in France (12th April, 1915).

The list of officers who accompanied the 4/K.O.Y.L.I. to France is as follows:—Lt.-Col. H. J. Haslegrave, T.D.; Majs. H. Moorhouse, P. T. Chadwick; Capts. J. P. Critchley, L. M. Taylor, A. C. Chadwick, F. H. T. Cartwright, J. P. Firth, H. Hirst, G. Greenwood, H. C. Fraser, W. B. Creswick; Lts. G. Thomson, F. Wardley, J. I. Muirhead, W. M. Williamson, H. G. Fraser, C. H. Plackett; 2/Lts. J. C. Plews, A. E. Greaves, C. P. Sugden, R. W. Moorhouse, T. Chadwick, H. E. Sladden, F. G. Kaye, S. E. Pierce, F. E. Massie; Adjt. Capt. H. S. Kaye; Qr.-Mr., Lt. H. G. Stickley; M.O., Maj. G. S. Mill (R.A.M.C.).

Le Havre was the port of disembarkation. The battalion moved on by train to Berguette and Merville. Billets were allotted to it in the vicinity of Doulieu.

Progressive instruction in trench warfare commenced on the 18th April. The general lines for this instruction, which were followed at the time in the case of all newly-arrived troops, were after this manner:—On the first day the C.O., the Adjt., sixteen platoon officers, sixteen platoon N.C.O.s, the R.S.M., the Coy. S.M.s, and the Coy. Q.M.Sgts. proceeded for a tour of duty lasting twenty-four hours into the front line trenches held by the 25th Inf. Bde. of the 8th Div. at Fleurbaix. On the 20th each battalion sent twenty-five men of other ranks in the same way. On the 21st four platoons were sent up, one from each company. From the 23rd to the 27th April the instruction continued progressively, first by single companies, then by two companies at a time, finally by the battalion, alongside of regular units of the 25th Inf. Bde.

On the 28th April the battalion took over from the 2/Lincolns section 6 of the trench line. This was the left of the line held by the 8th Div., serving in the IV Corps of the First Army (Lt.-Gen. Sir Douglas Haig).

On the 30th 2/Lt. H. E. Sladden and two other ranks were wounded.

Local offensive operations on a small scale were started by the 49th Div. on the night of the 22nd May. Two companies of the 4/K.O.Y.L.I., under Maj. P. T. Chadwick and Capt. J. P. Critchley, traced out and commenced to dig a new trench in advance of the existing line on the Bois Grenier-Bridoux road. The new trench had to include two ruined houses situated on the road about half-way between the rival lines. The houses were occupied by the enemy, and the working parties were worried by rifle and machine-gun fire. 2/Lt. R. T. S. Gwynne was wounded and died the next day; five other ranks were killed and ten were wounded. Further progress was made on the 23rd. On the 24th the other two companies, under Capts. A. C. Chadwick and L. M. Taylor, went over the parapet at 8.50 p.m. under cover of a strong artillery fire. The enemy was just too slow in opening with rifle and machine-gun fire; the companies were well over and under cover; the companies quickly seized their position and completed their digging; the ruined houses were captured by a section under Capt. W. B. Creswick (who was wounded in the head) and put into a state of defence.

The battalion gained credit for this, its first operation, and the G.O.C. IV Corps conveyed his appreciation to the officers and men of the 'gallantry' and 'precision' with which the operation was carried out.

In retaliation the enemy shelled the new line, killing 2/Lt. C. B. Sugden and eight other ranks on the 26th and wounding twenty-one others. Capt. H. Hirst was killed by a sniper on the 24th June. Two days later (26th June) the battalion was withdrawn from No. 6 section and it marched to Watou (Belgium).

For six months the 49th Div. occupied this sector of the Ypres-Boesinghe front without any violently disturbing incident. The work of covering the bridges over the canal was arduous and many casualties were occasioned from time to time; several honours were conferred on officers and men of the 4th and 5th Bns. K.O.Y.L.I.—Maj. H. Moorhouse was awarded the Legion of Honour and Lce.-Cpl. Best of "Z" Company the D.C.M. in connection with rebuilding a bridge under a heavy fire. Maj. Moorhouse was wounded on the 31st August, as also was 2/Lt. J. C. T. Crowden.

Capt. and Adjt. A. C. Chadwick was killed in the trenches by a sniper.

On the 19th December a sudden catastrophe occurred to the 4th Bn. The enemy made a concentrated effort to overwhelm the trenches occupied by it. At 4.50 in the morning a hissing noise, like that of a 'fast-running motor-car' was heard in the German lines. Very shortly after the presence of cylinder gas was detected in the air. Warning was given, tube helmets were put on and rapid fire was opened on the enemy parapet. The message "S.O.S. GAS" was sent to our artillery who immediately opened fire. The expected infantry attack was not made, but later a German patrol, numbering about ten, was seen to be advancing towards our trenches and they were fired on. Throughout the day the enemy heavily bombarded our front line and support trenches. In the evening the battalion was relieved by the 4/Y & L. (Hallams.), but the relief was apparently observed by the enemy, who put up a barrage of gas shells along the canal bank, and heavily shelled the roads approaching it.

The casualties were numerous—2/Lt. D. L. Rickards and twenty-three other ranks died from gas poisoning, six other ranks were killed; Capt. H. C. Fraser and 2/Lt. J. C. Burrows, also 149 other ranks, were returned as 'gassed'; 2/Lt. S. E. Pierce died from wounds, while nineteen other ranks were wounded.

Four D.C.M.s were awarded, the recipients being Cpl. A. Barry and Ptes. W. F. Hooper, J. Gill and E. Atha. There were 'Gallantry cards' issued for 2/Lt. Pierce, Capt. A. C. Edwards, R.A.M.C., 2/Lt. J. C. Plews, and twenty-four other ranks.

THE 2/4TH BN.

On the outbreak of war, Col. E. Hind, V.D., offered to form another Territorial battalion in the Territorial recruiting district. The offer was not at the time accepted, as it was likely to interfere with the recruiting of the Service battalions. It, however, remained under consideration, and on the 1st October, 1914, Col. Hind was commissioned to form the Territorial battalion, to be designated the 4th (Reserve) Bn., K.O.Y.L.I. Recruiting was actively commenced and Capt. J. H. Greaves was appointed Adjt. Help was obtained from the Right Hon. J. Compton-Rickett, M.P., Mr. Marshall, M.P. for Wakefield, the Mayors of Wakefield, Dewsbury, Batley, Morley and Ossett, and the Chairman of the Urban District Council of Normanton, and after a very vigorous campaign, during which addresses were delivered at the various Town Halls and music-halls, and from illuminated tramcars, the battalion rapidly attained its full strength and on the 5th March, 1915, was removed to Bulwell near Nottingham, its numbers totalling about 1,700. On the 6th April the battalion, now known as the 2/4th Bn. K.O.Y.L.I., was brigaded with similar units in the 2/3rd Bde., West Riding Div., and was removed to Strensall to be ready to relieve the 1/3rd Bde. under orders for France.

The brigade remained at Strensall until the 6th June, 1915, when it was marched to Beverley Racecourse, and later in October to Doncaster, and again to Gateshead to winter quarters. About this time the reduction of their numbers to twenty-three officers and 600 other ranks came as a great blow, as it was feared that it portended their retention in England. However, fresh orders later on arrived for the new division to be moved to Larkhill, Salisbury Plain, for a final training and completion of personnel. The move took place in January, 1916. The men's ardour for active service was destined to be damped for some time yet, however, and in the meantime the division was moved in June to Suffolk till October, when it was transferred to Wellingborough in Northamptonshire for winter quarters. The 62nd Div., to which it belonged, had the honour of being inspected by H.M. King George in July, 1916. At Wellingborough all ranks deservedly became popular, and by the institution of Sunday concerts the bands raised money for prisoners-of-war funds of the regiments they represented. Repeated orders to hold themselves in readiness for active service were becoming monotonous until the men were suddenly fitted out with steel helmets, and then, and not till then, did they really believe that they would see France. The actual date of their departure for France was the 15th January, 1917.

The 5/K.O.Y.L.I., which had been formed in 1908 at the same time as the 4th, had its headquarters at Doncaster, which town was also the headquarters of the West Riding Div., to which both battalions belonged. They were in the 1st West Riding Bde. Lt.-Col. C. C. Moxon, T.D., who was commanding the 5th Bn. at the time of mobilisation, took it to France (arriving in France the 13th April, 1915), where he was destined to see it through a long period of hard and distinguished service.

THE 5TH BN.

The following officers accompanied the 5/K.O.Y.L.I. to France:

Lt.-Col. C. C. Moxon, T.D.; Maj. C. G. Bradley; Capts. F. L. Parkin, E. H. Walker, T. G. Mackenzie, T. Shearman (jun.), J. W. Walker, A. W. Taylor, A. Tucker, N. S. Walker; Lts. E. R. Creyke, A. E. B. Jackson, B. A. Beach, P. Bentley, M. M. Wadsworth, H. E. H. Clayton-Smith, C. R. F. Sandford; 2/Lts. W. L. Lister, H. Williamson, F. K. Robinson, G. C. Anne, J. N. Walker, W. Crawford, R. A. C. Prevett, W. Bentley, J. O. Atchison. Adjt., Capt. G. K. Sullivan; Qr.-Mr., Lt. H. Barker; M.O., Surg.-Maj. V. Graham; Chaplain, Rev. H. F. Elgood.

On arrival in France the West Riding Div. came under the orders of Gen. Sir Henry Rawlinson, commanding the IV Corps, whose headquarters were at Merville. The division disembarked at Le Havre the 13th April, 1915, and on the 19th parties of officers and N.C.O.s went into the front line of trenches of the 20th and 21st Inf. Bdes. (7th Div.) for instructional purposes, to the sound of the guns which portended the opening of the second battle of Ypres, which commenced with the German gas attack on the 22nd. The 1st West Riding Bde. was made Army Reserve Bde. and was billeted from the 24th in La Gorgue, but the following day the 4/K.O.Y.L.I. was moved up nearer the line, having one company in the trenches, and this battalion took over a section of the trench line (No. 6) on the 27th April. On the 30th April the 5th Bn. relieved the 4th in the trenches near Bois Grenier, sustaining their first casualties on the 2nd May, when Pte. H. Hepworth was killed. During the nights of the 22nd-24th May, the 5th Bn. were in close support of the 4th, who were engaged in cutting new trenches seventy yards ahead of their position—a delicate operation skilfully carried out and successfully completed on the night of the 24th. The 5th Bn. lost twelve men killed and eleven wounded from shell-fire during the two succeeding days in the new trenches.

THE 4TH AND 5TH BNS. IN FRANCE

On the 12th May the 1st West Riding Bde. became designated the 146th Inf. Bde. and the division was numbered the 49th. The two K.O.Y.L.I. battalions henceforward took their share of the front line operations. Temporarily their division was taken into the Indian Corps, with the 8th Lahore and Meerut Divs., until in the redistribution of the 29th June, the 49th Div. moved a little northwards to the vicinity of Proven (Belgium) to join the VI Corps. Here, on the 3rd July, they were duly inspected by the Second Army Commander, Gen. Sir H. Plumer, and by their new Corps Commander, Maj.-Gen. Sir John Keir.

There was a period of considerable activity early in July. The 12th Inf. Bde. attacked and captured a line of trenches, which it handed over to the 146th Inf. Bde. on the 7th July. The Germans were restless for some time to come. On the 9th July, Lt. M. M. Wadsworth, machine-gun officer, was killed. 2/Lt. J. O. Atchison was killed on the 13th. Unfortunately, Gen. Baldock was wounded by a fragment of shell on the 16th July, and Maj.-Gen. E. M. Perceval was appointed to command in his place. The trenches occupied were near Boesinghe, the rest area being about Elverdinghe.

At this period all kinds of measures were being practised to defeat the deadly gas attacks. For instance, on the 21st July, there was a test of gongs and klaxon horns sounded by the Div. Headquarters, which was the signal to prepare for a gas attack. But it had a double effect; the men in the front line trenches duly put on their helmets, but the weird sound of the warning was equally well heard in the enemy's line and it so alarmed him that he opened all down his lines with artillery fire on the Canal and support trenches.

One wretchedly cold day the Yorkshiremen were marching up to their trenches and they passed some German prisoners. One man 'passed the time of day' to one of the prisoners, and he was rather taken aback to receive the response, "*It's colder here than Briggate, Leeds, isn't it?*"

The 31st July and 1st August, 1915, were made memorable by the German attacks on Hooge with liquid fire—creating a splash of lurid colour in the record of frightfulness. There was sustained activity in the line, which was near Hooge, for many days, the 5th Bn. losing on the 8th August alone Capt. Tucker and Lce.-Cpl. Williamson killed, and twenty-seven other ranks wounded.

With September there commenced the period of heavy rains which in this low-lying district flooded the trenches and were the cause of so much desperate discomfort and difficulty. Here is a record of the effect of the rain on the 3rd September: "*In places the water in the trenches was standing two feet deep, and deeper still in particular hollows and dips in the ground where there was no outlet for the water. The communication trenches held water three or four feet deep. In several places in the front line the parapets and parados had been washed down, but had been rebuilt with sandbags and revetting frames before the evening. Many of the dug-outs were flooded out or had collapsed through the wet. The men, however, were all without exception cheerful.*" It is a notable trait in the character of Yorkshiremen—I do not infer that they have a monopoly of it—that the more direful the discomfort, the more determined is their optimism; when conditions are too favourable, they 'grouse,' for want of something better to do; but when weather, temperature and the enemy are displaying their utmost savagery, they burst into song.

The 2/5th Bn. was raised as a reserve unit to supply the 5th Bn. with drafts soon after the mobilisation of the 49th (Territorial) Div., when the latter volunteered for foreign service. Lt.-Col. J. R. Shaw, Hon. Col. of the 5th Bn., was entrusted with the work of recruiting for the new reserve battalion in Pontefract, Castleford and Doncaster, and the recruiting began on the 1st October, 1914. Col. Shaw brought great enthusiasm and very considerable influence as a mine-owner to the work, and the recruiting went exceedingly well. The battalion was brigaded along with the 2/4th Bn. in the 2/3rd West Riding Inf. Bde. (Commanded by Col. H. B. Lasseter), whose movements have already been chronicled up to the time when the division to which they belonged received orders to proceed to France.

THE 2/5TH BN.

Col. Shaw was not destined to take his battalion to the front as his health broke down, and the command went in March, 1916, to Lt.-Col. W. Watson, who took the battalion to France in January, 1917.

THE 6TH BN.

The greatest war in the history of our country found Great Britain prepared to put into the field on the continent of Europe, six complete and regular divisions on the outbreak of hostilities, and it took some weeks to assemble three more. At the outbreak of war the Prime Minister had instantly called Lord Kitchener into office as Secretary of State for War. Lord Kitchener to the day of his death was ever a staunch upholder of the voluntary army system for Britain; one of his earliest actions was to call for 500,000 volunteers to reinforce the Expeditionary Force in France. The word had already gone the round of the country that, having been asked his opinion at a private dinner-party, Lord Kitchener had given it as his conviction that the war would last certainly for three years. Half-a-million volunteers was a staggering number to contemplate in those days; three years of war were well-nigh incredible. Still the faith reposed in the War Minister by his fellow countrymen was then absolute, and fortunately so; the answer to his call was a rush to the colours. The numbers were immediately forthcoming when the call was understood. Officially the new battalions were designated the 'Service Battalions.'

The 6th (Service) Bn. K.O.Y.L.I. was formed of men who were the first to answer the call. The battalion was recruited chiefly in Doncaster and the district. One complete company was got together by Capt. F. B. Brewis with the loyal assistance of the Mayor and Corporation, who in the name of Doncaster sent the following telegram to the Colonel of the regiment: "25th August, 1914,—To Sir Arthur Wynne, Tower, London:—Mayor and Corporation Doncaster present complete double-company to Sixth Battalion."

The story of the battle at Le Cateau, which was fresh in the minds of Yorkshiremen, affected the recruiting profoundly. Each recruit when he came forward said that he wished 'to take a dead man's place.'

Recruits from Doncaster, Wakefield, Huddersfield, Sheffield and Dewsbury rushed to the colours with enthusiasm. The Depôt at Pontefract was overwhelmed. Each company was organised to assemble men according to the district in which they resided, thereby ensuring close comradeship and local interest in their welfare.

On the 18th August, 1914, a move was made to Inkerman Barracks, Woking, and on the 28th the 6/K.O.Y.L.I. came into being as a complete unit. At the time it was commanded by Maj. C. R. Ingham Brooke, who had been in command of the regimental depôt. Capts. G. G. Ottley, J. E. Munby, and F. B. Brewis, Lts. C. R. T. Thorp and W. M. Tempest were among the 1st and 2nd Bn. officers posted to it in the early days: Lt. T. E. F. Penny also was Adjt., Lt. A. Barker was

Qr.-Mr., R.S.M. W. T. Brown and R.Q.M.S. J. W. Lamb were also appointed to it. Nine months of training followed at Woking, Witley and Aldershot. On the 5th March, when at Aldershot, the battalion was inspected by Gen. Sir Arthur Wynne. On the 21st May, 1915, the battalion entrained at Government Siding, Aldershot, for Folkestone, and crossed to Boulogne under the command of Maj. E. H. Rigg, in the temporary absence of Lt.-Col. R. E. Boulton, due to an accident. The passage was made in a S.E. & C.R. steamer, escorted by a destroyer. There were many officers in the battalion who were already well known to their men in civil life, who had answered the call, and who were destined to prove, as the men did, that though not soldiers by profession they were none the less soldiers in the field when the country had need of them. Capts. G. B. Wilson, W. M. Tempest, E. Bernard Wilson and A. W. Long were company commanders. The battalion was brigaded in the 43rd Inf. Bde., 14th (Light) Div., with the 6/Som. L.I., 6/D.C.L.I. and 10/D.L.I., and marched up to the front, arriving near Bailleul, some twelve miles south-west of Ypres, on the 30th May, 1915, having landed in France on the 21st May.

The further career of the battalion subsequent to its landing is traced in Chapter VIII (Hooge and Loos).

The list of officers who accompanied the 6/K.O.Y.L.I. to France is as follows:—Lt.-Col. R. E. Boulton; Majs. E. H. Rigg, A. E. Pery-Knox-Gore; Capts. W. H. Charlesworth, E. B. Wilson, G. de Hoghton, G. B. Wilson, W. N. Tempest, A. Waithman-Long, A. C. E. Elborough; Lts. H. G. Kaye, T. W. Warlow, L. Chalk, W. F. Burrows, E. G. Bartlett, R. E. Tennant, A. T. Shelton, A. Arrigonie, O. H. C. Shelswell; 2/Lts. E. D. Badcock, P. R. Rayner, C. E. R. Heaton-Ellis, C. E. H. Knapp-Fisher, C. B. Leatham, H. B. Stokoe, A. L. Badcock, E. A. L. Sturridge, W. J. Tempest, R. G. Royle, P. K. Buckley, E. J. Priddey; Adjt., Capt. T. E. F. Penny, and Qr.-Mr., Lt. A. Barker, who as Cpl. A. Barker, 2/K.O.Y.L.I., had won the D.C.M. in S. Africa in 1900.

The number of men who rushed to join the 6th Bn. was so great that, shortly after that battalion had moved to Woking in August, 1914, it was found that there were sufficient men to form two battalions. The 6th Bn. accordingly moved away as a complete unit and left the personnel to form a second, which became the 7th Bn. Many old officers of the regular battalions of the regiment, who had been on the retired list, returned to the colours to form the new battalion. The command was first given to Lt.-Col. B. Witherby, well remembered as an efficient and successful adjutant of the 1st Bn.: Majs. G. G. Ottley (transferred from the 6th Bn.) and R. M. D. Fox, and Capt. B. B. Robinson were old 2nd Bn. officers. Capt. J. Beddington was

THE 7TH BN.

Adjutant. Drilling was at once in full swing. In these days men were too much in earnest to be shy about coming on parade 'improperly dressed,' and tailors were unable to supply uniforms fast enough to equip the newly joining officers. As a result one officer drilled his company for several weeks in a Norfolk jacket and a straw hat, until the latter collapsed after repeated rainstorms and had to be replaced by the jauntier 'Homburg.' But for a true picture of what the Service battalions underwent during those early days, one should read 'The First Hundred Thousand,' by Ian Hay, a book which is full of vivid painting and interesting detail.

The men of the 7th Bn. were mostly Yorkshire miners; although military discipline was an entire novelty to them, discipline of some sort soon appeared. At first a man in the ranks, after being cautioned not to answer nor to 'argue the point' out on parade, would wait till the end of parade and would then buttonhole his officer and claim to 'have a word with him' in quite an aggressive tone; but he soon showed how reasonable and admirable a character is that of the Yorkshire miner when it was explained quietly how the officer's word had to be accepted, or the machine would never work like a well-oiled piece of mechanism.

Another old officer who was with the battalion for a short period in command, until a staff appointment claimed him, was Lt.-Col. W. B. Butler, who made his *début* as an officer in the 1st Bn. originally, when that battalion was marching up the Kyber Pass in the Afghan War in 1878.

The battalion shortly found itself a unit of the 61st Inf. Bde., being associated with the 7th Bns. of the D.C.L.I., Som. L.I. and D.L.I. A battalion of the King's (Liverpool) shortly afterwards took the place of the D.L.I. when the latter became a Pioneer battalion.

Whilst at Woking, H.M. The King made an inspection accompanied by Queen Mary, Queen Alexandra and Princess Mary.

Early in 1915, Lt.-Col. H. P. Creagh-Osborne of the King's Own took over the command, and the brigade moved by route march to Witley Camp and there underwent further training until May, 1915, when it was moved to Salisbury Plain. Here it joined the 20th Div., under Gen. Davies, and the final polish was put on what had proved to be a most admirable training. The battalion Qr.-Mr. at this time was Capt. T. Shearwood, late of the D.L.I., who was to prove that in spite of his sixty years of age, no night in France was so bad as to prevent him from coming forward to the trenches, nor was any issue of rations too early for him to attend, nor any task too difficult for him to tackle. He eventually had to return sick in 1917.

Another man in the battalion whose reputation soon became established was the C.O.'s groom, Pte. (Jack) Johnson, whose qualifications for the position included never-failing good humour, a bantam weight, a reputation for boxing, and the seat on a horse (in the early days) of the proverbial pea on a drum.

From July, 1915, Lt.-Col. V. A. M. Fowler, late The King's, commanded the battalion until February, 1916.

The officers of the battalion who accompanied it abroad were: Lt.-Col. V. A. M. Fowler; Majs. G. G. Ottley, B. B. Robinson; Capts. W. T. Brown, E. J. Smith, A. C. White, G. H. C. Manuk, J. T. Janson, A. W. Studd, R. St. C. Brooke; Lts. R. H. C. Ward, A. Furze, W. E. B. Wright, G. H. A. Lowe, A. J. Harvie, W. G. Barnaby, H. E. Holmes, V. G. Starkey, C. Tilley, H. V. Jones; 2/Lts. E. H. Frank, A. N. Wade, A. F. McC. Riggs, D. Tyson, C. N. Newcombe, F. C. Haskins, E. M. Williams, E. G. Foulston, J. S. Hollis, W. Johnstone, E. R. Broadbent, R. E. Leach, C. H. Adwick; Adjt., Capt. J. L. Beddington; and Qr.-Mr., Lt. T. Shearwood.

Before leaving for France the division was inspected by H.M. The King. Lord Kitchener also paid it a visit to speed it on its way. The departure from Larkhill, Salisbury Plain, took place the 24th July, 1915: the crossing was made to Boulogne and the 61st Inf. Bde. moved by route march to Steenwerck on the 29th, where it came into Gen. Pulteney's Corps, and on to Armentières for a course of instruction in the trenches, being attached for that purpose to the 80th Inf. Bde. On the 6th August it experienced its first casualties, and 2/Lt. D. Tyson was killed the day following. This short period of instruction proved to be of the utmost value for their morale generally and for their knowledge of trench routine. Under such tutors as the 3/K.R.R.C., officers and men of the K.O.Y.L.I. companies not only met with the utmost kindness and careful tuition, but they learnt a lesson in trench camaraderie and unselfishness which they had occasion to remember later on when it became their turn to befriend similarly other freshly joining units. Education in trench routine was no simple matter. It included not merely the military duties, but self-control, trench manners, and above all trench hygiene. The pupils, when they arrived, wondered at the absence of all excitement when shells were falling thick and fast; they soon learnt, from example, to walk upright and to disregard danger; they learnt, also, to remember to leave their trenches, on relief, as far as possible in the state in which they would wish to find them.

It is well to dwell for a moment upon this and such-like aspects of life at the front, for these tutorial duties were not always so punctiliously and heartily carried out as they were in the present case by the representatives of the famous K.R.R.C.

A fortnight later the 7/K.O.Y.L.I. took over trenches of its own in the line as a fully-fledged fighting unit, and the battalion had a part, though a very minor one as it happened, in the battle of Loos at the end of September, 1915.

During the period before Loos the 7th Bn. was in the trenches in the Laventie sector (three miles north of Neuve Chapelle). There is a story of these trenches which is possibly worth preserving. The incident referred to occurred in "D" Company (Capt. B. B. Robinson in command). Several messages had recently been received from the Bde. Headquarters calling for reports of the flights of any carrier-pigeons observed from the forward line. This became the subject of many facetious messages, such as an indent for salt to put on the tails of the birds. One evening a sentry saw a bird settle on the barbed wire. The sentry was no ornithologist; he was even rated as a third-class shot, but he knocked the head off the bird with his first shot. When the bird was brought in after dark it was found to be a young owl. It was decided to send it in to the Adjutant. The officers of the company composed this sentence in German, which was legibly written on a label by the best writer of their number (not the Captain!) and attached to the bird's leg: 'Ich habe eine taube gewesen,' meaning 'I have become a pigeon.' It was sent in with the Captain's compliments. Imagine the surprise when next morning a message was received from the Bde. Headquarters, marked 'Secret and Urgent,' calling for full particulars of the bird incident. Not long afterwards the Brigadier came round the trenches: he said "*I was immensely interested in that bird you sent down last night; at first I thought it was a leg-pull.*" "*As a matter of fact it was, Sir,*" was the reply. "*Good lord, get on to the 'phone at once: it has gone on to the division, and the Corps Intelligence are enquiring into it!*" History does not carry the story any further, but as the Brigadier was Gen. Walter Ross, well known to his many friends not only for his manifest qualities as a soldier but also for his ready sense of humour, the punishment meted out to the culprits no doubt was being made to fit the crime, namely, that of attempting to 'pull the leg' of authority. Incidentally, be it noted that within six months of the date, the senior culprit was appointed to command the battalion, being the youngest of his rank in the army at the time. Good temper and a sense of humour were recognised as invaluable qualities in the trenches.

After the Loos period the 7th Bn. was moved to trenches in front of Fleurbaix. Here Maj. G. G. Ottley left in order to command a battalion in another division, Capt. Robinson taking his place as second-in-command.

THE 8TH BN.

Col. E. Hind, who had been responsible for the organisation of the 2/4th Bn., was called upon to form the 8th Bn. also. When its numbers were complete he took the battalion to Frensham, near Aldershot, where its training commenced. The training was completed at Bordon, and the battalion left that camp for France early in September,

1915. It was in the 70th Inf. Bde. (Brig.-Gen. H. Gordon), which went out as a part of the 23rd Div. (Maj.-Gen. J. M. Babington).

Lt.-Col. H. T. Manley went out in command, with Lt. G. St. J. Coventry as Adjutant. The other officers of the battalion were Majs. E. C. St. G. Stockwell and T. H. Owen; Capts. A. C. Benson, K. E. Poyser, E. C. Moorhouse, H. L. Willey, H. C. H. Bull and G. L. Pyman; Lts. R. L. H. Salter, F. Else, R. S. P. Mackarness, E. A. Martin, M. R. H. Morley, A. G. Keyser, E. B. B. Speed, J. H. Bingham and B. H. Horsley; 2/Lts. V. F. Gordon, W. L. Browne, E. V. H. Bradley, J. Nelson, O. H. Cooke, E. Gould, W. B. Preston, H. Bertin, G. W. Morris, A. H. Hack, R. H. Hurst, J. E. L. Marshall, G. A. Holmes, M. G. Donahoe, C. W. Shepherd, M. D. Barber and H. J. Cooke; Qr.-Mr., Lt. D. Smith.

After its arrival, for some weeks the 70th Inf. Bde. was alternately in the trenches and in billets just south of Armentières, a fairly quiet sector for the time being and not much affected by the storm when it burst further south in the neighbourhood of Loos at the end of September. As soon as the pressure could be relaxed, and the fighting had died down, the 70th Inf. Bde. on the 18th October moved from Estaires to Sailly to derive instruction in that part of the line from the experienced battalions. The brigade was attached to the 8th Div. for the period of its new training. The 8/K.O.Y.L.I. was instructed by the 2/Devon. of the 23rd Inf. Bde. Lt.-Col. Manley was succeeded by Lt.-Col. H. E. Trevor at the end of October.

The 9th and 10th Bns.

The 9th and 10th Bns. were formed at the beginning of September, 1914. Drafts were sent from Pontefract to Berkhampstead and collected into two battalions numbered as above. Lt.-Col. R. C. Dill, a retired regular officer of the regiment, was the first commanding officer of the 9th, while Lt.-Col. A. W. A. Pollock, of 'Spectator Company' fame, commanded the 10th. Capt. C. K. Butler and J. Buckley were the adjutants respectively. Both battalions were placed in the newly forming 64th Inf. Bde. in the 21st Div., the other two units being the 14th and 15th battalions of the D.L.I. From Berkhampstead they went into new huts at Halton Park, Wendover, and thence temporarily to Maidenhead in billets, until April. Both battalions were upwards of 1,000 strong on parade on the 27th March, 1915, at Maidenhead, when Gen. Sir Arthur Wynne inspected them. In August they marched to Witley Camp in Surrey, being inspected by H.M. The King in passing Windsor. From Witley Camp they went to France.

The battalions were at first clothed in blue with buff equipment and the men carried dummy rifles. Just before Christmas, 1914, an issue of fifty serviceable rifles per battalion was made, and a corresponding number of men were immediately specially trained in their use: this was due to a fear of invasion when a large number of German divisions were temporarily lost sight of and were supposed to be unaccounted for by the Intelligence Department. In June a complete issue of new rifles, equipment, and mule transport was made. Maj.-Gen. Sir E. Hutton was originally posted to the command of the 21st Div., and was succeeded in April, 1915, by Maj.-Gen. G. T. Forestier-Walker. In July ammunition for musketry was received, and the men were put through a hurried course before their departure for the front in September, 1915. The story of the 9th and 10th Bns. is continued in Chapter VIII (Hooge and Loos).

The officers who accompanied the 9th Bn. to France were as follows:—Lt.-Col. C. W. D. Lynch; Majs. A. E. Fitzgerald and F. B. Brewis; Capts. H. Greenwood, W. Walker, G. Haswell and G. E. Griffin; Lts. D. J. Bethell, B. W. Cook, L. D. Head, E. M. B. Cambie, A. N. Richardson, B. L. Gordon, H. E. Yeo, L. D. Spicer and C. D. Jones; 2/Lts. N. L. Alexander, E. F. S. Graham, H. A. Teffer, F. G. Morris, C. W. Howlett, J. J. F. Oldershaw, W. F. Keay, A. G. Spark, C. A. C. J. Hendriks, E. R. Nott, G. L. Sly, H. F. Kingston, F. N. Smith, J. C. Sayers, J. P. Stevens, H. M. Green, W. R. Stokes, F. J. Powell, A. E. Day, R. A. Stokes, T. H. Ibbetson and A. Stephenson; Adjt., Capt. C. K. Butler; Qr.-Mr., Lt. W. K. Pethed.

The officers who accompanied the 10th Bn. to France were as follows:—Lt.-Col. A. W. A. Pollock; Majs. W. R. J. Ellis and H. C. Akroyd; Capts. A. M. Dale, H. T. King, F. S. Laskie, L. A. Day, C. Bethell and E. R. Santer; Lts. H. M. Laskie, O. P. Hill, A. S. Mills, J. Sheffield, A. R. Dugmore, I. L. Harrison, C. F. W. Wait, E. A. Franklin and A. A. V. Scudamore; 2/Lts. C. de L. Jacob, F. H. Lee, E. A. Stoddard, K. J. P. Asher, H. Burkett, A. Stretton, A. L. Kennedy, A. Mein, J. W. Bamber, A. R. F. Simpson, J. R. Caldwell, P. A. T. Ellis, G. C. Pilgrim, B. van S. Taylor, A. L. Jack, P. T. Lister, F. Noddle, E. G. R. Wingham, L. Bisset, J. A. A. Fountain, H. M. Shaw, W. D. Barnett, H. W. Whiteman and L. F. Sharp; Adjt., Lt. C. H. Page; Qr.-Mr., Lt. J. Allen.

The 11th Bn. was formed in October, 1914, a month later than the other service battalions. The command was given to Lt.-Col. S. C. Taylor, formerly Adjutant of the 2nd Bn., who for some years had been employed under the Colonial Office in Nigeria. The formation, organisation, and training as a service battalion proceeded normally at Harrogate. In April, 1915, the designation was changed from 11th (Service) Bn., King's Own (Yorkshire Light Infantry) to 11th (Reserve) Bn., King's Own (Yorkshire Light Infantry). As in the case of the 3rd Bn., being a reserve battalion there was no prospect of the battalion being sent as a unit to the front; officers and men served

THE 11TH BN.

their time in it and passed on to the 7th, 8th, 9th and 10th Bns. whom it was destined to feed.

Capt. W. N. Tempest,[1] who had been wounded and had gained distinction and promotion on the field in France, was posted to the battalion on its formation. Home employment was not destined long to claim his gallant and adventurous spirit.

In May, 1915, Lt.-Col. S. C. Taylor[2] exchanged with Col. J. W. Stead to the command of the 15/W. Yorks (the 'Leeds Pals').

On the 1st September, 1916, the 11th Bn. became the 8th (Territorial Reserve) Bn.

THE 12TH BN.

The War Office Authority for the formation of the 12th Bn. as the Miners Bn., King's Own (Yorkshire Light Infantry) was dated 5th September, 1914. In November, 1914, the title was altered to the 12th (Service) Bn. (Miners) (Pioneers), King's Own (Yorkshire Light Infantry). It completed its training in Yorkshire, and was sent abroad in December, 1915, at first for service in Egypt, but was subsequently moved to France in March, 1916, when it became incorporated in the 92nd Inf. Bde (31st Div.). The list of the officers of the 12th Bn. in January, 1916 (taken from the Army List), is as follows:— Lt.-Col. E. L. Chambers; Majs. J. S. Charlesworth and C. B. Charlesworth; Capts. H. F. Chadwick, J. C. Crawshaw, G. S. Leach, J. H. Frank, W. Cooper, D. E. Roberts and G. M. Stockings; Lts. F. H. White, H. D. Gaunt, P. C. Binns, B. Mason, J. S. L. Welch, R. England, W. S. Vincent, W. H. Roberts, J. Gaunt and P. T. Crowther; 2/Lts. W. E. Oliver, J. K. Partridge, G. Walker, J. J. McGroarty, L. Forsdike, V. Mossop, H. R. Dixon, A. V. Skevington, H. R. Skevington, N. L. Bennett, J. N. Blenkin and J. A. Hinchliffe; Adjt., Capt. S. G. Newton; Qr.-Mr., Lt. W. Parkin.

OTHER BATTALIONS

The 13th (Reserve) Bn. was raised in October, 1915, and became a reserve to the 12th Bn. (Miners). It was raised for home service only. It was disbanded at Otley in Yorkshire, 31st August, 1916.

Other battalions were raised later during the war for home and field service; to the former category belonged the 1st (Reserve) Garrison Bn. and the 3rd (Reserve) Garrison Bn., the latter of which was raised in 1916 and re-named the 14th (Home Service) Bn., King's Own (Yorkshire Light Infantry).

[1] *Maj. W. N. Tempest, M.C., was killed on the Somme, September 25th,* 1916 *when leading the 9th Bn. in attack.*

[2] *Brig.-Gen. S. C. Taylor, D.S.O., died 11th October,* 1918, *from wounds received on October 1st when in command of the 93rd Inf. Bde. Active, energetic and optimistic, with an extraordinary devotion to duty and to the welfare of those under his command, he inspired confidence and devotion in all with whom he came in contact.*

This battalion was disbanded at Bury St. Edmunds at the end of the year 1917. The 2nd (Reserve) Garrison Bn. went to France and became the 16th Garrison Bn., King's Own (Yorkshire Light Infantry). It served with the Fifth Army under the order of the Provost Marshal.

The 15th Bn., King's Own (Yorkshire Light Infantry) was raised in France, the 6th June, 1918, from various details, and served in the line in the 120th Inf. Bde. of the 40th Div. as a service battalion, to the end of the war.

HOOGE AND LOOS. 1915

VIII

AFTER the second battle of Ypres the armies on both sides in France settled down to trench warfare. Under the fire of the guns, exposed to view and attack from the air, in merciless weather often, despite gas-clouds and sheets of flame, the soldiers in the forward positions fought doggedly on to complete the chain of defence, here coupling up the links that had yielded temporarily to pressure, there bringing pressure to bear to rend asunder the links of the enemy's chain; incessantly testing the enemy's chain for weak spots, penetrating between the links to gain local information, forging fresh links in their own, camouflaging weak ones, inventing new methods and new weapons to counter the inventions of the enemy; elaborating the chain, to render it elastic and in order to give security to the troops behind the line. The business of the infantry soldier varied little in its outlook; periods in the trenches, of discomforts, anxiety and activity, endured stoically, recklessly, or tragically as the case might be, succeeded periods of comparative quiet and preparation in billets or camps behind the line: variety occasionally was found in raids by night, in organised local attacks to improve a tactical point, in resistance to the like attacks on the part of the enemy, occasionally in pitched battles when a battalion would go over the top into an inferno created by artillery barrages and reassemble later reduced to the strength of one company, sometimes more, sometimes less. The wider outlook, of which the infantryman at the time knew so little, had to do with higher commands, but needs explaining.

After their failure to penetrate to the coast by way of Ypres, the weight of the German armies was thrown against Russia in the east, where the German High Command now hoped to achieve a decisive victory such as they had failed to accomplish in the west. Hindenburg's star was in the ascendant, and Hindenburg looked to the east as the field of promise, where he was most in his element. The war had now been in progress almost a year. So far the military rulers of Germany had failed to redeem their promises to the German people, and so it had become necessary, in order to keep up the fighting spirit of the nation, to distract attention from the west, to feed the nation on success, exciting its enthusiasm by publishing news of successive victories over the Russians, and creating a frenzy of excitement by the publication, through the censored Press, of extra sheets each night with figures in large type headed by the message of victory 'Flags out.' So Galicia was swept by the German armies in the spring, and the Balkans were swept in the autumn.

In the western field they were content to remain on the defensive.

On the part of the Allies in France and Belgium, comparative inactivity was enforced by the necessity of accumulating larger supplies of guns and ammunition for contemplated activity in the autumn, while, as far as the British armies were concerned, the gain of strength was not so rapid as it otherwise might have been, owing to the drain made on the country's resources in order to feed the Dardanelles Expeditionary Force.

However, while the battle of Ypres was being fought, Gen. Foch, who was on the right of the British, had been engaged in maturing plans for a big French attack to seize the Vimy ridge. He looked to the British army on his left to co-operate. The battle of Neuve Chapelle had been fought early in March by the British First Army (Haig) chiefly with a view to securing a more favourable position for the further battle that was to be fought later in co-operation with the French. The second battle of Ypres had weakened the British forces and had exhausted a great part of their accumulations of ammunition.

The undertaking given to the French had to be carried into effect, and accordingly the British First Army under Gen. Haig fought two ineffectual battles, the first about Fromelles commencing on 9th May, and the second at Festubert, which ended the 25th May, while Gen. Foch was slowly and at great cost working forward to the Vimy Ridge.

Foch determined to continue the operation, with French troops only, in the autumn, but Gen. Joffre, his chief, stipulated that, in order to permit Foch to concentrate his strength for the effort, the British front should be widened, for Joffre intended to conduct still larger operations himself in Champagne to the east of Rheims, and he had reason to fear that, unless he made his requirements known to the British government in no uncertain language, the new divisions which had been training in England might be diverted to the Dardanelles. His representations resulted in the extension of the British front to its right and left and in relieving de Castelnau's Sixth Army on the Somme front. As the British New Army arrived during the summer months these changes were gradually effected. A British Third Army was formed under the command of Gen. Sir Charles Munro. This army took over seventeen miles of front from a point south of Arras up to, and later including, the Somme river. At the same time the front of the First Army was prolonged southwards to the neighbourhood of Lens, while the Second Army on its left (now commanded by Gen. Plumer) took over the sector of the Flanders front which the French had been holding between the British and the Belgian armies.

In addition, the British C.-in-C. was enabled to form another corps, consisting of the freshly constituted Guards Division and two of the New Army divisions, which he held as a reserve.

Now let us return to the trenches of the British front.

After the month of May, on two particular occasions in the year 1915, the smouldering fires were fanned into flame and there were eruptions of first-class intensity. First, for a fairly prolonged period between the middle of June and the 10th August at Hooge immediately east of Ypres, in the famous salient; and later, on the 25th September and for some days subsequently, at Loos, some thirty miles further south in the line and four miles south of La Bassée.

The object of the earlier operation was purely local, for it was made in order to improve a very cramped and difficult position; that of the later one was to assist the French, who were making their grand attack in Champagne, by preventing the Germans from detaching troops from the north and so concentrating against the French assaulting columns.

In June, 1915, the VI Corps (Keir) was the left corps of the British line. Of the three divisions which composed this Corps the 49th held the right sector, a little to the north of Hooge; the 4th and 5th Bns. K.O.Y.L.I. belonged to this division.

Next in line to the right came the V Corps (Allenby) with the 14th (Light) Div. in its centre sector; the 3rd and the 46th Divs. were on either flank. This Corps held the line about Hooge.

South of Hooge again came the II Corps (Fergusson), of which the 5th Div. (Morland) held the northern sector, with the 28th Div. next in order to the south.

The 6/K.O.Y.L.I. was with the 14th (Light) Div.; the 2nd Bn. was with the 5th Div., and the 1st Bn. was in the 28th Div. Though the corps on either side of Gen. Allenby's V Corps were not actually included in the Hooge operations, they were involved to some extent by the increased activity which resulted from those operations.

It will be remembered that the 6th Bn. (with the remainder of the division to which it belonged) had landed so recently as the 21st May.

The 6th Bn. at Hooge.

In the first week the men were employed in digging trenches half a mile west of Neuve Eglise. On the 12th June the battalion marched to Locre, there to be attached, by companies, for instruction, to units in the front line, the 6th and 8th Bns. of the Sherwood Foresters acting as their tutors. On the 13th June the first casualties were reported, Pte. L. A. Beedon being the first man to lose his life. On the 15th June the Germans fired two mines under portions of their trenches; Capt. A. Waithman-Long was wounded; 5 other ranks were killed, 8 wounded, and 5 were 'missing, believed killed.' The German trenches were only 25 yards distant at the nearest part of the trench known as J.3. Right, where the mine did the greatest damage. The companies behaved with all possible steadiness. Lts. R. E. Tennant and A. T. Shelton, 2/Lts. P. R. Rayner and H. B. Stokoe were commended by the G.O.C. 139th Inf. Bde. for their services, and Pte. A. Clark was reported for gallant conduct in mending the broken telephone wires under fire. The battalion had a short rest. The killed were buried at Kemmel cemetery. A draft of forty men arrived from the base.

On the 16th June the 3rd Div. assaulted and carried in brilliant fashion the line of German trenches to the immediate north of Hooge.

On the 24th June the 6th Bn. returned to the front trenches, advancing to positions to the north and south of the Menin Road, the relief of the unit in occupation being completed by 11.30 p.m. This part of the line was now the scene of great activity, and the 6th Bn. was in the thick of it until the 30th June, when it was again withdrawn for a rest to Busseboom. Throughout July and part of August there was constant activity in attempts to re-take the same line of trenches by Hooge on the Menin road.

On the 19th July the 3rd Div. opposite Hooge made an organised attack and took some further trenches; the consequent activity affected the trenches to the south occupied by the 6th Bn., and their casualties that resulted numbered 3 officers wounded, 4 other ranks killed and 29 wounded.

On the 30th July, owing to a German attack preceded by gas made on the 41st Inf. Bde. hard by Hooge, the battalion was again turned out of its bivouac to take up position in support. The German artillery, searching the approaches by which reinforcements might come to the units in the front line trenches, inflicted casualties on the 6th Bn. again. Capt. A. C. E. Elborough, 2/Lt. C. E. H. Knapp-Fisher and Sgt. Callan were killed or died of their wounds; 24 other ranks were wounded.

The Zouave and Sanctuary woods were in the immediate rear of the trenches that were attacked. The Germans had followed up their gas attack, which had obliterated the defenders belonging to the 41st Inf. Bde., by occupying the undefended trenches, but the supports held on to the edge of the woods. Two companies of the 6th Bn. relieved the 8/K.R.R.C. in the woods, Maj. E. H. Rigg being in command. The other companies followed, Lt. L. Chalk being wounded in getting into position. In the early morning of the 31st July the battalion helped to repel a heavy attack. The 41st Inf. Bde. suffered very heavy casualties; many wounded had been left lying out between the lines, some of whom were rescued when darkness made it possible on the following nights. On the 1st August Lt. T. W. Warlow was reported to have died of wounds. The trenches of Zouave Wood were heavily shelled during the night. Capt. W. H.

Charlesworth and 2/Lt. R. S. M. Beatson were wounded; other ranks, killed and wounded, 10. 2/Lt. P. R. Rayner was sent forward to be attached to "C" Company, but was wounded before reaching the trenches, where Lt. R. E. Tennant was now the officer in command.

The trenches by Hooge were again carried in brilliant fashion by the 6th Div. on the 9th August, and the new line which was the objective of the successive operations, was properly consolidated.

It is notable that the 14th (Light) Div. was the first division of "Kitchener's Army" to be regularly engaged, and very nobly it acquitted itself throughout this, its earliest ordeal. A complimentary message was received from the Army commander on the 3rd August on the manner in which the ground was held and the position improved, by the division.

On the 4th August, Brig.-Gen. Wood assumed command of the 43rd Inf. Bde.; there was a bombardment of the trenches, chiefly by "whizz-bangs," that night as if to celebrate his assumption of office. The following day "C" Company again suffered and lost its new C.S.M., W. Shaw, who was killed.

After the relief of the battalion, Pte. W. Maddox was recommended for the D.C.M. As a stretcher bearer he had been wounded, but in spite of this he walked under heavy fire to report where his fellow was lying wounded also, before going to have his own wounds dressed. Lce./Sgt. H. Buckley was also recommended for the D.C.M. for his splendid example to the stretcher-bearers, dressing and bringing in wounded men under a hot fire.

Thus did the 6th Bn. graduate as a fighting unit and take its place as a seasoned battalion in the stern fighting of the ensuing years of the war.

THE BATTLE OF LOOS

By autumn of 1915 the French and British forces were sufficiently equipped to assume the offensive on a grand scale. The French made their chief effort in Champagne. The question they were out to solve was, how to pierce a modern trench line and, when pierced, how to maintain possession of the gap. They were not destined in this instance to advance very far towards its elucidation; it was a problem that had still to wait another three years for its satisfactory solution. In order to give the French armies in Champagne every chance of success, attacks were simultaneously delivered in other parts of the line, notably by the British forces in the neighbourhood of Loos. The great attack on Loos and Hulluch was made on the 25th September on a front of about seven miles, including the La Bassée canal to the north, and the village of Grenay (south of Loos) to the south; subsidiary attacks were made at the same time all the way up the line to the coast in order to obscure the point of main

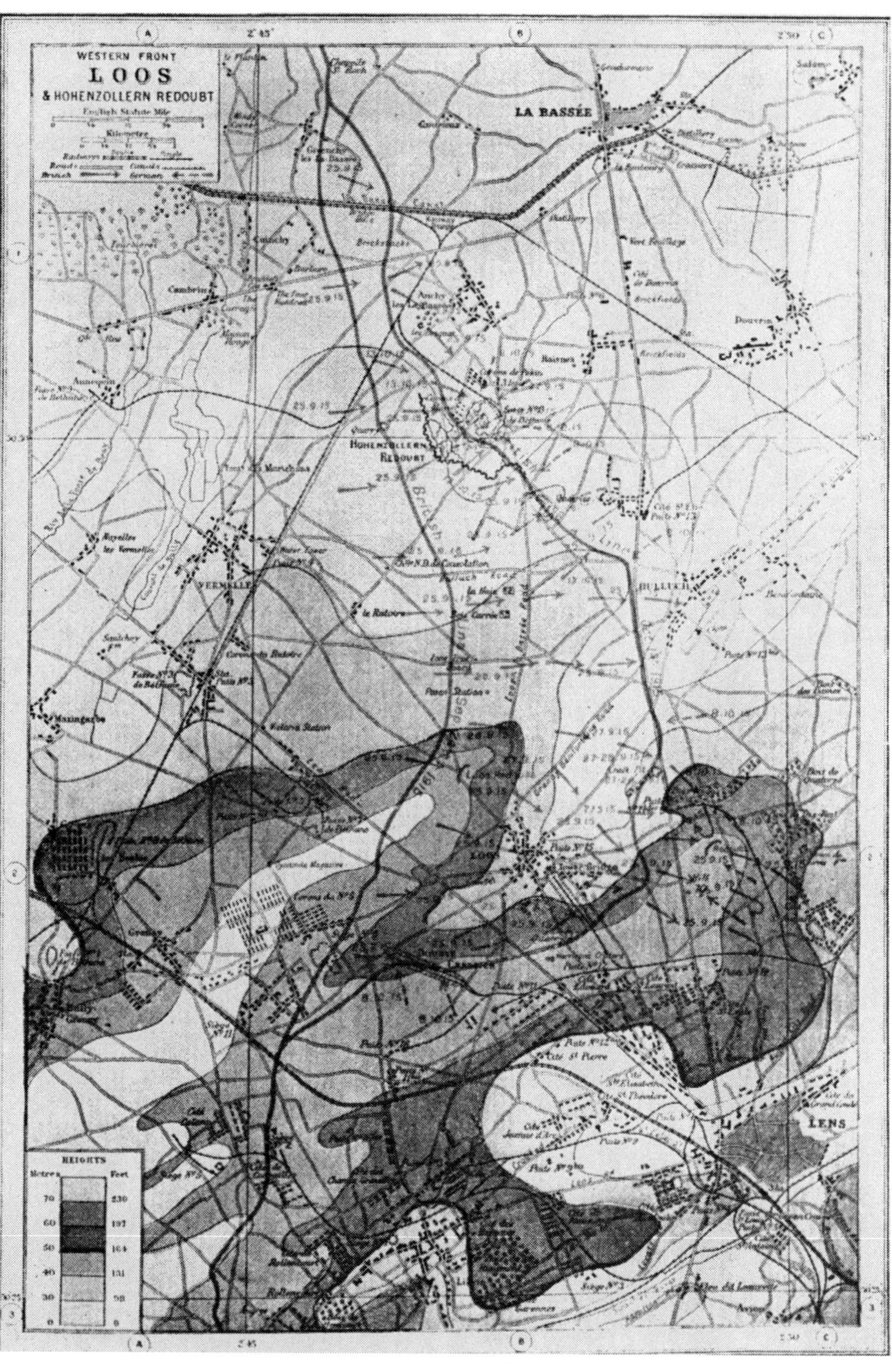
WESTERN FRONT
LOOS
& HOHENZOLLERN REDOUBT
LA BASSÉE
HOHENZOLLERN REDOUBT
VERMELLES
HULLUCH
LENS
HEIGHTS

importance. The two corps engaged were the I (Gough) and the IV (Rawlinson) of the First Army (Haig).

The road leading from Vermelles to Hulluch bisected the front to be attacked, and this road was the boundary line between the two attacking corps, the I Corps being north, the IV Corps south of it. This was the first occasion when divisions of "Kitchener's Army" were used in a great operation (that by Hooge being in comparison of minor importance).

The divisions of the I Corps were the 2nd, 7th and 9th; those of the IV were the 1st, 15th and 47th. The 47th (London) Div. was commanded by Maj.-Gen. C. St. L. Barter, who had commanded the 2/K.O.Y.L.I. throughout the campaign in S. Africa, 1899 to 1902.

The general attack was commenced on the 25th September, 1915. The 2nd Div., attacking on the left, was held up by Auchy, the artillery preparatory fire having failed to cut the wires covering the German trenches. Part of the 9th Div. next to the right shared the same fate, but the remainder of the 9th Div. captured the Hohenzollern redoubt and went beyond it, past the "Fosse 8" defences. To the right of the 9th the 7th Div. reached the village of Hulluch but had to fall back again to the Quarries, a strong post in their line of advance.

South of the Vermelles-Hulluch road, the 1st Div. got as far as the village of Hulluch, the 1st Inf. Bde. on the left penetrating three lines of German trenches. The 2nd Inf. Bde. was held up by uncut wire for a time, but managed to prolong the line now occupied by the 1st Inf. Bde., who were in touch with the 7th Div. on their left. The 15th Div. reached the same line with its left Brigade, while its right penetrated the village of Loos and pushed on to Hill 70, taking up a position considerably in advance of the next Brigade to the left. The 47th Div. fought its way past Loos and, with its left shoulder forward, took up a position forming a defensive flank for the troops of the attack.

The most forward of the captured positions could not, however, be held, and at nightfall the salient formed was considerably contracted, for the failure of the left division of the attack allowed the enemy to take the attackers further south in flank.

The 21st and 24th Divs. of the new reserve Corps were brought up to support. This brings us to the point where the 9th and 10th Bns. of the K.O.Y.L.I. were introduced (with their 21st Div.) to the field of the attack. Sir John French in his dispatch says: "To ensure the speedy and effective support of the First and Fourth Corps in the case of their success, the Twenty-First and Twenty-Fourth Divisions passed the night of the 24th and 25th on the line of Beuvry-Nœux-les-mines." The 64th Inf. Bde. had landed in France so

The 9th and 10th Bns.

recently as the 12th September. The Brigade had left Whitley Camp and entrained at Milford, the 10th Bn. proceeding first to Southampton Docks, and thence to Le Havre, the 9th Bn. going to Boulogne *via* Folkestone. The Brigade was billeted about Nielles les Ardres, our two battalions being at Zutkerque at first. Gen. Forestier-Walker was in command of the 21st Div.

On the nights of the 20th, 21st and 22nd September, the division was marching from Nielles les Ardres to Ames; after a rest of thirty-six hours there followed a fresh night march to Four aux Chaux, which was immediately succeeded by a day march to Mazingarbe, three miles west of Loos. Thence three hours later it marched by night to the position of deployment, whence it made a very arduous march by night to the battlefield, over country intersected by trench lines, where no transport could accompany it.

Before they had heard a shot fired at close quarters, in total ignorance of the look of the positions ahead of them, the battalions of the 64th Inf. Bde. found themselves moving up in support of the 63rd Inf. Bde. in the direction of Hill 70 (the right of the British attack) where the battle was in progress. They crossed the front system of the British trenches by night in brigade mass of company columns, a laborious process, as each crossing of a trench entailed a halt and a re-formation of each unit on the far side.

At 2 a.m. the 26th September, the German front system was crossed. The 63rd Inf. Bde. had gone ahead during the night and were out of touch; so with daylight coming on, being in a proper position from which to support the 63rd, should the latter have reached the Lens-Hulluch road and have occupied the position that it had been ordered to occupy, the 64th took up a position and made what use it could of the existing cover in the German trench line. The information given was that the greater part of Hill 70 was in British hands with supporting troops in Loos. The 62nd Inf. Bde. received orders to advance in the morning against a redoubt on Hill 70, which was still in German hands. The Brigade was taken to the south and east of Loos to operate with the 15th Div., who had in reality been unable to make themselves masters of the crest of Hill 70, while the 63rd and 64th Inf. Bdes. were ordered to join in an attack on 'Puits 14,' immediately east of Loos and just north of Hill 70, the 64th Inf. Bde., however, being held in Divisional reserve at first. The 24th Div. came next in line to the north, and the 1st Div. was further north of them. The 62nd Inf. Bde. was itself attacked in its new forward position on the right of the division at 5 a.m., and throughout the day of the 26th was engaged in a desperate fight to maintain its ground. This brigade was practically detached from the remainder of their division, and sustained very heavy casualties in the fighting, which was often hand to hand. The 63rd Inf. Bde. suffered equally heavily and was driven back from the positions gained in their early advances. The two D.L.I. battalions of the 64th Inf. Bde. were about noon sent forward to reinforce the 63rd Inf. Bde., while the two K.O.Y.L.I. battalions were still held in reserve. At about 2.30 p.m. the 63rd Inf. Bde. and the two D.L.I. battalions were driven back west of the Lens-Hulluch road. The Germans had received large reinforcements, and appear to have been themselves attacking, so that the conflict swayed to and fro, positions being gained and lost as the weight of reinforcements on either side began to tell. The position held by the two battalions of the K.O.Y.L.I. became a rallying point behind which the shattered remnants of the attacking battalions were enabled to pull themselves together.

No ground was gained to be held for any length of time in these sanguinary advances. To the men of the K.O.Y.L.I., who were in the dark as to the general trend of movements and who were faced by an enemy position which they had not seen before in daylight, much less reconnoitred, there was a mystery about the whole proceedings. The regular attack had commenced at about 9 a.m., two hours earlier than was expected, up the slopes of Hill 70 and the high ground to its north. On the right, in the face of heavy opposition, the attackers were observed to disappear into trenches and folds of the ground along the summit of the high ground. But apparently owing to some misunderstanding the 63rd Inf. Bde. commenced to retire from the hill, as did large bodies of other troops. The IV Corps troops were apparently executing a steady retirement, which was general. This was understood to have been chiefly due to heavy shelling by our own guns and to being attacked in rear by the troops of the 9 a.m. attack, whose information as to the position of our troops appeared to have been faulty. It gave the impression that Hill 70 was being evacuated, especially when our own guns again commenced to shell it indiscriminately. It was then that the retired troops re-formed behind the position held by the 64th Inf. Bde. By 12 noon a second attack directed against Hill 70 was in full swing, and again the left battalions of this attack were apparently drawn to the left from their original objective in an advance towards our own troops, who were still holding on to part of the high ground. In fact, the attacks were hastily organised and orders were but half understood; there was doubt and hesitation, for the position was very obscure. Again the troops commenced a regular retirement from Hill 70, crossing the front which the 21st and 24th Divs. occupied. Again the units were re-formed behind the trenches of the 64th Inf. Bde.; they had been followed by a heavy enemy fire. Another attack was about to be launched when suddenly the 9/K.O.Y.L.I. moved forward independently to a counter-attack. Apparently a call had come when their C.O., Lt.-Col. Lynch, was at Bde. Headquarters getting instructions from his

Brigadier, and it was never discovered who had given the order for the advance. The battalion was over the top and was already irretrievably committed to an advance; all that could now be done by the senior officers on the spot was to adapt themselves and their orders to the unexpected turn of events, and the 10th Bn. was ordered hastily to follow in support, with instructions not to proceed beyond the Loos-Hulluch road. The advance was timely in the way that it came in time to cover the re-organisation of the battered units, but as an attack it was seen that where so many other units had failed to make an impression two battalions were not likely to succeed. Unfortunately the order to stop at the road failed to reach the advancing lines, or was ineffective as the units were too widely extended, for other troops, too, had hurried forward to share in the advance. The attackers pressed on up the hill, in the direction of a part which was found later to be held by our own troops; as before, the lines were crumpled up by the enemy machine gun and shrapnel fire, which took them in flank, and the troops were forced to retire. The men were pursued by a very destructive and intensified artillery fire. Once more the original line of the 64th Inf. Bde. had to be held till dusk, and all the time under a destructive bombardment which caused many further casualties. The enemy seized the opportunity to attempt to get into Loos, but our dismounted cavalry succeeded in preventing this.

Finally, the troops who had been holding on to Hill 70 all day under these unhappy conditions were seen to be coming away, and only then was it realised that the position which the three attacks had attempted to reach had been held all the time by our own advanced troops. The fact that these troops were wearing blue smoke-helmets and that they were being shelled by our own guns, possibly completed the illusion that they were Germans.

The 9/K.O.Y.L.I. suffered in casualties, two officers wounded; other ranks, killed 13, wounded 167, missing and unaccounted for 34.

The 10/K.O.Y.L.I. lost 3 officers wounded; Lt.-Col. A. W. Pollock and 2 other officers gassed; other ranks, killed 5, wounded 113, missing and unaccounted for, 28. 2/Lt. E. R. Nott of the 9th Bn. was awarded the M.C. "*for conspicuous gallantry and determination during operations at Hill 70 on Sept. 25th and 26th. Although twice wounded he continued to advance, leading and encouraging his men.*"

The Brig.-Gen. commanding the 64th Inf. Bde., in his subsequent report on the battle, described the march of his brigade as having been "*carried out over heavy plough in necessarily irksome formation by compass-bearing. The absence of all transport necessitated the man-handling of machine-guns with their ammunition, also 1,000 bombs per battalion, and 50 additional rounds per man. After two nights and a day under arms on the march, it is not too much to say that the men arrived on the battlefield in an exhausted state. Nevertheless there was never a word of complaint, and the* élan *with which the advances were made was nothing short of astonishing. The spirited way in which the* 14/*D.L.I. returned to the attack three times, and the* 15/*D.L.I. twice, is in my opinion also deserving of the highest commendation. That the attack failed was no fault of the men's or their training.*"

Those people of Yorkshire, whose feelings are stirred by evidence of the 'sporting spirit' in the lads of that county, should indeed find their hearts warmed by the story of the two K.O.Y.L.I. battalions of young miners, who had been forced during the day to witness the slaughter of their gallant cousins of Durham county in their repeated attacks, and who, becoming restive in inaction, poured "over the top" without word of command, like colts at the starting-gate that break the tape and get away down the course before the starter's flag is down.

The whole action in which the 21st Div. had been engaged during the day had taken place in a valley between a spur running from the village of Maroc to Hulluch and the spur from Hill 70 towards Wingles. The trenches held by the 64th Inf. Bde. were on the forward eastern slope of the first spur; along the crest of this spur the original German front line of trenches ran. Except for the cover afforded by these trenches, by the village of Loos and by the ditches alongside the Loos-Hulluch and Lens-La Bassée roads, also by the woods north and east of Puits No. 14, the terrain was smooth grass and was without cover. The valley lies wide and open and had been under cultivation: the undulations are very slight and gradual. The weather had been foggy in the morning but it cleared about 9 a.m. The new troops had been full of eagerness to join battle, and all eye-witnesses agreed that they behaved with splendid courage and steadiness, for their preliminary training in England had been of exceptional value, but no troops could have achieved success under such conditions as these battalions were faced with. In writing of the re-formation of the 21st Div. after their abortive attacks, Conan Doyle in his *British Campaign in France and Flanders* says: "*This re-establishment was materially helped by the action of the* 9*th and* 10*th Yorkshire Light Infantry battalions previously mentioned of the Twenty-first Division, who had become a Divisional Reserve. These two battalions now advanced and gained some ground to the east of Loos on the enemy's left flank . . . . The movement covered the re-organisation which was going on behind them. One small detachment under Captain Laskie of the* 10*th K.O.Y.L.I. did especially good work.*"

By the evening the of 26th September the general line was contracted rather than advanced, and part of the Lens-Hulluch road was lost. Fresh troops were hurrying to the front. The Guards Div. (Lord Cavan) had reached Sailly la Bourse on the 26th and was brought in on the morning of the 27th to the relief of the shattered divisions, including the 21st, on the front extending from the Vermelles-Hulluch road to Loos.

The 28th Div. (Maj.-Gen. E. S. Bulfin) was sent in to restore the fight north of the Vermelles-Hulluch road, in the same way that the Guards Div. was directed south of it.

THE 1ST BN. The 1/K.O.Y.L.I., commanded by Lt.-Col. C. R. Ingham Brooke, had been billeted during September at Scherpenberg in the Ypres district; the 83rd Inf. Bde., to which it belonged, was then commanded by Brig.-Gen. Ravenshaw. It started on its journey down behind the lines to Outersteene *via* Locre and Bailleul on the 23rd September. On the 26th it marched *via* Merville to Robecq. On the 27th it 'embussed' at Robecq for Noyelles les Vermelles, where it occupied reserve trenches behind the line on the Vermelles road on the morning of the 28th.

Gen. Thesiger, commanding the 9th Div., had been killed. Fosse 8, a commanding position, had been re-occupied by the enemy; Hohenzollern redoubt only partially remained in our hands, and the Quarries position was in danger of being lost. The 1/K.O.Y.L.I. was moved up into the trenches on the 29th. At 10.15 a.m. "B" and "D" Companies under Maj. H. Mallinson occupied Sussex trench: Bn. Headquarters with "A" and "C" Companies were in Lancashire lines. The 2/King's Own moved forward at the same time.

At 2.15 p.m. "B" and "D" moved again and came under the orders of the 85th Inf. Bde., "D" being in the firing line in Big Willie, "B" close behind in support.

At 5 p.m. the remainder of the battalion moved up into reserve trenches, also under the orders of the 85th Inf. Bde. The battalion helped to repel the enemy counter-attacks. The Germans were making a great effort to recover the piece of their line which had been lost and were bringing fresh divisions.

While resisting the attacks south of the Hohenzollern redoubt, C.S.M. J. W. Lawn was specially recommended for his conspicuously gallant conduct, and was later awarded a bar to his D.C.M.; he had won his medal originally when serving in the South African war with the 2nd Bn.

Sgt. R. Hill also received a D.C.M.

While these events were taking place Capt. C. E. C. Rabagliati, a representative of the 1st Bn. serving in the R.F.C., won his M.C. for a particularly fine reconnaissance carried out far into the enemy's lines under difficult conditions.

On the 30th September the battalion was relieved and went back to the old British front line trenches north of the Hulluch road, but it returned to the former German front line trenches at 5.45 for a few hours on the morning of the 1st October.

The casualties this day included Lt. J. L. Heath, killed; Lt. S. A. Milner, wounded; other ranks, 5 killed and 31 wounded.

That night the battalion was relieved by the 2/H.L.I. and it proceeded to billets at Annequin, but returned to the trenches opposite Hohenzollern redoubt on the 3rd October, taking them over from the 6/Welch by 6.10 p.m.

It had been determined that the 1st Bn., together with the 2/E.York., should make an attempt to recover lost portions of the Hohenzollern redoubt early in the morning of the 4th. The distance to be traversed before reaching the German trenches was about 200 yards. Each battalion furnished two companies for the operation. Of the 1/K.O.Y.L.I., "A" and "D" Companies were detailed. In accordance with their orders the first two lines went over the parapet in the dark at 4.15 a.m., advanced thirty yards and lay down; the third line followed at 4.30 a.m. and the fourth at 4.45 a.m. This was the moment for the commencement of the attack; it was also the signal for a hurricane of rifle and machine-gun fire on the part of the defenders. Capt. Hon. H. A. Law with the second wave almost immediately overtook the first, which had already lost in casualties half its strength; forming one line of the two waves he continued the advance in the face of devastating fire until about half the distance had been covered; by this time he had some twenty men remaining, and no further headway was possible. It was evident that the enemy was fully prepared for this counter-attack on the redoubt from the intensity of the fire from the moment that an attempt was made to advance. The essential element of surprise, on which an attack of this kind must always be dependent, was absent; also the preliminary bombardment, although it had been carried out with pre-arranged care, had not effected its purpose of decreasing the volume of the enemy resistance.

The companies of the E.York. met with a similar fate.

The casualties in the K.O.Y.L.I. were:—Officers, 2/Lt. A. H. Martindale, killed; 2/Lt. C. L. Pearn, wounded; Lt. F. W. Graham (4/D.L.I. attached) and 2/Lt. P. T. C. Simpson returned as missing. Other ranks, 10 known to be killed, 65 wounded, 101 missing.

There was little doubt that the men who were reported to be missing were lying dead on the field. It was found possible to recover a few of the wounded during the night.

In Sir John French's dispatches of the 1st January, 1916, the following members of the 1/K.O.Y.L.I. were mentioned for services at Loos:—

Maj. H. Mallinson, Capt. J. A. Jervois, Capt. W. H. Brooke, Capt. and Qr.-Mr. J. C. Brasier; Q.M.S. H. Knight, C.S.M. F. Setterfield, and Cpl. R. Hill. Also, Maj. H. W. B. Thorp and Maj. F. J. G. Agg, both serving on the Staff.

Awards: D.S.O., Majors Thorp and Agg; M.C., Capt. Brooke, D.C.M., No. 1028, Pte. H. Smith.

The 28th Div. was now withdrawn for a rest and their place was taken by the Guards Div. The 1/K.O.Y.L.I. moved by route march to Gonnehem, where large drafts met it.

It was in the trenches again by Hulluch on the 17th when it relieved the 2/Queen's.

On the 21st October the division was finally withdrawn, the 1/K.O.Y.L.I. going to billets in La Vallée.

It was here that the division received orders to proceed to Macedonia. All unfit men were promptly weeded out, and the change in prospect was heralded with excitement. No man living could have regretted leaving France for fresh fields, however much the prospect might be wrapped in mystery. A repetition of the experience gained at Loos was not a thing to be anticipated gladly.

The battalion entrained at Fouquereuil at 12.30 a.m. on the 25th. Marseilles was reached at 10 a.m. on the 26th October and the battalion straightway embarked in *H.M.T. Kyarra*, sailing at 6 in the evening for Alexandria. It arrived at that port at 2.30 p.m. on the 31st October, after a pleasant voyage "with nothing of interest to report."

Loos was the last action of importance for the British troops on the western front in 1915. The armies settled down to trench warfare and to incessant local activity, which no amount of rain and cold and bitter conditions were allowed to interfere with.

Heavy fighting, in order to maintain and consolidate the position which had been gained in the face of fierce counter-attacks, broke out again and again before the end of October, notably on the 8th and 13th. All along the British line to the north, fighting was meanwhile occurring in connection with the battle of Loos, for as the attack by Loos was subsidiary to the great attack of the French to the south of them, so again minor British attacks north of it were subsidiary to that by Loos. All were made with the primary object of preventing the Germans from detaching troops to the south.

The 20th Div. was engaged in the fighting in the line some distance north of La Bassée, involving the 7/K.O.Y.L.I.; and again further north the 6th Bn. was engaged, where the 14th (Light) Div. took its share in the holding attacks. Since its arrival in France in May, 1915, this battalion had, by the 31st December suffered in casualties, killed and wounded, a loss of 538 men of all ranks.

The net result of the fighting at Loos to the British was an advance of line extending to some 7,000 yards of front, with about 3,000 prisoners and twenty-six captured guns. It proved that with sufficient artillery preparation, with the use of gas and smoke clouds, no fortified line held by the enemy was impregnable. But it also proved that the more difficult task was the holding and consolidation of the line subsequently under the concentrated enemy gun fire and his organised attacks by bombers. Also that further advances could only be gained if the gap created could be enlarged sufficiently to allow the attackers to roll up the flanks of the hostile lines and so force a retirement on a considerable front.

The French meanwhile had had a success in the Champagne country which was commensurate with their larger forces engaged, and with their more adequate equipment in guns and ammunition. They gained a valuable position and drove the Germans off the ridge along which runs the Chemin des Dames. In their case, too, the gains were almost entirely made in the first spring, when they made substantial hauls of prisoners (25,000) and guns (125). The prestige of the victory was of far higher value than the count of the spoil.

THE SOMME. 1916

IX

AFTER the battle of Loos in the autumn of 1915, throughout the winter and the spring of the new year, in the British line in France there were no serious departures from the state of dogged resistance that had supervened. As a state of "passive" resistance it certainly could not rightly be described, for the lesser units were constantly engaged in active operations on a minor scale.

Taking a wide survey of the theatres of war, it is plain that, notwithstanding the loss of her colonies, Germany (with the other Central Powers) had considerable reason for feelings of satisfaction. October, 1915, had seen Bulgaria ranged 'on the side of the victors,' following the successful campaign of Germany in the east. Poland, Bukovina and Galicia had been overrun. The British expedition to the Dardanelles ended in complete withdrawal on the night of the 8th-9th January, 1916. Gen. Townshend was blockaded in Kut from the 8th December, 1915, and was finally forced to surrender on April 29th, 1916. On the western front Germany was in possession of almost the whole of the soil of Belgium, and of a great slice of northern France in addition.

The initiative, that all-important factor in military operations, was in the hands of the Central Powers, who possessed interior, and shorter, lines of communication.

In anticipation of any attempt to wrest the initiative from her, Germany broke the spell of uncertainty by hammer blows directed on Verdun. Twenty-six divisions were concentrated for the attack. On the 21st February, 1916, the first blow fell. French soldiers are traditionally famous in the attack; they were now to prove to the world, in the fighting round Verdun, that they are capable of fighting no less gloriously in the defence. Verdun must supply for all time the noblest page of national sacrifice in the annals of France.

In a letter dated 11th November, 1920, addressed to the writer of this record, Col. E. Hind, who had commanded the 4/K.O.Y.L.I. early in the war, wrote "*I remember once when my men were going up into the line some German prisoners accosted them, and one said, 'It took many ships to bring over the British army but one will take them back!' It seems to me that the Hun was right, and the name of the ship is 'Verdun'.*"

It will be remembered that in July, 1915, a British Third Army had been formed, and that the part of the line between the Ancre and the Somme had been handed over by the French to this Third Army.

Later in the year the remaining portion of the northern line by Arras had been handed over, when the British Fourth Army was formed. So the whole front from Ypres to the Somme was now held by British troops. The Third Army held the line including Hébuterne as its southern limit, the Fourth Army held from that point almost to the northern bank of the Somme.

The battalions of the K.O.Y.L.I. serving in the line on the western front at the commencement of the year were the 2nd, 4th, 5th, 6th, 7th, 8th, 9th, 10th and 12th.

THE 2ND BN.

The 2/K.O.Y.L.I. in January, 1916, was transferred from the 13th Inf. Bde., 5th Div., to the 97th Inf. Bde., 32nd Div. Some of the brigades of seasoned warriors were being broken up and battalions were being posted to brigades of the new armies in order to introduce the element of experience into the young formations. The 2/D.W.R. in this way also left the 13th Inf. Bde. The parting was keenly felt; the battalions of this brigade had been quartered together in Dublin before the war and had been inseparably connected in the field for nearly eighteen months; it was a matter of great pride with them to wear the distinguishing badge of the 5th Div.

If the breaking away from old associations was fraught with regret, the prospect was not necessarily depressing, for the change brought new friends, fresh scenes and fresh responsibilities.

The 97th Inf. Bde. included also the 2/Border, the 16th and 17th Bns. of the H.L.I. and the 97th Inf. Bde. Machine Gun Company. Brig.-Gen. Jardine commanded it, and Maj.-Gen. Rycroft commanded the division. After their training period behind the line the division was destined for the trenches by the river Ancre, becoming a unit of the X Corps (Morland), of the Fourth Army (Rawlinson).

On the 18th June when at Contay Wood, where the 97th Inf. Bde. was training, Gen. Rycroft addressed the men after church parade and referred to the coming offensive (on the Somme) in which they were, so he said, to play a prominent part. The 2/K.O.Y.L.I. was held up as an example to the new battalions, and its record since 1914 was reviewed.

By the 24th June the battalion was in dugouts by Crucifix Corner, over against that well-known landmark, which overlooked the trench to which it gave its name. This was the position of readiness before proceeding to the front line trenches which extended from Skinner Street to Mersey Street. Lt.-Col. E. H. Rigg was in command of the battalion, with Maj. G. H. Kent as his Adjutant.

The 4th and 5th Bns. K.O.Y.L.I., with the rest of the 49th Div., had been moved from the Ypres salient into the X Corps also. The third division of the X Corps was the 36th. For the opening of the Somme attack the 49th was detailed to act in support of the other two divisons. Our two battalions, centred on Bois d'Aveluy had, throughout the month of June, 1916, been employed in 'assisting' the 32nd Div., and both battalions were placed at the disposal of the 96th Inf. Bde. in its attack on Thiepval. Lt.-Col. H. J. Haslegrave still commanded the 4th Bn., having Capt. J. I. Muirhead as his Adjutant; Col. C. C. Moxon also was with his own battalion; Capt. P. Bentley had been appointed Adjutant (9th November, 1915) *vice* Capt. G. K. Sullivan appointed to command the 4/D.W.R.

THE 4TH AND 5TH BNS.

The 6/K.O.Y.L.I. (43rd Inf. Bde., 14th (Light) Div.) was now at Agny, three miles south of Arras. On the 21st June the companies went up into the line by S. Nicholas, occupying trenches J88, J91, J84, and J90. Lt.-Col. E. Meynell commanded and Capt. T. E. F. Penny was Adjutant.

THE 6TH BN.

In January, 1916, the 7/K.O.Y.L.I. had left the Fleurbaix sector for Poperinghe, and from this place, greatly to the regret of the battalion, Lt.- Col. V. A. M. Fowler was forced to return home owing to ill-health. Capt. B. B. Robinson succeeded to the command. In mid-February the battalion was in the trenches in the north part of the Ypres salient; this was always recognised as the hot spot of the British line, and casualties were frequent. Lt.-Col. Robinson was wounded and was sent to England to hospital for a time. His return to the front a few weeks later was a little accelerated by the fact that an order for a passage back to France, made out for some other officer of the same name, was sent to him in error; however, thinking (to use his own words) that "*one Robinson was as good as another*" he did not worry the authorities with explanations, and crossed to Boulogne. Col. Lyon of the 18th Hussars had commanded the battalion during his absence. The 20th Div. was now incorporated in the XIV Corps, under Gen. Lord Cavan. It is recorded that the 7/K.O.Y.L.I. at an early date had the pleasure of receiving in their trenches a visit from Maj. Deedes[1] who was now on the Headquarters Staff of the XIV Corps and acting temporarily as Bde.-Maj. to the Brigade. In May the battalion went back to Calais for its long rest. While there, a not too arduous training was carried out by day, and every facility was given to the men after working hours to rid themselves of the memory of trench life in the enjoyment of the amenities of the town.

THE 7TH BN.

[1]*Now Maj.-Gen. C. P. Deedes, C.B., C.M.G., D.S.O., Colonel of the King's Own Yorkshire Light Infantry* (1927).

But there came a sudden call to proceed back to Poperinghe by route march one sweltering day, and they went back forthwith into trenches on the left of the Menin road in the centre of the Salient. Here Maj. R. T. A. Ball-Acton (who had retired from the army after serving in the 2/K.O.Y.L.I. in South Africa) joined as second-in-command. He was killed very shortly afterwards. Capt. J. L. Beddington, the Adjutant, was wounded on the 2nd June, during a heavy bombardment, which had been followed up on the part of the enemy by the temporary occupation of Sanctuary Wood and Hill 62. On the 6th June the 7/K.O.Y.L.I. was moved in response to a S.O.S. message by train from Poperinghe to Vlamertinghe; the Germans had exploded several mines and were in Hooge. The battalion relieved the 12/R.B. in the trenches, with its headquarters in Potijze Wood. On the 13th June, at 1.30 a.m., gas was discharged from our trenches on either flank of the 7/K.O.Y.L.I., and the divisional artillery bombarded the German front line opposite. At 1.45 a.m. the gas discharge ceased and raiding parties were sent across. These parties left the trenches of the 7/K.O.Y.L.I. front, as no gas had been used there. The Canadians then attacked and were entirely successful in regaining their old position. Later in the evening the 12/King's relieved the 7/K.O.Y.L.I., who went back to billets in Ypres. These were chiefly cellars in the barracks, convent and Boulevarde Malou.

The battalion had had Capt. Moss-Blundell wounded and 15 other casualties in this last episode.

Until the 20th August, while the earlier stages of the Somme battle were being fought, this battalion remained in the same sector. After that date it was called upon to take its share in the battle operations.

THE 8TH BN.

The 8/K.O.Y.L.I. had been undergoing an extended training under Lt.-Col. H. E. Trevor near Albert, all with a view to the great attack. The 70th Inf. Bde. (Brig.-Gen. H. Gordon) was temporarily attached to the 8th Div. (Maj.-Gen. H. Hudson). On the 22nd June, 1916, Sgt. J. T. Waldron of the battalion was decorated by the G.O.C. the 8th Div. with the D.C.M. The battalion finally moved into the trenches in front of Authuille Wood on the 29th June while the preliminary bombardment of the German lines by our guns was in progress.

THE 9TH AND 10TH BNS.

Since the battle of Loos the composition of the brigades of the 21st Div. had been altered, as in the case of other formations of the new army. The 64th Inf. Bde. now had the 1/E.York. in place of the 14/D.L.I. The 9th and 10th Bns. K.O.Y.L.I. and the 15/D.L.I. thus remained. The division was in the XV Corps (Horne), which occupied a sector of the line opposite Fricourt and Mametz.

The HQ. of the 64th Inf. Bde. was in Meaulte, one and a half miles south of Albert, but for practices in attack formation, over ground marked out to represent the actual features in the intended operations, the brigade went to La Neuville. These were varied by such duties as gas-cylinder carrying parties, 300 strong, who carried the stuff by train to Meaulte and on by hand to the trenches. On the 26th June both 9th and 10th Bns. moved up to Buire to make their final preparations before moving into the trenches for the attack. To the 9/K.O.Y.L.I. Lt.-Col. C. W. D. Lynch (on whom the D.S.O. had recently been conferred) here addressed his last words of advice and instruction. The following officers of this battalion went with him into the trenches:—("A" Company) Capt. L. D. Head, 2/Lts. C. W. Howlett, N. L. Alexander, R. A. Stokes, A. Hardman and C. E. Vassie; ("B" Company) Capt. G. Haswell, Lt. B. L. Gordon, 2/Lts. C. W. Ellis, D. Williams and G. A. Kemp; ("C" Company) Capt. W. Walker, 2/Lts. J. J. F. Oldershaw, G. F. Ellenberger, A. D. Maconachie, and F. W. Golding; ("D" Company) Capt. G. Griffen, 2/Lts. A. E. Day, R. F. Frazer and J. R. Wood; also 2/Lt. F. G. Morris, Bombing Officer; 2/Lt. G. H. Featherstone, Signals; and 2/Lt. E. R. Nott, Scout Officer. Other ranks numbered 750. The following were left in reserve at Buire:—Lts. L. D. Spicer and B. L. H. Hart; 2/Lts. W. F. Keay (Adjt.), W. W. Shepherd, H. F. Kingston, K. W. Sutcliffe, A. M. L. Hart and E. G. J. Jenkins; also the Qr.-Mr., Lt. W. K. Pethed, and the Transport Officer, 2/Lt. T. H. Ibbetson.

In the evening of the 30th June by 11 p.m. the two battalions, 9th and 10th, moved up into positions of assembly for the attack, side by side (the 9th on the right). Lt.-Col. H. J. King had commanded the 10/K.O.Y.L.I. since the 6th April, 1916.

THE 12TH BN.

After its short period of service in Egypt the 12/K.O.Y.L.I. (Pioneers) arrived in France in March, 1916, and was incorporated in the 31st Div., now part of the VIII Corps (Hunter-Weston).

Lt.-Col. E. L. Chambers was in command of the battalion whose Headquarters were in Bus-les-Artois, about ten miles north of Albert. By the 20th June preparations for the attack on the German line were in full swing in the division, and the companies of the Pioneer Bn. were allotted: "A" to the 94th Inf. Bde., "D" to the 93rd, while "B" and "C" were detailed for work connected with clearing out the German communication trenches leading to the line which it was hoped to capture in the first bound.

When a division entered upon a general attack, there was no vast distinction made between an infantry soldier and a pioneer infantry man; the ordinary soldier carried 220 rounds of ammunition, the pioneer carried 170 rounds plus a pick or a shovel; their other impedimenta were very much the same in detail.

The officers of the battalion who went into action on the 1st July were:—Lt.-Col. E. L. Chambers, Maj. C. B. Charlesworth, Capt. S. G. Newton (Adjt.), Capt. E. Forbes, R.A.M.C. ("A" Company) Capt. J. C. Crawshaw, Lt. J. S. L. Welch, 2/Lts. N. L. O. Bennett and P. Atkinson. ("B" Company) Capt. D. E. Roberts, Lts. H. D. Gaunt and J. T. Underhill, 2/Lts. W. E. Oliver and W. Baird. ("C" Company) Lts. W. H. Roberts and J. H. Partridge, 2/Lts. J. J. McGroarty, L. Forsdike and G. R. C. Adams. ("D" Company) Capt. H. F. Chadwick, Lt. R. E. England, 2/Lts. P. T. Crowther and V. Mossop.

The remaining officers of the battalion were ordered to stay in Bus Wood under Capt. G. M. Stockings and to be prepared to reinforce at a moment's notice.

R.S.M. L. Shackleton and Sgt. Andrews also waited in the wood.

The troops of the division allotted to the successive waves wore distinguishing strips of coloured cloth tied to the right shoulder-strap. This practice was universally adopted at this period of the war and ensured that each individual knew the objective which he was to reach during the course of the attack. The successive waves passed through each other, and thus the objectives which were first captured were consolidated, while fresh troops went forward to the later objectives.

By 5.50 a.m. on the 1st July all companies were present in their assembly posts.

Having now traced the movement of the battalions of the K.O.Y.L.I. up to the moment when they waited in their trenches for the final barrage to create the opportunity for them to step 'over the top' into No Man's Land, we will leave them for a few minutes to sketch in outline an explanation of the scheme of the series of battles known comprehensively as the battle of the Somme. Without such a sketch the series of offensives could hardly be intelligible.

THE SOMME BATTLEFIELD

The part of the German line which was the object of attack extended from the Ancre to the Somme, with a few miles also of their line north of the river Ancre. From Hébuterne to Fricourt the line ran north and south, but from Fricourt for about six miles it ran in an easterly direction, turning southwards again at that point to join up with the French who were on the north bank of the river Somme.

Behind this portion of the German line the ground rose steadily to a ridge which forms the watershed of the Somme and the Ancre; the highest point is near the northern end above Bazentin-le-Petit.

About twenty-five miles of front was included in the attack. The British Fourth Army was opposed to this frontage, and to Gen. Sir H. Rawlinson, the Commander of the Fourth Army, was given the direction of the operations. The right Corps (the VII) of the Third Army (Allenby) co-operated on the left of the attack.

COMPOSITION OF THE ATTACKING ARMY.

The five corps which composed the Fourth Army stood in order from left to right as follows:—VIII Corps (Hunter-Weston), X (Morland), III (Pulteney), XV (Horne) and XIII (Congreve). The divisions of the VIII Corps in the front line were the 31st, 4th and 29th, with the 48th in reserve. Of the X Corps the 36th and 32nd were in the front line, with the 49th in reserve; General Pulteney had the 8th and the 34th in front line, with the 19th in reserve; the three divisions of the XV Corps all occupied portions of the front line, *i.e.*, the 21st, 17th and 7th; while of the XIII Corps the 18th and 30th divisions were in the line and the 9th was held in reserve.

That an offensive on a large scale was impending was of course obvious to the Germans. What they could not have known was the exact portion of the line where the blow was to be delivered. It is presumed that they expected it further to the north than it actually came, for they appear not to have given the French credit for making a further great effort at the very time that they were displaying such wonderful energy in the defence about Verdun. The British offensive was in fact very materially assisted by the French Army operating on its immediate right. As it turned out, the resistance met with on the right of the British attack was not so adamantine as it was on the left.

FIRST PHASE COMMENCING 1ST JULY, 1916

In the battle of the 1st July the left Corps of the Fourth Army the VIII, attacked the German lines from Serre to Beaumont Hamel, but were unable to hold any part of the enemy's front line though the 4th Div. penetrated for some distance. The same fate met the X Corps, which had a desperately strong position in Thiepval to encounter. The 8th Div. (III Corps) fared no better in the attack on Ovillers, but from this point southwards the attackers met with signal success. Though La Boiselle itself was not taken, the trenches north and south of the village were captured and held by the 34th Div., and the 21st, which was on its right, took Crucifix Trench and the Sunken Road in dashing style. All the other divisions of the XV and XIII Corps made considerable advances, capturing Mametz and Montauban, while beyond them to the right the French, who operated on both banks of the Somme, reached Hardecourt and Curlu north of the river, and penetrated deep into the German lines south of it.

The second forward bound was made on the 14th July. The careful preparations enabled the attackers to achieve success. They established themselves on the ridge, capturing the two Bazentin villages, and penetrated as far as Delville Wood and even to High Wood; Ovillers fell into their hands, as did Longueval. Unfortunately, reserves could not be brought up fast enough to secure the two woods against the tremendous counter-attacks which ensued, and several weeks elapsed before the coveted line, which included the woods, was won. Progress on the right was sufficient to bring the British advance up into line with the French, but Ginchy and Guillemont were too strongly defended to be taken this time.

THE SECOND PHASE COMMENCING 14TH JULY, 1916.

By the beginning of September fresh dispositions had been made of the British troops. A new Fifth Army, under Gen. Sir Hubert Gough, had been created. This was pushed into the line between the Third and Fourth Armies. Even now the left could make no progress, but the right gradually made themselves masters of the important positions ahead of them. Guillemont fell, then Ginchy and Falfemont Farm.

On the 15th September, the Fifth Army on the left, with the Fourth Army on its right, opened a third great offensive. In this attack tanks were employed for the first time. Courcelette, Martinpuich, High Wood and Flers were all captured on the left and centre, but further to the right the Quadrilateral resisted successfully till the 18th, and Les Bœufs and Morval were not taken till the 25th September. Meanwhile Thiepval resisted the Fourth Army till the 26th, after which the advance was rapid for a time and the Fourth Army registered successes on both sides of the Albert-Bapaume road.

THE THIRD PHASE COMMENCING 15TH SEPTEMBER, 1916

The general direction of the British advance had been north-east. Throughout October constant heavy rain made operations extremely difficult; the ground was a sea of mud; when trenches were taken it often became impossible to strengthen and consolidate them. Some progress was made in spite of all difficulties, but progress was slow and the gains were very costly. Gueudecourt in the right centre was reached; Eaucourt l'Abbaye and Le Sars further east were captured on the 2nd and 7th October respectively; thus the greater part of the Bazentin ridge was cleared of the enemy.

On the left of the British attack no ground had been taken, for the defences about Beaumont Hamel and Serre were so strong that the left was forced to wait until the high ground south of the Ancre was completely in our hands, and so to render Beaumont Hamel untenable to its defenders.

The fourth and last phase of the Somme operations commenced the 13th November with an attack in which seven British divisions took part, which cleared the northern end of the great ridge and resulted in the capture of Beaumont Hamel itself, and of Beaucourt-sur-Ancre. This operation was confined to the troops of the Fifth Army under the command of Sir Hubert Gough. It is referred to officially as the battle of the 'Ancre, 1916,' but was actually the last of the series of battles which constituted the battle of the 'Somme,' and formed the final successful effort of the left flanking army to straighten the northern portion of the line that had been the object of attack.

THE FOURTH PHASE COMMENCING 13TH NOVEMBER, 1916

The season had been notable for the vileness of the weather and further operations were suspended.

Briefly the 1916 campaigns, 'Verdun' and the 'Somme,' had far-reaching results, for the mass of the German forces were pinned to the western theatre of war, and the period proved to be a turning point; up to this point the German High Command had been possessors of the initiative; from this time onwards, except for the period of their great offensive in 1918, they were obliged to think first about 'the defence of their own goal.'

The various actions of the Somme period in which battalions of the K.O.Y.L.I. were engaged, will be detailed in the following chapter.

THE SOMME OFFENSIVE FIRST PERIOD. 1916

X

THE left division in the Fourth Army in front of Albert, *i.e.*, in the attack on the Somme on the 1st July, 1916, was the 31st. The left-most battalion of the K.O.Y.L.I. consequently was the 12th Bn.

The pioneer battalions might well have borrowed that old proud motto 'Ich dien' (but that it is expressed in a language that could find no favour in 1916). Compare this motto in its brevity and simplicity with the official account of its experiences written in the diary of the 12/K.O.Y.L.I. opposite the date 1st July, which runs:—

12TH BN. K.O.Y.L.I.

"*Battalion reported present in assembly posts at* 5.50 *a.m.*"

"*Battalion reassembled at assembly posts at* 4.30 *p.m.*"

"*Casualties sustained:* 1 *officer killed,* 3 *wounded,* 188 *other ranks killed and wounded.*"

Such a diary demands amplification for this record. The 94th and 93rd Inf. Bdes., to which "A" and "D" Companies of the 12th Bn. were allotted in the attack, had Serre for their objective. At 7.30 the whistles blew; each brigade went over the top in waves on a front of two companies; the left brigade of the Fourth Army was the 94th Inf. Bde. They were met by a destructive fire from the German infantry (who had been sheltered from our artillery barrage), from numerous machine-guns, and, most serious of all, from an immense concentration of heavy guns, especially from the direction of Bucquoy, east of Hébuterne, on their left front. To quote Conan Doyle: "*These guns formed successive lines of barrage with shrapnel and high explosives, one of them about* 200 *yards behind the British line, to cut off the supports; another* 50 *yards behind; another* 50 *yards in front; and a fourth of shrapnel which was under observed control, and followed the troops in their movements. The advanced lines of assault were able in most cases to get through before these barrages were effectively established, but they made it difficult, deadly, and often impossible, for the lines who followed.*"

The companies of the 12/K.O.Y.L.I. had their duties to perform among 'the lines who followed.' The waves of the attack melted under the hail of metal: they advanced at the only pace they were permitted—the quick time, never the double. Those 'who followed' had to rebuild trenches that were crumbling under heavy gunfire, forward supplies of ammunition, dig new trenches, and help in the later hours to save some of the wounded. That these duties did not render them immune from danger to life is obvious from their casualty list: that they found opportunities of displaying high military qualities may be judged from an entry made in the diary on the following day: "*Lts. W. H. Roberts and H. D. Gaunt, 2/Lts. W. Baird and L. Forsdike, specially recommended for the coolness and energy they displayed during the 1st July attack. C.S.M. R. E. Freakes was a splendid example of discipline and pluck, rallying the men with the assistance of C.Q.M.S. R. Keer. Sgt. A. Adams, though wounded early in the day, continued to give his utmost assistance.*"

On the 2nd July the battalion was acting in divisonal reserve, in position in Hittite trench. On the 4th July it marched to Bus-les-Artois; thence on the 6th to Beauval, on the 7th to Prouville, the 9th to Conteville and by train to Berguette; then on to billets at Mollinghem. For four months or so it was to be occupied in work under the R.E. Its varied occupations included the unloading of coal barges, the digging of drainage systems in the forward area, making tramways, tunnelling, building strong posts, and the duties included under the head of 'forest control.'

We have seen that little progress was made by the VIII Corps north of the Ancre. On its right came the X Corps with its 36th Div. attacking on the left, the 32nd Div. on the right, and the 49th Div. in general support. The objective of the 36th Div. was that part of the great ridge lying between the Ancre and Thiepval. The village of Thiepval with a portion of the ridge south of it was the goal for which the 32nd Div. was to strive. The ground slopes down from Thiepval gradually and forms a glacis, but a spur of the ridge descends below the village in a direction south-west-by-south towards Authuille Wood, and the lines of German trenches footing this spur formed a salient, which was very strongly fortified and was known as the Leipzig salient.

THE 2ND BN.

From the 26th to the 30th June the 2/K.O.Y.L.I. held the front line trenches from Skinner Street to Mersey Street over against the western front of the salient. The British bombardment had continued since the 24th June and had been heavily replied to, so heavily that the front line trenches were so badly damaged by gun-fire as to make it impossible to move along them. Two platoons of "C" and two platoons of "D" Company, which had suffered most severely, were relieved and sent back to Bouzincourt on the 28th. At noon on the 30th the battalion was relieved by the 16th and 17th Bns. H.L.I., who entered the line and took up battle positions for the assault. The battalion took up its own battle positions in Kintyre and Caithness trenches, in immediate support of the H.L.I., about 300 yards east of the village of Authuille. The casualties had been 5 killed and 54 wounded up to date.

Of the brigades of the 32nd Div. the 96th (left) and 97th (right) were front line, the 14th was in support. Of the 97th Inf. Bde. the 16/H.L.I. was on the left and the 17/H.L.I. on the right in the front line, with the 11/Border in right support, and the 2/K.O.Y.L.I. on their left.

The K.O.Y.L.I. trenches were 400 yards in rear of the front line. The companies advanced to the attack in line in the following order:

(LEFT)

2 platoons of "C" Company	2 platoons of "D" Company	"B" Company	"A" Company	2 platoons of "D" Company	2 platoons of "C" Company

The flanking platoons of "C" Company were to consolidate strong points when the second objective should be reached: the platoons of "D" Company carried materials, wire, etc.

The company commanders were Capts. C. K. Butler ("A"), T. Wells ("B"), G. A. Gamble ("C") and E. J. Millin ("D"). "A" and "B" Companies were ordered to follow close behind the leading battalions, to pass through after the capture of the third objective, and to attack the fourth objective. They were to have the 11/Border on their right, to whom a particular objective, the capture of the Ferme du Moquet, had been allotted.

The task of the 36th Div. was a notably formidable one, yet the dash of the Irish brigades carried them over every obstacle, even past the northern outskirts of Thiepval; the left company of the 32nd Div., belonging to the 15/L.F., was drawn to the left and carried on past the left of the village, but the right company of the same battalion, which was more exposed in its advance, was held up in front of Thiepval village. The 16/N.F. being next on the right, exposed to the full blast on the open glacis, was unable to make headway. Next on the right came the H.L.I. Bns.

At 6.25 a.m. our guns put an intense barrage over, which lasted for sixty-five minutes.

Under cover of a smoke screen the leading battalions advanced at 7.30, and the barrage then lifted on to the hostile support line. At 7.30 also the 2/K.O.Y.L.I. left the Kintyre trenches and advanced at a steady pace across the open. On reaching a ridge just behind our own first line trenches the left of the battalions, platoons of "C" and "D", with "B" Company, came under a very heavy machine-gun fire from the direction of Thiepval, and suffered heavily. On reaching our front line these companies came up with the 16/H.L.I., who had attempted to advance, but owing to the terrific machine-gun fire had been compelled to fall back again to our own front line, leaving many dead and wounded behind in No Man's Land. Capt. Wells led his men forward to the attack, but was wounded immediately after clearing the parapet. 2/Lt. E. Hicks, R.G.A., who had volunteered to accompany Capt. Wells as forward observing officer, gallantly continued to lead the men of "B" Company forward until he also fell wounded. 2/Lt. H. G. Walker of "C" Company, who had been previously wounded but would not go back, led his men over the parapet but was instantly killed. The hostile machine-gun and shell fire was so intense that all efforts to cross the fire-swept zone between the opposing lines failed, and the survivors here were forced to remain in our own front line trenches. Capt. E. J. Millin was killed while attempting to advance in this part of the field.

Meanwhile on the right "A" Company, under Capt. Butler, with halves of "C" and "D" Companies, had been able to advance with less difficulty and, following close on the heels of the 17/H.L.I., captured the German front line trench in the Leipzig salient; after passing over this they established themselves near the quarry in the German support line, opposite Fort Hindenburg, where the enemy was in great strength. Here they established themselves firmly with the Highlanders, and the fighting developed into a series of bombing attacks and close fighting. Capt. Gamble brought a Lewis gun into action at close range and did great execution with it until he was severely wounded in the face. Capt. Butler led a bombing attack up a communication trench leading from the enemy's support line to his reserve; he was killed by a bullet through the head. The position held in the Leipzig salient became isolated, as the troops to the right and left had been unable to make headway; however, the grip was not released and the place was held against all bomb attacks.

At 9.30 a.m. Bn. Headquarters, including Lt.-Col. E. H. Rigg, Maj. G. H. Kent (Adjt.), 2/Lts. E. D. Donnell and H. Gresham (Lewis gun officer), with two Lewis guns as a battalion reserve, moved forward up Campbell Avenue and across No Man's Land to the German front line trench of the salient, in order to see what could be done to assist the troops in the trenches ahead. There were roughly some 150 men of the battalion, with men of the 17/H.L.I., who were fighting against attacking parties on their left, front, and right. Judging it to be impossible to go deeper into the enemy's position without reinforcements, the position was consolidated as far as possible and defensive flanks formed. Lt. M. H. Garrard was now in command of the forward party and he had with him 2/Lts. A. R. Ramsden and P. Lambert; these officers for hours led the bombing parties, throwing bombs themselves, until about 11 a.m., when the supply of bombs and ammunition began to run short. At once arrangements were made to organise carrying parties under R.S.M. Wall, from all available men, and with their help a steady flow of bombs, ammunition, food and water found its way to the salient, where the detached troops were kept supplied until relieved thirty-six hours later. These carrying parties, who worked up across the open under heavy fire, deserve special notice. C.Q.M.S. C. Healey did particularly good work, and Cpl. W. Druggitt was conspicuous.

In the Leipzig salient the situation remained unchanged. Reinforcements from the 1/Dorset (14th Inf. Bde.) came in during the day. No serious counter-attack was made by the enemy, but the bombing duels were continuous.

Late in the evening two companies of the 2/Manch. under Lt.-Col. Luxmoore came in, and the latter took over the command locally. In the morning of the 2nd July the position was unchanged. The men of the 17/H.L.I. had been withdrawn during the night to their old lines.

The left half of the 2/K.O.Y.L.I. were suffering great losses throughout the day and night from shell-fire, and the trenches which they held became gradually obliterated. Accordingly, in the morning, they were ordered back into the old support line trenches. At this stage about 100 men survived, under 2/Lts. A. O. Purdon and W. A. Smith.

Many gallant deeds were performed by individual men during the time the trench line was being held. Wounded men who were lying out in shell-holes were brought in under heavy fire of snipers and machine-guns. In some cases it was only possible to bandage the men by day, and these were brought in after dark. L/Cpl. A. Holding did fine work, saving many lives; there were many others, including the regimental stretcher-bearers.

Throughout the 2nd July there was no special incident in the Leipzig salient; the position was held securely; for thirty-six hours the men, without a chance of sleep, were engaged constantly in bombing; they showed the greatest endurance and never relaxed in their efforts until, at 9 p.m., they were relieved by the 14th Inf. Bde.; they then went back to the dug-outs at Crucifix Corner. At 10.30 p.m. the companies of the left half battalion joined the others, having been withdrawn by way of Caithness trench.

Of casualties in these two days' fighting the battalion had, besides the officers already mentioned, 2/Lts. R. Smith and O. R. Ilberry, killed; Lt. T. Thwaites and 2/Lts. R. S. Turpin, F. O. Skidmore, E. H. Harrison and M. H. Garrard, wounded; of other ranks, 42 were killed, 242 wounded, 7 shell-shocked, and 42 were missing.

On the 3rd July the 97th Inf. Bde. moved *via* Aveluy, Bouzincourt and Senlis, to Contay Wood, where it found huts. On the 7th the brigade went into billets in Senlis, but it remained here long enough only to re-organise, and at 8.30 p.m. marched back *via* Bouzincourt to the trenches in front of Authuille Wood. The 2/K.O.Y.L.I. was made up for the time into two companies; Capt.

G. H. C. Palmer was put in command of the 11/Border R. temporarily, as that battalion had no senior officers left. The K.O.Y.L.I. took over the Nab Valley sub-sector from the 6/Buffs.

The shelling was very heavy on the 9th, especially in Authuille Wood. The nights of the 9th to the 12th were occupied by the battalion in digging a new trench out in front, which was completed to a depth of 4 ft. 6 in. On the 13th a demonstration was made to draw the enemy's fire and to attract his attention from the operations further south. At 6.30 p.m. on the 15th the battalion was relieved by the 4/Glosters., of the 48th Div., and the battalion retired to billets in Bouzincourt. There had been 4 men killed and 48 wounded in this period.

THE 4TH BN.

The 4/K.O.Y.L.I. arrived in their assembly trenches in Aveluy Wood at 3 a.m. on the morning of the 1st July. The 49th Div., being in reserve that day, did not participate in the first great advance, but at 6 p.m. orders were received which placed the 4th and 5th Bns. K.O.Y.L.I. at the disposal of the 96th Inf. Bde. in their attack on Thiepval. By 8.15 next morning they were holding trenches in Thiepval Wood, a position which had been won within the first line of the enemy trenches (known as the A line) on the previous day. They were shelled heavily in this position till 5 a.m. the next morning. During the night "X" and "Y" Companies of the 4/K.O.Y.L.I. were sent forward to relieve the 5/Y. & L.; "W" and "Z" Companies remained in support. On the 4th July there was a bombardment, followed at 2 p.m. by rapid fire; under cover of a thunderstorm the enemy launched an attack on the defenders of A trench line in which the 5/K.O.Y.L.I. was chiefly involved; however the defenders remained in possession of the trenches and the attack was driven off; the 4/K.O.Y.L.I. had Capt. H. C. Fraser and 45 other ranks wounded.

The 5th July was occupied in bombing attacks on both sides; after one of our attacks Capt. C. H. Plackett, who had been leading, was reported missing. 2/Lts. T. H. Riordan and E. T. Archer were wounded; 3 other ranks were killed, 20 wounded. "W" and "Z" Companies were employed in carrying bombs and ammunition up to the men in A line.

On the 6th the 4/K.O.Y.L.I. relieved the 5/K.O.Y.L.I. in the A line trenches. At 12.30 a.m. on the 7th the enemy opened an intense bombardment of the original British front line and of the A line. A furious fight with bombs ensued till 6.30 a.m. Casualties were numerous. Maj. Moorhouse (who had already won the D.S.O.) was in command of the sector; he was wounded at 4 a.m., but held on till 5.30, when he was forced by loss of blood to seek the dressing-station. Capt. W. M. Williamson and Lts. S. R. E. Carter, F. E. Massie, F. W. Mackay, A. A. F. de Jonquet and J. W. Huntington were also wounded; Capt. H. G. Fraser took command and continued the fight till 6.30 a.m. when, having no more bombs, he was forced to retire his men by way of the communicating trench to the original British front line, which he continued to hold with the 4th and 5th Bns. Y. & L. He had thirty-five men only of his two companies. At 9.30 a.m. he had orders to move to the assembly trenches in Thiepval Wood. The casualties in other ranks of his companies numbered 20 killed and 181 wounded. The battalion was relieved at 9 p.m. by the 5/D.W.R. It proceeded to Martinsart Wood, where the men had huts. Here it went through the process of re-organisation, and started training for further efforts later in the month.

THE 5TH BN.

The 5/K.O.Y.L.I., at the same time as the 4th, moved from their assembly trenches in Aveluy Wood at 6 p.m. on July 1st in order to assist the 32nd Div. in its attack on Thiepval. They had twenty casualties from shell-fire on the way, and not being required in the forward trenches, as the 36th Div. were coming back a little, they were directed to relieve the 9/R.U.R. in the Thiepval Wood sector.

On the 3rd "C" and "D" Companies replaced two companies of the 4/Y. & L. in the German A line trenches.

On the 4th there was heavy rain and a thunderstorm after 1.30 p.m., when the enemy attacked but were repulsed after a big bombing encounter. Lt. J. N. Walker was killed by shell-fire.

At 4 a.m. on July 5th an attempt was made to seize more of the German A trench system northwards by the Ancre. The attack was made by "A" Company, with "B" in support. The assault was met by shrapnel-fire and by rifle-fire from the shell-holes. All the officers of the leading company quickly became casualties; Capt. J. W. Walker was missing, 2/Lt. W. Royle was killed; Lts. W. L. Lister, W. R. Allen and J. N. Smith, wounded. The Germans were not only prepared to meet this assault, but they followed up with three violent counter-attacks; they got into some of our trenches and fought hard before being ejected. Capt. E. R. Creyke, Lt. H. W. P. Emerson and 2/Lts. S. D. Somerville and R. A. Harpley (M.G. Officer attd.) were killed; Lts. H. Butler, B. M. Tatham and C. C. N. Wade, 2/Lts. E. G. Simpson and S. H. Stokes, were wounded. Of other ranks 269 were killed, wounded or missing.

The 5th Bn. was relieved in the trenches next day (July 6th) by the 4th Bn.

On the 7th, soon after midnight, the enemy guns were very active in shelling the trenches now occupied by the 4/K.O.Y.L.I. Our own guns responded; enemy bombing parties became dangerous, so two companies of the 5/K.O.Y.L.I. were sent up to reinforce, and the others also were held in readiness in Ross Street. After severe losses the A line trenches were evacuated. The three weeks that followed were spent in and out of the trenches in the same sector with no very notable incident to be chronicled in the case of the 5/K.O.Y.L.I.

THE 8TH BN.

Gen. Pulteney's III Corps occupied a central position in the general attack, being immediately east of Albert on the line between Ovillers and Bécourt. Of his three divisions the 8th held the northern half, while the 34th held the southern; the 19th was in support. The 70th Inf. Bde., in which was the 8/K.O.Y.L.I., held the left position; of its battalions the 8/ Y. & L. was the left, the 8/K.O.Y.L.I. the centre, and the 2/Lincolns. the right. The German guns, including the machine-guns, had fatally favourable positions and were too well posted to give this division much chance of success. The story is a tragic one, for the fate of our 8th Bn. is the fate that overtook the other battalions of the division with little variation.

The battalion diary, which was written up immediately after the events, from all the evidence that could be collected from survivors on the spot, by Capt. G. L. Pyman, is of greater value then one might have expected. All the officers who were with the battalion when it attacked, were killed or wounded in the first few minutes, so that no officer who took part in the operations was available to give evidence of what the battalion had done.

From the 29th to the 31st June the 8/K.O.Y.L.I. occupied trenches in front of Authuille Wood, waiting to make the great attack. Capt. K. E. Poyser was temporarily in command of the battalion. At 7.27 a.m. the 1st July, under the British artillery barrage, the leading companies went over the top. During the preliminary bombardment the losses from hostile shell-fire had been considerable, estimated at 10 per cent. of their numbers. The first two waves that left the trenches reached the German lines with only slight loss. The succeeding waves lost heavily in No Man's Land from the machine-gun fire from both flanks, and these waves must have lost probably 50 per cent. of their strength before they arrived at the German front line trenches. The diary is careful to record the fact that no casualties occurred owing to the fire of our own artillery, in order to disprove any incorrect statements which might be made to the contrary. The men of the battalion soon found themselves intermingled with men of the other battalions of the brigade. After passing over the first enemy trenches severe fighting took place for the possession of the second or supporting line, which several times changed hands. At one time some of the men of the battalion penetrated into the third line, but both second and third lines were under heavy fire of machine-guns; the opposition was almost wholly from machine-gunners and bombers, who gave few chances to the attackers of coming to close quarters with the bayonet.

At about 8.30 a.m. the order to retire was being passed along; this probably originated with the enemy, and created some confusion temporarily. A retirement from the right was actually in progress, in conjunction with the extreme left of the 25th Inf. Bde., until the troops were picked up by the 9/Y. & L., the oncoming battalion in support. They were then carried forward into the enemy's line of trenches once more.

By 10 a.m. the whole of the 70th Inf. Bde. was across No Man's Land, fighting in the German front and support trenches. Communication with the headquarters of the division by way of No Man's Land had ceased, for communication was impracticable.

Soon after midday orders were issued by the division for a fresh attack, which was fixed for 5 p.m. The 70th Inf. Bde. was ordered to renew its attack at the same time. By 3.30 p.m. reports regarding the situation had been received from all three brigades in the fighting line, and the fresh attack had to be abandoned. The remnants of the 8th Div. retired to occupy the old front line trenches, supported by the 56th Inf. Bde. which had been held in reserve.

All of the officers of the 8/K.O.Y.L.I. having become casualties, the men were re-organised for the repeated attacks by their N.C.O.s and by officers of the 2/Lincolns. of the 25th Inf. Bde., who operated on the right of the 70th Inf. Bde.; sometimes prominent private soldiers took the initiative in rallying parties of men. Time after time the survivors followed the lead of any man who assumed authority, and fought to recover the ground which they had temporarily lost.

In the end the objectives could not be held owing to the tremendous losses that were incurred, but it was not till about 6 p.m. that the last man of the battalion, of those who were known to have recrossed the intervening 350 yards or so of No Man's Land, got back to the original first line of British trenches. It was considered established that no other men of the battalion were then alive in the trenches of the German line.

The battalion had gone into action in the morning with 25 officers, 1 medical officer and 659 other ranks. Of these numbers the medical officer and 110 other ranks reported present after the battle. Very few of the officers reached the second line of German trenches. Over the flat rising ground the enemy machine-guns acted like so many reapers, and wave after wave of men was mown down in this harvest of the manhood of the nation. Fortunate were those sections of the line to whom the conformation of the ground offered some slight depression or fold of the ground into which men disappeared temporarily from view. It is customary to attribute the failure to capture the enemy's position either to insufficient artillery preparation or to the inexperience of the troops of the new armies, but no skill in leadership or individual resourcefulness of the men could have rendered these men immune from the storm which they faced unflinchingly, or transported them alive across the beaten zone in sufficient numbers to render it possible for them to hold the positions which handfuls of them were able to reach.

The casualties in the 8/K.O.Y.L.I. during the day amounted to 10 officers killed, 14 wounded and one reported missing; of other ranks, 35 were returned killed, 122 missing, and 365 wounded reached the dressing-stations.

The names of the officers are: (Killed) Lts. and 2/Lts. M. R. H. Morley, C. W. Morris, P. G. Boswell, H. S. Drury, A. H. Hack, W. I. S. Hartley, H. S. Jackson, G. H. Kernaghan, R. W. K. Oakley and H. Ormrod. (Missing) Lt. E. M. B. Cambie. (Wounded) Capts. K. E. Poyser, B. H. Horsley and H. L. Willey; Lts. G. St. J. Coventry and E. B. B. Speed; 2/Lts. R. B. Crankshaw, W. L. Browne, G. Elliott, L. A. Welch, P. B. P. Robinson, J. Downs, H. Child, O. S. Stevenson and J. Nelson.

During the night of the 1st July the battalion was withdrawn to Long Valley. On the following day it marched to Dernancourt to entrain for Bruay to be rebuilt and refitted.

Brig.-Gen. H. Gordon, commanding the 70th Inf. Bde., in his report said: "*I cannot speak too highly of the gallantry and determination shown by the regimental officers and men. All of them were inspired with the one idea to get forward and attack the enemy . . . . Though severe losses were suffered both in our own trenches and in crossing No Man's Land, the ranks remained firm and no hesitation or wavering could be seen. The enemy's artillery would not stop them, but with nothing on their right and less on their left, except hostile machine-guns, when supports from behind were exhausted, and when from in front and flanks fresh enemy reinforcements were engaging them, they fought for over six hours in positions they had won, till they died.*" (Dated, 9th July, 1916.)

Maj. C. H. M. Imbert-Terry of the 2/Devon, was brought in to command; Lt.-Col. Trevor had taken over the command of the 103rd Inf. Bde.

At Bruay Maj.-Gen. H. Hudson, commanding the 8th Div., addressed the battalion (July 10th); he congratulated the men warmly on the manner in which the battalion had done its duty, and thanked them for the gallant and skilful manner in which they had supported him on the 1st July.

A record is kept also in the diary of the words addressed to the survivors of the battalion by their Brig.-Gen. (H. Gordon). He said that the battalion had done its duty in the recent operations magnificently. It had sustained the high traditions of its regiment. It had held trenches for several months and he always knew that those trenches were safe in its keeping. His expectation had been more than realised in the splendid manner it had borne the brunt in the recent battle. Lewis gunners, signallers, bombers, riflemen, all had done well; the stretcher-bearers also had done their duty finely. They had lost many comrades and all their officers, but fortunately many only for a short time. The battalion must not think that because it could not keep the enemy's trenches, it had failed. They had not failed, but had paved the way to success and even now their deeds were bearing fruit.

On the 16th July the 70th Inf. Bde. rejoined its own division, the 23rd. The 8/K.O.Y.L.I. had entrained at Houdain for Amiens, and marched to billets in Poulainville.

(The list of casualties in the 8/K.O.Y.L.I. is taken from the diary of the 8th Div. for July, 1916.)

The 34th was the right division of Gen. Pulteney's Corps in the attack. Immediately on the right of the 34th came the 21st Div. of Gen. Horne's XV Corps. This division advanced eastwards from the direction of Bécourt. The 50th Inf. Bde. was detached from its own division, the 17th (the remainder of which was held in reserve), to operate with the 21st in the attack.

THE 9TH AND 10TH BNS.

Of the 21st Div. the 64th Inf. Bde. was the left of its fighting line, the 63rd coming next, with the 50th on its right. The front to be attacked extended almost from La Boisselle to Fricourt, the latter village itself being the objective of the 50th Inf. Bde. Beyond Fricourt, where the German line bent eastwards, the 7th Div. faced the north. If the 50th Inf. Bde. 'contained' Fricourt, which was near the apex of the salient, and if the attacks on either flank of Fricourt were successfully pressed home, it was hoped that the enemy troops defending the salient would be squeezed so as to render their position untenable.

Of the 64th Inf. Bde. the 10/K.O.Y.L.I. held the left position, in touch with the 101st Inf. Bde.; the 9/K.O.Y.L.I. came next on its right; the 1/E. York. supported the 10/K.O.Y.L.I., the 15/D.L.I. supported the 9/K.O.Y.L.I. The objectives were, first, a sunken road which was roughly 1,100 yards from the British front line; secondly, a trench some 400 yards further on, which was Crucifix trench.

The line in that part of the field opposite the two K.O.Y.L.I. battalions formed a small but marked re-entrant, across which a Russian sap had been dug, the roof of which was broken in a few days earlier. By using this the two leading companies were able to make their start from a distance of 180 yards from the enemy trenches. The method of advance in each battalion was with a front of two platoons in ten waves, the two extra waves being the Headquarters (the 6th) wave, and the Stretcher-bearers (the 10th). Thus in the

9/K.O.Y.L.I. a platoon of "A" Company went over side by side with a platoon of "C" in extended line, followed by the nine other waves at one-minute intervals. Advances were made in quick time, otherwise men would become 'blown' and so be useless on arrival on the far side. The other companies of each battalion started from our front line proper. Parties had been sent out at midnight before to cut our own wire in front of the trenches.

The men had tea and a ration of rum before setting out.

At 7.25 a.m., five minutes before "Zero" time, the leading platoons (in the case of the 9/K.O.Y.L.I. they were led by 2/Lts. Alexander and Oldershaw) left the Russian sap, crawled forward as far as possible under the barrage from our guns, and then advanced in quick time when the barrage lifted. They were greeted by a hail of machine-gun and rifle fire; the enemy, in spite of our guns, brought their machine-guns out of their dug-outs and opened fire from the top of their parapet. "A" and "C" Companies were the chief sufferers, while "B" and "D" had to endure a heavy artillery barrage. When the leading troops were close enough the enemy employed cylindrical stick-bombs also. The waves in rear pressed on, and some were soon up with the leading platoons. In spite of heavy losses the battalions carried the first line without delay; when they had passed the front trench the 15/D.L.I. came up to reinforce splendidly; within a quarter of an hour of the start the whole brigade was united, irrespective of battalions, and was driving the enemy rapidly out of his support trenches. From here to the sunken road the attack became a running fight or a series of small fights; much work was done with bomb and bayonet, prisoners were taken, but men were falling in great numbers. A subsidiary line of German trenches lay in front of the sunken road; the khaki flood poured into this; the senior officer on the spot was Lt.-Col. Fitzgerald, the officer commanding the 15/D.L.I. A pause lasting for some hours was necessary to allow the 63rd Inf. Bde. to get up; then another advance was made and Crucifix trench was carried.

Conan Doyle records that a lieutenant of the 9/K.O.Y.L.I., though wounded by shrapnel, was the first to lead a party into this advanced trench, and that it was soon strongly occupied; also that another lieutenant of the K.O.Y.L.I., also wounded, took over the direction of the work of consolidating the position, until a captain of the 10/K.O.Y.L.I. took over the command. Later, help came from the 62nd Inf. Bde., and the men of the 64th Inf. Bde. were withdrawn to the sunken road.

Out of the twenty-four officers of the 9/K.O.Y.L.I. only five subalterns (Gordon, Day, Ellenberger, Frazer and Featherstone) succeeded in passing the first German trench; of these five, Featherstone was hit later in the morning and died in the afternoon in

Lozenge Alley. Undoubtedly 2/Lt. A. E. Day was the officer who first led a party into Crucifix trench. He was reinforced by Lt. B. L. Gordon about 1.30 p.m., with other survivors of the two battalions. As the evening wore on it became obvious to Lt. Gordon that Day, his junior, was becoming incapacitated by his wound. Argument would not suffice to induce him to go to the dressing-station; nothing short of a positive order could make him leave his post.

This incident of the capture of Crucifix trench is worthy to rank with the most glorious deeds of the Regiment, even with the storming of Badajoz, the memory of which is kept green in the officers' mess of the 1st and 2nd Bns. on Band Night in the toast 'Dyas and the Stormers.'

Capt. E. R. Santer, of the 10/K.O.Y.L.I., arrived in the forward position during the afternoon and took over the command. Brig.-Gen. Headlam had his headquarters in the sunken road for some time.

The work of consolidation went on steadily and steps were taken to secure the flanks. Pte. J. Kearford performed a risky and invaluable piece of work by proceeding down the sunken road towards Fricourt until he found and established communication with the 4/Mx., of the 63rd Inf. Bde.

About 6 p.m. 2/Lt. R. F. Frazer was hit in the head by shrapnel and was forced to go back. Shortly afterwards Capt. Santer, who had been wounded in the chest some hours previously, was compelled to get his wounds dressed. Then Gordon was sent for to Bde. Headquarters to report on the situation, and Ellenberger carried on until he, too, received a summons to repair to the sunken road, and left R.S.M. A. Crossland in charge of the men of the 9/K.O.Y.L.I. (about 8.30 p.m.). Lt. Gordon was now the senior officer with the battalion and it fell to him to arrange the relief which was now due. At 8.45 p.m. five officers, of whom the senior was Lt. L. D. Spicer, reached the sunken road from the reserve left at Buire.

In the 10/K.O.Y.L.I. Lt.-Col. King had been wounded and Maj. F. S. Laskie was in command.

The relief in both cases was not actually carried out till early in the morning of the 2nd July.

The following is a list of the officers of the 9/K.O.Y.L.I. who were killed or wounded on the 1st July: (Killed) Lt.-Col. C. W. D. Lynch, Capts. L. D. Head, G. Haswell, W. Walker and G. Griffen; 2/Lts. C. W. Howlett, N. L. Alexander, C. E. Vassie, C. W. Ellis, D. Williams, J. J. F. Oldershaw, A. D. Maconachie, F. W. Golding, G. H. Featherstone and E. R. Nott. (Wounded) 2/Lts. R. A. Stokes, A. Hardman, G. A. Kemp, A. E. Day, R. F. Frazer, J. R. Wood and F. G. Morris.

The official "Q" diary of the 21st Div. gives the total casualties in the two battalions for the period 30th June to midnight 3rd July as under:

9/K.O.Y.L.I.: officers, 12 killed, 7 wounded and 4 missing; other ranks, 43 killed, 263 wounded and 126 missing.

10/K.O.Y.L.I.: officers, 8 killed and 17 wounded; other ranks, 50 killed, 265 wounded and 162 missing.

1916. THE SOMME OFFENSIVE
THE LATER PERIODS

XI

THE SECOND PHASE

SIR Douglas Haig, Commander-in-Chief of the British Armies in France, ordered the second great concentrated effort to be entered upon by the Fourth Army in the morning of the 14th July along the line from the Leipzig salient in the north to the point of junction with the French forces in the south. The high ground of the ridge east of the Bazentin villages and to south-east of them, was the objective; the hold on the Leipzig salient was to be extended and Thiepval was to be threatened, but this northern end of the ridge was too strongly fortified to be carried by direct attack for the present.

The 4th and 5th Bns. K.O.Y.L.I. had undergone re-organisation while in huts at Martinsart Wood and they returned to the trenches on the 21st July. On the 23rd at 2.30 a.m. part of the 4/K.O.Y.L.I. was ordered to attack with a view to extending the position in the salient. Heavy casualties were suffered while crossing No Man's Land and the enemy were found to be in force in their lines; the attackers were too much weakened to put up a fight and were forced to withdraw, having Lt. J. C. Plews wounded and 2/Lts. A. J. Mountain, E. T. Archer and J. C. Jubb killed.

THE 4TH AND 5TH BNS.

The enemy bombers counter-attacked up trenches leading to our lines, but were driven back by the 4th Bn. bombers, assisted by those of the 5/K.O.Y.L.I. and of the 4th and 5th Bns. Y. & L.

In addition to the officers mentioned there were 66 casualties in other ranks, of whom 6 were killed. Lt.-Col. H. J. Haslegrave was wounded the following day.

The 5/K.O.Y.L.I. was concerned in a very similar incident on the 28th July. "B" Company assaulted an enemy trench east of the salient without success. The attack was carried out admirably, but the assaulting platoons were met by very heavy bomb fire from both sides of the trench and suffered heavily. Two bombing squads effected an entrance, but were in their turn bombed out again or left behind as casualties. 2/Lt. A. W. Baker was missing. "B" Company lost 10 men killed and 49 wounded.

The two battalions remained in the sector till the end of September.

The 64th Inf. Bde. was back in the line at Bottom Wood, in reserve to the 110th Inf. Bde. This latter brigade attacked the German line in Bazentin-le-Petit Wood at 3.45 a.m. on the 14th July. Its two objectives were carried with entire success. On the 15th the 10/K.O.Y.L.I. came again into action in Bazentin-le-Petit village, where Lt. A. R. F. Simpson was killed. Maj. F. S. Laskie was wounded and Lt. C. F. W. Wait died of wounds. On the 18th both battalions were withdrawn to corps reserve near Meaulte.

THE 9TH AND 10TH BNS.

On the 26th July the 8/K.O.Y.L.I. was brought back to the line again into trenches immediately to the left of Bazentin-le-Petit Wood. Large drafts of officers and men had been received from time to time during the month.

THE 8TH BN.

The 6th was the next of the K.O.Y.L.I. battalions to be brought into the Somme area. We have seen that the 14th (Light) Div., to which it belonged, was acquiring experience in that hard school, the Ypres salient. In June, 1916, the battalion was still north of the Somme area in the neighbourhood of Agny, three miles south of Arras. Here it was occupying trenches when on the 23rd July a heavy day was experienced. The enemy started bombarding oppressively with minenwerfer, etc., at 8.50 a.m., and continued doing so till 1.30 p.m. The trenches were demolished and the front line was temporarily evacuated. From 4.30 p.m. till 6.30 the bombardment was repeated. The front line was merely occupied by sentries, but these were all lost. At 9.15 p.m. there was a further repetition, and at 10.10 the barrage lifted on to the line of the supports, while a raid was made by the enemy, who pierced our line as far as the supports and bombed the dug-out in which the company headquarters were. However, they were beaten back to their own lines.

THE 6TH BN.

Lt. F. Roberts was killed in the bombardment; 2/Lt. H. W. Hayward was missing, almost certainly buried; of other ranks there were 9 killed, 6 missing and 32 wounded.

The remainder of the night was spent in feverish work, repairing trenches.

On the 28th July the battalion was relieved and it marched at noon to Warluzel, a great strain on the men who had been forty days in the trenches without having their boots off! Many men fell out, for in addition to the excessive heat they had to wear their steel helmets. The battalion was on the line of march till the 7th August, when trains carried it from Candas Station *via* Flixecourt to Amiens, where there was a short halt before the trains carried the brigade to Méricourt l'Abbaye on the Ancre. Here it detrained at 1 p.m. The brigade marched *via* Ribecourt and Buire to Dernancourt, two and a half miles south of Albert. The next five days were spent in training, bathing and getting fit.

On the 12th August the 14th (Light) Div. went into the line to relieve the 17th Div. in Delville Wood. On the march up to the line through the battle area it was found that all the villages were flattened out and all trenches were obliterated. Our guns seemed to be everywhere and the gun-fire was continuous. Transport wagons were on the move in all directions. When the 6/K.O.Y.L.I. arrived it was seen that tents, wagons, cookers, guns and troops were all out in the open, but the enemy seemed to make no attempt to shell them. Obviously our airmen had achieved complete mastery of the air for the time being, and our balloons were up always.

On the 15th, trenches were taken over by the 6/K.O.Y.L.I. in the wood, having Longueval on its left in rear. Very few trees were standing, and a small portion of a wall of the church was all that could be seen of the village. There were great 'crump-holes' everywhere; trenches were shallow and all communication trenches had been obliterated. Our field and heavy howitzers were bombarding the enemy trenches which ran through the north salient of the wood.

During the night 16th-17th, Capt. E. B. Wilson and 2/Lt. H. J. Atkinson with a patrol reconnoitred the wood; they were discovered by the enemy, who opened fire, killing 2/Lt. Atkinson and wounding Pte. Morton. Later Capt. Wilson managed to bring in Lt. Atkinson's body. The casualties of other ranks in these two days numbered 6 killed and 26 wounded.

The 18th August opened with an intense bombardment prior to a simultaneous attack on the enemy's line delivered by troops of the XIII, XV and III Corps. The 6/K.O.Y.L.I. acted in support of the 6/D.C.L.I., who suffered heavily, but reported by 4.15 p.m. that the objectives had been gained. The infantry advance had been timed to commence at 2.50 p.m.

The 6/K.O.Y.L.I. lost Capt. L. Chalk and Lt. J. A. Jowett, wounded; of other ranks 12 were killed and 56 wounded.

That night the 43rd Inf. Bde. was temporarily relieved in the front line.

The efforts to gain full possession of Delville Wood were tremendous and were never relaxed, and the enemy were no less determined not to give ground. An impression of the concentration of the enemy gun-fire may be gained from the fact that, in order to establish communication between bn. headquarters and brigade battle headquarters, a cable was buried five feet deep under the superintendence of the brigade signalling officer, and even so the cable became disconnected from time to time.

Fricourt and Montauban were on the road up to Delville Wood, at intervals of about two and a half miles. The 6/K.O.Y.L.I camped at Fricourt, advanced to Montauban, acted as carriers to the 42nd Inf. Bde. on the 24th August during that brigade's attack, and in the night of the 25th itself went into the front trenches in Delville Wood in relief of the 5/Oxf. Bucks. and 5/K.S.L.I., with "X" and "Y" Companies in the first line. The 10/D.L.I. relieved the remainder of the 42nd Inf. Bde. During the night of the 26th August by concerted action the 6/K.O.Y.L.I. succeeded in establishing a line of posts in advance of the present line in order to conform to that of the 10/D.L.I., who improved their position with a new trench about fifty yards outside the wood. This was effected in response to a report made by Lt. H. D. Davidson and his patrol.

In the morning of the 27th the 10/D.L.I. again attacked and gained its objectives; the 6/K.O.Y.L.I. reinforced and occupied its former trenches. There was a counter-attack at 6.30 p.m.; the D.L.I. sent an S.O.S. message for our guns to assist in repelling it, and a barrage very quickly opened and scattered it. When the men of the D.L.I. went over the parapet in the morning two platoons of "X" Company of the 6/K.O.Y.L.I. accompanied them. 2/Lt. J. H. Hurst was wounded; of other ranks 6 were killed or missing, 20 were wounded.

At 4.45 p.m. on the 28th, all the officers of "Y" Company were buried by a shell. A party under the C.S.M. at once attempted to dig them out, several more great shells landing close by. Sgt. Gollick, Cpl. McDonough and Pte. Hill continued to try to reach them, but their efforts were unavailing. C.S.M. O. Maltby deserved great credit for his attempt under the heavy bombardment that was proceeding; he eventually brought his company safely out of the trenches under heavy fire when the battalion was relieved after midnight by the 5/K.S.L.I. Both the front line companies had had all their rations buried and had subsisted on their iron rations.

The battalion went back to Pomières trench by Mametz in the rain. It had sustained the following casualties:

(Killed) Capt. R. E. Tennant, Lt. E. M. Gosschalk, 2/Lts. H. D. Davidson, M. K. Grey, H. Mayson, J. R. Whittaker. Other ranks, 10.

(Wounded) other ranks, 30, missing, 2.

The 43rd Inf. Bde. was then withdrawn to Airaines in the neighbourhood of Amiens to refit; bathing and sports were indulged in, leave was opened to officers for a few days, and the men had a rest which was designed to dim the memories of Delville Wood. The brigade returned from Airaines *via* Méricourt, Dernancourt and Meaulte to take part in a big attack on Gueuedecourt and Gird trench which commenced in the morning of the 15th September.

July, 1916, found the 7/K.O.Y.L.I. still in the Ypres salient. The battalion had not arrived in France in time to take part in the heavy fighting in 1915; it had now been twelve months in the country. A summary of the casualties it had experienced in this period can be given, and is as follows:—Officers: killed in action, 6; died of wounds, 2; wounded, 6; sick and off the strength, 8. Other ranks: killed in action, 45; died of wounds, 21; wounded, 209; sick and off the strength, 145; died of natural causes, 2.

THE 7TH BN.

On the 20th August, 1916, the battalion, which was training at Courcelles, received orders to entrain at Candas for Méricourt *via* Amiens; thence to Morlancourt, and on to Happy Valley. The 20th Div. (Maj.-Gen. W. D. Smith) was destined for an attack on Ginchy, having the 5th and 7th Divs. on either side of it. Lt.-Col. B. B. Robinson commanded the battalion; the 61st Inf. Bde. was commanded by Brig.-Gen. W. E. Banbury.

The battalion was in the trenches opposite Ginchy from the 22nd to the 26th August. Lt. W. G. Barnaby was killed, and there were fifty casualties in the other ranks. After a second tour of duty it was relieved in the trenches at 10 p.m. on the 2nd September by a battalion of the 57th Inf. Bde.

The division attacked Guillemont next day. The 61st Inf. Bde. was in the support line. The battalion moved up at 12.25 p.m. ("Zero" hour, for the attack had been 12 noon) to occupy trenches between Trones Wood and Bernafay. German prisoners were coming down in considerable numbers, the majority of whom were acting as stretcher-bearers. Guillemont and the sunken road beyond, the objectives, had been duly reached. At 6 p.m. the battalion was placed under the orders of the G.O.C. 47th Inf. Bde. to carry up rations and bring back the wounded from Guillemont. 2/Lt. Matthews was wounded and there were about fifty casualties in other ranks.

On the 14th September the 61st Inf. Bde. was brought into the line left of Guillemont in readiness for an attack to be made on Les Bœufs by the Guards, the 6th, and the 51st Divs. The 20th Div. at first was to be held in reserve.

THE THIRD PHASE

When the 8/K.O.Y.L.I. rejoined the 23rd, its own Div., it went into billets for a time in Poulainville, three miles north of Amiens, so remaining in the Somme sector. The ranks of the battalion were rapidly refilled by drafts. By the 26th July the battalion was back again in the trenches, where it relieved a battalion of the Black Watch on the

THE 8TH BN.

immediate left of Bazentin-le-Petit Wood. For some weeks it was learning its business in the usual routine of trench life, varied by that of support and reserve. It was while billeted at Rue de Sac that a list of awards was issued which included the M.C. for Capt. B. H. Horsley and Lt. G. St. J. Coventry; D.C.M.s for Lce./Cpl. G. Musgrove, Sgt. T. Priestley and Lce./Cpl. A. Marr; M.M.s for Lce./Cpl. J. T. Johnson, Ptes. C. Goodwin, F. C. Gaylor and A. Landrels.

While still at Rue de Sac on the 9th September, the battalion was addressed by Maj.-Gen. J. M. Babington, who told the men that they were returning to the Somme trenches and foreshadowed early participation in a further offensive. The next day the battalion marched to St. Omer and entrained there.

The 1st October found the battalion in trenches near Martinpuich, almost two miles beyond Bazentin-le-Petit Wood, so deeply had the continued offensives eaten into the German line. It was under orders to attack, the objectives being two lines of trenches known as O.G.1 and O.G.2.

The 70th Inf. Bde. of the 23rd Div. was concerned in this attack with the 151st Inf. Bde. of the 50th Div., both divisions being in the III Corps.

Assembly trenches behind Destremont Farm were occupied just before dawn. The attack was timed for 3.15 p.m., and the trenches which were the objects of attack were in front of the village of Le Sars, having a frontage of about 300 yards; the advance had to be made over 600 yards of open ground. At dawn the position of the assembly trenches stood revealed to the enemy, who shelled them continuously. Under this shelling about 25 per cent. of the strength of the battalion was already lost before the attack was delivered. At 3.15 p.m. our artillery put up an intense barrage, the signal for the departure of "A" and "D" Companies, who attacked with "C" in support; "B" Company remained in reserve. The objectives were both carried despite a counter-barrage by the German gunners, and the work of consolidation of the two lines forthwith commenced. The new trenches were held against all counter-attacks, and the work went on into the night. At 2 a.m. "B" Company was brought into the line to reinforce; at 4 a.m. two companies came in from the brigade reserve and took over O.G.2, the more advanced trench, the survivors of the 8/K.O.Y.L.I. being withdrawn to O.G.1. On the following day they were relieved by the 10/D.W.R. of the 69th Inf. Bde. The battalion was withdrawn to bivouacs in the Dingle.

The casualties amounted to: officers, 1 killed, 2 missing and 8 wounded; other ranks: 248 killed, wounded or missing.

Immediate awards for gallantry were announced, which included: M.C., 2/Lt. O. H. Cooke, 2/Lt. F. Noddle; M.M., No. 21128 Sgt. White, No. 15650 Sgt. Whitehead, No. 12983 Lce./Cpl. Lund, No.

12291 Pte. Holmes, No. 17497 Pte. Crossland, No. 3609 Pte. Shields, No. 8359 Pte. Goldsby, No. 16415 Pte. A. Norgate, No. 20029 Pte. Hall, No. 21157 Pte. Gregg. Bar to M.M., No. 15269 Sgt. Holberry (attached).

The following letter was received from Maj.-Gen. Babington, G.O.C. 23rd Div.:

My dear Colonel, *3rd Oct., '16.*

Will you please tell all ranks how very pleased I am at their behaviour on Oct. 1st. I congratulate them most heartily on their success, which was due to their gallantry and the fine spirit they showed. Good luck to you all.

(sd.) J. M. Babington.

On the 17th October the 23rd Div. moved north to the Ypres salient.

As the 6/K.O.Y.L.I. made its way to the front on the 15th September the signs preparatory to a great effort were in evidence on all sides.

THE 6TH BN.

The battalion marched to Bernafay Wood, then on to York Alley, between Trones Wood and Crucifix Alley. The battalion was detached from its own brigade to go in support of the 42nd Inf. Bde. Each man carried two Mills bombs in addition to those carried by the bombers; he carried also three sandbags, while red ground flares and blue rockets formed part of the equipment of each company. Ordered to attack soon after midnight, the companies advanced in single file round the eastern edge of Delville Wood, under the searching fire of the enemy artillery all the way. 2/Lt. Pearn was wounded, and there was a fair number of casualties in the ranks, but the objectives were reached by 1 a.m. The men commenced vigorously to dig themselves in. The battalion had been subdivided previous to this advance, for Maj. W. H. Charlesworth, with "W" and "X" Companies, was detached to co-operate with the 41st Inf. Bde.

In the morning of the 16th September, the 6/Som. L.I. and the 10/D.L.I. were ordered to attack Gird trench at 9.25, while "Y" and "Z" Companies of the 6/K.O.Y.L.I. and the 6/D.C.L.I. were to follow up and occupy the line left by the others. The former battalions were then to take Gueudecourt while the others occupied Gird trench. The advance of the second line companies was made in small columns of half-platoons in file after the first line had 'gone over.'

The first objective was reached, but the second part of the programme could not be carried out. The enemy issued from Gueudecourt but were thrown back.

At 6.55 the attack was renewed, the two companies of the 6/K.O.Y.L.I. co-operating with the 6/Som. L.I.; "Y" Company was led by Capt. J. Clegg and "Z" by Lt. J. A. Jowett, for Capt. Wilson had been wounded in the morning. The two companies had to cross the open in order to come into line with the Som. L.I. This they did and they were caught by machine-gun fire after crossing Bull's road, but the Som. L.I. had not received their orders yet to go forward, and as there was no room in their trenches the K.O.Y.L.I. had to lie in the open under heavy fire. Eventually the further advance was cancelled, so 2/Lt. A. G. Patterson, the only officer left with the K.O.Y.L.I., withdrew his companies.

Capt. J. Clegg, Lt. J. A. Jowett and 2/Lt. W. D. Bentall had been killed; Capt. E. B. Wilson and Lt. A. T. Shelton were wounded; of other ranks there were 20 killed and 80 wounded.

The failure was due to the Som. L.I. not having received the orders which had been communicated to the K.O.Y.L.I., and to inadequate artillery support, for the enemy rifle and machine-gun fire were unaffected by our barrage.

In the meanwhile "W" and "X" Companies had been working with the 41st Inf. Bde. Their attack on the 15th September was started by three tanks at 5.20 a.m. (This is the first mention of tanks in the K.O.Y.L.I. diaries of the war.) Both companies went over the top and made progress until within 100 yards of Pint trench when they were caught by machine-gun fire. A halt was made while a bombing party under Sgt. Vaughan went back to clear Vat Alley in the right rear, from which the machine-gun fire appeared to come. Heavy casualties were meanwhile sustained and all nine officers were put out of action; the N.C.O.s were left to carry on the attack. During the next forward move the Guards, who were on the immediate right, took ground to the left, and from this point onwards the units became intermingled. Considerable resistance was met with in Pint trench, bombing and bayonet work were freely resorted to, and the majority of the enemy in the trench surrendered. Two machine-guns and about thirty prisoners were taken.

Our two companies then advanced as far as Switch trench, "X" Company bringing up its right shoulder in order to clear the left of the Guards. Isolated machine-guns were opposed to them, which were captured with about fifty prisoners, including a major, a captain and several subalterns. After bombing a few dug-outs the men went still further, but on advice from an officer of the Guards, who told them that they had overshot their objective, they returned to Switch trench and proceeded to consolidate it. When their own ammunition became exhausted the men collected the German rifles and ammunition to resist a threatening counter-attack, but this latter never materialised as other troops were now working up into line with them on the left, their exposed flank.

The two companies held on in Switch trench till 3 p.m. on the 16th, when relief came and they rejoined their battalion headquarters in Pomières redoubt.

The casualties had been: killed, Maj. W. H. Charlesworth and 2/Lt. A. L. Levick; 2/Lt. A. A. Maiden died of wounds; wounded, 2/Lts. R. Foulkes, O. M. Holmes, J. F. B. Abson, A. C. L. Goldman, J. W. Henderson and B. H. C. Hettler. Of other ranks 180 were killed or wounded.

It was C.S.M. Jacobs who took command of the two companies at the critical time and led them in a masterful way, greatly assisted by Sgts. Whatmore, Vaughan and Boyd.

The 14th (Light) Div. was withdrawn from the line *via* Amiens and Doullens to Le Souich, and later into the line by Achicourt, a much quieter section of the front; indeed the battalion diary refers to it as being 'rather dull and damp!'

A letter from Gen. Sir Henry Rawlinson, commanding the Fourth Army, was read on parade by the G.O.C. 43rd Inf. Bde. in which he said: "*HQ Fourth Army, 20th Sept.,* 1916. *It is with very sincere regret that I hear the 14th Div. are leaving the Fourth Army, and before they do so I desire to convey to every officer, n.c.o. and man my gratitude and congratulations for the admirable work they have done. Both in Delville Wood and the attacks of the 15th and 16th September they displayed a fighting spirit and a dash which is worthy of the best traditions of the British Army, whilst their discipline and self-sacrifice has been beyond praise.*

The artillery support has on all occasions been adequate and well-directed, and is the result of careful and thorough training.

I have been struck by the keenness and good comradeship which exists among all ranks of the 14th Div. It is a most valuable asset in war and shows that both Staff and Regimental officers are working in harmony.

In some future time I hope that it may be my good fortune again to find them under my command."

The 21st Div. had been moved north to the neighbourhood of Arras for a tour of less strenuous duty. Early in September the 64th Inf. Bde. was addressed by Maj.-Gen. Campbell, G.O.C. 21st Div. when at Manin, who said that the division would shortly be moving down to the battle area of the Somme again. The move commenced on the 11th. Lt.-Col. C. E. Heathcote arrived to command the 9/K.O.Y.L.I.; Lt.-Col. B. C. Bridge had been in command of the 10/K.O.Y.L.I. since the 11th July.

THE 9TH AND 10TH BNS.

The brigade arrived in Pomières redoubt through Fricourt on the 15th, and at 2 a.m. on the 16th it started in the rain to move up to Flers trench in front of Gueudecourt. The 9/K.O.Y.L.I. took up its position in the centre of the brigade, while the 10/K.O.Y.L.I.

moved into Switch trench in close support of the 15/D.L.I. Flers trench was exactly five miles from Pomières, and it was reached by 5.45 a.m., as it was getting light; another 2,000 yards of country separated Flers trench from the first objective of the proposed offensive.

The attack on Gueudecourt by the 64th Inf. Bde. was timed to commence at 9.20 a.m. In front of Gueudecourt were two main enemy trenches, Gird trench and Gird support; these were the objects of attack. Brig.-Gen. Headlam had a difficult problem before him. The battalion commanders had had no opportunity for making any kind of preliminary reconnaissance. In order to take advantage of our artillery barrage when it opened, it was necessary to get the troops forward to a position near enough to the barrage line for them to get cover from it. As it was not possible to get the barrage line altered the assaulting battalions had to advance twenty and twenty-five minutes before the "Zero" time in order to get across the intervening open country and be up behind the barrage when it started. This was done under fire, and the 9/K.O.Y.L.I. advanced well and in fair formation to approximately fifty yards from the objective, where it occupied the shell craters which were everywhere existing. The losses had been very heavy and the attack which followed was not made in sufficient strength to prevail. The position in the craters was held throughout the day, but under cover of darkness the troops were withdrawn to the road running from Flers village towards Les Bœufs. The casualties during the day had amounted to:

Officers: killed, 4; wounded, 6; missing, 3. Other ranks: killed, 43; wounded, 180; missing, 153.

The officers killed included Lt. and Adjt. F. W. Keay, 2/Lts. K. W. Sutcliffe, A. S. Jackson and E. Asquith.

Capt. L. D. Spicer, Capt. W. C. Woollett, Lt. G. F. Ellenberger, 2/Lts. A. Simpson, S. Wilkinson, T. H. Leason and H. G. Cross were wounded.

The 9/K.O.Y.L.I. was relieved at midnight on the 17th September by the 7/King's.

Meanwhile the 10/K.O.Y.L.I. had conformed, in close support of the 15/D.L.I., and had come under the barrage which the enemy had put down to prevent the supports from reaching the front line of attackers. When the troops were withdrawn at night the battalion occupied Flers trench.

The brigade diary gives the losses in the 10/K.O.Y.L.I. as:

Officers: wounded, 6. Other ranks: killed, 23; wounded, 117; missing, 39.

Many of these casualties occurred in Flers trench on the 17th, due to the bombardment which followed.

On the 25th September the 21st Div. returned to the attack on Gueudecourt. This time the preliminary arrangements were more elaborate and the New Zealand Div. co-operated on the left by forming a defensive flank which faced north-west. In the 64th Bde. the 10/K.O.Y.L.I. was right attacking battalion, having the 1/E.York. on the left, while the 15/D.L.I. and 9/K.O.Y.L.I. were in support. The leading battalions were held up in front of Gird trench and occupied a line of shell-holes, but when the supporting battalions came to their assistance the enemy's front line of trenches was gained and consolidated. The next day, the 26th, a tank was brought up to co-operate, as Gird trench was reported by our airmen to be full of the enemy, and by 8.58 a.m. the 15/D.L.I. was able to report that Gird trench was captured. In the meanwhile the 9/K.O.Y.L.I. and the 10/K.O.Y.L.I. had been withdrawn to the support line to re-organise. 400 of the enemy were taken in Gird trench. In consequence of the surrender in Gird trench the front was declared "clear" and the 9/K.O.Y.L.I. was ordered up in order to occupy Gird support; it was found that this trench had been obliterated by our guns, so at 2 p.m. the battalion commenced to dig a line connecting up shell craters; at 3 p.m. the 15/D.L.I. passed through the line and occupied the Gueudecourt-Les Bœufs road; the 9/K.O.Y.L.I. then advanced at 6 p.m. and occupied a piece of the road to the right of the D.L.I. and touching the Welch Guards on the right.

Both battalions of the K.O.Y.L.I. were relieved at night and withdrawn to bivouac between Trones Wood and Bernafay Wood.

Of the 9/K.O.Y.L.I. Maj. W. N. Tempest was killed and Capt. G. A. Gamble, 2/Lts. V. H. Wells-Cole, J. Caldwell and G. Panton were wounded. Of the 10/K.O.Y.L.I. Capt. T. E. Sayer, Lt. (acting Capt.) A. H. Thompson, and 2/Lts. C. H. C. Winkworth, A. E. Watts, A. V. Skevington, C. J. Eversfield and C. M. Armstrong were killed, while 2/Lts. H. R. Dixon, E. P. Short, H. R. Bradshaw, E. R. Graham, P. D. Rooke, C. K. Moseley and F. P. Nilen were wounded. Capt. R. Clibborn, N.F. (attd.), had been missing since the night of the 24th, when the patrol he was leading was bombed by the enemy.

The 21st Div. was subsequently taken out of the line and moved north to the region of Béthune.

For the period 21st-27th September the casualties in other ranks were given as under:

9/K.O.Y.L.I.: killed, 6; wounded, 65; missing, 29. 10/K.O.Y.L.I.: killed, 51; wounded, 162; missing, 110; while for the whole period July-September the total numbers were: 9/K.O.Y.L.I., officers killed and wounded, 44; other ranks killed and wounded, 955; 10/K.O.Y.L.I.: officers killed and wounded, 49; other ranks killed and wounded, 1,097.

THE 7TH BN.

We left the 7/K.O.Y.L.I. on the 14th September, as a unit of the 61st Inf. Bde. of the 20th Div., in the position of reserve in the XIV Corps (Lord Cavan). With daylight on the 15th September there commenced the third great effort from the Pozières ridge on the left to Combles on the right, in which twelve divisions moved forward to force the German line back from their superior positions. The portion of the line with which the XIV Corps was concerned extended from Ginchy on the left to Combles on the right, next door to the French. The Guards Division occupied the left half of this front, while the 6th Div. attacked on the right; they were supported by the 56th Div.; the 20th Div. was, as stated above, held in reserve. Les Bœufs was the objective, but between the British front line and the village of Les Bœufs was an intricate network of trenches, and, most important of all, the system of trenches known as the Quadrilateral. The Quadrilateral was destined to hold out till the morning of the 18th, after it had been outflanked by the Guards Div. on the left and by the 56th Div. on the right, and by this time the whole position that was the object of attack was overrun.

About noon on the 15th September orders came for the 61st Inf. Bde. to be attached to the Guards Div., the Bde. Headquarters to be in Waterlot Farm. The 61st Inf. Bde. was at first to be used in protecting the right flank of the Guards, but later the whole division might be used to form a wedge between the Guards and the 6th Div. By 4 p.m. the 7/K.O.Y.L.I. was established in Trones Wood.

On the 16th September an attack was delivered in the direction of Les Bœufs by the 61st Inf. Bde. There appeared to have been some misunderstanding, for it was expected that the Guards would be attacking at the same time on the left of the 61st Inf. Bde., but this attack did not materialise, and the 61st Inf. Bde. set to work to consolidate the line which it had gained about 400 yards west of Les Bœufs. During these operations the 7/K.O.Y.L.I. lost by one shell all its Bn. Headquarters' officers. Capt. and Adjt. A. Furse and 2/Lt. Smith, signalling officer, were killed; Lt./Col. B. B. Robinson and Capt. R. H. C. Ward were wounded; in other ranks there were about thirty casualties.

On the 18th September the 7/K.O.Y.L.I. came again into active participation, being in support of the 59th Inf. Bde., who attacked left of the position gained on the 16th. Lt. L. O. Johnson was wounded and about sixty casualties in other ranks were sustained, chiefly while coming up soon after dawn through a fierce barrage of shells and machine-gun fire. The 6th Div. meanwhile was engaged in completing the capture of the Quadrilateral.

Operations in the next few days were pursued by the III Corps and the Reserve Army, assisted by the guns of the XIV Corps, with the ultimate object of attaining a definite position from which a view of the whole of the le Transloy system of the enemy defences could be overlooked. On the 7th October a final combined thrust was delivered by which the required position was won. For this the 61st Inf. Bde. was again introduced.

At 12.30 a.m. the 7/K.O.Y.L.I. changed places with the 10/K.R.R.C., whose Headquarters were in Rose trench. Our artillery proceeded to cut the wire in front of Rainbow trench, the first objective; the second objective, Cloudy trench, was not wired. "Zero" time for the attack was 1.45 p.m. "D" Company under Capt. R. St.C. Brooke directed the divisional attack, which consisted of two brigades.

The first objective fell into our hands at 1.48 p.m. and the 7/K.O.Y.L.I. was re-formed in Rainbow trench by Lt. Wright, the senior surviving officer. As soon as our barrage permitted, Cloudy trench also was successfully taken (about 2.10 p.m.) and the battalion dug itself in, for there were merely slight indications of the trenches existing. Two companies of the Som. L.I. prolonged the line on the right, while the 12/King's on the left threw back a defensive flank as far as Rainbow trench.

This operation had been carried out with great vigour and success in spite of the fact that there had been only four company officers to conduct the attack. In the evening the R.E. came up and established very strong posts all along the line.

On the 8th October at midnight, the 7/K.O.Y.L.I. was relieved by the 2/D.L.I. of the 6th Div. and fell back, through Montauban, to billets in Meaulte. The casualties in the battalion included: Killed, Lt. F. H. Moore; wounded, Capt. R. St.C. Brooke, Lt. E. F. S. Graham, 2/Lts. F. P. Hargreaves, H. H. Haddlesey, R. Forster, H. R. Prust, R. E. Sayer, D. S. Wyllie, and E. Keel; 180 other ranks were killed or wounded.

An appreciation of the part played by the 7/K.O.Y.L.I. in the Somme fighting is contained in the address of the Earl of Cavan, commanding the XIV Corps, made to the 61st Inf. Bde. on the 13th October, 1916. The following is the text of the address:

"*Gen. Banbury, Officers, N.C.O.s and Men, I have come here this morning to say 'Thanks' to you from the bottom of my heart for the excellent work you have done for the Fourth Army and the XIV Corps. I will read out to you first to remind you what I am thanking you for.*

The 61st Inf. Bde. took a prominent part in the capture of Guillemont on Sept. 3rd.

The brigade was attached to the Guards Division from the 15th to the 17th September, and it attacked on the 16th, when it gained the whole of its objectives in spite of the fact that the units attacking both flanks were held up.

On the 1st October the brigade advanced the line for about a quarter of a mile by means of posts pushed forward which were afterwards joined up.

On the 7th October the brigade attacked with the 60th Inf. Bde. and once more gained the whole of its objective, and I may tell you that you were the only division in the whole of the Fourth Army that gained and held its objectives on that day.

Now these four facts will live for ever. Your children will be taught what you did at the Battle of the Somme in exactly the same way that you were taught what your ancestors did at Waterloo and in the Crimea, and the Battle of the Somme is a very much harder battle than any battle which was fought out there.

I am also very proud indeed to see that in spite of your being in the middle of a battle, the brigade can turn itself out in the extremely smart and soldierlike manner that you have this morning, and it is because you do that as well as fight that you are the magnificent brigade that you are.

In about two days' time the 8th Div. will, I understand, be coming up here, and directly they come I hope to get you out and send you back to nice billets near Amiens, where you will be thoroughly comfortable, and can thoroughly train once more for another push.

I have asked the Army Commander and the Commander-in-Chief not to take away the 20th Div. if they can help it, and they have both promised to do their best. I would not lose the 20th Div. for crowns and crowns.

I look with enormous admiration on the 20th Div., and especially the 61st Brigade. I thank you one and all from the bottom of my heart for what you have done for England, and I wish you Good Luck!"

THE FOURTH PHASE

THE 12TH BN.

On the 13th November the II Corps (Jacob) and the V Corps (Fanshawe) stormed the German line north of the Ancre. The II Corps on the right was directed northwards across the valley of the Ancre; the V Corps simultaneously attacked from the west with its left almost as far north as Serre. In the V Corps the 31st Div. attacked in line with the 3rd Div. on its right. Two battalions of the 92nd Inf. Bde. were in the first line and with them went half of the 12/K.O.Y.L.I., the pioneer battalion, numbering twelve officers and 356 men. The attack was successful in reaching its objectives, but the troops had to withdraw at night from the captured positions owing to the pressure in front and from both flanks. In fact, their rôle had been primarily to draw the fire of part of the enemy artillery on themselves in order to assist the advance of the II Corps. Capt. G. M. Stockings, who was in command of the K.O.Y.L.I. companies, was instructed to withdraw them in the night, but he left 2/Lts. W. Collings and W. A. Hunter with seventy other volunteers behind to help to bring in the wounded of the 92nd Inf. Bde., who were lying out on No Man's Land.

In acknowledgment of the services of this party the following message was received: "*The Brig.-General has asked me to write and thank you for the great help your men rendered to the brigade last night in bringing in wounded. From several sources he has heard of their good work, and how extraordinarily hard they worked. He hopes that his thanks will be conveyed to the officers and men who volunteered last night.*"

The casualties in the 12/K.O.Y.L.I. were: Lt. H. C. Williams, wounded; one other rank killed, and eleven wounded.

2/Lts. W. Collings and A. W. Hunter received the M.C. by the immediate award of the G.O.C. 31st Div.; Sgts. A. Grace and G. H. Richards, Lce./Cpl. R. Metcalfe, also Ptes. G. Hughes and R. W. Charleston, were awarded the M.M.

THE 2ND BN.

While the attacks by the II and V Corps had been proceeding north of the river Ancre, as we have just seen, other divisions south of the river facing Grandcourt had been pushing forward their lines, with the result that the right of the Fifth Army was becoming drawn away from the left of the Fourth Army. Into the gap the 32nd Div. was introduced in the part of the line facing Pys. The forward movement of the 97th Inf. Bde. of this division on the 18th November was the occasion of very severe fighting and of heavy losses to the 2/K.O.Y.L.I.

The 97th Inf. Bde. attacked at dawn on a front of 1,125 yards, having the Munich and Frankfort trenches as its first and second objectives. The four battalions of the brigade advanced in line from a tape, in four waves, companies abreast in column of platoons. Their order from the left was, the 2/K.O.Y.L.I., the 11/Border, the 16/H.L.I. and the 17/H.L.I.

The 17/H.L.I. never reached Munich trench owing to overwhelming machine-gun and rifle-fire, which our barrage had been unable to reduce. The 16/H.L.I. got in, but being unsupported, had to retire with a loss of 90 per cent. of its strength. The Border battalion met with a similar fate to that of the 16/H.L.I. The two right companies of the 2/K.O.Y.L.I. were also held up, but the two left ones not only reached the first objective, but pressed on to Ten Tree Alley with the Manchester battalion of the 14th Inf. Bde.; here they were heavily attacked from south and south-east and fought till they died.

At about 5.30 p.m. 2/Lt. H. R. Forde, who commanded the right company, had come back to Bn. Headquarters to report on the situation; he could give no information of the two left companies which had advanced out of sight. As there was now no line for the right companies to hold, for their flanks were unprotected, Lt.-Col. E. H. Rigg decided to withdraw to the original line. It was a mere remnant of the battalion that he had to bring back, for there were, in addition to the Adjutant and the Intelligence officer, only 2/Lt. Forde and about 171 other ranks.

The battalion lost fourteen officers and 351 other ranks killed or wounded.

The officers of the 2/K.O.Y.L.I. who had gone into action in the morning were:

Lt.-Col. Rigg, commanding, 2/Lt. D. A. Scott (Adjt.), 2/Lt. W. K. Elles (Intelligence officer).

"A" Company. 2/Lts. H. R. Forde, J. A. Williams (missing), J. W. McMordie (missing), F. Mountain (shell-shock).

"B" Company. 2/Lts. G. B. E. Reynolds (missing), J. S. Hollis (shell-shock), S. Mills (missing).

"C" Company. 2/Lts. C. L. M. Battersby (missing), A. E. Rylatt (missing), R. F. Corlett (missing), A. L. Westwood (missing).

"D" Company. Capt. H. Whitworth (wounded), Lt. P. A. Chubb (wounded), 2/Lts. H. C. Hotson (missing), J. A. Armitage (missing).

Two men of the 11/Border, who managed to make their way back at night, reported that some sixty men of the brigade under 2/Lt. A. E. Rylatt, K.O.Y.L.I., were holding on in the German second line; repeated fruitless attempts were made to discover them and to bring them out, if found, but without success, and in the morning there was no sign of them.

On the night of the 19th the 2/K.O.Y.L.I. was relieved by the 16/L.F., and went back to billets in Mailly-Maillet. It received a visit from Gen. Sir Hubert Gough on the 21st November, who presented M.M.s to four sergeants (out of twelve to whom that honour was awarded).

So ended the prolonged fighting in what is historically known as the Battle of the Somme, 1916. A new type of battle had been introduced, the laboured but remorseless advance by attrition. When reviewing the prospects for 1917, General Ludendorff in "My War Memories, 1914-1918," says that the Central Powers "*had to face the danger that 'Somme fighting' would soon break out at various points on our fronts, and that even our troops would not be able to withstand such attacks indefinitely.*"

As a consequence of the Somme campaign Field-Marshal von Hindenburg was forced to shorten his line by strategic retirements and to economise men; his measures were carried out in the following year.

THE 1st BATTALION IN SALONICA

XII

WE have seen that the 1/K.O.Y.L.I. arrived at Alexandria on the 31st October, 1915, on its way to Salonica. A force composed of French and British divisions was being assembled under the supreme command of the French Gen. Sarrail. Some divisions were being diverted from the front in France, other British divisions were transferred from the Gallipoli peninsula when the force which had been engaged in the abortive attempt to open the road to Constantinople was finally withdrawn.

1915 The object of the Salonica campaign was twofold, namely, to save gallant Servia from total annihilation, and to check the growing influence of Germany in the Balkans.

Gen. Sarrail had arrived on the 12th October. His troops first came into conflict with the Bulgarians, who had thrown in their lot with the Central Powers, on the 14th October at Strumitsa Station. The Bulgarians now stood in the path of the retreating Servians, who were thus forced to alter their course and to head for the Adriatic. Gen. Sarrail decided to retire to the immediate neighbourhood of Salonica and there await the arrival of reinforcements, for his position was complicated by the uncertain attitude of the Greek army in his rear.

Taking advantage of the delay on the part of the Central Powers in pushing their expected offensive, the Allies continued to assemble their forces until, by July, 1916, they had about 300,000 men in the field. Half this number was provided by the Servians, who had been transported down the Adriatic to Corfu, rested there, and brought by sea to Salonica. The British army, now under the command of Gen. Milne, consisted of six divisions, the 10th, 22nd, 26th, 27th, 28th and 60th. The British force occupied the front east of the river Vardar and acted as a containing force, while the rest of the allies on the west of the river, with the Servians on the extreme left, assumed the offensive without great success in the later months of 1916.

The 28th Div., of which the 1/K.O.Y.L.I. was a part, was included in the XVI Corps, which was under the command of Lt.-Gen. C. J. Briggs. Until the division returned to France at the end of June, 1918, the line held by the British troops remained much the same. The day had not quite arrived when the Allied armies engaged in the Balkan campaign were to make their great and final offensive, by which the chain-armour of the Central Powers was pierced and the long-disputed diversion of a portion of the Allied strength claimed its justification.

The 1/K.O.Y.L.I. spent a month very pleasantly in camp at Sidi Bishr, about 7 miles from Alexandria, on the seashore. On the 1st December the battalion embarked in *H.M.T. Ulysses* with the 1/Y. and L. and various details, and sailed at 12.30 p.m. on the 2nd. The beauty of the isles of the Ægean was a revelation, and, coming after the rest at Alexandria, it served to increase the conviction in the minds of the men that the new field was going to prove much more attractive than the battlefields of France. It was well that it could not be foreseen that 2½ years later it would be recorded in a private diary, "*At last we are to get away from this pestilential country!*"

After lying outside during the night the transport passed through the torpedo boom into Salonica harbour on the morning of the 7th December. There was a fog outside and the view of the shore and town was very misty; the harbour was full of troopships waiting to land the troops, but for seven days disembarkation was held up owing to the hostile attitude of the Greeks. The time was mostly spent by the soldiers in watching the weird native craft in harbour, whose crews (judged by the men to be all pirates) were engaged for the time in the simple arts of commerce, belying their cut-throat appearance.

Seen from the harbour the town rose spotless and picturesque with its buildings of white stone or whitewashed mud; to the east is the residential quarter, principally occupied by the consuls and merchants; the west is the Turkish quarter, and this stretches northward up the hill until it meets the walls of the old citadel which encircles the crest of the hill, with its towers and battlements frowning down on all sides. The centre of the town is the business portion populated by Greeks and Jews.

The quay accommodation was found to be very poor. Most of the disembarkation was done in lighters; later this was remedied when the British built two more piers.

However, when the battalion landed on the 14th, closer acquaintance with the streets corrected impressions that had been gathered from a distance. There was a ceaseless din of traffic, rough wheels jolted over the loose granite cobbles, bullock carts moved laboriously forward, modern three-ton lorries, brought by British and French, threaded their way through the crowd, while loaded camels and strings of donkeys, looking like moving haystacks with their colossal burdens, approached the docks from all directions. The only touch of modern civilisation, apart from that introduced by the Allies, was afforded by the electric tramcars of shabby and uninviting appearance

The dress of the native population was varied and generally dirty, many of the men looking like animated ragbags; the Greek soldiers, who were to be met everywhere, looked slovenly and badly dressed, a great contrast to their officers. The imported Cretan policemen, by their smartness and the cleanliness of their turnout, introduced a tone of efficiency which would otherwise have been lacking, and it was obvious that these men at any rate maintained authority with the crowd.

The battalion marched out of Salonica by the western exit to the junction of the Monastir and Lembet roads. It followed the latter, which is the beginning of the road to Seres, climbing the hill to the Lembet plain, where the Allied camps were pitched. The first camp was by the side of the Seres road about four miles from Salonica. The weather was wet and there was always a mist; by night the frosts were severe. The battalion at once settled down to road-building, of which there was a crying need, for there was no railway running in the direction of the Struma and no possibility of building one; if an advance were made in this direction the Seres road had to be made fit for the heavy traffic of supply columns or the troops would starve.

The troops found this to be a most barren and uninviting country at the time of year. Also the inhabitants regarded them with unfriendly looks, and the Serbian refugees who passed down the road wore such woebegone expressions that, in their depression of spirits, the men turned for consolation to making pets of the tortoises which were discovered during digging operations enjoying their winter sleep. Tortoise-racing became the rage, and being suitable as an in-tent sport, it served to wile away the hours. Many little tortoises that were packed away to sleep in mossy beds in matchboxes, awoke some weeks later in Batley maybe, or Dewsbury, in Doncaster or Pontefract.

On the 22nd December the battalion moved about two miles up the Seres road to assist in digging the new defence line which was being made across the neck of the peninsula for the protection of Salonica from the landward side. This line was destined to take four months to construct and it occupied a position of great natural strength, running along a high ridge where it was not protected by the Beshik and Langaza lakes. It rested on the sea on the right and on the marshes of the river Vardar on the left. It had a total frontage of about 70 miles, of which twenty-five were occupied by the two lakes. In addition to trenches there were dug-outs, aid-posts, gun positions, roads and light railways to be constructed, telephone lines to be buried, water supply and sanitary arrangements to be completed. The work of digging and blasting the rock was sometimes stopped by the bitter weather, for there was a piercing wind which blew from the Vardar which was accompanied at times by falls of snow, so that the ground would be ice and snow bound. At night when the troops came in the camp was aglow with charcoal braziers put outside to be fanned by the wind. A pantomime produced by the Field Ambulance proved an outstanding attraction in the cold dark nights.

1916 The battalion moved on the 2nd February to Besch Chinar gardens in Salonica down by the seashore close by the pier.

Two companies daily found guards and other duties in the town, while the other two had duties in camp. Strict supervision was necessary over the Greek labourers on the docks, whose pay amounted to 3 drachmas a shift (drachma = 10d.), but who were credited with stealing on the average 20 drachmas' worth of stuff every time. The guard at the gates had the unpleasant and unsavoury job of searching these plunderers, who had hitherto been in the habit of stuffing their baggy breeches between garter and cummerbund with tins of bully beef, milk and other commodities. The process was carried out by tapping the suspect all round with the flat blade of an entrenching tool, and if this struck metal, an order was given to loosen the cummerbund, when out would fall a shower of useful articles from the folds of the cummerbund itself or from the now unsupported trousers. To those soldiers who were interested, this period in other ways was an education in itself in supply and disembarkation work. The following is a letter written by Brig.-Gen. H. Poett, Base Commandant Salonica, to Maj.-Gen. C. J. Briggs, commanding 28th Div.:—

My dear General Briggs, *2nd March,* 1916.

I cannot let the 1*st Bn. K.O.Y.L.I. leave the Base without letting you know how much I have appreciated having such a good smart battalion on duty in the town. They have been an excellent example to men coming into the town. Col. Brooke has been most helpful and has given my Staff the greatest assistance in getting the guards and the guard camp into shape.*

Sincerely yours (sd.) H. POETT.

Letter from Maj-Gen. C. J. Briggs, comdg. 28th Div., to Lt.-Col. C. R. Ingham Brooke, comdg. 1/K.O.Y.L.I.:

My dear Brooke, *Headquarters, 28th Division.*

I was very pleased to receive the enclosed which speaks for itself. It reflects great credit on you and your excellent battalion.

Very sincerely (sd.) C. J. BRIGGS.

On the 6th March the 8/K.S.L.I. relieved the 1/K.O.Y.L.I. in the Besch Chinar gardens and the latter went to a new camp just below the Baldza pass, from which a glorious view of the country southwards and westwards, with the harbour and Mount Olympus snow-capped beyond, helped to create a more cheerful prospect. The battalion took up a section of the new line, which was nearing its completion, so that much time could now be devoted to training.

Early in April Maj. Mallinson assumed command, when Lt.-Col. Ingham Brooke took over that of the 82nd Inf. Bde.

From the 11th to the 17th April up-country manœuvres were carried out, which proved of the greatest interest to all, for the country was now looking its best with a wonderful wealth of spring flowers blooming, while the unfamiliar nature of this rough country was exciting to contend with as a battle ground.

The Macedonian inhabitants were unconcerned in the war, as the German and Bulgarian armies in the north were merely maintaining the positions of their furthest advance, which in the case of the Bulgarians ran east and west through Strumitsa Sta., including the point where the Struma enters Bulgaria. These country people were cleaner in appearance than their Salonica brethren, but they obviously practised the same habit of piling new garments over their old ones. They wore brighter colours, but all had the sallow complexions which spoke of indigenous malaria.

The village houses, two-storied as a rule, are constructed of timber, wattle and daub, the roofs thatched with reeds or maize straw, the ground floor commonly used for storeroom and granary with a small annexe for donkeys and chickens. The upper storey usually has a verandah facing east, where the family take their mid-day siesta. Agriculture was in full swing when the British troops came through, and the men were much amused to note the crudity of the ploughs and other implements in use; it was a common sight to see a donkey and a small ox harnessed side by side. One village was keeping festival, the villagers being attired in their brightest garments of which the brilliant coloured aprons of the women were a conspicuous feature; every inhabitant of the village joined in the country dances with a great deal of hand-clapping; the music accompaniment was supplied by two or three flutes and a drum.

The 1/K.O.Y.L.I. returned to its training and digging. As the days grew longer, football matches took place nightly. The days were becoming hotter, indeed hotter than the warmest summer's day in England, but as yet the climate had appeared kind and the men were fit and were beginning to wonder when the fighting was going to commence.

In May the German aircraft were busy. On the second occasion of a visit paid by a Zeppelin it was struck by a 12-pounder shell from *H.M.S. Agememnon* and brought down in the Vardar marshes. There was a great stampede to view the raider at close quarters, and one Canadian doctor was unfortunately drowned when riding out to the wreck. The Zeppelin was removed to the White Tower gardens in Salonica, where it was erected for the population to see.

Throughout the month of May the Allied force was constantly being augmented. Not only had the splendid little army of the

Serbians arrived from Corfu, re-organised and re-equipped, but there were two brigades of Russians and a fine Italian division fresh from the fighting on the Trentino. The Allied force was very cosmopolitan and in the streets of Salonica there might be seen Annamites, British, Canadians, French, Indians, Italians, Moors, Russians, Senegalese and Serbians, jostling one another merrily.

Towards the end of May, as the result of diplomatic intervention on the part of the Allied governments with that of Athens, it was arranged that the Greek corps (five in number) distributed in the region 'for the protection of the Macedonian frontier,' but in reality a source of great embarrassment, should be withdrawn. The Bulgarians seized the opportunity to occupy Fort Rupel and to advance through the pass, which was their gate into Macedonia.

On the 3rd June there was a Greek revolution in favour of Venizelos in Salonica, and the French took control of the town.

On the 4th June our 83rd Inf. Bde., including the 1/K.O.Y.L.I., started to march up country in the direction of Seres. There were no railways and practicable roads did not exist. In order that supplies could be brought on, roads and light railways had to be constructed on the way. Ten days were spent between the 13th and 24th June on making a light railway between Lahana and Mirova. The heat now was appalling and work could be carried on only in the early morning or after 4.30 in the evening. The nights were sultry and the mosquitoes and other insects descended in swarms on the unprotected troops. By day the men found shelter from the sun under the bivouac sheets.

On the 15th July the battalion marched into the valley, taking over from the 2/Buffs a portion of the outpost line.

There followed, from the 16th July to the 7th October, a period of inactivity, monotony and fever. Three companies were constantly in the outpost line facing the wide bed of the river, where they were shelled daily. The outpost line occupied the foothills, with advanced posts at the bridge-heads; behind the outpost line was a mountain range, which would be the main resistance line if the outposts were driven back. On the north or left bank of the Struma the plain extended for some miles before it reached the higher ranges of Bulgaria.

Malarial fever soon began to play havoc and the battalion strength became very much reduced. It was difficult to find a sufficient number of men for the sentry line, so that even the transportmen had to be called in to furnish mounted patrols by night in order to reduce the number of posts by three. Officers and men suffered alike. Men dreaded reporting sick, for the Field Ambulance was many miles away and owing to a shortage of ambulances the journey to it was accomplished in very rough conveyances. Quinine was a daily issue; mosquito nets did not arrive till the end of the summer; the routine of work in the early morning, lying in the sweltering heat by day, and being on outpost duty by night, became wearisome in the extreme.

The first move which bore the semblance of active operations occurred on the 7th October, when "C" Company, now fifty strong, attempted to take Cavdarmah, a village standing about one mile from the left bank of the Struma. The Bulgarians were found to be holding it in strength, backed by artillery, and the attack was not pushed home. This had merely been a reconnaissance, and was followed on the 8th by an advance of the battalion, who took up a position on the left bank of the river and attacked Cavdarmah at the first streak of dawn. The Bulgarians did not wait for the attack and they withdrew their guns. Cavdarmah was then occupied by "A" Company and one platoon of "B," who were left as garrison.

Next morning a squadron of the Surrey Yeomanry joined this little garrison to assist it in making a further reconnaissance towards Barakli Dzuma; the object was to make the enemy disclose his strength; he was strongly entrenched, with several machine-guns in the houses, and was supported by guns. The left reconnoitring platoons were caught by his fire and suffered a loss of three other ranks killed and five wounded, while the right platoons retired unscathed.

This was all part of a concerted move of the XVI Corps under Gen. Briggs, coincident with an attack on the main front by the French and Serbians. The British front was carried forward to Ormanli on the far side of the river. Two fresh bridges had been thrown across the Struma, gun positions had been dug, and trench stores had been collected in the forward area on the left bank of the river. The appearance of a battery of 6-in. howitzers and a battery of 60-pounders indicated to the troops that there would be a battle in the near future.

On the 26th October the battalion assembled at Kopriva bridge and on the 30th moved forward to Ormanli, the position of assembly, about 400 strong. The weather had now become vile and the troops were soaked by the rain, while the plain had become a morass.

From 2 a.m. until 7.15 the battalion lay waiting while the guns delivered a bombardment. Then the infantry advanced, meeting with little opposition. The Bulgarians were taken by surprise and did not await the assault. By 8.30 a.m. the infantry were consolidating on the far side of the Bulgarian position. The 1/K.O.Y.L.I. had 320 rifles in the attack and captured two officers and 296 other ranks, with two machine-guns and a considerable amount of telephone and other equipment; there were no casualties in the battalion. On the 3rd November the 2/Cheshire relieved the battalion in the front line. On the 16th November the battalion moved up again to Ormanli in support of the 85th Inf. Bde., which was attacking Barakli, and it relieved the Suffolks in the line at Barakli on the 18th. The brigade went forward on the 26th to Lozista, and on the 28th the 1/K.O.Y.L.I. relieved portions of two battalions of the Italian 35th Div. in Radeli, near Lake Doiran.

The Italians expressed great surprise at the weakness of the taking-over battalion; they had 1,400 men in the position which was now being occupied by 400. They were most friendly and hospitable, taking every possible care and interest in handing over; they actually left a party behind for a few days to show the country to the new-comers. Rain was incessant; trenches and dugouts fell in in consequence in all directions. Opposed to this new front, three miles away across the valley, the Belashitza mountain range commenced to rise like a great rock wall, to a height of over 6,000 feet. The main line of the Bulgarians was high up on these mountains, but they held a strong outpost line in the foothills, also a strong advanced post at Peroi station on the Salonica-Constantinople railway in the centre of the valley.

While the operations of a minor character were taking place along the right front a great offensive was being launched in the eastern portions of the line. A Franco-Russian offensive ended in failure, but the Serbians, under Gen. Michich, advancing eagerly over familiar country, pressed on in spite of all opposition until they were able to re-occupy Monastir.

December and January were wretched months. The battalion suffered a great loss on Boxing Day in the death of Capt. and Qr.-Mr. J. C. Brasier, who went down to hospital sick on the 12th December and died at Salonica.

There was always a certain amount of shelling of the trenches, but luckily casualties due to the enemy's fire were few. A quotation from Capt. F. K. Lambert's diary of this period will best illustrate the story of these trenches in the wet season: "*The roads, which looked so nice when we first arrived, soon began to break up under the heavy downpours and became quagmires, in which men, horses and mules sank to their knees. Rations were extremely bad, and were brought for twenty miles on pack animals. In fact some days not even half rations were drawn. For ten days we had neither milk, jam, nor candles, the tea was mouldy, also the bread, and it was a case of tightening one's belt daily. The mules were much worse off, for no forage was sent for them at all, and they lived on oak scrub, harness, horse-rugs and their own tails. On Christmas Day we had not a mule with a complete tail, whilst there was scarcely a rug left which was fit to use. Mails were overdue, and this, combined with the sodden conditions, lack of food, etc., provided the worst Christmas any of us had spent.*"

It may be inferred from this account that the highly-trained and intelligent mules were expecting a more sumptuous feed on Christmas Day, and that they were disappointed in their hopes; 'transport' animals might be expected to be more highly-strung than the common agricultural beasts of burden!

An incident which relieved the monotony of existence
1917 occurred on the 15th March, 1917. "B" and "D" Companies, together with one company of the 2/E. York., attacked and captured Peroi station and secured twenty-five prisoners, with a loss of three wounded in the case of the K.O.Y.L.I.

It was not until the 26th March that the battalion was relieved from their long spell of trench work, which had started on the 29th October, 1916, by the arrival of the 22(Garrison)/R.B.

Some good sport and recreation for the officers had been provided by Capt. W. H. Brooke, who returned from leave early in January. Emulating a famous example in the Peninsular War, he brought with him from home three couple of beagles to hunt hares or whatever quarry they should in their waywardness prefer. One morning, on the line of what the Master concluded to be a wolf, the pack went 'over the top,' through the wire, and in full cry headed for the Bulgarian lines. The hounds were in view from both trench lines, and the excitement became tense to discover what action the enemy would take; the Bulgarian showed that he was a good sportsman, for far from interfering with the hunt, he cheered the beagles on until they were lost to sight behind the lines. The pack returned in the early hours of the following morning, very tired and dirty but unharmed.

The battalion remained in the neighbourhood of Lake Doiran with the rest of the 83rd Inf. Bde. till the 15th August, 1917, when it marched eastwards to rejoin the 28th Div. in the same camp at Gumus Dere, from which it had set out on the 26th November, 1916, in order to relieve the Italians. The heat during the march was intense, and the men's energy was greatly reduced by malarial fever, from which everyone suffered. The majority of the men were quite unfit to carry their packs, which were carried for them in the extra transport provided for the purpose, despite the fact that all marching was done after sundown.

The battalion remained in the line holding two bridgeheads for the remaining months of the year. Except for a certain amount of shelling daily and for occasional patrol actions, there was not much war. More recreations were now provided for the troops, and the officers played polo on the transport ponies. A Y.M.C.A. tent appeared; mosquito nets, sun helmets and plentiful supplies of quinine were available, and a few officers and men obtained leave to England.

1918 From the 14th to the 19th May, 1918, the battalion was engaged in a march to Ereselli spur *via* Paprat, Krusova and Karamudli, where it became attached to the 85th Inf. Bde. and found working parties for clearing Dova Tepe fort and moving guns from it in preparation for the evacuation which was imminent. During this period the air was thick with rumours of moves to France on the one hand, and on the other, of big approaching Bulgarian attacks on our front, designed to drive the British from the heights of the Krusa Balkan mountains into the sea. However, on the 18th June the battalion marched to Karamudli, and the joyful news leaked out that the battalion was on its way down country to Salonica *en route* for France. It seemed almost too good to be true; the men brightened up, straightened their knees and marched 'with faces wreathed in smiles.'

Salonica was reached on the 20th June. The next few days were spent in handing stores in to Ordnance depôts and in packing baggage for a journey. The battalion was inspected at Sarigol by Gen. Milne, G.O.C. in C., on the 26th.

The battalion was greatly pleased by the publication of the following letter from their Corps Commander on leaving his command for France:

From Lt.-Gen. Sir Charles J. Briggs, K.C.B., K.C.M.G., to Lt.-Col. H. Mallinson, D.S.O., commanding 1st Bn. K.O.Y.L.I.

Headquarters, XVI Corps,
Macedonia,
21st June, 1918.

My dear Mallinson,

I much regret that stress of work getting the Greeks into the line has prevented my running over to wish you all 'God-speed,' and to thank you all for the excellent work you have all done for me during the past two years and nine months.

I think you know that I have always had a warm corner in my heart for the 1st *Bn. K.O.Y.L.I., largely due to your smartness and efficiency in your duties, and I can never remember having taken anyone's name on my black book, which I cannot say of all others.*

I shall miss you all very much and I hope we may serve again together. Will you please express my sincere thanks to all and my best wishes for every possible success and a safe return to the old country.

Yours very sincerely,
(sd.) C. J. Briggs.

The battalion entrained on the 27th and 28th June in two trains for Bralo on the road to Athens. The line follows the seaboard till it leaves Macedonia and runs inland by way of Larissa; then down through old Greece. At Bralo Sta. lorries picked the men up and carried them over the mountains under the shadow of Mount Parnassus to the little port of Itea on the Gulf of Corinth. This road was a fine piece of engineering work, made serviceable by the French; the scenery is magnificent.

The 1/K.O.Y.L.I. embarked at midnight the 30th June in the *S.S. Odessa*, a dirty little boat which all were glad to see the last of on arrival at Taranto in Italy on the 2nd July. From the 3rd to the 9th the battalion was travelling overland, through Italy to Ventimiglia and then on through France *via* Marseilles, Lyons and Paris to Dieppe.

At Dieppe the 1/K.O.Y.L.I. was incorporated in the 151st Inf. Bde. of the 50th Div., together with the 4/K.R.R.C. and the 6/Inniskg. The 50th Div. had lost nearly all its personnel during the German spring offensive, and was being reconstituted from nine battalions which were being brought to France from Macedonia and Palestine.

THE ADVANCE TO THE HINDENBURG LINE. 1917

XIII

THE campaigns of 1916 about Verdun and the Somme, in the western field of action, had resulted in forcing the German armies to act on the defensive. The German armies were weakened and there was considerable depression as a consequence of those battles. These considerations led the German Commander-in-Chief to shorten his line and so to enable him to economise his available forces. On the 16th March there commenced the German retreat from the salient existing between Arras and Soissons, over country that had been carefully prepared beforehand. The new line ran from the Scarpe by the village of St. Laurent, west of Cambrai, west of St. Quentin, through La Fère, to the Aisne just west of Vailly; this new line had a length of about 85 miles and was called by the Germans the Siegfried Line, but is referred to in British accounts always as the Hindenburg Line.

SPRING, 1917.

The retreat of the Germans was carried out very cleverly, and rearguard actions were reduced to the minimum; also a certain amount of dislocation of the British plans was occasioned, for all preparations for the Spring offensive, to commence early in April, were in an advanced stage at the time when, towards the end of February, it became apparent that the Germans were contemplating an evacuation of the salient.

Previous to the offensive on the Arras front, the only battalion of the K.O.Y.L.I. which was seriously engaged in the first quarter of the year 1917 was the 2nd Bn., but there was a very fine example of a successful raid carried out by one company of the 6th Bn. which deserves recording also.

THE 2ND BN.

Immediately north of the Ancre the forward bend of the German line was still very pronounced, and efforts were being made by the Fifth Army to gain a tactical advantage of position in February, 1917, by biting a little deeper into the extremity of the salient. The 2/K.O.Y.L.I. was called upon to take part in a minor operation with this end in view, just north-east of Beaumont Hamel.

The divisional order read: "*The 97th Inf. Bde. will drive the enemy off the ridge from R.I.a.8.6 to R.I.a.0.9, and out of Ten Tree Alley, on the night of Feb. 10/11th.*"

The action that ensued was later described in dispatches as a "*highly successful local operation north of the Ancre; trenches on a front of more than ¾ mile captured.*"

The 11/Border was the right battalion of attack, the 2/K.O.Y.L.I. the centre, and one company of the 16/N.F. was on the left. "Zero" hour was 8.30 p.m. The battalion paraded at 4.15 p.m. and proceeded to Beaumont Hamel by platoons; hot soup was provided at Auchonvillers on the way. After drawing stores and ammunition in Beaumont Hamel, owing to the flooded state of the traffic-congested wagon road, up which the platoons had to pass in order to reach the tape, the battalion reached its position only just in time. The four companies attacked in line in the order "D," "C," "B," "A," "A" being on the right. Our artillery barrage opened at 8.30, and the infantry advanced in four waves close up behind it; it was a creeping barrage, lifting (after the first five minutes) 100 yards every three minutes, and finally resting on the ridge beyond Ten Tree Alley until 9.30 p.m. The distance from the jumping-off line to the objective was approximately 600 yards.

In Lager Alley, about 400 yards from the starting line, a series of strong enemy posts existed; these were in the line of advance of "C" and "B" Companies. Near to, and south of, the objective, was another series of enemy posts in front of "A" Company; and again in Ten Tree Alley itself there was a formidable series of strong posts at the point where "C" and "D" Companies were finally to consolidate; the Bn. Headquarters were in Munich trench in the old front line.

At 8.30 p.m. the leading troops went over the line and stepped out into the night. The night was dark and the ground was frozen hard. Their progress could not be watched, but could be judged from the reports which commenced to come back, the first to be received arriving at 10.17 p.m. The following extracts tell the story:—

10th Feb. 10.17 *p.m. from "C" Company, reporting the capture of one enemy post in Ten Tree Alley.*

10.20 *p.m. from "D" Company, sending in ten prisoners.*

10.50 *p.m. from "B" Company, reporting capture of fifty prisoners.*

11.15 *p.m. from "B" Company, reporting capture of more prisoners and arrival at their objective.*

11.50 *p.m. reported that "C" and "B" Companies were in touch in Ten Tree Alley, but had no news from "D" Company.*

11th Feb. 12.30 *a.m. Two machine-guns were sent forward to reinforce Ten Tree Alley in response to a request from O.C. "B" Company.*

2.0 *a.m. The whereabouts of the right company ("A") being uncertain,*

R.S.M. Wall was sent forward from headquarters to reconnoitre. In carrying out this duty R.S.M. Wall was mortally wounded.[1]

2.25 *a.m. from "A" Company, reporting having gained its objective and occupying crater and shell-holes on crest of ridge* 80 *yards from enemy line.*

2.45 *a.m. from "C" Company, reporting capture of two enemy machine-guns, and that the company is engaged in bombing enemy out of two posts in Ten Tree Alley; also, contact with "B" Company is established.*

4.20 *a.m. from "D" Company, reporting contact with* 16/*N.F. on its left; that enemy had extended for counter-attack but were dispersed by our machine-gun fire.*

At 4.50 *a.m. the O.C.* 2/*K.O.Y.L.I.* (*Lt.-Col. Ingham Brooke, who had been in command since the* 4*th January*) *conferred with the Brig.-Gen. on the phone with reference to a post still held by the enemy in rear of the left of the Borderers, and a post in front of "C" Company's objective. C.O. did not recommend any withdrawal.*

4.55 *a.m. Bn. Headquarters called on the Brigade for a further supply of bombs and small arms ammunition. An adequate supply was promptly sent up.*

5.55 *a.m.* 219*th Field Coy. R.E. reported it had commenced the formation of strong points at* 1.30 *a.m. in rear of our new line.*

7.15 *a.m. "C" Company sent down twenty-seven prisoners and reported having one enemy officer and seven other ranks wounded in their hands.*

By 9.15 *p.m. the O.C. Bn. was able to report to Bde. Headquarters that communication was established between all companies and with all units on right and left.*

12th Feb. 6 *a.m. The battalion was relieved by the* 17/*H.L.I. and retired into reserve at Beaumont Hamel.*

In all, 193 prisoners were captured by the 2/K.O.Y.L.I.

The battalion suffered casualties as follows:—Officers wounded, 2/Lts. F. J. Steele, A. H. Glynn, H. T. Curtis, H. F. Mountain, H. J. S. Cole and J. S. Copeland. Died of wounds: R.S.M. G. B. Wall. Other ranks: killed, 15; wounded, 52; missing, 117; total 185.

On the 18th March the 2/K.O.Y.L.I. was reserve battalion in the division, which advanced *via* Fresnoy-les-Roye to Battencourt and again to Herly on the 19th, and Nesle on the 20th.

The Bn. Headquarters were established for some days in Nesle

[1] *R.S.M. G. B. Wall had been with the* 2/*K.O.Y.L.I. since the day of its arrival in France. He had succeeded R.S.M. John Moore, M.C., D.C.M., who had lost his life owing to the premature explosion of a bomb of a new pattern, with which he was demonstrating to a class of N.C.O.s behind the lines on the* 8*th June,* 1915. *R.S.M. Moore might have cast the bomb from him when he saw that the fuse had ignited, but realising the danger this would entail to others, he retained his hold on it till it exploded, and he was killed.*

while the men were employed in clearing the roads, and then moved forward to Quiquéry, where a bridge had to be rebuilt; thence to Languevoisin on the 24th March, where the list of honours in connection with the recent attack was published. It included:—
M.C.: Capts. J. W. Woods, G. A. Gamble and H. R. Forde. D.C.M.: C.S.M. J. Bramley, C.S.M. J. Hearn, Lce./Cpls. J. Abbott and A. Lumb. M.M.: Cpl. J. Breheny, Lce./Cpls. A. E. Dowling and H. Bewsey, Sgts. G. Langham and F. R. Swift, Lce./Cpls. W. Murray and J. W. Coleridge, Pte. G. F. Bugg.

In accordance with the general advance of the IV Corps the 2/K.O.Y.L.I. moved forward to Toulle on the 28th March, and later to a line running through Douchy-Germaine, where it received orders to prepare for greater efforts connected with attacks on Savy and Fayet beyond.

Here, for the time being, we must leave the battalion to record other incidents in the story of the Regiment, which occurred within the period of the first quarter of the year 1917.

The 6/K.O.Y.L.I., commanded by Lt.-Col. G. Meynell (43rd Inf. Bde., 14th Div.), was in the Arras sector. Arras was at the time a centre of great activity, for it was intended by the British Commander-in-Chief to deliver the first great stroke of the spring campaign from this sector of the line. It was about Arras that the tunnelling companies had prepared the underground quarries for the reception of two whole British divisions which were to remain concealed and to be sprung on the enemy at a critical moment of the offensive.

THE 6TH BN.

Throughout March, the month that preceded the great attack, it was necessary for the British forces to be kept up-to-date in their information concerning the enemy line. One of the methods adopted in such cases was that of conducting organised raids. Capt. C. B. Leatham, with "Z" Company and the battalion bombers 6/K.O.Y.L.I., carried out a successful raid on the brickfields north of Beaurains, a village two miles south of Arras, in the early morning of the 12th March.

The raid was carefully planned and supported by gunfire; "Zero" time was 7 a.m. All the objectives were reached; the enemy were in dug-outs, and as they would not come out and surrender there was no option left but to deal with them by using Stokes mortar bombs and 'mobile' charges. The raiding party remained in the German trenches until 7.30 a.m., and the withdrawal was carried out with precision, parties covering one another's retirements in succession, the Lewis-guns being in action all the time. All were back in the trenches by 7.45 a.m.

The German front lines were found to be 8 or 9 feet deep, and there were numerous deep dug-outs found in them all along the raided area; these were blown in after the occupants had been called on to come out and surrender.

When they got into the German lines Capt. Leatham directed operations from the top of the "Brickstack," where he was wounded; the bullet which wounded him killed his sergeant-major, C.S.M. Sharpe, who had twice previously been decorated for gallant conduct in the field, and was a great loss to the company. The trenches were occupied by the 100th Saxon Reserve Regiment.

All our wounded were brought in, the stretcher-bearers working splendidly.

The attack had been organised in five parties, each with its particular objectives and duties. The commanders of the parties were 2/Lts. L. C. Clews, T. G. Mayne (N. Staffs. attd.), — Hill, J. W. Benn and A. S. Newborn.

The casualties were heavy: Capt. C. B. Leatham and 2/Lt. J. W. Benn were wounded, and of other ranks 28 were killed and 26 wounded; also 1 R.E. (attd.) was killed.

Brig.-Gen. P. Wood, commanding the 43rd Inf. Bde., and the G.O.C. 14th (Light) Div., sent congratulatory messages; the VII Corps Commander conveyed his very high appreciation of the gallant behaviour of the raiding party. "*He considers that the enterprise reflects great credit on the battalion. The damage done to the enemy was heavy, and valuable information was gained. He particularly expresses his appreciation of the parts played by Capt. Leatham and 2/Lt. Clews, and his regret at the loss of C.S.M. Sharpe and those men who fell with him.*

(sd.) J. Burnett-Stuart, Brig.-Gen.,
Gen. Staff, VII Corps."

Two new battalions of the K.O.Y.L.I. arrived in France on the 16th January, 1917. These were the 2/4th and the 2/5th, both in the 187th Inf. Bde. of the 62nd Div. The brigade was commanded by Brig.-Gen. R. O. B. Taylor, the division by Maj.-Gen. W. P. B. Braithwaite. The division was assigned to the V Corps (Fanshawe) in the Fifth Army (Gough).

THE 2/4TH BN.

The 2/4th Bn. K.O.Y.L.I. disembarked at Havre early the 16th January, 1917. The officers serving with the battalion were:—Lt.-Col. E. Hind, V.D.; Majors E. H. Walker and J. H. Greaves; Capts. G. Beaumont, N. Lee, W. H. Smith, A. L. Pyrah, F. Brook, W. Bell; Lts. A. E. Pilley, A. G. Russell, A. R. Mosley, F. MacCunn, G. L. Hudson, G. S. Day and S. S. Wainwright (attd.); 2/Lts. M. McNicholl, J. H. Wellington, M. O. Walsh, E. J. S. Mees, C. A. Lepine, A. L. Taylor, A. Morris, C. A. Ireland; Adjt. Lt. V. C.

Green; Qr.-Mr. Lt. J. Lockwood; Med. Officer Capt. F. W. Hird, R.A.M.C. (attd.).

The battalion proceeded by rail to Neuvillette, near Doullens, and on to St. Leger, near Authie, on the 27th January. Here, parties went up to the trenches in turn for attachment, and the battalion was employed on railway construction duty till the 15th February. The frost at the time was so severe that the earth had to be blasted, an occupation that was congenial to the miners from Yorkshire. On the 20th the 187th Inf. Bde. took over a portion of the line, the battalion moving into Mailly Wood East as brigade reserve. The Germans were now showing signs of retiring from this part of the line, and the brigade began a forward movement towards Puisieux. In the tentative operations which ensued, the 2/4th K.O.Y.L.I. suffered their first casualties, but the battalion did all that it was asked to do, and did it well.

After a rest the battalion, on the 12th March, moved up again by way of Bois d'Hollande and took over a position in brigade reserve at Miraumont, a position which was unpleasantly near to the enemy's artillery in Irles. Lt. Wainwright was killed by a shell on the 11th, and seven other ranks were killed and seventeen wounded on the 13th during an advance on Bucquoy trench, which had to be occupied in order to straighten the line. Capt. Bell was killed on the 16th; also in other ranks there were one killed and six missing. After this the battalion was moved back to Beaumont Hamel and was engaged on railway work here and at Achiet-le-Grand till the end of the month.

The strength of the 2/5th K.O.Y.L.I. on its arrival in Havre on the 14th January, was 34 officers and 977 other ranks.

THE 2/5 BN.

The officers who had embarked at Southampton were:—

Lt.-Col. W. Watson; Major O. C. S. Watson; Capts. F. Mellor, H. G. Bracey, E. G. L. Whiteaway, C. R. Bramley, W. J. Oswald, S. S. Chappell, R. J. Preston, B. Sykes, J. Mailer, E. B. Bilton; Lts. T. F. B. Hall, H. O. Brown, B. M. Tatham, J. L. Summers, C. H. Wilson, C. C. Snow, E. R. Woodrooffe, C. Boden, E. P. Pattinson, A. C. Lynn; 2/Lts. A. R. Rose, C. H. Webb, S. D. Lang, A. Butler, J. Atkin, B. S. Brewster, O. G. Platt, J. Ingle, G. C. High; Adjt. Lt. A. Robinson; Qr.-Mr. Capt. G. A. McNally.

The experiences of the 2/5th K.O.Y.L.I. were similar to those of the sister battalion in the same brigade. The journey from Havre to Frévent, in the Somme area, was made by train, and Beauval was reached by route march on the 22nd January. At Bus, while the battalion was under training and instruction, the 2nd Bn. sent a party of officers over to welcome the newcomers. This visit was paid on the 10th February; on the 18th the battalion took over a section of the line, which here consisted of small posts in occupation of shell-holes, from the 188th Inf. Bde. It suffered losses two days later; Capt. C. R. Bramley was killed in the trenches, and 2/Lt. S. D. Lang died of wounds; of other ranks there were one killed and seven wounded. The shell-holes were wet, cold and exposed; when relieved on the night of the 22nd forty-three men were suffering from 'trench feet.'

When the enemy showed signs of retiring from his positions in front of Serre and Puisieux, the battalion joined in the advance made by the brigade on the 25th February, passing through the 2/4th Bn. the following day to take its place in the front line. The brigade had now received its baptism of fire and was withdrawn for a rest on the 28th to Mailly-Maillet Wood.

Life in the other battalions of the K.O.Y.L.I. during the first quarter of the year 1917 was fairly normal. Their places in the general line will now be briefly traced.

Some ten miles north of Serre and Puisieux, where the 2/4th and 2/5th Bns. had entered the line, the original 4th and 5th Bns. were with their division (the 49th) in the sector which had Bailleulval for its headquarters. Lt.-Col. B. Musgrave (Loyals) was now in command of the 4th Bn., the 5th being still commanded by Lt.-Col. Moxon.

THE 4TH AND 5TH BNS.

The 4th Bn. lost 2/Lt. A. E. Gardner, killed, and 2/Lt. A. C. Richardson, wounded, towards the end of January, while in the right sub-sector of the brigade front at Blaireville.

From the 25th February to the 4th March, the 148th Inf. Bde. was on the line of march to take up a new position in the Neuve Chapelle sector. A considerable détour was made *via* Frévent, St. Pol and Merville, in order to reach this more northerly sector, for it was necessary to give Arras a wide berth. The brigade relieved the 167th Inf. Bde. of the 56th Div., and it was still in this sector at the end of March.

The New Year found the 7/K.O.Y.L.I. at Meaulte, just South of Albert. In the honours list Lt.-Col. B. B. Robinson and Maj. A. C. White were awarded the D.S.O.; Maj. J. T. Janson also was mentioned in dispatches among the "Somme" awards.

THE 7TH BN.

Alternately resting and taking its place in the line east of Combles, the battalion had been holding trenches in Sailly-Saillisel, Le Transloy and Morval.

According to Lt.-Col. Robinson, the trenches opposite Le Transloy were, without exception, the worst he met with as regards mud and water. The misery the men suffered in them from mud and cold during the two or three months of that winter was beyond description. Several men were lost through being drowned in the mud; many others got bogged in the mud up to their shoulders, and in their efforts to drag them out others of their comrades became engulfed. It took twelve hours to take over the trenches and twelve hours again to get through the work entailed in handing them over. While in reserve at Carnoy (five miles east of Albert), the battalion had to contend against the severest spell of cold weather it ever experienced. Bread was frozen to the semblance of a brick; ice had to be thawed for cooking; washing oneself "*was reduced to a thought, and a painful thought at that.*" He bears witness to the fact that "*the spirit of the men during these trying months was marvellous.*" Complaints were never heard; the men realised that all that could be done for them was being done.

Two incidents which occurred during this period are illustrations of the thoughtfulness and care on the part of superior officers, which met with due appreciation in the trenches. They are given in Col. Robinson's words (written in March, 1921):—

"*On one occasion before going into the trenches a draft arrived for whom I had no jerkins. I could obtain none from brigade or division, for none were to be had, so I took upon myself to telephone direct to Corps Headquarters. Unexpectedly I was put through to Lord Cavan in person. I explained my difficulty and he replied that he would do his best. Before we went to the trenches I received the necessary jerkins, which had been collected by a special lorry from various hospitals. I was, personally, much gratified, and I took care that the action of the Corps Commander should be known to all ranks. I feel certain that this interest in our welfare on the part of the Corps Commander did much to endear him to officers and men. On another occasion, four very weary and muddy privates were returning from these trenches at about 4 o'clock in the morning, when a passing car pulled up and an officer in the car told them all to jump in; the men were driven almost all the way to their camp, and they were very grateful to the young officer, but they were still more gratified when they learnt that it was the Prince of Wales who had befriended them.*"

Col. Robinson proceeds to write: "*We spent that Christmas in a small village behind the lines, where we received and enjoyed a large consignment of oranges, nuts, cigarettes, socks, etc., sent out by the Regimental Comforts Fund to all the battalions, and other parcels from kindred Yorkshire organisations. All ranks were very grateful to those who so kindly remembered us. After a rest the battalion went into a much more comfortable and equally quiet sector in front of Combles, and here it remained until the enemy retirement in the spring of 1917. The long-expected retirement of the enemy in front of us then commenced. The Germans offered no real resistance to our advance, that is, in our immediate front. We were only opposed by very young troops, led by mature N.C.O.s. The battalion was much struck by the wanton devastation wrought by the enemy before retiring, who had not only destroyed houses, roads and railways, which, being of military value, was excusable, but had gone to the length of cutting down the apple and pear trees, and even the currant bushes. We came across numerous booby traps, some ingenious, but many very obvious. I saw one consisting of a live cat nailed to a board, which, had it been touched, would have exploded a bomb. An ingenious one was a nail sticking out of the wall of the stairs leading down into a dug-out. It was in such a position that anyone passing it was in danger of tearing his clothes. It was connected with a bomb which could have blown the dug-out to pieces. There was one dug-out that no one dared to enter. In it on a table, visible from the entrance, could be seen an attractive lunch displayed, a plate, knife and fork, a newly-cut ham, and a bottle of wine!*

We found that any house that appeared to be in a state of repair was mined with fuses set to ignite charges, in some cases as much as six weeks later. One house in which I spent three nights went skywards four days after I left.

Our advance led through Le Transloy, where I came across a tall tree lined with steel, an enemy observation post, in which I found a notice fixed bearing the words, 'You get a good view of Morval from here.' Later, we were occupying 1,200 yards of frontage in a wood, when we were ordered to carry out what I think was one of the most difficult manœuvres required of us during the war. The wood was so thick that one could hardly make one's way through it by day. We were ordered to advance 500 yards through it by night and change direction half-right. The operation was to commence at 7.30 p.m. and be completed by 10.30 p.m. At midnight I could hear nothing definite of my battalion and the majority of my messengers failed to return; however, as all was quiet I decided to report 'All's Well' and await the dawn. At dawn I found all four companies facing in different directions, one being almost back at the starting point facing rearwards. We got things in order in time to continue the advance later in the day. A day or two after this we obtained a good view of the famous Hindenburg Line, and the advance was at an end. During the advance I had had with me one man who had retired in the reverse direction over the same bit of country with the remnants of the 2nd Bn. in 1914. During my absence for a month, owing to an attack of fever, Maj. White commanded the battalion when it moved to the vicinity of Bourlon Wood; this had recently been the scene of some very hot fighting, but was now comparatively quiet. A few days after my return to duty the battalion was visited by Col. Basil Spragge, who accompanied me round our camp. Both officers and men much appreciated an unofficial visit of this kind from one of the old regular officers of the Regiment."

The 8th Bn.

The 8/K.O.Y.L.I. was now on duty in the Ypres sector, being, at the opening of the year, in corps reserve near Vlamertinghe, some three miles west of the city. Lt.-Col. T. H. Owen commanded, and he had Lt. E. B. B. Speed as adjutant. On the 23rd February, Lt.-Col. Imbert-Terry resumed command.

Among the 'Somme' honours Maj. G. L. Pyman and Capt. K. E. Poyser both received the D.S.O.

On the 23rd January a company of the 8th Bn. raided the enemy line at 9 p.m., after a short but very intense barrage. The enemy realised that the barrage would be followed by a raid and the trenches were vacated. No German prisoners were taken but the information that was collected was of value. The raiding party was perfectly timed and finely led; the enemy trenches were occupied for fifteen minutes under very heavy gun-fire.

The casualty list was heavy; all three officers concerned were wounded, namely, Capt. H. C. H. Bull, 2/Lts. H. A. Dinsdale and —. Horwood. Other ranks, eight killed, forty-nine wounded.

Capt. Bull and 2/Lt. Dinsdale received the M.C. Sgt. M. White was awarded the D.C.M.

On the 24th January Capt. M. G. Donahoo was mortally wounded.

The 9th and 10th Bns.

Some twenty miles to the north of Arras the 21st Div., in the VIII Corps, held its place in the line east of Béthune. In the early part of 1917 the 9/ and 10/K.O.Y.L.I. were occupied chiefly with their reorganisation and training after their splendid efforts in the Somme offensive. The 9th was at Nœux-les-Mines, and the 10th at Fouquereuil throughout the month of January; they were then moved by train to Esquelbecq, and by road to Ledringhem for more advanced training, and on the 13th February returned through Béthune to Annequin in order to take their turn in the line. This was the sloppy period of thaw and mud. The trenches were in a terrible state, reliefs were carried out under the worst conditions, and on occasions whole platoons would stick fast in the mud. On the 22nd February, Capt. C. R. F. Stanford, of the 9th Bn., was killed in the trenches by a stray bullet during relief, and on the 24th 2/Lt. R. A. Stokes, of the same battalion, met with a like fate.

Lt.-Col. C. H. Milward was now in command of the 9th Bn., and Lt.-Col. F. J. M. Postlethwaite commanded the 10th.

The 12th Bn.

The 12/K.O.Y.L.I. was still employed as Pioneer battalion in the 31st Div. under the command of Lt.-Col. E. L. Chambers. On the 11th January it marched from Sailly au Bois to Beauval, with a strength of 27 officers and 880 other ranks; from Beauval it moved to Bernaville on the 22nd, and again to Aveluy Wood on the 6th February to take over work on the roads. Later in the month it was employed under a Canadian construction company on making railways. The battalion was at Coigneux (near Hébuterne) in March till the 19th and then had several changes of camp.

At the German General Headquarters, a continuation of the British attack on the Somme, perhaps extending to the north, was expected, and that this would be accompanied by a simultaneous offensive on the part of the French, was within the calculations, but it was not foreseen where either blow would fall. Ludendorff writes: "*We had to be prepared to offer a stubborn resistance at any point along our whole front. It was impossible to tell what was going to happen.*" The initiative rested with the Allies.

SOME DAYS OF SUSPENSE.

On the other hand, by the end of March, 1917, on the British front, there was little that was obscure as to the location of the Hindenburg Line. In following up the retiring German troops between Arras and the Aisne, resistance tended, during those days of March, to grow increasingly formidable, and strong points were found to be more strongly held as the new line was approached, until it came to be realised by our leading brigades that they were up against a solid stone wall of opposition, fenced in by the familiar protection of barbed wire.

As the result of ceaseless activity in England and behind the lines during the winter months, there was a vast improvement in the quality and quantity of the equipment in guns, ammunition, and the new engines of war; tremendous expansion of the air services; a network of new railway lines, increased means of transport and advancement in all the technical services for use behind the fighting lines.

The scene was now set; the troops that were concentrated about Arras awaited the signal for the raising of the curtain with some impatience.

Imperial War Museum Photograph. Copyright Reserved

Battle of Arras, April, 1917. Men of a K.O.Y.L.I. Battalion at dinner in the ruins of Feuchy.

To face page 863.

THE BATTLES OF ARRAS AND THE SCARPE. 1917

XIV

THE chief part in the attack on the Arras front was assigned to the Third Army, commanded by Sir E. H. H. Allenby. The river Scarpe, which rises west of Arras, flows for some distance eastwards past the north of Arras, cutting through the British line. Of the five corps which made up the Third Army, the XVII operated north of the Scarpe, and the VI and VII were in the front line south of the river, while the XVIII and the Cavalry Corps were held in reserve. On the left of the Third Army the Canadian Corps and the 13th Bde. of the 5th Div., being portions of the First Army (Gen. Sir H. S. Horne), were directed to attack the Vimy heights and Thélus. Of the Fifth Army (Gen. Sir H. Gough), the Australian and the V Corps operated on the right of the Third Army.

The battle was designed to take place on a frontage of twelve miles, having Croisilles as the extreme southern boundary. South of this boundary the British troops had already advanced across the now abandoned Gommecourt salient, and the hardly-won Somme battle area. With the exception of some spasmodic efforts to clear away some remaining strong points of the enemy, such as at Savy and Fayet, the fighting south of Croisilles, as well as that north of Vimy ridge, was the normal activity of troops on either flank who fought to support the corps engaged in the Battle of Arras.

The 6th, 9th and 10th Bns. of the K.O.Y.L.I. were in the front line of battle in the Arras offensive. Within the period of the battle the 2/K.O.Y.L.I. also was heavily engaged in the affairs at Savy and Fayet, further down the line in the neighbourhood of St. Quentin.

Though the Battle of Arras proper may be said to have terminated in the middle of April, there was no sudden diminution of pressure in the Arras sector and its neighbourhood. Indeed, the wave of low pressure which was accompanied by the storm of early April was followed by 'secondaries' such as that of the 3rd May, when the 2/4th, 2/5th, 6th, 9th, 10th and 12th Bns. were among the troops that stormed the Hindenburg Line.

The 14th (Light) Div. fought in the VII Corps in the attack on the strong position of Telegraph Hill, which is some four miles south-east of Arras.

THE 6TH BN.

During the first week of April the 6/K.O.Y.L.I., with the remainder of the 43rd Inf. Bde., was preparing for the battle, and the battalion was billeted in Berneville; practice attacks were carried out on ground alongside the Arras-Doullens road against dummy trenches marked out to represent the first and second objectives in the advance. At night, assembly trenches were being dug to be occupied prior to the assault, to the east of Beaurains.

Maj. W. H. Micholls commanded the battalion temporarily in the absence of Lt.-Col. G. Meynell; the latter returned on the 8th May. Capt. E. G. Bartlett was adjutant.

In the night of the 7th April the battalion proceeded through Arras to the caves at Ronville, and remained in the caves until 8 p.m. on the 8th, when it took up its position in the assembly trenches. The silence in the caves, which muffled the roar of the guns engaged in a huge preliminary bombardment, together with the weird surroundings underground, added awe and mystery to the proceedings. Throughout the move and during the time the men were in the assembly trenches, such good discipline was maintained that (as was afterwards recorded) the enemy had no idea the assembly trenches were occupied until after the attack started. "A" Company of the 6/Som. L.I. had taken over the assembly trenches in advance and was then attached to the battalion for purposes of 'mopping up' in the attack.

From midnight till 3 in the morning of the 9th April, parties consisting of twenty men from each company crept forward to cut wire in front of the first objective. These parties were continuously sniped and a machine-gun was brought to bear on them. They suffered a few casualties, among them, 2/Lt. A. C. Churchill was wounded.

At 5.30 a.m. the attack commenced away to the north and gradually worked southwards to the region of the Scarpe until it became general.

At 7.15 six tanks reached the K.O.Y.L.I. trenches to co-operate with the infantry.

The 43rd Inf. Bde. was on the right, the 42nd on the left; the brigades of the 56th Div. attacked on the right of the 14th (Light) Div.

At 7.34 a.m., under an artillery barrage, the leading wave left the assembly trenches, "Y" Company on the left and "Z" on the right, supported by "W" and "X." Each company occupied a front of one platoon. The Som. L.I. company followed the second wave, while the 10/D.L.I. attacked simultaneously on the immediate left of the battalion.

The 12/London (Rangers) of the 56th Div. were directed to commence their attack at 8.12 as soon as these battalions had come level with their position on the southern slope of Telegraph Hill.

The first objective, Pine Trench, was taken at about 8 a.m. without difficulty, and with only slight casualties, about thirty-five prisoners being taken. After passing Pine Trench companies deployed to the right to cover a company front of two platoons, the right following the line of the NeuvilleVitasse-St. Sauveur road, and proceeded to the attack of Fir Alley Redoubt. This was a triangular system of strong deep trenches, very heavily wired. The defences had not been much damaged by the bombardment; however, under cover of our barrage, and with the assistance of the three tanks, the men were able to penetrate the wire and to capture the redoubt. The enemy put up a moderate resistance only and left about twenty-five prisoners to be taken, a few others being taken out of a dug-out afterwards. One heavy trench mortar and two machine-guns were captured; by 8.15 the redoubt was in the hands of the 6/K.O.Y.L.I.

Two platoons were left behind to consolidate while the remainder of the battalion, following the lifts of the barrage, proceeded to the attack of Telegraph Hill trench, a further sidestep to the right being required to bring the battalion on to the new objective. At this point there was a wide gap between the right of the battalion and the left of the 56th Div., the gap being further increased when, after leaving Fir Alley Redoubt, a slight swing was made to the left which involved the battalion left with the right of the D.L.I.

Some casualties were suffered during this advance owing to machine-gun and shell-fire.

Telegraph Hill trench was taken at about 8.40 a.m. in the face of a moderate resistance; about fifteen of the enemy remained to become prisoners.

Two platoons were again left in this line and the rest went on to the capture of the Cojeul Switch trench. Both this and Telegraph Hill trench formed part of the Hindenburg Line, and each consisted of a very deep and wide trench with a few deep dug-outs (mostly in course of construction) and was well provided with communicating trenches.

The Cojeul Switch was taken at about 8.50 a.m. with thirty-five prisoners. Touch with the Rangers had now been lost and the enemy in the untouched portion of Telegraph Hill trench gave some trouble, until a bombing attack drove them back 100 yards or so, when a strong post and a block were established with two Lewis-guns.

At 1.30 p.m. the enemy attempted a counter-attack on this flank but were driven off with loss. At 2.30 2/Lt. K. H. Coulson went into Neuville Vitasse and procured two companies of London Scottish and some London Rangers, and an attack was organised on the portion of the line between the right of the 6/K.O.Y.L.I. and the 56th Division. This attack was successful and the enemy here were driven out of the Hindenburg Line. Consolidation then continued without further interference.

About 12.30 p.m. the 6/Som. L.I. had passed through to the attack of the Wancourt line, but owing to the fact that the 56th Div. was not yet up, for they had met with very severe resistance, the

Som. L.I. battalion was unable to reach its objectives, and had to be content with holding on to a position about 1,000 yards east of the Cojeul Switch.

The following morning (10th April) at about 10.20, orders reached the battalion to attack the Wancourt line at noon. This attack was conducted as on the day previous, with the D.L.I. on the left of the 6/K.O.Y.L.I. and the 56th Div. on the right. Our artillery covered the advance with a creeping barrage. The advance of the 56th Div. was delayed by the amount of opposition it encountered; the Wancourt line was found to be very heavily wired, and the wire was mostly undamaged, so that the men had to cut gaps through it under fire. However, the trench was carried at 1.30 p.m. and the 6/K.O.Y.L.I. made thirty prisoners. Enfilade fire from the right continued for some time, causing casualties, especially where men were waiting in shell-holes outside the wire before they could get into the trench.

At 2.30 the enemy were observed to be leaving Wancourt and moving to higher ground towards the right front.

At 3 p.m. the 56th Div. moved against this high ground and cleared it.

About 4.30 p.m. the 41st Inf. Bde. came in to relieve the front line troops, shortly followed by the 5th Cav. Bde. to the left of the 41st Bde. After the relief the 6/K.O.Y.L.I. returned to the old British front line.

The casualties in the battalion during the two days' fighting had been:—Killed, 2/Lts. A. H. Loxley and J. F. W. Lord; other ranks, 26. Wounded, 2/Lts. H. D. Liversedge, A. Rhode, R. B. Nicholson, A. S. Newborn and C. Pickering; other ranks, 126. Missing, other ranks, 7.

Next day the battalion was relieved in the line by the 5/Border, and marched to Agnez les Duisens by night in a blizzard. By the 14th April it had marched to Sus St. Leger, where it was reorganised, and on the 27th it marched to Ronville.

Maj.-Gen. V. Cooper, commanding the 14th (Light) Div., issued the following complimentary order on the 10th April: "*The Commander-in-Chief has personally requested me to convey to all ranks of the 14th (Light) Div. his high opinion of the excellent fighting qualities shown by the division. The commencement of the great offensive of 1917 has been marked by an initial success in which more than 11,000 prisoners and 100 guns have been taken on the first day alone. The division has taken a prominent part in the achievement of this success and has maintained the reputation gained last year on the Somme and added to the laurels of the gallant regiments of which it is composed.*"

On the 2nd May the battalion moved back into the Cojeul Switch. Before dawn on the 3rd there was a general attack by the First, Third and Fifth Armies. The 43rd Inf. Bde. was in reserve, while the 41st and 42nd were in the first line. The 6/K.O.Y.L.I. moved up from the Cojeul Switch to a line of trenches west of Wancourt as soon as the 6/D.C.L.I. vacated that position at 5 a.m., and it remained there during the attack. Both the 41st and 42nd Brigades reached their objectives, but eventually had to retire in the evening to their old front line as the 56th Div. on their left and the 18th Div. on their right were unable to take their objectives. During the night of the 4-5th May, the 43rd Inf. Bde. relieved the others in the front line and remained in occupation of the trenches till the night of the 14th, when the 7/K.R.R.C. relieved the 6/K.O.Y.L.I.

Though there had been no further infantry action during this period, shell-fire accounted for seventy-four casualties in the battalion between the 4th and the 14th May. Among the number 2/Lts. S. J. E. Callcott (7th May), C. J. Morton (13th May), and C. F. Hadfield (14th May), were wounded; the latter had been twenty-two hours only in the line before he got his wound.

On the 9th May Lt.-Col. G. Meynell, who had returned to the battalion the day before, was wounded, but after inoculation at the field ambulance he returned at once to duty.

On the 13th June the 43rd Inf. Bde moved to Monchiet and on to Bus-les-Artois by the 17th for training and organising, where it remained for some weeks to come.

THE 9TH AND 10TH BNS.

Only three or four miles south of Telegraph Hill, where the 6th Bn. was attacking, the 9th and 10th Bns. went into the fight on the morning of the 9th April, their brigade, the 64th, being on the extreme right of the VII Corps. For some days both battalions had been practising attacks near Boisleux-au-mont, on the Cojeul river, for an assault on the Hindenburg Line.

Two days before the assault they went forward into the trenches from which the attack was to be delivered. In full daylight on the 7th, at about 3 p.m., under the protection of our bombardment, which was heavy at the time, and covered by a Lewis-gun in the hands of 2/Lt. A. W. Hobbs of the 10/K.O.Y.L.I., a close reconnaissance was made of the Hindenburg Line by C.S.M. J. W. Gill and Cpl. A. Hammond. After creeping 1,500 yards to the wire, and all along it, they brought back valuable information of the effect of our gun-fire. C.S.M. Gill for this and previous instances of coolness and bravery, was awarded the D.C.M.; Cpl. Hammond received the M.M. Unhappily, 2/Lt. Hobbs was killed two days later.

In the assault of the 9th April, which was made in the afternoon, the 9th Bn. was the left of the brigade in the front line, while the 10th Bn. was in brigade reserve at first. The objectives were positions in the Hindenburg Line about the Hénin-Héninel road. The artillery preparation had been insufficient to cut the wire thoroughly in front of the 9th Bn.; however, the companies in the first wave managed to get through the gaps in the case of the first objective, which was taken; the wire covering the second was impenetrable, and here there was a severe check; heavy losses were incurred while endeavouring to find and to cut gaps; both the companies of the second wave, which had passed through the first, had lost their leaders; an endeavour was made to blow a passage with Stokes mortars, but the officer with them was wounded and but little damage was done to the wire. When Lt.-Col. Daniell went forward at 6 p.m. he found most of his men established in shell-holes in front of the wire. The men were gradually withdrawn to consolidate the first position which was immediately south of Héninel.

Shortly after dusk the 10th Bn. arrived to reinforce. 2/Lt. R. H. Box, who had, during the afternoon, been most useful in visiting and reporting on the whole of the front, again did admirable work in collecting wounded after dark from the exposed ground outside and from the enemy wire. This was very essential as the position was to be bombarded by our guns again the following day.

"B" and "D" Companies of the 10th Bn. in support had, meanwhile, been digging new trenches just behind the sunken road where Lt.-Col. Postlethwaite had made his headquarters. Under the personal supervision of Maj. A. T. Shakespear, R.E., the 126th Fd. Coy., R.E., with the 14/N.F. Pioneers, worked at this new trench and by 3.30 a.m. on the 10th this position was ready for occupation and a new communication trench joining up with the front line, which had been the German front line, was established.

In the night the men of the 9th Bn. were ordered to fall back to the line of the sunken road, and the forward line was occupied by the 10/K.O.Y.L.I. with the 15/D.L.I. and the 1/E. York. "C" Company, 10/K.O.Y.L.I., held the left of the forward position; as this position was actually in the enemy's line, the extreme left flank was held by a bombers' block. This block had to be held at all costs or the enemy's bombers could have penetrated our front trench.

Two very strenuous counter-attacks were delivered in the morning of the 10th April, the first at 8 a.m., but they were beaten off with notable loss to the enemy. The attacks of the enemy bombers against the block were, however, continuous, and it was here that Pte. H. Waller, of the 10/K.O.Y.L.I., so greatly distinguished himself; his little party was gradually reduced in numbers till finally he was left to hold his important position single-handed; this he did successfully, keeping the enemy at bay alone for half an hour, in spite of his wounds. Finally, he was killed. The V.C. was awarded to him posthumously.

On the evening of the 10th the forward position had temporarily to be given up and the 64th Inf. Bde. was then relieved, but burial and salvage parties were sent up by the battalions, and many of their wounded were recovered during the night. While these parties were working and searching in the deep snow for their comrades they made the discovery that the enemy had evacuated the position ahead; thus, the line for which they had fought so hard in the last two days was finally won.

The casualties in the 9/K.O.Y.L.I. in the two days' fighting amounted to:—Officers killed, 3; wounded, 5; other ranks killed, 26 wounded, 99, missing, 49. The officers were: killed, Capt. A. G. Spark, 2/Lts. R. R. Akrill Jones and S. Harvey (4/N. Staffs., attd.); wounded, Lt. J. P. Shaw, 2/Ltd. W. E. Crick, A. C. Lupton and G. E. Matthews; Rev. A. Bouchier, C.F.

Twelve officers and 550 other ranks had taken part in the assault.

In the 10/K.O.Y.L.I. 2/Lt. A. W. Hobbs and 2/Lt. V. H. Wiseman were killed; 2/Lts. P. J. O. Morris, E. B. Yardley and H. E. Sharp were wounded. Of other ranks there were 10 killed, 54 wounded, 36 missing.

After recuperating at Blaireville for a few days the 64th Inf. Bde. moved to Boyelles just south of the Cojeul.

When the Third Army made a renewed attack on the Hindenburg Line on the 3rd May, the 9th and 10th Bns. were both engaged, but were in the second line of their brigade. No permanent gain of ground was made in their part of the line, though advances were achieved in northern sectors of the attack.

THE 12TH BN.

The 12/K.O.Y.L.I. (Pioneers) since the 2nd April had had its headquarters at Bray for work on the Fond du Vase railway. Here at midnight, the 30th April, the battalion received a summons to come up into the line in order to take part in the operations of the First and Third Armies.

The 31st Div. on the 3rd May attacked the Oppy-Gavrelle line with the 2nd Div. on its left and the 9th Div. (of the XVII Corps) on its right. On the divisional front the 92nd Inf. Bde. with one battalion of the 94th Inf. Bde., was the left of the attack, while the 93rd with another battalion of the 94th, was on the right; Oppy Wood and village were opposite the 92nd Inf. Bde.

"B" and "D" Companies of the 12/K.O.Y.L.I. were attached to the left brigade for work on trenches; the other two went to the 93rd Bde.

In pioneer trench making and in close support of the advancing line, the battalion bore its full share of the strenuous work of the offensive. The 31st Div. was relieved in the front line on the 18th May by the 63rd Div.

In the period the 12th Bn. had thirty-three casualties in other ranks, including Sgts. W. G. Macdonald (mentioned in dispatches) and N. Gomershall among the killed; while Capt. R. E. England, Lt. G. Walker and 2/Lts. J. M. Reynolds and O. B. Wilson, were wounded.

Lt.-Col. E. L. Chambers was in command, Capt. W. Cooper, adjutant, and the four company commanders who went into action were Capts. G. M. Stockings, D. E. Roberts, W. H. Roberts and H. F. Chadwick.

The battalion then returned to its work on the railways.

By the end of March the 2/K.O.Y.L.I. had reached the extreme south of the British line near the point of junction with the French in the neighbourhood of St. Quentin. The battalion now formed part of the Fourth Army (Gen. Sir H. Rawlinson), which consisted of the XV and III Corps. The 32nd Div. was in the latter and was now commanded by Maj.-Gen. Hon. A. R. Montagu-Stuart-Wortley. The French were engaged in what proved to be an unsuccessful attack on St. Quentin.

THE 2ND BN. AT SAVY AND FAYET.

Orders had been received on the 31st March for the 97th Inf. Bde. to capture Savy in the morning of the 1st April. At night the 2/K.O.Y.L.I. moved to a position north-west of Roupy by the Château de Pommery, where it was in brigade reserve; it dug itself in about the railway line between Douchy and Fluquières.

The 11/Border and the 17/H.L.I. attacked and captured Savy in the early morning in accordance with their orders, followed by the 2/K.O.Y.L.I. in support. An advance of 5,000 yards was made. The casualties in the battalion amounted to two other ranks killed and eight wounded. The weather was very severe, storms of snow and sleet falling throughout the day.

The battalion was now placed at the disposal of the 14th Inf. Bde. to attack (2nd April) the northern edge of the Bois d'Holnon from the east; meanwhile, the 14th Inf. Bde. itself was to attack the villages Francilly-Selency and Holnon, starting at 5 a.m. In abominable weather the advance was made successfully; the Bois d'Holnon was occupied, the enemy had retired. In the evening the 2/K.O.Y.L.I. left the northern edge of the wood and marched *via* Holnon to Francilly-Selency, arriving in their bivouac there by 11.30 p.m., being in a position of readiness to support either the 14th or the 96th Inf. Bde. if called upon. The men were engaged all the next day in digging a support line trench; at 4.30 p.m. an enemy aeroplane appeared when they were at work and dropped three bombs among them with disastrous effect, for the battalion had seventeen men killed and thirty wounded. The battalion had to move its quarters to a railway cutting in order to avoid the inevitable shelling which followed the discovery of their position. With grim satisfaction the men were in a position to watch the effect of a heavy bombardment of their old bivouac, which was delivered between the hours of 4 and 6.15 in the morning of the 4th April.

On the 7th the battalion relieved the 1/Dorset in the line to the east of Holnon and Selency. From the new position St. Quentin could be seen plainly two miles distant. At 10 p.m. that night the battalion attacked, led by "B" Company under Capt. J. W. Woods, which went over the top 'as one man' and stormed an enemy position; the enemy made a hurried retirement from this, his rearguard post; the captured position was consolidated and listening posts were sent forward.

On the 8th April, while accompanying the O.C. Bn. round the new position, Capt. G. A. Gamble was wounded; Capt. L. R. McDougall was killed by a shell in Holnon; he was in command of the Trench Mortar Battery.

The battalion was withdrawn for a short rest on the 9th to Auroir, by way of Savy, Vaux, etc.; snow fell; the men were exhausted by the trying weather and the constant hard work of the week. The divisional commander visited the battalion and thanked the men for their good work.

The attack on Fayet, a village west of St. Quentin, was made by the 97th Inf. Bde. on the 14th April; the battalion had marched back from Auroir to Holnon to take up assaulting formation on a tape line the previous evening. The advance was timed for 4.15 a.m. In the front line the 2/K.O.Y.L.I. was on the left, the 16/H.L.I. on the right. Of the former, "A" Company was left attack, "B" Company was right; "D" supported "A," and "C" supported "B." There were two objectives given. All the available artillery was concentrated to support the attack.

The officers of the 2/K.O.Y.L.I. who took part in this attack were:—

Headquarters, Lt.-Col. C. R. Ingham Brooke, commanding, Major E. H. Rigg, senior major, Lt. H. S. Howard (adjutant), 2/Lt. A. O. Purdon (Intelligence Officer), and Lt. R. H. Jackson (Signalling Officer). "A" Company, Capt. G. H. Staveley, 2/Lts. S. J. G. Dibblee, F. Underwood and C. P. Halliday. "B" Company, Capt. J. W. Woods, 2/Lts. J. F. Cadman, W. J. Pickering and C. E. Seaman. "C" Company, 2/Lts. F. Johnson, C. R. Brutey, V. G. Ballard and E. E. E. Cass. "D" Company, 2/Lts. A. F. White, M. W. Richmond and J. G. Kennedy.

At 4.30 a.m. the companies advanced against their first objective; on the left "A" met with little opposition and arrived at a sunken road leading from Fayet to Fresnoy-le-Petit by 5 a.m., being closely followed by "D." There were several dug-outs in the line, the occupants of which were either killed or captured; forty prisoners were sent back to the rear. At 5.20 a.m. "A" Company re-formed and moved forward. As the company went over the bank of the sunken road Capt. Staveley was killed and 2/Lt. Dibblee assumed command in his place. The advance was considerably impeded by wire and machine-gun fire; "D" Company was close up, rather to the right of "A."

On the right of "A" the village of Fayet was captured by "B" Company, who cleared the dug-outs and sent back many prisoners. Assisted by the barrage put down by our guns, the company then headed for the second objective, which also was carried by 5.30 a.m. "C" Company had come up on the left of "B" as the two leading companies had appeared to be drawing apart, but in spite of this "B" Company had now lost touch with both "A" and "C." The opportunity for counter-attack was not wasted on the enemy, who struck a shrewd blow and turned the unsupported flank of "B." The company experienced many casualties and Capt. Woods was killed; it was forced to give ground a little; a new line facing east was held, and here, with the aid of two Lewis-guns, the enemy was held.

Meanwhile, "C" Company had attacked and gained (at 6 a.m.) the second objective line between the two leading companies which had drawn apart. "C" Company was in touch with "D" Company on its left. At 6.40 "C" had to repel a counter, and, finding that their new position was being badly enfiladed, the commanders of "C" and "D" conferred and agreed to withdraw to a better position a short distance in the rear.

"A" Company also conformed in order to form a solid offensive and defensive line. So, by 9 a.m. these three companies were in line along the Fayet-Fresnoy le Petit road, facing about north-east.

"A" Company of the 17/H.L.I., ever watchful to assist, came in on the right of "C" and filled the existing gap, thus bringing all companies of the 2/K.O.Y.L.I. into line. However, "B" Company, which was in the Château grounds, had its hands full and could not participate in the next advance which was carried out by the other three, who awaited the result of an attack by the 11/Border on its own objective, the Twin Copses. As soon as this battalion had gained its objective, the three K.O.Y.L.I. companies advanced once more, with the faithful company of the 17/H.L.I. supporting them and protecting them from counter-attack from their right flank. This advance was made at 1.50 p.m. under cover of an artillery barrage. By 2.15 p.m. the companies were in possession of a new line, having the right flank still protected by two platoons of the H.L.I. for the time being. At 2.30 p.m. 2/Lt. Pickering, the sole remaining officer of "B," found it possible to conform, and decided to advance his company to its place in line. At the outset he was wounded and Sgt. Ormsby took command. The advance was successfully carried out and a position was consolidated in line with the other companies. The whole battalion, now in line, dug away furiously under the fire of the enemy's rifles and machine-guns.

At 9.30 p.m. the whole battalion advanced yet again and took up a further position, which brought the left flank in close touch with the 11/Border, while the right rested on the 17/H.L.I.

Quoting the words of the O.C. 2/K.O.Y.L.I., written in the battalion diary at this date: "*This narrative would be incomplete without an acknowledgment of the admirable support provided by the companies of the 17/H.L.I. placed at my disposal. Under the command of Capt. Dobson, these companies of the 17/H.L.I. not only supported the battalion, but in every emergency filled in all gaps between my companies in the front line.*"

At 9.30 p.m. on the 15th April, the battalion was relieved in the front line by the 16/Lan. Fus. of the 96th Inf. Bde., and it retired to billets in Beauvois.

The casualties on the 14th April had been: Officers, Capts. G. H. Staveley and J. W. Woods, killed; 2/Lts. Underwood, Cadman, W. J. Pickering, C. E. Seaman, Johnson and A. F. White, wounded; other ranks, 36 killed, 69 wounded, and 14 missing.

Military medals were awarded for the action of the 1st April to Lce./Cpl. J. A. Auty, "C" Company, and Pte. R. Goward, "B" Company, for conspicuous bravery. For their services on the 14th a long list of awards was published, including the names of 2/Lt. Pickering (M.C.), who led his company till wounded in three places and then had himself carried to Bn. Headquarters, in spite of his pain, in order to explain the situation; to 2/Lt. C. P. Halliday (M.C.), for skilful leading and "services of the utmost value" when the final objective was reached; to Sgt. S. E. Andrews, "B" Company, for his "inspiring leading" and handling his Lewis-guns in a masterful manner throughout the operations (D.C.M.). Also twelve Military Medals were granted to N.C.O.s and men of the battalion.

On the 19th April the battalion was withdrawn to Voyennes for re-formation and training. The weather had become fine and sports were held on the 29th. Maj. E. H. Rigg left on the 13th May to take command of the 2/Inniskg. At the close of the month of May, the battalion was transferred to the XIV Corps (Lt.-Gen. Lord Cavan), and proceeded by train northwards, arriving in billets near Doulieu on the 2nd June.

On the 10th April, when the 4/K.O.Y.L.I. was in the Neuve Chapelle sector, a raid on the enemy's trenches was carried out by "Y" Company, which had for its objectives (i) to obtain identifications; (ii) to inflict casualties; and (iii) to bring back machine-guns and destroy their emplacement.

4TH BN.
CAPT. MOORHOUSE'S RAID.

The party was under the command of Capt. R. W. Moorhouse, and it consisted of 4 officers and 87 other ranks, with flanking parties in addition; four sappers were also attached from No. 456 Company R.E.

The party blackened their faces and were fitted with body shields.

At 10.25 p.m. our barrage opened. The enemy sent up S.O.S. signals all along their line. Under cover of the barrage the company advanced; on reaching the enemy parapet it was discovered that the trenches had been vacated in order to leave a clear field for the counter-barrage, which immediately ensued. The trenches were deep in water and were filled with barbed wire. The enemy's machine-gun emplacement was duly destroyed, but the gun had been withdrawn previously. A few men jumped down into the trench, only to become at once caught in the barbed wire; the task of extracting them was no easy matter, and a few casualties occurred during the process.

The withdrawal was conducted with great precision, and great credit was given to Capt. Moorhouse, who was wounded, for the manner in which the raid was conducted from start to finish, though the results were not material. He was ably assisted by Capt. G. A. McG. Ricketts (Scout Officer) and 2/Lt. D. G. Horsfield; 2/Lt. H. Scholefield was wounded on reaching the enemy wire.

In other ranks 6 were killed and 11 wounded, including two of the R.E.

Lce./Sgt. F. Hatton was awarded the M.M. and five gallantry cards were issued.

The 62nd Div. received orders to attack the Hindenburg Line at Bullecourt, in co-operation with the Third Army on its left and the 2nd Australian Div. on the right, the attack to be launched at 3.45 a.m. on the 3rd May. Thus the 187th Inf. Bde., which included the 2/4th and 2/5th Bns. K.O.Y.L.I., entered on its first important attack.

THE 2/4TH AND 2/5TH BNS.

By 1.45 a.m. the brigade was in readiness in attack formation between the railway cutting and the front line of posts. At the "Zero" hour our artillery barrage descended at once on the enemy trenches. The 2/5th Bn. was in the front line, and with it went "A" and "B" Companies of the 2/4th, who were attached for the operations. The 2/4th Bn. Headquarters, with the remaining companies, were moved to St. Leger Wood.

The night was pitch dark and a strong wind blew the smoke and the dust of the barrage back in the faces of the attacking troops. It became most difficult to keep direction, and there was consequent confusion when the enemy front line was reached. In places the wire had not been cut by the gun-fire, and masses of men were moving laterally to find a passage where the wire was cut. Into the scene of confusion went Lt.-Col. W. Watson, already severely wounded, to rally his men and lead them through; with the help of other officers he restored order and re-organised the advance, seeking to carry the trenches by weight of numbers. He was killed at about 4.20 a.m. and most of the officers near him became casualties. With the loss of the gallant leader the attack again became disorganised.* Small parties reached the front line trenches but failed to make headway.

At about 8.30 a second attack was attempted by Maj. O. C. S. Watson with a force which he had rallied from the carrying parties and details of all units of the brigade. Maj. Watson was severely wounded; the men succeeded in reaching the enemy wire but were held up by machine-gun fire and occupied a line of shell-holes opposite the trenches for the remainder of the day. At about 8 p.m. a withdrawal was carried out to the original line, but Maj. Watson was not brought in till dusk the following day. The 2/4th Bn. re-established its headquarters in the railway cutting and took over the brigade front from the 2/4th Y. and L.

The attack, in which so many divisions participated, thus ended in failure, not only on the front of the 187th Inf. Bde., but on all points of attack.

Maj. (actg. Lt.-Col.) R. E. Power was in command of the 2/4th Bn., and Maj. F. Mellor assumed command of the 2/5th, with 2/Lt. C. H. Webb acting as his adjutant.

The casualties had been heavy. The 2/4th Bn. lost: Officers, killed, 2/Lt. M. O. Walsh; wounded, Capts. N. Lee and A. L. Pyrah; Lt. A. R. Mosley, 2/Lts. C. A. Ireland, W. B. Diver, J. E. V. Hill, T. R. P. Butcher, G. N. Smith and C. H. Johnson; other ranks, 11 killed, 94 wounded, 15 missing.

* *Lt.-Col. William Watson, born 17th June, 1880, at Hedon, near Hull, entered the Som. L.I. in India. He went to France with his regiment in the first Expeditionary Force, and was in the retreat from Mons. He was at this period twice mentioned in dispatches, and early in 1915 was promoted Brevet Major. Being wounded near Ypres in June, 1915, when in command of his battalion, he was invalided home. He returned to France in January, 1917, as Lt.-Col. commanding 2/5th K.O.Y.L.I. In the "London Gazette" of 1st June, 1917, he was again mentioned in dispatches for gallant and distinguished service in the field. After the war at a regimental dinner of the Som. L.I. on 3rd June, 1920, Lt.-Gen. Sir Walter Braithwaite, in speaking of Lt.-Col. W. Watson, said that "he went into the open in full view of the enemy under very heavy fire, and was killed while making a heroic effort to put things straight."*

The 2/5th Bn. had the following casualties: Officers, killed, Lt.-Col. W. Watson, Lt. E. P. Pattinson, 2/Lts. B. S. Brewster (Norfolk R., attd.) and F. A. Moorcock; wounded, Capts. S. S. Chappell, T. W. Mottram and W. J. Oswald ("H" Cyclists Bn., attd)., Lt. and Adjt. A. Robinson, Lts. C. C. Snow, E. R. Woodrooffe and J. L. Summers; other ranks, killed 35, wounded 156, missing 69.

2/Lt. P. Holroyd was killed by shell-fire also on the 5th May when in support.

In the Battle of Arras, which had commenced on the 9th April and had lasted for a week, Sir Douglas Haig had attained the objects which he had set out to attain in order to assist the French offensive on the Aisne. In the constant fighting which ensued up till the end of May, though the losses were great and the results limited, the increased forces of the enemy were kept pinned to this front, and though the operations were devoid of spectacular successes, the same object was all the time being relentlessly pursued.

OPERATIONS AFTER THE BATTLE OF ARRAS. 1917

XV

THE Battle of Arras had given the British the command of the Vimy position. This success was followed by that in the Battle of Messines on the 7th June, when Gen. Sir Herbert Plumer with the Second Army, after long preparation and mining of the enemy position, scored a brilliant success and established his line on the far side of the Messines ridge.

No battalion of the K.O.Y.L.I. was greatly involved in the battle, but, as we have seen, the 2nd Bn. had been brought temporarily into this part of the line on the 2nd June. The 32nd Div. was in general headquarter reserve to the force which captured the Messines-Wytschaete ridge. The services of the division were not required in the fighting line.

During the short stay of the 2nd Bn. in this area, a succession of gratifying awards and incidents occurred; it was notified that Capt. M. H. Garrard and Capt. L. H. W. Iredale, R.A.M.C. (attd.), had received the M.C. in the King's Birthday Honours list; also the battalion was congratulated on the high standard of efficiency attained by their signallers and on it continuing to be 'the best signalling battalion in the division'; and a letter dated "*War Office, June* 8th, 1917," notified it that "*The King has been graciously pleased to approve the award of the V.C. to the following N.C.O.:*

No. 1836, *Sgt. John William Ormsby,* 2/*K.O.Y.L.I., for most conspicuous bravery and devotion to duty during operations which culminated in the capture of an important position on the* 14*th April.*"

The V.C. was pinned to Sgt. Ormsby's breast (11th June) by the Divisional Commander, Maj.-Gen. Hon. A. R. Montagu-Stuart-Wortley, who made the interesting announcement at the same time that another V.C. was awarded in the Regiment by the same gazette (posthumously), to the late Pte. H. Waller of the 10th Bn. The story of Pte. Waller's devoted services has already been told in the preceding chapter; he had been well known in the 2nd Bn. in which he had served for fifteen months on active service, and in which he had been wounded on the Somme in 1916.

Lt.-Col. Ingham Brooke presented a cup to the Sergeants' Mess, to be called the Ormsby Cup, to be competed for annually by sergeants of the battalion as a musketry trophy.

Lt.-Col. C. C. Moxon came over from Neuve Chapelle to the presentation with a concert party of the 5th Bn., who entertained their brethren of the 2nd Bn. with a capital entertainment.

Throughout this period a vast reshuffling of the forces on the western front was going on. It was due to this reorganisation that we have seen the 2/K.O.Y.L.I. fighting in the neighbourhood of St. Quentin early in April, transferred to the Messines area early in May, and now, in the middle of June, again under orders to move northward to the coast.

On the 14th June it became known that the 32nd Div. was being transferred from the XIV to the XV Corps, in the Fourth Army (Rawlinson), to hold the Dunkerque area. Hitherto, for some months, the armies had faced eastwards (commencing from the left) in the order: Belgians, (British) Second, First, Third, Fifth, Fourth Armies, up to the left of the main French armies. Henceforth till the end of the year they would stand with the British Fourth Army on the left by the sea, then the Belgians, with a newly-interpolated French Army on their right, then the British Fifth Army in the Ypres area; then the Second, First and Third Armies (in that order).

The same day the battalion marched, in hot and sunny weather, to Eecke; on the 15th to Steenvoorde, where it was met by 'bus transport and conveyed to St. Pol-sur-mer. When marching the last stage, owing to the fine white dust on the road, the men assumed the appearance of a battalion of millers, causing great amusement to the inhabitants.

That the German General Headquarters appreciated the significance of the movements in the British armies in France, soon became evident. Ludendorff (*vide* his *War Memories*) felt the magnitude of the loss of the Wytschaete salient, for, as he writes, "*as long as it remained in German hands every British attack at Ypres and to the north of that town, was outflanked from the south.*" He noted, too, that the British army did not press its advantage, and, apparently, only intended to improve its position for the launching of the great Flanders offensive. There followed a great strengthening of German forces to resist any attempt on the part of the British to advance along the coast, and a great concentration of guns, which was used, incidentally, to destroy the bridgehead on the right bank of the Yser, at its mouth in the neighbourhood of Nieuport.

THE 2ND BN. AT NIEUPORT

Under the new British arrangement Gen. Strickland's 1st Div. held the extreme left of the British line from the sea to Lombartzyde, a frontage of 1,400 yards; the 32nd Div. held the next sector to the right or south. The River Yser, running northwards into the sea, was the line held, but the town of Nieuport, being close up to the river, battalions of each division were pushed across the river and held a line of trenches on the eastern side some 600 yards from the river, which could be crossed only by floating bridges.

The position of the battalions on the far side was obviously very precarious should the Germans make a determined effort to destroy them; the position was not of their choosing, but was that recently taken over from the French troops who had been relieved. The Germans made their effort on the 10th July. If the number of guns employed, as represented in Conan Doyle's account (*viz.*, 182 German batteries against 13 British batteries) is approximately correct, the affair may be compared to the use of a hydraulic steel hammer to crack a nut! It was no great strategic victory for the Germans; its military consequences were not far reaching, and the effect was merely local, but it was reported in the German press as a notable victory, and, as the German people were in need of a stimulant, the affair of Nieuport was paraded to counterbalance the loss of the Wytschaete Ridge.

Ludendorff (*My War Memories*, page, 431, Vol. II) dismisses the action in a few words, nor is he accurate in these, for the clarity of his vision appears often to become obscured when a British incident enters into the picture; he writes, "*On the front of the 4th Army the British had been established ever since 1914 in a narrow bridgehead close to the coast, on the right bank of the Yser. This point had always been the Naval Corps' weak spot. The 4th Army, which was supported by this Corps, received permission to take this bridgehead. The attack took place on July 10th, and was successful. The Yser effectively prevented all enemy counter-attacks.*"

Let us now view the action from the opposite side of the Yser, from the point of view of the defenders of the river bank. To the battalions in the post of danger, notably to the 2/K.R.R.C., next the sea, and to the 1/Northamptons on their right, who represented the 1st Div., the overwhelming storm of projectiles and shells of all calibres was a sudden and dire calamity. From the outset these battalions were effectively isolated, the floating bridges behind them were obliterated and communication was cut off. There is a brook running parallel with the coastline which meets the Yser at right angles just east of Nieuport; this brook was the dividing line between the troops of the 1st and 32nd Divs.; the trenches occupied by the Rifles and Northamptons were unprovided with dug-outs, for they were constructed in the sand dunes which filled the interval between the sea and the canal. The battalions, without any means of retaliation, simply endured the devastating shell-fire and the attacks by low-flying aeroplanes till they were practically destroyed.

The comparatively humble part played in this tragedy by a battalion of the K.O.Y.L.I. will be overlooked in history if it is not proclaimed in these chronicles of the Regiment.

From St. Pol-sur-mer, where the battalion enjoyed a short rest and the 97th Inf. Bde. was in the divisional reserve, the 2/K.O.Y.L.I. moved into the front line on the 25th June in the Lombartzyde sector, 'recently taken over from the French.' On the 1st July the battalion was withdrawn from the trenches on the east side of the Yser into billets in Nieuport. Fortunately for the historian, it had become traditional in this battalion for the adjutants to keep accurate and illuminating diaries of the events of the war, and the diary of this period was no exception to the rule.

The men were, in all cases, accommodated in house cellars. Many of these cellars contained wire beds which had been fixed in by the French troops; they formed comfortable, if dark, quarters. Nieuport was, at this time, daily shelled by the enemy, and the little town was in a state of ruin. On the east side of the town the stagnant Canal de Dunkerque reeked unwholesomely. Along the centre of several of the streets communication trenches had been constructed for the passage of troops, and these had been covered with sandbags and camouflaged with earth on which grass was growing luxuriantly. The streets were cobbled, but grass-grown also, and pitted with shell-holes; some of the streets were hardly distinguishable as such from the ruins caused by the shells of the enemy; grass grew freely over all débris. Here and there a roof was delicately balanced on the surviving bricks of a burst-in wall; here a street lamp-post, distorted by impact, appeared to be wriggling out of the way of further shells, there a noble town pump, painted a gorgeous blue, stood up unscathed.

Battalion Headquarters were accommodated in the cellars of the Nieuport Hotel. On the rails near the station was a long screen on which the picture of a train was painted (by a French artist?), and a real old locomotive stood on the lines at its head. Now it is handed down to us in history as a crowning triumph of realism in pictorial art that, in the days of the ancient Greeks, the artist Apelles achieved an equestrian portrait of Alexander the Great, which was so lifelike that, when the picture was displayed, Alexander's charger, mistaking the horse in the picture for a rival, advanced neighing and with a ferocious air to attack it. It is also related that Alexander expressed disapproval of the picture, but, as Apelles is said to have remarked, that proved nothing except that the horse was a better judge than his master! This story has been resuscitated in order to compare the value of the art of the ancient artists with that of the modern, for it is noted in the diary that the German observers were deceived by the painted screen, and that "*the number of shells expended by the enemy on our train was quite incalculable.*" Witty Tommy Atkins christened this the 'Leave Train,' partly, no doubt, in derision because it didn't, and partly, perhaps, because in his hectic surroundings it pleased him to jest about so sacred a subject as Leave.

Perhaps the strangest billet in the town was that taken up by No. 13 platoon of the battalion. This platoon defied superstition by occupying the cellar of the Mortuary, and it held its claim obstinately against all rivals desiring the protection afforded by this stoutly-built edifice.

The main street of the town was provided at intervals with screens as protection from observation, but no ingenuity could save Nieuport from being considered what it was in truth—a thoroughly 'unhealthy' spot.

The 2/K.O.Y.L.I. had already done one tour of duty lasting four days, in the trenches on the far side of the Yser; a second tour was completed and the battalion was back in the billets in Nieuport by the time that the intense bombardment was put down by the enemy commencing on the 9th July. Our reply to the artillery bombardment was feeble owing to the fact that the French heavy batteries had been withdrawn and our own heavies had not yet been brought into position. Even before the shelling had become intense the 2/K.O.Y.L.I. had recorded that the trenches were daily bombarded with every conceivable form of shell and that many other casualties were inflicted by aerial darts and rifle grenades.

Though the attack on the sector held by the 32nd Div. was not so intense as on that in the dunes, and the defences in the former sector were more solid and furnished with dug-outs, Gen. Shute and his battalions had an anxious time in resisting the desperate attacks which followed the bombardment.

On the 10th, when in Nieuport, the 2/K.O.Y.L.I. at 12.56 p.m., received orders from Bde. Headquarters to move companies up into the sub-sector held by their old friends the 16/H.L.I., to take the place of casualties. By this time there was only one bridge available over the Yser by which the sector could be approached. One after another the companies were hurried across to reinforce, first the 16/H.L.I. and then the 11/Border, until at last only the headquarters of the battalion remained on the Nieuport side. All the battalions of the brigade became involved in the struggle to hold or recover the trenches, till finally, in the evening of the 11th, the enemy desisted from his attacks.

The casualties in the 2/K.O.Y.L.I. during this and the previous days in these trenches amounted to:

Officers killed, 2, wounded, 9; other ranks, killed, 52, wounded, 140, missing, 6. In the officers' list the following casualties are recorded:—On the 5th, killed, 2/Lts. C. A. Brown and J. C. Robins; wounded, 2/Lts. C. S. Nash and J. G. B. Draper (the latter within a week of joining). On the 6th, wounded, 2/Lts. A. W. Stark and W. G. Penn-Simkins. On the 7th, 2/Lt. N. E. Carden; on the 8th, Capt. M. H. Garrard.

Also, on the 16th July Maj. Hon. E. P. J. Stourton, K.O.Y.L.I., who was D.A.Q.M.G. 32nd Div., was wounded in Nieuport by shell-fire.

H.M. King George visited the divisional area on the 5th.

The official announcement of the battle was as follows:—"*After a very intense bombardment, lasting for twenty-four hours, the enemy made a determined attack on our positions on the Nieuport front yesterday evening (July 10th) at 7.45 p.m.*

Owing to the concentrated and heavy nature of the enemy's fire the defences in the Dunes sector, near the coast, were levelled, and the sector was isolated by the destruction of the bridges across the River Yser.

The enemy succeeded in penetrating our positions here on a front of 1,400 yards and to a depth of 600 yards, thus reaching the right bank of the River Yser near the sea.

Further south, opposite Lombartzyde, after gaining temporarily some of our advanced positions, the enemy was driven back to his own lines by a counter-attack."

On the 16th July the 2/K.O.Y.L.I. was sent by route march to Ghyvelde to be billeted in comfortable huts, and on to Bray dunes on the 20th. Here the companies were allotted to certain portions of the coast in support of the French defenders, and sea bathing was permitted.

On the 23rd the 97th Inf. Bde. paraded under Brig.-Gen. Blacklock for inspection by the Divisional Commander, Maj.-Gen C. D. Shute. The Corps Commander, Lt.-Gen. Sir J. P. Du Cane, then inspected it and presented some decorations to N.C.O.s who were on parade, *viz.*, M.M. ribbons to Sgt. E. Dudley, "*for conspicuous courage when in charge of the food-parties in continuous duty for twenty-two hours, whereby he maintained the battalion's tradition of getting food to the men regardless of obstacles,*" and to Pte. H. Healey; also a Bar to M.M. to Cpl. J. Mair "*for his devotion to duty as Signalling Corporal, working all through the intense barrage to keep the companies in communication with headquarters.*" Cpl. Mair was one of the original Expeditionary Force.

The 2/K.O.Y.L.I., though it returned again to the front line trenches in what was known as the St. George's sector towards the end of August, was not called upon for any further notable effort until the fighting near Passchendaele at the end of the year.

While operating in the Neuve Chapelle area, both 1/4th and 1/5th Bns. suffered many casualties. The 49th Div. remained in the XV Corps, Fourth Army, till the 22nd September.

THE 1/4TH AND 1/5TH BNS.

Lt.-Col. B. Musgrave, commanding the 4th Bn., was wounded by a sniper on the 13th May, and Maj. H. Moorhouse took over command until he rejoined on the 26th July, while Maj. A. E. Blythe Jackson commanded the 5th Bn. temporarily in parts of June and July, when Lt.-Col. Moxon was in hospital.

In the 5th Bn. on the night of the 23rd April, when in the front line at Neuve Chapelle, Capt. A. Ferguson, 2/Lt. Pringle and two runners, were attacked by a German patrol when they were visiting posts. 2/Lt. Pringle was missing; Capt. Ferguson and both runners were wounded.

On the night of the 13/14th June a raid was carried out in which parts of all companies were concerned, under the command of Maj. Jackson. Though "C" and "D" Companies failed to get into the German trenches on account of wire, "A" Company got in after cutting through the protecting wire. The raid gained both its objectives, it inflicted heavy casualties on the enemy, accounting for twenty-three killed, and obtained the identifications required of it.

On the night of the 21/22nd June, a similar raid was carried out. Parties started at 10.45 p.m. with the object of placing six Bangalore torpedoes in position. A stout opposition was put up by the enemy, and it was only by the determination and devotion to duty of the Bangalore parties that five were successfully fired. "Zero" hour for the actual raid was 12.30 a.m. The artillery barrage was excellent, and the object of the raid was achieved. Casualties included Capt. J. Anderson (7/H.L.I. attd.), who died of his wounds; other ranks, 1 killed, 1 missing, 38 wounded.

Three of the R.E. who accompanied the raid were awarded the M.M., which was richly deserved. Sgt. J. T. Fletcher, of the battalion, acquired a Bar to his M.M., and nine other M.M.s were awarded in the ranks.

The raid was the occasion of letters of congratulation from the corps, division and brigade commanders.

On the 13th July our two battalions marched from Annezin to Béthune station to entrain for Dunkerque, where they arrived in the course of the afternoon. They proceeded in barges to Zuydecoote (spending the night in the barges). Next day they marched to Bray Dunes, taking over some of the coast defences there. On the 18th July, a week after the 2nd Bn. had experienced their hard fighting there, both Territorial battalions were in occupation of the Nieuport defences. The 5th Bn. were in front line with the 4th Bn. in support. The former had several casualties in its "A" and "C" Companies on the 18th. Capt. M. M. Simpson (H.L.I., attd.) and 2/Lt. F. E. Carrington, were wounded. Capt. Q. H. Campbell was killed in a daylight raid, and 2/Lt. F. G. Hobbs was wounded, on the 19th. The enemy attacked the front line and were driven off, 2/Lt. R. H. Ward being wounded.

On the 20th there was again a destructive bombardment; 2/Lts. E. Taylor, Bennett and R. E. Beall were wounded.

A heavy bombardment descended on the defences in the night of the 21/22nd. The enemy used shells of all calibres and included a large quantity of his new (mustard) gas shells. The 4th Bn., in support, were the chief sufferers. The gas attack was repeated twice. The gas smelt of garlic or mustard, and was the chief cause of an overwhelming number of casualties. The immediate effect was a slight irritation of the nose and throat. Sneezing ensued, followed by vomiting, and the eyes became acutely inflamed and very painful. Coughing and symptoms resembling bronchitis followed and prevailed for a week, at least, after contact with the gas.

In the 4th Bn. the casualties were:—killed, 7; wounded, 9; gassed, Capts. F. G. Kaye and A. C. Edwards (R.A.M.C., attd.), Lt. G. A. McG. Ricketts, Lt. B. Barnes, 2/Lts. S. G. Paget, G. Heggs, O. W. Appleyard, C. H. Taylor and E. A. W. Gordon; other ranks, gassed, 413, missing, 3.

The following day there were further casualties; Lts. J. W. Glew, F. C. Bishop and H. E. Richards were gassed; in other ranks there were 73 gassed and 1 killed.

In the 5th Bn. the total casualties for the period, including Capt. R. Dow (R.A.M.C. attd.) who was gassed on the 22nd, and Capt. H. E. H. Clayton-Smith, who was killed in the bombardment of the 23rd, amounted to:—Officers, 4 killed or died of wounds, 10 wounded and 1 missing; other ranks, 35 killed, 11 died of wounds, 2 missing, 143 wounded, and 124 gassed.

Both battalions were then moved in motor lorries to billets near the coast, and thence into the coast defences about Zuydecoote.

C.S.M. Sutherland and Cpl. Brain of the 5th Bn. were awarded the D.C.M.

On transfer to the Second Army in September, the 49th Div. was posted to the II Anzac Corps, commanded by Lt.-Gen. Sir A. J. Godley.

THE 8TH BN.

The Flanders Offensive (June 7th to November 10th, 1917) opened with the Battle of Messines. This battle was most skilfully and elaborately planned by Sir Herbert Plumer, and resulted in a complete success for the Second Army which he commanded. It began with the explosion of huge mines, whose existence had been triumphantly kept secret, and it effected the capture of the whole of the Messines-Wytschaete ridge at a comparatively small cost. It freed the low country south of Ypres from the domination of these commanding heights, and straightened the salient into line.

The 23rd Div., to which the 8/K.O.Y.L.I. belonged, was part of the X Corps in the Second Army.

Lt.-Col. D. Quirk had come from the 8/Y. and L. to command the 8/K.O.Y.L.I. from the 1st March *vice* Lt.-Col. Imbert-Terry, who went to Divisional Headquarters. Maj. S. D. Rumbold from the same regiment joined for duty on the 5th April as second-in-command.

In the first days of June, from camp near Ouderdom the 8/K.O.Y.L.I. moved up to battle concentration area for the Messines offensive.

The 70th Inf. Bde. was allotted the part of pivot brigade on the extreme left of the X Corps. The directions issued to the brigade were, to bring its right shoulder up till its line should be facing north-east, and to form a defensive flank for the general line of operations.

There were five days of bombardment prior to the attack. Mines at Hill 60 and the Caterpillar were fired at "Zero" hour and were the signal for the assault.

The 8/K.O.Y.L.I. was right support battalion of the brigade, with orders to capture and consolidate the second objective. The first objective was Image trench and part of Illusive trench in the enemy's front line, the second being Image crescent.

The 8/K.O.Y.L.I. moved in rear along a tunnel towards Hedge Street, with "B" Company in advance. This company was responsible for seeing that the front line was fairly clear before the battalion emerged at the Winnipeg exit. The battalion then moved down the front line trench into Living trench, where it came in touch with the 8/Y. and L. Two hours after "Zero" "B" and "A" Companies advanced in line of sections in file to their assembly positions in Image reserve, followed by "C" Company.

Three hours and forty minutes after "Zero" the battalion advanced to capture its objectives. When that was successfully accomplished Image crescent was consolidated under the protection of the Lewis-guns, while bombing parties were immediately pushed forward up the communicating trenches. The 8/Y. and L. combined in the attack.

From June 8-10th the battalion remained in the front line trenches. It was relieved on the night of the 10th and proceeded to camp near Meteren till the night of the 27th, when it went back into the front line again.

In the four days June 7-10th the battalion had 250 casualties in other ranks, and of its officers 2/Lts. P. K. Powell and J. F. Hall were killed or died of wounds, while 2/Lts. C. Fawcett, G. A. Holmes, I. D. P. Stephens and G. W. Franks were wounded.

Capt. G. F. B. Handley received a Bar to his M.C. Capt. A. W. Becher, Lt. G. T. Nye and 2/Lt. W. Dowland were awarded the M.C. There were 1 Bar to D.C.M., 2 Bars to M.M., and 22 M.M.s given in the battalion.

In an operation undertaken by the 94th Bde. on the 27th June, two companies of the 12/K.O.Y.L.I. were ordered to assist. "B" and "D" Companies each found 110 men. The officers were Capt. D. E. Roberts, 2/Lts. J. N. Blenkin, L. E. Cole, W. Read, F. Lobel and H. P. Morgan. Their task was trench-digging. They commenced work before dusk on a new communication trench in the front line between the railway and Cadorna, and in spite of many casualties, did such excellent work as to elicit the warm approval of Brig.-Gen. G. Carter-Campbell and of Lt.-Col. W. B. Hulke, who commanded the 14/Y. and L. They lost 3 killed and 33 wounded in other ranks. Cpl. A. Hirst, Lce./Cpl. A. Wright and Pte. G. Parkinson, gained the M.M.

THE 12TH BN.

To face page 887

THE THIRD BATTLE OF YPRES. 1917

XVI

IN the comprehensive title "The Third Battle of Ypres," is included all the fighting on the arc having Ypres as its centre, which took place in 1917 between the 31st July and the 10th November.

Of this battle one can here describe in detail only those events in the series of fights with which the various battalions of the K.O.Y.L.I. are directly concerned. A general survey, however, of the conditions which governed the offensive will assist to render coherent the individual actions of those battalions.

The Fifth Army had been moved north into the Ypres salient, into position, for the purpose of the great attack. It had on its left, opposite Bixschoote, a French army under Gen. Antoine. On the right of the Fifth Army was the Second Army under Sir Herbert Plumer.

The Fifth Army consisted of four Corps, the XIV to the north, the XVIII upon its right, next the XIX, and the II to the right of that. Each corps had two divisions in the line and two in reserve.

In the XIV Corps the Guards Div. was on the left, in touch with the French; the 38th (Welsh) Div. was on the right, in touch with the XVIII Corps; the 20th and 29th Div. were in support.

The immediate tactical object of the offensive was to capture the Flanders ridges which dominated the Ypres sector on the north and east. The strategical object was to compel the Germans to leave the French alone and give them time to recuperate; the period during which it became necessary to force the Germans to send more and more divisions into the blazing furnace of Ypres was prolonged, long after the French had made good their line, by the defeat which the Italians had sustained at Caporetto (October 24th), for it became still more urgently incumbent on the British to pin the Germans to the Flanders area.

The British troops, battling in the mud, often in darkness, choked by suffocating fumes, oppressed by the thunder and destruction created by their own guns and by those of the enemy, liable to be blown skywards at one moment or bombed or stricken from the air at another, could know little of the reasons for the almost superhuman efforts they were called upon to make, but they rose grandly to the occasion and fought, not blindly as men fighting body to body in the melée, but with calculating bravery as men who had to use their utmost ingenuity to get into the enemy's trenches and to hold them when they had reached them.

They were confronted now by a new departure in the system of enemy's defences; continuous trenches had given place to short lengths of trench supported by strong points at uncertain intervals, where machine-guns had free play. These strong points were either old buildings converted and solidified out of all recognition, or were newly-built forts of cement and iron with walls so thick that even direct hits from 5.9 guns had little or no effect on them. Entrance to them was gained by tunnel, and the only vulnerable points were the inward-splaying embrasures of the machine-gun emplacements. The garrisons of some of these forts were caught like rats in a trap, and more than one V.C. was gained by some daring soldier who contrived, single-handed, to outmanœuvre the machine-gun men and approached near enough to use his bombs through the embrasure and summon the survivors to surrender.

The achievements of the troops is summed up in the words of the Commander-in-Chief of the British armies in France:—

"*This offensive, maintained for three and a half months under the most adverse conditions of weather, had entailed almost superhuman exertions on the part of the troops of all arms and services. The enemy had done his utmost to hold his ground, and in his endeavours to do so had used up no less than seventy-eight divisions, of which eighteen had been engaged a second or third time in the battle, after being withdrawn to rest and refit. Despite the magnitude of his efforts it was the immense natural difficulties, accentuated manifold by the abnormally wet weather rather than the enemy's resistance, which limited our progress and prevented the complete capture of the ridge.*"

BATTLE OF LANGEMARCK. THE 7TH BN.

The 7/K.O.Y.L.I. reached Proven on the 21st July, having come north by train from Doullens. Here, for ten days or so, it underwent an intensive training. On the 4th August it entrained for Elverdinghe, and went on by road to Malakoff Farm. This area was familiar to the battalion, and it was now possible to see something of the stupendous preparations which had been made behind the line, new roads and new bridges everywhere; the strength in artillery was something to marvel at. There was line after line of field batteries, supported by more lines of howitzers, both light and heavy, standing wheel to wheel; further back still were heavy guns of every class.

The bombing at night was a constant annoyance, for even when out of range of shell-fire, the enemy planes were continually overhead dropping bombs, which, perhaps, were more nerve-wracking than damaging.

After the initial success of the Guards and Welsh Divisions on the 31st July, parties of officers of the supporting units went forward to the Pilkem ridge to survey the positions they were destined shortly to take over. It was on the first occasion of his going forward that the O.C. 7/K.O.Y.L.I. viewed the village of Langemarck, which the battalion was due to attack shortly. The village appeared to be almost undamaged, but even while he was there to see it, our massed guns opened fire on it, and when he left, within three hours, there was no sign of the existence of the village. He said that the ground seemed simply to rise in the air and fall as dust; it was difficult to describe the impressions gained from watching such artillery power. He saw the ridge in front of him studded with concrete strongposts; a few days later he was destined to be inside one of these posts at the time when it was under the enemy barrage, and it received three direct hits from a 5.9, which merely made the building tremble.

On August 5th the battalion went forward for a short tour in the trenches on Pilkem ridge. There was heavy shelling and mustard gas was experienced for the first time. In two days there were 7 men killed by shell-fire, 22 wounded, and 28 gassed. After this the battalion was withdrawn, was given its definite orders for an attack on Langemarck to be carried out on the 16th, and handed over to its officers for a particular and detailed preparation for the attack with a full knowledge of the position of the objectives.

On the 14th the battalion moved up under Maj. Janson (Lt.-Col. Robinson was in temporary command of the brigade). The battalion rested for the day near Malakoff Farm and at dusk moved up further and dug into position near Norman Junction, between the Steenebeke and Pilkem ridge. It was now actually on the forward slope of the ridge, and throughout the 15th the men had to lie absolutely still, as their newly-made trenches were in full view from the enemy's side.

The 59th Inf. Bde., after very hard fighting, had managed to establish posts on the further side of the Steenebeke, and the crossings were consequently in our hands. The attack of the 61st Inf. Bde. was to be on a two-battalion front, with the 7/Som. L.I. right of the first line, and the 7/K.O.Y.L.I. left, in touch with the 2/Hamps. of the 29th Div., the dividing line between divisions being the Staden railway (Ypres to Bruges). There were three objectives given for the day; the first two were to be dealt with by the leading battalions, and the third by the supporting battalions who had to "leap-frog" through the leaders. Early in the night of the 15-16th, the R.E. laid a "jumping-off" tape line on the east side of Steenebeke, and at midnight the companies began to move up into position. The enemy shelled the approaches to the river all night, using Véry lights; there were a few casualties in "B" Company, which was caught when crossing by one of the two footbridges available. It was a pitch dark night, but by 3.30 a.m. all companies were ready, "C" and "D", who were given the first objective, being in front. Each company was organised in three platoons, two in front and one in rear to 'mop up'; each was about 100 strong; there were two officers per company only. The frontage covered by the battalion was about 400 yards.

At about 3.30 a.m. our own guns and those of the enemy ceased firing, and there was an impressive silence until the French gunners away to the left opened with a barrage about 4 a.m. in support of their attack. At 4.45 a.m. our own gunners started an intense barrage just as it was growing light enough to see; this remained stationary for five minutes and then commenced to creep forward. The ground ahead of the troops was a mass of shell-holes which were half-filled with water; 700 yards had to be covered before arriving at the first objective, which was a line just short of where the village of Langemarck had stood; the second objective was 600 yards further ahead, to be reached by passing through the château grounds, about 300 yards beyond the village. There was a slight rise to start with; as soon as the leading lines reached the crest of the ridge they came under very heavy machine-gun fire, chiefly directed from two large concrete forts, one at Reitres Farm, the other at the railway station on the left front. There was also a cross-fire from a strong post on the right. It was very difficult to keep up with the barrage, although it was made to creep slowly, for occasionally a man would become completely stuck in the mud and required the help of several men to draw him out. By the time that the front line had arrived within 100 yards of the objective nearly half the battalion had become casualties, including all the company officers except Lt. A. C. H. Robinson. As battalion headquarters was moving up, the Adjutant, 2/Lt. R. C. W. Smithers, also, was mortally wounded.

For a time the machine-gun fire produced a serious check. Reitres Farm, with its deadly armament, stood right opposite the centre of the attack. It was at this juncture that Pte. W. Edwards, of "D" Company, greatly distinguished himself. On his own initiative he crawled ahead alone, reached the building and threw a bomb in; the machine guns were silenced; he then appeared on the top of the building and waved to the men to come on, so saving a critical situation; there was a rush and the fort was taken; two German officers and forty prisoners were taken out of the farm and the dead and wounded were numerous. About the same time a part of "D" Company, led by Cpl. Joseph Havenhard, attacked the station fort, another concrete building, with bombs, and forced the garrison to put up the white flag after putting their machine-guns out of action. Three officers and thirty other ranks were made prisoners here, and eight machine-guns were taken; there had been four machine-guns taken in the farm.

The ground between the first and second objectives was practically one great swamp and was impassable. The men of "A" Company led on mostly in file round the right of the swamp, till they came to the second village road where bits of a few houses were yet standing; "B" Company were pushing on up the railway meanwhile, round the left of the swamp. Both companies went on determinedly until they reached the second objective line, where the men proceeded to dig themselves in. The 7/Som. L.I. was in touch on the right.

Bn. Headquarters were established in Reitres Farm, and the place was consolidated. Lt. Robinson, having seen his own company into shelter, was sent on to take charge of the forward line.

The Lewis-gunners had done great work in the second advance. There had been considerable opposition from some railway trucks on the line, as also from the ruined houses on the second road. The fall of the strong points was the signal for a retirement from these points; the Lewis-gunners were quick to seize the opportunity and the retirement became a stampede, so that no further real opposition was encountered.

There was only one bit of hard ground near the station. C.S.M. A. Taylor, although wounded, collected about twenty men and set to work to construct a strong point there.

Just behind the second line a prize in the shape of three 4.2 howitzers fell to the battalion.

The 7/D.C.L.I. had followed close up in lines of sections, and passing straight through reached the third objective.

The day's operations on the brigade front were entirely successful.

The enemy shelled both lines vigorously for the rest of the day. Lt.-Col. Priaulx, with the 11/K.R.R.C., arrived about 11 a.m. at Reitres Farm to be in readiness to reinforce; the battalion dug itself in.

The night was comparatively quiet and rations were got up to the front line.

The 7/K.O.Y.L.I. was relieved in the night of the 17/18th.

Throughout this operation the N.C.O.s and men had shown a fine spirit and had worked splendidly. The signallers kept communication open with the brigade in spite of repeated damage to the wire. The stretcher-bearers worked incessantly, and by the night of the 17th had carried back all the wounded. Sgts. S. Goodman, of "A" Company, and G. H. Jackson, of "B" Company, both of them acting C.S.M.s, deserve special mention for their leading against the second objective.

Pte. Wilfred Edwards was awarded the V.C.

Lt. A. C. H. Robinson received the D.S.O.

A long list of further awards was subsequently published.

The following casualties were returned by the battalion: Officers, killed, Lt. R. C. W. Smithers, 2/Lts. J. Napier and L. Whitaker; wounded and missing, 2/Lt. C. D. Yearwood; wounded, Capt. R.

Wright, D.S.O. (died August 17th), 2/Lts. C. E. Hinchcliffe, H. R. Prust and W. H. Haddlesey; other ranks, killed, 20; wounded, 173; missing, 8.

The strain of periods like this was very great, and the health of officers and men suffered accordingly. Among those who were taken out of the line for a well-earned rest was Lt.-Col. Robinson, who for the next six months was placed in command of a young soldiers' battalion at home. Maj. Janson, who had been with the battalion from its earliest days, succeeded him in the command.

That patient friend of man, the transport mule, also deserves mention. He went through the same danger to life and limb, it may be thought without apprehension or realisation of the danger, but the following little anecdote taken from an officer's letter, may tend to dispel the illusion that he was entirely unappreciative of the exigencies of life at the front. The officer writes: "*On the way up (to the front line before Langemarck) the enemy were shelling fairly heavily, and I noticed a transport party with ammunition mules under what appeared to be a concentrated shell-fire. The drivers threw themselves on the ground, and, to my astonishment, the mules promptly lay down too!*"

The same officer shortly afterwards was leaving his command for another, and, being anxious to do something for his soldier-servant, asked the latter if there was any job he would like to be recommended for; somewhat to his surprise the answer was, "*I would like to have charge of a mule, sir!*"

The Second Army (Plumer) was on the right of the Fifth Army (Gough), and during the early stages of the third battle of Ypres, it fought to defend the right flank of the attacking army. The 14th (Light) Div., including the 6/K.O.Y.L.I., left the VII Corps (in which the 6/K.O.Y.L.I. had fought at Arras), to join the IX Corps, Second Army, on the 12th July.

THE 6TH BN.: INVERNESS COPSE.

The 6th Bn. entrained at Doullens, detrained at Bailleul, and marched into camp near Montnoir. Here, Lt.-Col. C. E. Atchison arrived from the K.S.L.I. and assumed command of the battalion. Gen. Sir H. Plumer paid a visit of inspection on the 26th.

On the 6th August the battalion left Montnoir for billets between Caestre and Hazebrouck, for an intensive training before going up into the front line.

On the night of the 21/22nd, the battalion moved into Sanctuary Wood in close support. This move was made under the fire of the enemy's guns, and the battalion encountered the gas shells for the first time. Box respirators had to be worn and progress was slow owing to the extreme darkness and the narrow way.

At 7 a.m. the 22nd August, the other two battalions of the 43rd Inf. Bde. attacked Inverness Copse and the north side of the Menin road. The 6/K.O.Y.L.I. followed in support and dug itself in under fire. At 11 a.m. "Y" and "Z" Companies were ordered forward to occupy a position near Stirling Castle, recently held by the 10/D.L.I., and while "Y" held the previous British front line, "Z" formed a defensive flank facing south. A counter-attack on the position which this company was holding was promptly made by the enemy, but it was successfully driven off. A little later the 8/K.R.R.C. relieved these companies, who then advanced to reinforce the 6/Som. L.I., coming under the orders of the O.C. that battalion.

During the day 2/Lt. W. F. Pogson was wounded; in other ranks there were 3 killed, 72 wounded, 1 missing.

The 23rd August was spent in improving and consolidating the new position which was on the north side of Inverness Copse, but this was done under the fire of the enemy guns, which harassed them with an intense bombardment from 9 p.m. till 5 a.m. the next morning, inflicting many further casualties. 2/Lts. G. C. Robinson, J. P. Hanes, F. W. Stirk and D. I. Jones, were wounded; in other ranks 7 were killed, 73 wounded, and 2 were missing.

The fierce bombardment by the enemy was followed up by a massed attack on the Inverness Copse position. As early as 2.30 a.m. the O.C. 8/K.R.R.C. gave notice that an attack was imminent. At 5 a.m. our front line sent up the S.O.S. signal, which was repeated from Stirling Castle. At 5.15 a.m. the left battalion of our front line was forced to give a little ground, and the right defensive flank was also in danger. The headquarters of the 6/K.O.Y.L.I. sent a party to reinforce the right, and the remainder of one company to the left, where it joined up with the D.L.I. and its own "X" Company. By 9 a.m. three strong points had been established on the left in an endeavour to keep touch with the D.C.L.I. beyond, and, since our artillery had temporarily ceased firing, an open infantry battle was taking place. Timely reinforcements arrived and the enemy was repulsed; in his retirement it was noticed that he was pulling hand-carts. At 11 a.m. our artillery again opened, but our infantry had, in the meantime, advanced as far as the extreme edge of Inverness Copse, and coming under the fire of our own guns, suffered heavily; the men had to retire to the western edge of the wood. Directly the guns ceased fire they returned again.

At 12.30 p.m. Lt.-Col. Atchison was killed, and Maj. E. B. Wilson was left in command, with Maj. C. B. Leatham second-in-command.

About 1.30 another massed attack was again dispersed. At 2 p.m. Bn. Headquarters and three platoons of the 8/K.R.R.C. came up into Stirling Castle, bringing orders to hold on to that position at all costs. The enemy bombardment with guns of heavy calibre became terrific; flammenwerfer and trench mortars were freely used, and his infantry attacks were pressed right up to our lines. However, by the evening his extreme energy was spent and the danger temporarily past.

At 9 p.m. the 6/K.O.Y.L.I. was relieved and the battalion retired to dug-outs on the western side of Zillebeke bund. By the 4th September it had moved back to the La Crêche waterworks area *via* Bailleul, there to be billeted in huts for reorganisation and training.

In addition to the loss of the C.O., on the 24th Capt. G. W. F. Birch and 2/Lt. A. Bradley were killed; 2/Lts. A. S. Lowe and O. M. Holmes died of wounds; Capt. E. G. Bartlett and 2/Lts. W. S. Hill and R. T. Corke were wounded. In other ranks 22 were killed, 129 wounded, and 31 were returned as missing.

In short, the battalion had gone into action on the 22nd August with a strength of 20 officers and 523 other ranks; it came out on the evening of the 24th with 7 unwounded officers and 183 other ranks.

By the 20th September the battalion was back in the line. A list of honours published that day contained the names of 2/Lts. B. H. C. Hettler and W. S. Hill and Lt. S. Vidot, R.A.M.C. (attd.), as recipients of the M.C., while C.S.M. Cooke, Sgt. Bonser and Pte. Smithson received D.C.M.s; and Cpl. Rotherforth and Pte. C. Simms were awarded M.M.s.

This was only one list of several which affected the 6/K.O.Y.L.I.

In October the battalion was in the line near Poldehoek Château (Lt.-Col. W. H. M. Micholls had resumed command on the 1st October), and it suffered about fifty casualties, mostly from shell-fire near Sanctuary Wood. From the 24th onward it underwent a special training for Passchendaele, but by the time that it arrived (December 8th) in the front line, just north-east of that sinister region, the fighting had died down, and immediately after Christmas Day the battalion moved by train and route march, first to Acquin, and then into the Noyon area, where it did trench duty until February, 1918.

The 6/K.O.Y.L.I. was disbanded in February on a reduction of the number of battalions. The members of the battalion were mostly drafted into the 10/D.L.I. and 6/D.C.L.I. Lt.-Col. E. B. Wilson went on to win fresh honours in the 34/London (K.R.R.C.).

About the middle of September the 21st Div. was transferred to the X Corps, Second Army (Plumer). The Second Army was preparing for a great offensive on a front of eight miles, from Langemarck on the left to Hollebeke in the south.

THE 9TH AND 10TH BNS: POLYGON WOOD.

The 64th Inf. Bde. left Simencourt and trained to Casel, *via* Aubigny, on the 16th September, the 9th and 10th Bns. K.O.Y.L.I. being billeted about Hendeghem. Here, an intensive training was undergone with a view to the attack of the 4th October. Both battalions

Imperial War Museum Photograph.

Men of the K.O.Y.L.I. fusing Stokes Mortar Bombs, near Ypres. 1 October, 1917

To face page 894.

moved up into the line on the 1st October, the 9th passing through Polygon Wood to be at the disposal of the G.O.C. 110th Inf. Bde., who was holding the eastern edge. The Bn. Headquarters was established at Clapham Junction. The 10th Bn., being in brigade reserve, occupied dug-outs for two days by the railway embankment south-west of Zillebeke lake.

The 64th Inf. Bde. was on the right in the attack, and the 62nd on the left; the 110th was in divisional reserve. The 21st Div. had on one side (left) the 7th Div., and on the other the 5th Div.

The 9th Bn. spent the 3rd October in the front line under continuous shelling, and in the morning of the 4th formed up to attack the German front line. The objective was a portion of the road just west of Reutel. The 10th Bn. formed up behind the 9th for the capture of the second objective, which included the village of Reutel. "Zero" hour was 6 a.m.

The back area was being heavily shelled all the time, so the rations and rum were late, but the carrying party pushed up with great determination.

The 9th Bn. attacked with "D" Company on the right and "C" on the left; "B" was behind "D," and "A" behind "C." Half an hour after the start German prisoners began to come back, but Bn. Headquarters could discover little of what was going forward in front, for the enemy barrage was intense over the area extending from the eastern edge of Polygon Wood back to Clapham Junction. All communication was consequently cut off.

At 8 p.m. the Adjutant, Capt. C. A. C. J. Hendriks, was able to work his way up to the front with a small carrying party under 2/Lt. H. N. Teaz, taking water and small arms ammunition. He found the battalion in possession of its objectives and in a sound position as regards the left, but strung out on the right owing to the failure of troops on that flank to make good their objective.

At 9.30 p.m. our front line sent up the S.O.S. signal; our guns opened and were replied to by the enemy, who again searched the back area; it was during this bombardment that at about 10.30 p.m. a shell exploded at the entrance of the 9th Bn. Headquarters, which mortally wounded the C.O., Lt.-Col. Daniell, killed the signalling corporal, and wounded the signalling and intelligence officers. The O.C. the 10th Bn. was ordered by the Brig.-Gen. to take command of the remnants of the 9th in addition to his own battalion.

The story of the fortunes of the troops up in the front was told later by Capts. A. E. Day and J. H. Frank, who were there leading their companies; in a joint narrative they explained that when the British barrage opened at "Zero" hour, the companies leapt from the shell-holes they were occupying and went forward 'in snake formation.'

It was the darkness that precedes the dawn, and no man could recognise his neighbour. A withering machine-gun fire at once caught them and men were falling, but the one idea was to get forward. Joist Farm was the first stumbling block and proved a tough nut to crack. As soon as the swamp in the low ground was reached, white Véry lights had been fired from this point to show the stormers up. Two sections of "D" Company under Capt. Sykes 'mopped up' this post with the help of one section of "B" under Sgt. Pigott. One officer, twelve men and four machine-guns were taken.

There was a swamp to be crossed in the low ground, which proved to be a death trap; the men were up to their knees in slush and were subjected to an enfilade machine-gun fire from the right. A small strong point, not concreted, on the west bank of the swamp, was taken by surprise and the garrison surrendered. On the east side the ground rose rapidly and contained a number of concrete forts, two of which were in the battalion's area. The garrisons were bombed or shot, and the survivors surrendered. The one on the left was the headquarters of a battalion; each contained two machine-guns.

Juniper trench was strongly held, but the garrison retired before our men reached it. However, 2/Lt. L. B. Spicer, by a quick manœuvre, cut off the majority of the garrison, who surrendered to him. On the right the Germans made a better fight and attempted a counter-attack. "D" Company dealt with these successfully.

Three more strong points were attacked, after which there was little real opposition before the objective was reached. All the troops of the brigade were then mixed up, and a considerable number of Northumberland Fusiliers and men of the Queen's were with the battalion. For an hour and forty minutes the troops in the captured trench were subjected to a bombardment, and were also much troubled by a strong point on the east edge of Reutel; this was at last knocked out by a tank.

It was realised that the right flank was in the air. As reinforcements, consisting of remnants of a company of the D.L.I. and of a company of the E. York., arrived, they were directed to the right to form a defensive flank, while the men in the first line dug themselves in about 100 yards ahead of the road running north and south on the western extremity of the village, which had been their objective.

About noon the enemy was seen to be advancing in force from the south-east and to be massing near Polderhoek Château; a party under 2/Lt. Spicer was sent out with two Lewis-guns and one Vickers to get on their flank; this party entirely disappeared and nothing was seen of it again. It was later established that 2/Lt. L. B. Spicer, who had displayed so much daring and initiative, was killed.

The 10/K.O.Y.L.I. had started at 6 a.m. close on the heels of the 9th Bn. When the 9th Bn. had been temporarily checked by the strong

Men of the K.O.Y.L.I. resting on the way down from the trenches. Wieltje, 1 Oct., 1917

To face page 897.

posts, the 10th soon found themselves mingling with the ranks of the other battalion, and, owing to the number of casualties, they were required in the front line for the work ahead. The right support company of the 10th, which had gone round by the road and so avoided the swamp, actually reached the first objective before the right "front" company. All the officers of these two companies had been killed or wounded by machine-gun fire from Joist Farm; there were two officers only of the four companies who were not hit. Our barrage remained stationary for one hour and forty minutes over the second objective while the troops were clearing up the first line and digging in; as soon as the barrage advanced again the remnants of the 10th Bn. went ahead to the number of about fifty, but as there were no signs of attackers on their right the senior officer on the spot decided to stop and dig in 150 yards ahead of the first objective and to throw his right back to watch the flank. Some cover was obtained by connecting the shell-holes by day; during the night the 9th and 10th Bns. combined to dig one line of defence. The 1/E. York. continued this line southwards and faced south-east, for there was still a gap of 700 yards between it and the next division.

Throughout the next day this position was held against repeated counter-attacks, and in the night of the 5-6th some of the reserve officers of the battalions were sent forward by Lt.-Col. H. W. Festing, who had commanded the 10th Bn. since the 22nd August and was now in command of the survivors of both.

The next night the tired soldiers were relieved by the 7/Leicesters and went back to Ouderdom to be entrained for Ebblinghem.

The 9th Bn. came out of the trenches 120 strong, including officers. Maj. H. Greenwood was the senior officer left with the battalion and now commanded it until Lt.-Col. A. J. McCulloch took over the command on the 10th November.

The casualties in the battalion during this short experience of the offensive amounted to: Officers, killed, 3; wounded, 12 (2 still at duty); missing, 6 (2 at least were believed killed); other ranks, killed, 35; wounded, 274; missing, 51.

The 10th Bn. suffered equally; its losses were: Officers, killed, 4; wounded, 5; missing, 1; other ranks, killed, 25; wounded, 247; missing, 41.

The Brig.-General came to address each battalion on the 12th October with a few words of congratulation; he reminded them that this was the third time when the 64th Inf. Bde. had fought with its right flank in the air, the other occasions being the 1st July, 1916, and the 9th April, 1917.

By the 15th October the brigade was sufficiently rested to take some voluntary exercise. Sports were arranged to be held in the brigade camp, which included several events which afforded a little fun for the mules, such as musical chairs, pig-sticking, and mounted wrestling!

The 21st Div. was not seriously engaged again in 1917, though it continued to hold its sector of the line until the 17th November, when it was transferred from the Second to the First Army.

Our two battalions were five days on the road to Ecoivres, arriving there on the 21st November. After ten days they entrained at Hubigny for Tincourt, and moved up into the front line once more. The end of the year found them in camp at Saulcourt.

The 148th Inf. Bde., including the 1/4th and 1/5th Bns. K.O.Y. L.I., proceeded on the 22nd September to St. Pol-sur-mer and on by 'bus on the 24th to Lederzeelle. The division was now leaving the XV Corps, Fourth Army, and joining the II Anzac Corps (Godley), which was the left corps of four in the Second Army (Plumer).

THE 1/4TH AND 1/5TH BNS. AT PASSCHENDAELE.

In the last chapter it has been seen that a great attack commenced along the front of the Fifth and Second Armies on the 4th October, and how the 9th and 10th Bns. K.O.Y.L.I. were engaged near Polygon Wood. These two battalions were also in the Second Army, in Morland's X Corps. The I Anzac Corps stood in the line next to the X Corps on its northern flank, while the II Anzac came next again on the left. The left of the II Anzac Corps was in touch with the XVIII Corps of the Fifth Army (Gough).

The 49th Div. was put in as left division on the front held by the II Anzac Corps. The Australians had been making considerable advances in the direction of Passchendaele; the 49th Div., with the 66th on its right and the 48th on its left, was brought in to carry the advance further. The division was fitted out with everything necessary for the attack when still behind the line, and on the 7th October received its orders for the attack.

Two brigades of the 49th Div. were in front line, the 146th on the left, the 148th on the right; the 147th was in reserve. In the attack, which was made on the 9th October, the 4th and 5th Y. & L. Bns. and the 5/K.O.Y.L.I. were in the first line of the 148th Inf. Bde., and the 4/K.O.Y.L.I. was in reserve.

At 12.15 a.m. the 4/K.O.Y.L.I., led by Lt.-Col. H. Moorhouse, moved from the old German front line, following in the footsteps of its sister battalion. The night was intensely dark, the track was in bad repair, and progress was consequently slow. The head of the supporting battalion reached the support line behind the little ridge which had the high-sounding name of the Abraham Heights, at "Zero" hour. This was 800 yards behind the position of assembly.

The leading battalions duly made their advance, but from the outset were hopelessly far behind our barrage, which travelled too fast to be overtaken. None the less, as Conan Doyle expresses it, the battalions struggled forward with splendid courage, and, if they did not win their utmost objective, at least they gained a broad belt of new ground. Before the 4/K.O.Y.L.I. could close up to the leaders, the enemy put a heavy barrage on the ridge which had to be crossed, causing delay and numerous casualties.

The 4th Bn. went forward in two waves of attack, two companies on the right and two on the left. In the advance down the forward slope of the ridge many casualties were inflicted by machine gun fire, which came from a strong position on the Belle Vue spur. The leading battalions suffered very heavily, and at this stage of the operations the 4th Bn. lost 2/Lt. P. F. Beaumont, who was killed, while Capt. J. W. Morehouse, 2/Lts. H. Nichols, J. Bramald and W. B. Greaves were wounded. Companies were forced to close on to the Meetcheele-Gravenstafel road on account of the impassable condition of the ground, due to the overflowing of the Ravebeek stream, whose banks had been knocked about by shell fire.

In the front line, while on the left the machine gun and rifle fire was causing heavy losses, on the right men were becoming temporarily lost owing to the impossibility of getting through the mud. The battalions on both left and right were shouting for reinforcements; "Z" and "Y" Companies were sent forward from the 4th Bn. to reinforce the left, under Capts. T. Chadwick and R. W. Moorhouse, while "W" and "X" Companies went to the right, led by Lt. G. H. Brook and 2/Lt. G. E. Parsons. The whole brigade was now in one line.

The line had to advance up a long slope under rifle and machine gun fire; the advance was made as far as possible by sections, but the fire from Wolf Copse on the left and from Belle Vue on the top of the slope was devastating. Capt. R. W. Moorhouse was killed while gallantly leading his company. Half an hour later Lt.-Col. H. Moorhouse was killed by a bullet when leaving his headquarters, a great loss to the Regiment.

There came a time when the companies no longer carried sufficient weight to carry a position; the strength of a company now averaged from thirty to forty men. A position was occupied on the slope, the extreme left of the brigade being held by "Y" and "Z" Companies of the 4/K.O.Y.L.I. about 400 yards north-east of the point where the Ravebeek crosses the road, while "W" and "X" Companies of the same battalion formed a defensive flank on the right of the 4/Y. & L. There was a considerable gap between the left companies and the 146th Inf. Bde.

About 7 p.m., Capt. T. Chadwick with "Z" Company made an attempt to capture two pill-boxes on the crest of the slope, which were giving particular trouble, but they were so heavily wired that the attempt had to be abandoned.

In the night the brigade was relieved by the New Zealanders, and it went back to bivouac in fields near the Asylum at Ypres.

The casualties in the 4/K.O.Y.L.I. included Lt.-Col. H. Moorhouse, Capt. R. W. Moorhouse, 2/Lt. P. F. Beaumont, and 17 other ranks, killed; also Capt. J. W. Morehouse, Lt. J. W. Huntington, 2/Lts. H. Nichols and W. B. Greaves, and 147 other ranks wounded; 2/Lt. J. Bramald was wounded and missing, and 19 other ranks were returned as missing.

The 5/K.O.Y.L.I. had 2/Lts. F. E. Davies and H. Wade killed; 2/Lts. J. D. Drummond and C. W. Uncles missing; other ranks, 33 killed and 18 missing; wounded, Capt. J. Shirley, Lt. E. Roberts, 2/Lts. W. Crow, J. Siddle, D. K. Ward (Manch. R. attd.), R. H. L. Davis, B. O. Davis, G. P. Cranmer, and S. C. Bywater; other ranks, 116.

Capt. and Adjt. P. Bentley was wounded on the 20th October.

On the 11th October the brigade retired for a brief rest to billets in Winnezeele, but was back again in the line on the 18th. The 4/K.O.Y.L.I. had Lt. F. C. Bishop and 2/Lt. S. J. Yates, with 9 other ranks wounded while holding the position in the line, by the 21st October; after that it was occupied for some nights in working at the formation of an assembly position for an early attack to be made by the Canadian Corps; 2/Lt. G. E. Parsons and 5 other ranks were wounded in this period.

Capt. H. C. Fraser assumed command of the 1/4th Bn. on the 14th October, taking over from Capt. T. Chadwick, who had brought it out of action on the 10th.

On the 1st November Lt.-Col. C. C. Moxon relinquished the command of the 1/5th Bn., and proceeded home for duty, after a long and successful command of his battalion in the field.

To the end of the year 1917 these two battalions were busy in the usual routine of duties in their section of the front in the Ypres front. There was no special activity to record.

Field Cooker of the K.O.Y.L.I. beside a camouflage-screened road near Ypres, 1 October, 1917

To face page 900.

THE BATTLE OF CAMBRAI AND SOME OTHER INCIDENTS. 1917

XVII

THE third battle of Ypres ended on the morning of the 6th November, when the Canadians finally made themselves masters of the village and ridge of Passchendaele. The extent of country gained in the battle was not great; the channel ports were almost as far away as ever, and there was now no hope this year of a combined attempt by sea and land to capture them; the sacrifice of life had been very great. On the other hand, Ypres was now free from domination, for the enemy was driven from the semi-circle of commanding ridges. More German divisions had been engaged and shattered in the fighting than had our own, while the French had been given time to reconstruct their front and reorganise their armies. But the collapse of Russia and the disastrous defeat of the Italians at Caporetto on the 24th October convinced the British Commander-in-Chief of the necessity to continue the pressure upon the Hindenburg Line. However, there was a change in tactics.

Up to this period, in 1917, there had perforce been an absence of the element of surprise. The preparatory artillery bombardment and the preliminary arrangements for attack on a large scale gave the enemy warning of an impending offensive. The intensity of the heavy shell fire, which was designed to overcome the hostile defences and so assist the infantry, did in fact so plough up the sodden soil that an infantry advance became a matter of extreme difficulty. The disadvantage of this method of attack reacted still more unfavourably on the tactics of the new arm, the tanks.

Accordingly Sir Douglas Haig evolved a new tactical plan and decided to deliver the assault with tanks, unheralded by artillery fire, and to break through the wire defence without cutting it with shell. The portion of the Hindenburg line chosen for the attack was of the strongest, and lay between the Cambrai-Bapaume road in the north and the Escaut river by Banteux in the south; Cambrai lay about six or seven miles behind.

The concentration of more than 400 tanks was effected in such a manner as not to attract attention; cavalry were brought up too, in the hope of a complete break-through. There was one factor which acted prejudicially to the chances of a great success; six French and five British divisions were taken out of the line and dispatched hurriedly to Italy just before the event, thus reducing the force available for exploiting success, should initial success be achieved.

In the event surprise was complete, the tanks achieved their task admirably by crushing lanes through the wire, and bridging the marvellous system of trenches in places with the huge bundles of timber and faggots which they carried for the purpose. The first day's fighting was notably successful, the second marked some additional gains, the third day was spent chiefly in consolidating; after that some stern fighting ensued for days to capture Mœuvres and Bourlon. The successful counter-attack which was made by the Germans on the 30th November more than neutralised the gains in the southern area, but in the northern part left the British in possession of six miles of the Hindenburg Line.

The 7/K.O.Y.L.I. and the 2/4th and 2/5th Bns. were engaged in the Cambrai battle. The action of the 7th Bn. will be followed first.

THE 7TH BN.

The 20th Div. had been brought south into General Sir Julian Byng's Third Army early in October. On the 2nd October the 7/K.O.Y.L.I. had moved by train from Proven to Bapaume and went to the front in the Gonnelieu sector. Throughout the month of November until the 19th life was normal in and out of the front line.

Lt.-Col. J. T. Janson was in command of the battalion, but in his temporary absence the command was given on the 20th to Maj. L. P Storr, of the 12/King's, who took it into action.

The battalion found the trenches in this area, with their capital dugouts, a welcome change from the trenches in the Salient. The line was very extended and consisted of small posts; there was a wide stretch of no man's land and active patrolling had to be kept up. All seemed very peaceful, with very little shelling from either side. In the evening of the 18th November the battalion came out of the front line into reserve. The next evening it moved up into battle position just east of Gonnelieu. At dawn on the 20th the great surprise attack was launched.

The 7/K.O.Y.L.I. formed the third wave of the 61st Inf. Bde. in the attack; the brigade was the right brigade of attack, being opposed to La Vacquerie with its right on the Escaut river.

The leading wave was composed of the 7/Som. L.I., with two companies of the 7/D.C.L.I.; thirty tanks co-operated with it.

The second wave consisted of the 12/King's and the rest of the 7/D.C.L.I.

At 4.40 p.m. on the 19th, after having been fitted out with battle equipment at Revelon, the battalion had marched to its position.

At 6.20 a.m. the 20th November, the attack commenced. The 20th Div. had the 6th Div. on its left, and the 12th Div. on its right. The 12th Div.'s duty was to form a defensive flank in the south. The

29th Div. was held in readiness behind the 6th and the 20th, until the way was clear for it to pass through and make a further important advance.

All went well; La Vacquerie was taken in the first bound. At 8.10 a.m. the 7/K.O.Y.L.I. passed through the 7/D.C.L.I., who were busy consolidating the line which they had captured, and attacked the Hindenburg support line. Casualties became frequent from machine-gun fire, and the leading officers were killed or wounded; the support line was captured as designed; there was a second objective allotted to the battalion and the barrage, on which it counted for protection, was now 1,000 yards ahead. Some time was necessarily occupied in mopping up pockets of the enemy, and some reorganisation of companies had to be effected before advancing to another attack. As soon as possible the line went on under Capt. F. P. Hargreave. The barrage was too far ahead to afford any protection and the tanks were also away in front, so that the line came in for heavy machine gun fire and suffered many casualties before it reached its goal at 11.30 a.m. Capt. Hargreave was among the killed.

The brigade had gained all its objectives and had made secure all the ground within the limits of its allotted task.

At 11.30 a.m. the 29th Div. passed through on its way to the capture of Marcoing and Masnières, where there were important bridges over the canal.

Maj. Storr did fine work in personally directing the companies on their objectives and dealing with the situations rapidly as they arose, and was awarded the D.S.O. later.

2/Lt. W. Joffe, with Sgt. Roberts and about a dozen men, distinguished themselves by rushing an enemy 77 mm. gun, which continued firing point blank until they were within fifty yards of it. 2/Lt. Joffe was wounded. A second gun of the same calibre was also captured by the battalion.

The companies consolidated their position and spent the night on the line of their final objective.

Besides the officers already named the 7/K.O.Y.L.I. had Capt. H. R. Prust killed, and Capt. E. C. Gripper, and 2/Lts. J. G. Hurst and W. Watson wounded.

From the 21st to the 28th the battalion remained in the forward area, the position of the brigade being that of a prolongation of the defensive flank thrown back by the 12th Div. On the night of the 28th the battalion went back into brigade reserve, and Lt.-Col. Janson took over his command from Maj. Storr. The 7/Som. L.I. and the 12/King's were holding the front posts, the 7/D.C.L.I being in support. In case of an attack by the enemy the orders to the 7/K.O.Y.L.I. were to hold on to the reserve line.

By the evening of the 29th the Commander of the German Second Army, which occupied the Cambrai sector, had collected sufficient troops to make a great counter-attack. He made one drive southwards west of Bourlon, and another, his main attack, westwards in the direction of Banteux and Gouzeaucourt.

Early in the morning of the 30th November the enemy brought a heavy barrage to bear on the front line posts. At about 8 a.m. the S.O.S. signal went up from our front line. A strong attack followed the barrage and both the battalions in our front line were surrounded and almost completely wiped out. A few men managed to trickle back to our support line. Very soon the enemy reached the support line, and the remnants fell back and came into line on the right of the reserve line. Every available man was rushed up to the right by the Brigade Headquarters, for the right was exposed, and the reserve line managed to hold firm. The advance was checked.

The situation, however, was full of danger.

On the right of the 61st Inf. Bde. the 59th had been forced back, and further to the right the enemy had broken right through the line and had reached Gouzeaucourt in rear of the 20th Div. The left of the 55th, the division on the right, had been obliterated, the 12th and 20th Divs. were shattered, the enemy had pierced between the 20th and the 29th Divs. for a time. The 29th Div. had desperate fighting but, together with the 6th on its left, it stood its ground.

The Guards Div. came to the rescue. It had been taken out of the battle around Bourlon and was resting in rear when the call came. By a splendid counter-attack the enemy were driven from Gouzeaucourt; by the afternoon the situation was rendered a little clearer by their efforts; the 29th Div. had also closed up the gap on the left of the 20th Div.

The 7/K.O.Y.L.I. took up a new line on the right flank. The men were now thoroughly weary, and practically every man had to be in the trenches to hold it. Throughout the night they worked at strengthening the position; the arrival of a small supply of rations helped things on.

During the 1st December there were no developments; as the commanding officers of the 7/D.C.L.I. and the 12/King's had both been killed on the 30th, and the O.C. 7/Som. L.I. wounded, all the remnants of these battalions were attached to the K.O.Y.L.I. together with all available Headquarters' troops. The composite battalion so constructed numbered in its ranks 30 men of the King's, 60 Som. L.I., 140 D.C.L.I., and 60 men of the 84th Fd. Company R.E., besides 320 of the K.O.Y.L.I. There were a few machine gunners and trench mortar men also. On the 2nd the enemy renewed his attacks. The brigade on the right of the 7th Bn. was heavily assailed, and "A" Company was called in to assist several times.

In the night the battalion was relieved, and the following day the whole division was moved by rail from the area.

It was only realised afterwards how narrowly the division had escaped being entirely cut off, and that the divisional transport had been packed and had started to move to the rear. The Commander of the Second German Army had struck a shrewd blow; he had also unfortunately learnt a lesson by the experience, which would be of service to him in the event of making any future attack on a line thinly held by a system of small posts.

We have seen how the 7th Bn. fared in the right of the attack directed on the Hindenburg Line; in the left of the offensive the 2/4th and 2/5th K.O.Y.L.I. also earned imperishable fame.

THE 2/4TH AND 2/5TH BNS. AT CAMBRAI.

The 62nd Div., so ably commanded by Maj.-Gen. Walter Braithwaite, had been collected about Havrincourt Wood while the 36th (Ulster) Div. continued, up to the 17th November, to make elaborate preparations in the front for its reception.

The story of the 62nd Division has been finely and graphically told in *The History of the 62nd (W.R.) Division*, by Everard Wyrall, a book which should be read by all who had friends in the division. No attempt will be made here to recapitulate the whole story, but the share that the two K.O.Y.L.I. battalions had in the capture of part of the Hindenburg Line will, it is hoped, be made intelligible.

The 62nd Div. had in the line of its first objective (called the Blue line) the village of Havrincourt, in its second (the Brown line) it had Flesquières and part of the Hindenburg Line to deal with. The division attacked with the 187th Inf. Bde. on the left, and the 185th on the right; the 186th Bde. was in close support, ready to pass through and assault the further lines. Of the 187th Bde. the 2/5th Bn. K.O.Y.L.I. (Lt.-Col. B. J. Barton) was in the left of the front line, the 2/4th (Lt.-Col. R. E. Power) in the right; the 2/4th Y. & L. supported the 2/5th K.O.Y.L.I., while the 2/5th Y. & L. was behind the 2/4th K.O.Y.L.I.

On the 17th November the two K.O.Y.L.I. battalions moved up into the Havrincourt sector. It was well for our battalions that the business of reconnoitring by patrols was carried out in no perfunctory manner. In particular Capt. A. C. Lynn and 2/Lt. W. G. James of the 2/5th Bn. made a minute reconnaissance of the position ahead of them by night on the 19th, cut some of the wires, and left guiding tapes to lead their men by at dawn.

At 6.20 a.m. in the morning of the 20th the attack was launched. Three wire-crushing tanks and eight fighting tanks had been told off to co-operate with each battalion in the fighting line. The first objective of the 187th Inf. Bde. was a section of the front Hindenburg trench between Vesuvius and Oxford road. (The dumps of the pits in the neighbourhood, owing to their conical shape in some cases, were given the names of well-known volcanoes.) The second objective was on a line running westerly from Havrincourt, and included the north-western half of the village. The 36th (Ulster) Div. fought on the left, the 51st (Highland) Div. on the right, of the 62nd Div.

Though the enemy had been restless in the early hours of the morning, and had kept up a lively bombardment intermittently, all this had died down, and the sudden tremendous tempest of our barrage, which opened at "Zero" hour, burst upon a quiet and unruffled morning. The attack was carried out according to plan, and the minutest detail had not been overlooked in the orders to the division. It is true that some of the tanks detailed to precede the 2/4th K.O.Y.L.I. were late, but the leading companies went forward without them; the tanks soon, however, came up and took the lead. The 2/5th were entirely without tanks in assaulting the first objective, and it was here that Capt. Lynn's work during the night was found to be of such paramount importance. Without tanks the battalion carried all before it, rushing the enemy posts and still keeping the general line. Capt. Lynn and 2/Lt. James gallantly led the way and were conspicuous in the close fighting in the enemy trenches. First the enemy outpost line was overrun. One machine gun post after another fell into the hands of the stormers; Boggart Hole, Snowden and Etna were rushed and taken, the last by a combined effort of flank platoons of the 4th and 5th Bns. K.O.Y.L.I., who would not wait for an expected tank to do the crushing part of the work for them. "C" and "D" Companies of the 2/4th Bn. were in the second wave of the battalion; a heavy machine gun fire was enfilading the leading companies from Château Wood on the right; the flank company of this second wave went for the wood, fought the garrison, and took seventy prisoners with two machine guns.

When "A" and "B" Companies of the 2/4th Bn. reached the German front trench and occupied it, the other two companies passed through to attack the left half of the village of Havrincourt. The 2/5th acted in like manner. Havrincourt was taken without a serious check. A machine gun had been mounted in the village square, the houses were manned and defended, but the suddenness of the offensive had taken the enemy at a disadvantage, and these important points were not too strongly held at the moment. By 8.30 a.m. the K.O.Y.L.I. battalions had captured their objectives in the Blue line and at once set to work on the business of consolidation.

The 185th Inf. Bde.'s left battalion had co-operated in the attack on Havrincourt,

The 2/4th Bn., of the two K.O.Y.L.I. engaged, had suffered most heavily. Capts. M. McNicoll and G. H. Roberts, Lt. A. R. Mosley, 2/Lts. H. A. E. Barker and C. P. Maddox, had been killed. Lt. R. Hale-White, 2/Lts. C. Hirst, A. G. Hill, H. Anderson, S. A. V. Butler, J. E. David and A. Kilner were wounded. Of other ranks there were 211 returned as killed, wounded or missing.

Of the 2/5th Bn., Capt. and Adjt. A. Robinson, 2/Lt. E. Morris and 2/Lt. J. H. V. Jago (King's Own, attd.) were wounded; 21 other ranks were killed and 101 were wounded.

When the 185th and 187th Bdes. had made good their hold on the Havrincourt line of trenches, the 186th Bde. passed through with a rush, under the leadership of its gallant young commander, Brig.-Gen. R. B. Bradford, V.C., and went on to the capture of Graincourt, well assisted by the tanks; the impetus of the attack carried the fighting lines even to the first houses of the village of Anneux, but there was not sufficient weight left in it to carry the village itself. There was no opportunity afforded for the regular employment of cavalry; two squadrons of King Edward's Horse, who watched for a chance of assisting the attack of the 62nd Div., were disappointed in their hope of mounted action. During the day 37 guns and 2,000 prisoners were taken by the 62nd Div.

The 2/5th K.O.Y.L.I. had taken 200 prisoners and 8 machine guns, as well as 2 granatenwerfer and 4 minenwerfer.

After the attack had surged on, both K.O.Y.L.I. battalions were left to occupy the Hindenburg support trench line, but on the 25th November were moved in order to relieve battalions of the 121st Inf. Bde. in the sector east of Mœuvres near the sugar factory. Meanwhile on the 21st, the second day of the operations, the 186th Bde. completed its task by driving the enemy before it out of Anneux and reaching the fringe of Bourlon Wood which clothed part of the Bourlon Ridge on its south side. The village of Bourlon lay on the far side of the ridge behind its north-west portion. Bourlon Ridge was in reality the goal towards which the attack was heading.

Early in the same day Flesquières, which had held up the 51st Div. on the right of the 62nd, was stormed and captured, and the 51st Div. then made an advance of something like three miles, taking Cantaing with 500 prisoners on the way, and going on to attack the village of Fontaine-notre-Dame.

Mœuvres on the left held up the 36th Div.; Bourlon Wood and hill were too strongly held to be rushed by the 62nd, and the 51st Div. had reached the limit of its strength.

There was no advance on the 22nd, and Fontaine was retaken by the enemy in a counterstroke. From Mœuvres to Fontaine, a difficult stretch of country, was a distance of six miles, and this now comprised the new front of the attack.

On the 23rd the 40th Div. went through and attacked Bourlon Ridge, capturing the wood for the time being. There was desperate fighting for the ridge in the next three days. The Germans had received considerable reinforcements. The 40th Div. and the cavalry, who were assisting it dismounted, were rapidly thinning. The Guards Div. relieved the 51st; the 62nd was brought in again to replace the 40th.

At 6.20 a.m. on the 27th the 62nd Div. attacked the Bourlon position; the weather was very bad, there had been a gale and a snowstorm in the night; the object was to recover Bourlon Wood and the village, which were both again in the hands of the enemy.

The 186th and 187th Bdes. attacked, the 187th being directed on the village, which it entered but could not hold. The Guards Div. attacked on the right of the 62nd.

At 1 a.m. "C" and "D" Companies of the 2/4th K.O.Y.L.I., under Maj. Beaumont, had marched to Bourlon Wood, followed by "A" and "B" under Lt.-Col. Power at 3 a.m. The brigade line of attack consisted of the 2/5th K.O.Y.L.I. on the left and the 2/5th Y. & L. on the right; the 2/4th K.O.Y.L.I. was in the support line, with the exception of its "D" Company, which was detailed to attack the extreme left of the village. The attackers made some headway, but after penetrating into the village the troops were forced back and had to withdraw to trenches south of Bourlon. Under most adverse conditions the troops behaved splendidly, and eventually finished the day holding the original line.

The casualties in the attack on Bourlon in the 2/4th Bn. amounted to 110 other ranks, killed, wounded and missing, while of the officers, 2/Lt. J. W. Berryman died of his wounds, and Lts. F. McCunn, H. L. Hollard (R.A.S.C. attd.), A. E. Earle, and 2/Lts. F. Cocker and A. Brealey (Green Howards, attd.) were wounded.

Those in the 2/5th Bn. numbered, in other ranks, 22 killed, 146 wounded, and 23 missing. Of the officers, Capt. O. S. Roper, 2/Lts. G. E. Eardley (King's Own, attd.) and L. Melhuish (Green Howards) were killed; Capt. H. O. Brown, Lt. C. H. Wilson, 2/Lts. R. A. Waters, P. Cartwright, C. E. Townend, W. McArthur, G. W. V. Hughes and H. L. Field, were wounded.

In the *History of the 62nd (W.R.) Division*, p. 117, Wyrall writes, "*Preceded by the Tanks the two battalions pushed on, and had succeeded in getting about half-way through the village when they found themselves confronted by street barricades. The barriers prevented further progress of the Tanks. Stiff fighting now ensued, heavy machine gun fire sweeping the streets, and many more casualties were suffered, especially in officers who, with great gallantry, made every endeavour to push their way forward . . . . The 2/4th K.O.Y.L.I., who had supported the attack, also succeeded in penetrating the village.*"

The battalions went back into reserve in the Hindenburg Line south-west of Graincourt the following day.

On the 4th December the whole brigade marched to Hendecourt, and on to Etrun on the 5th. The 19th found the brigade at Frévillers, where it spent the time for the remainder of the month in regular routine work.

Congratulatory messages from the C.-in-Chief downwards were received by the units of the 62nd Div. on the part played in the Cambrai offensive, and the following were recipients of honours published in the lists which were received on the 29th December:

2/4th K.O.Y.L.I.

D.S.O., Maj. (actg. Lt.-Col.) R. E. Power.

M.C., Lts. A. E. Earle, R. Hale-White (R.A.S.C. attd.), C. J. H. McCausland; 2/Lts. J. L. Rodger, F. Cocker and P. Scholes.

D.C.M., Lce.-Cpl. R. Elliott.

M.M., Lce.-Cpl. E. Simpson and 11 others.

2/5th K.O.Y.L.I.

Bar to D.S.O., Maj. (acting Lt.-Col.) B. J. Barton.

D.S.O., Lt. (actg. Capt.) A. C. Lynn and 2/Lt. W. G. James.

M.C., Lt. (actg. Capt.) and Adjt. A. Robinson, 2/Lts. E. Morris and W. C. Ibbott.

D.C.M., Sgts. J. W. Haskey, O. C. Thomas and F. Roberts; Ptes. E. Budby and H. J. Boam.

M.M., 17 N.C.O.'s and men.

December 11th: Lt.-Col. B. H. H. Perry, R. Scots, took over command of the 2/4th Bn. from Lt.-Col. Power, who went to command the 1/Buffs.

The great German counterstroke of the 30th November was, as we have already described, made in two sections, one at either flank of the gap made in the Hindenburg Line by General Byng with his Third Army. The enemy's design was that the two forces engaged, acting as a pair of pincers, should burst their way through the flanks of the new British line, the one from the south working in a north-westerly direction, the other from the north working south-westwards. If both had been successful there would have resulted a squeezing of the divisions of the Third Army which might well have ended in the loss of the portion of the Hindenburg Line which had been gained on the 20th. The south attack penetrated but failed to get behind the Third Army; the north was, happily for our arms, a complete failure, ending in great losses for the Germans; but there was a contraction of the British front due to the salient formed by the giving way at the south end of the line.

Thus the fighting in 1917 virtually came to an end, that is to say, the fighting of historical importance.

There was yet an incident on the Passchendaele front, dismissed in half-a-dozen lines in contemporary history, which involved a handful of battalions in dire distress, of which one happened to be the 2/K.O.Y.L.I. It is with the affairs of the battalions and with the lives of its gallant soldiers that this regimental record is concerned. In devoting a few pages to this incident, therefore, it can hardly be said that the treatment of the affair is bringing it out of its perspective.

On the 23rd November the 2/K.O.Y.L.I. relieved the 2/R. Sussex in the right sub-sector of the II Corps front. This was about three-quarters of a mile north-east of Passchendaele, one and a-quarter miles south of Westroosebeke, the scene of much recent heavy fighting. Some idea of the difficulties experienced in moving about this land of enduring hope may be gathered from the record that, before the forward companies completed the relief in the dark at 8 p.m., there were thirty casualties. The front line companies had to wade through mud knee-deep, and the weight of battle-stores carried was from 67 to 68 lb. per man. Each man carried two days' rations, and the battalion was supplied with 200 petrol tins of water and 400 home-made "Tommy Cookers." Hot food was conveyed to the men by night in "hot food containers," *i.e.*, petrol tins again, containing hot soup or tea, wrapped in straw and packed into the men's packs.

THE 2ND BN. NEAR PASSCHENDAELE.

On the 25th November the battalion was relieved by the 16/H.L.I. It had been making intimate acquaintance with the particular section of mud over which it was destined to spread itself in attack formation before a wakeful and active enemy in the middle of the night of the 1st–2nd December.

Our artillery was active through the night. No telephonic communication existed to the front line trenches, but Cpl. Mair and Lce.-Cpl. Groves worked throughout the night and laid a line, all the time subject to shell fire. Up to 12 noon the casualties numbered: other ranks, killed 11, wounded 23, missing 6. In the afternoon Lt.-Col. L. Lamotte, Sussex R., joined the battalion and assumed command.

On the 26th the battalion entrained at St. Jean for Dambre camp, north of Vlamertinghe, for reorganisation prior to an attack. It went back to St. Jean on the 30th, and before midnight of the 1st December was in position facing Westroosebeke, hoping to carry out its orders to drive the enemy off the ridge ahead.

The attack was made by the 97th Inf. Bde. together with two battalions of the 25th Inf. Bde. of the 8th Div. The 2/K.O.Y.L.I. occupied 400 yards in the front line of five battalions and was right battalion of the 97th brigade, having the 2/R.B. on its right. 2/Lt. H. L. Brigham was to have been the right directing officer, but he was wounded half an hour before "Zero," and Sgt. Davies took his place. "Zero" hour was 1.55 a.m.

The element of surprise was all-important for a successful attack. This night was bright with moonlight. The movement of the troops before "Zero" hour had been only too easily observed.

Promptly at the arranged moment the battalion advanced from the tape; equally promptly the enemy opened with a destructive machine-gun fire. Casualties among the leading officers and N.C.O.'s were numerous, and very soon there was no possiblity of keeping direction. The men floundered forward, but there was a long way to go and the machine guns were taking their toll all the time; the units all along the front were becoming mixed; in a few minutes the O.C. Bn. at his Headquarters ceased to have a battalion to direct. The reports subsequently made by the senior N.C.O.'s of the three leading companies and by the one remaining company officer, who commanded the support company, supply the story of this unmitigated misfortune. They were as follows:

In "A" Company, commanded by 2/Lt. H. J. Knight, the other two officers, 2/Lts. C. P. Halliday and J. V. Webb (who had joined the battalion only the day before), and the Company Sgt.-Maj., became casualties in the first five minutes. After proceeding a considerable distance the company dug itself in alongside a party of the 2/R.B., and so remained till the night of the 2nd–3rd.

In "C" Company within fifty yards of the start all the officers and senior N.C.O.s were *hors de combat*, with the exception of Sgt. Hayward, who led the men on 500 yards. Here they held on till dawn, when Sgt. Hayward withdrew his seven men who were still with him to a position in his left rear on the far side of the Passchendaele-Roosebeke road, where they dug themselves in.

"D" was the left company. The remnant were taken in hand by Sgt. Horne, who found himself in touch with the 16/H.L.I. upon his left. He joined up with the right company of that battalion, and went on with the Highlanders to attack two pill-boxes which were in their front. Nothing had been seen of Capt. Forde, who had been in command of the company, since going the first 250 yards. 2/Lt. J. N. Ellis of the company joined him and together they made two attempts to take the pill-boxes, but both 2/Lt. Ellis and his platoon Sgt. were killed and the attacks failed. The men dug themselves in, but later were driven out by a counter-attack. Sgt. Horne withdrew to a trench where he found three officers and twenty men of the 16/H.L.I., and he remained with them till they were withdrawn to Irish Farm at 5.30 a.m. on the 3rd December.

"B" was the support company, commanded by Capt. J. Hassell. His report stated that immediately after the start the enemy illuminated the ground with Véry lights and opened with machine-gun fire. He reached Hill 52, his first objective, with one platoon, the other three platoons being ahead, and established a strong post to support the others if they came back. 2/Lt. Corcoran came back to him here and reported that he had reached the two pill-boxes which were his objective, but had found them too strongly held for his numbers to take them. Soon after that there was a general retirement from the front, and his men were carried back to the jumping-off tape. He tried to re-organise, but found great difficulty, for men of all battalions of the brigade, except the 17/H.L.I., were mixed up, so he set them to work at consolidating their position, and then got all the K.O.Y.L.I. men together whom he could find. With these he established three strong posts, putting ten men in each.

Except for the Headquarters officers, Capt. Hassell was the only unwounded officer left with the battalion. All the Company Sgt.-Majs. were casualties and most of the senior N.C.O.'s also. The men whom Capt. Hassell placed in his posts were the only men of the battalion who were discoverable in the morning, but there were many others who had attached themselves to other units and were helping in other parts of the field.

The battalion was withdrawn to Irish Farm in the night of the 2nd–3rd, and back to Danbre camp by 'bus at 2 p.m.

The following is a list of the officers who went into action (the letter after each name denotes whether the officer was killed, wounded or missing):

Bn. Headquarters, Lt.-Col. L. Lamotte, Capt. and Adjt. H. S. Howard, 2/Lt. K. J. Box, 2/Lt. J. F. Evans.

"A" Company, 2/Lts. H. J. Knight (w), H. L. Brigham (w), C. P. Halliday (w), J. V. Webb (w).

"B" Company, Capt. J. Hassell, 2/Lts. A. W. Stark (w), A. T. Corcoran (k), E. Cain (m).

"C" Company, Capt. P. Lambert (w), 2/Lts. T. S. Goode (w), G. W. Asquith (m), C. S. Allen (w).

"D" Company, Capt. H. R. Forde (k), 2/Lt. J. N. Ellis (k), R. D. Abbiss (k). 2/Lt. J. S. Wilson, who was attached to the 97th T. M. Battery, was wounded.

In other ranks: killed 18, died of wounds 5, missing 41, wounded 120.

The battalion was back again in its old place opposite Westroosebeke by the 17th Dec., and the line was by this time comparatively quiet.

On the last day of the year it proceeded by train from Elverdinghe Station to Audruicq *via* St. Omer, and marched to Zouafques, near Calais, where the inhabitants gave the men a great welcome.

THE 8TH BN. IN ITALY.

In the latter part of 1917 the alarming situation of the armies of Italy became too pressing to be disregarded by the Allied governments, and finally was the reason for withdrawing six French divisions and five British from the western front, which were hurried with all speed to the assistance of the Italian armies on the line of the river Piave. As a reinforcement for the Italian spring offensive, eleven batteries of British 6-in. howitzers with thirty-five French heavy guns had previously been lent to the Italians. General Cadorna, the Italian Commander-in-Chief, had urged the Allies to send him the divisions early in the year, but until the crisis induced by the failure at Caporetto (October 24th) opened the eyes of the French and British governments to the urgency of the situation, there had been no real community of effort, and no unity of command. From this date forward efforts were made to ensure greater unity, and the Supreme Allied Council, which met at Versailles, became a permanent institution.

General Sir Herbert Plumer was appointed Commander-in-Chief of the British forces on the Italian front; he was succeeded by Gen. Lord Cavan in March, 1918.

The 23rd Div., in which the 8/K.O.Y.L.I. was included, was among the divisions which were ordered to Italy.

Throughout September the 8th Bn. had been in the front line in the Dickebusch area. The casualties during the month were: officers, wounded, Capt. G. T. Nye, 2/Lts. F. H. J. M. Keefe and F. Downes, and Lt. J. C. Pearce, M.D., R.A.M.C. (attd.)

Other ranks, killed 34, missing 3, wounded 84, and shell-shocked 16.

On the 4th October the battalion was transferred to the Ypres sector and for a time it was in the front line east of Polygon Wood. In this period the casualties were: officers, killed, Lt. H. S. Pettinger, attd. Headquarters 70th Inf. Bde., wounded, Capt. E. V. H. Bradley and Lt. O. H. Cooke; other ranks, killed 7, wounded 31.

Capt. A. W. B. Becher and Lt. O. H. Cooke won Bars to their M.C., 2/Lt. E. V. Coltar was awarded the M.C. 1 D.C.M. and 15 M.M.'s also were given in the battalion.

The battalion was at Esquerdes till the 10th November, when it received orders to entrain at Wizerne and at Arques for the move of the 23rd Div. to Italy.

The train journey through France, Piedmont and Lombardy occupied four days, and came to an end on arrival at Mantua, the birthplace of Virgil, an appropriate starting-place for the battalion on its Æneid. The rest of the journey was accomplished by road. The British divisions were assembling in the Montello sector on the river Piave, some fifteen miles from the place where that river issues from the great ranges of the Veneto Trentine mountains. The 8/K.O.Y.L.I. was from the 15th November to the 2nd December on the line of march, billeted from night to night in the villages and kindly welcomed by the inhabitants. It may be of interest to trace the stages of the march, and a list of the stopping-places is therefore given: they were Bigarello, Nogara, Vaugadizza, Villa Nuova, Montruglio, Rampazzo, Isola di Callura, Castello di Gorgon, Alberedo and Edificio.

The battalion went into the front line opposite Edificio and relieved the 2/136th Regt. of the 70th Italian Div., being left battalion of brigade, having an Italian division on the left and a battalion of the Foresters on the right.

On the 6th the front line was visited by H.R.H. the Prince of Wales, who was received at the Headquarters of the battalion.

On the 9th 2/Lt. Downes had the stimulating experience of crossing the Piave with an Italian patrol.

From the 13th to the 19th the battalion was in support trenches, and from the 20th till the end of the year was in reserve in billets at Biadene, mainly engaged in tactical exercises in the training area.

PRISONERS-OF-WAR.

The close of the year 1917 witnessed a new departure in the treatment of prisoners-of-war. Through the mediation of the Dutch government an arrangement had been sanctioned, by which the prisoners who had been over three years in captivity might be interned in Holland and Switzerland, in equal numbers representing Great Britain on the one hand and Germany on the other. By the terms of this arrangement the officers, N.C.O.'s and some men of the 2/K.O.Y.L.I., who had been captured in the retreat from Mons, had been assembled from the prison camps in the interior of Germany, at Aix-la-Chapelle (Aachen), and commenced to enter Holland by train in the New Year. Of their original number one, Maj. Yate, had lost his life in an attempt to escape from Torgau in Saxony; several of the officers and N.C.O.s had made attempts to escape and had been re-captured; but the majority had been in camps too distant from the frontier lines to render escape feasible except under exceptional circumstances.

Opposite this page will be found a print (from a photograph) of the original cheque by means of which the officers of this battalion from their prison in Torgau in 1914 effectually managed to let their next-of-kin know that they were alive in the hands of the enemy. The German government had not given any information on the subject of the prisoners who were in their hands before this cheque was depicted in the English press, and as, in the casualty lists published by the British government, all the names appeared under the heading of "killed," the prompt action taken by Messrs. Cox & Co., who received the old cheque after it had been cleared, brought relief in a dozen homes in England.

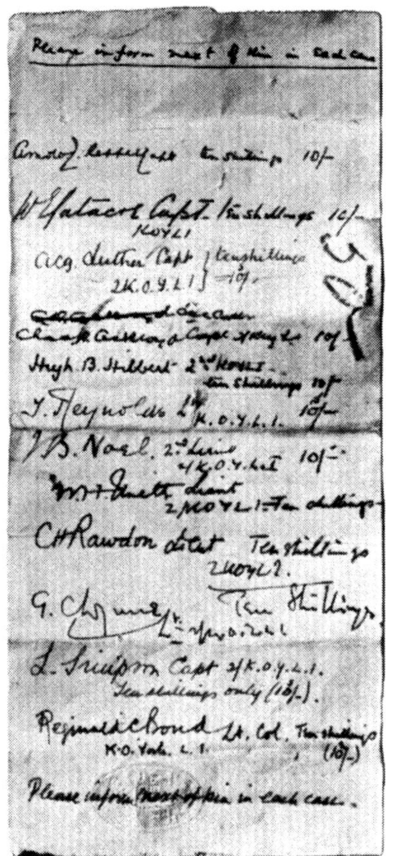

W. L. Gatacre Capt. Ten shillings 10/-
KOYLI
A. G. Luther Capt. ten shillings
2K.O.Y.L.I. 10/-
Hugh B. Hilbert 2nd KOYLI
Ten shillings 10/-
T. Reynolds Lt. K.O.Y.L.I. 10/-
J. B. Noel 2nd Lieut
2/K.O.Y.L.I. 10/-
C H Rawdon Lieut Ten shillings
2KOYLI
L. Simpson Capt 2/K.O.Y.L.I.
Ten shillings only (10/-).
Reginald C Bond Lt. Col. Ten shillings
K.O. Yorks. L.I. (10/-)
Please inform next of kin in each case.

THE PRISONER OF WAR CHEQUE

To face page 914.

THE EARLY DAYS OF 1918

XVIII

WITH the New Year (1918) the dull rumbling and clanking of heavily laden troop trains, moving from east to west, was constantly heard by day and night by people in Germany who lived within sound of the railways. The newspapers were silent on the subject of the great strategic movement that was in progress, but there was an air of expectancy. Russia had withdrawn from the struggle, swamped by the rising tide of Bolshevism, and there was a diminishing need for Germany to maintain an army on her eastern frontiers. A final great offensive was to be made on land at Ludendorff's bidding, while the German naval authorities were employing every possible means to increase the submarine output, in order to strike effectively at sea against the American transports engaged in bringing over to Europe the new troops for service in France.

Germany was an armed camp and her system of railways was built for such an emergency; every unit of man-power was put forth in the effort; her women had donned uniform to serve in the place of men on her railways and on her tramways in the cities; her copper-covered domes were stripped of their metal, her church bells had gone into the melting-pot, her national rationing system was calculated out to the last ounce in order to keep the fighting troops well-fed even at the expense of her population. The nation rallied to the call for a supreme effort, and for a time the disease which was attacking her body, the seeds of which had been sown by the enemies of her established authority and fed by insidious propaganda from outside, was arrested, and the development of a revolution was postponed to give her armies a last chance of dominating the situation in the west. In taking the offensive her spirits rose.

At Clausthal, in the Harz Mountains, out of hearing of the groaning troop trains, there was a British officers' prisoners-of-war camp, which had for its commandant a notable bully. It was this man's custom to arrive at the morning "Appel" or roll-call with a newspaper in his hand, and to greet the assembled prisoners with any item of news which he thought would be particularly unpalatable. One morning in March, 1918, in a loud voice and flushed with excitement, he greeted them with these words, "Have you read your newspapers this morning? I will tell you. You will soon hear great news. Five hundred thousand Germans *have gone west*, you know!" A cheer from the prisoners, and up went all their caps in the air. The

Commandant was puzzled; he shouted yet louder, "Five hundred thousand *gone west*, you know. I know what I speak!" Again cheers and renewed exhibitions of delight. The Commandant left the parade in wrath, and went back to his office to ponder over the singular ebullition of spirits which his communication had evoked.

The German preparations included the massing of from twenty to thirty batteries of artillery (about 100 guns) to every 1,100 yards of front to be attacked. Over forty divisions were withdrawn from the various eastern fronts and from the front in Italy, to be brought across Germany in trains to reinforce the armies in France and Belgium. The divisions already on that front which were destined to take part in the offensive were taken out and given a special training behind the lines. Great increases in the number of machine-guns and light trench-mortars were made, for great reliance was placed on these weapons. Ludendorff had no high opinion of the effectiveness of tanks, "except when employed in masses against troops who had lost their discipline," and as the output of the arsenals and workshops in other engines of war kept those establishments working at their utmost capacity, he had to be content with a limited number of tanks.

A change was made in the system of employing artillery fire. If the advantage of surprise was to be retained, it was impracticable to carry out registration beforehand. Errors of the gun were determined behind the line and reliance was placed on a sudden bombardment, short in duration but great in intensity. The manner in which the British artillery barrage had been conducted at the opening of the Cambrai offensive served as an object-lesson. The infantry were now taught to march close up behind the advancing barrage. Ludendorff realised that it was disastrous for infantry in an attack to allow the barrage to get too far ahead, and he fixed the normal rate for a barrage at 1,100 yards to the hour.

In the previous year the German armies on the western front had been specially trained in the principles of defensive fighting; this year they were trained for attack and for a war of movement. "*It was found to be no light task to teach the troops to adopt the necessary open formation*," wrote Ludendorff.

There were strikes in Germany at the end of January, which threw a lurid light on the activities and propaganda work of the Independent Socialists.

For the German High Command it was a race against time. Never at any time in the war had the Germans the same local preponderance of force as they had assembled on the western front in March, 1918, but the danger which had to be faced by the German High Command was that time would weight the scales in favour of the Allies with American troops (who were already arriving), while loss of weight at their own end would be effected by disintegration with every day which was allowed to the propagandists.

While the German army in the west was "*waiting for the opportunity to act*" and was facing "*the biggest task in its history*," confident in its strength, the Allies were feeling no less assured; the self-reliance of the British troops was unimpaired. Whether it was the experience of breaking through the Hindenburg Line at Cambrai, confidence in the leaders who had been proved by the successive years of continuous devotion to duty, or merely temperament, there was undoubtedly at the commencement of the New Year on the part of the troops a confidence and a will to win which exceeded any previous year's experience of like emotions.

There is a Latin motto *Possunt quia posse videntur* ("They can because they think they can"), and here on the western front the armies on both sides in the spring of 1918 were convinced that they could win; in the end victory would go to the fighting men who, through storm and sunshine, through reverse and renewed effort, were able to endure longest and keep that motto before their eyes.

One measure which the British Commander-in-Chief found he was forced to introduce was the reduction of the number of infantry battalions in a division from twelve to nine (or rather, from thirteen to ten, for the Pioneer battalion in each division was retained as the tenth battalion). This was necessitated by the falling off of the drafts from home. Three battalions in each division had to be broken up, and those had to be selected whose numbers were most reduced, whose ranks it was most difficult to fill; in many cases the units on whom the choice fell had sister battalions into which a large proportion of the disbanded personnel was drafted, which tempered the ill wind in their case, but it was when the portions of a battalion were drafted into other divisions that the blow was painful, and the "axed" felt that they had lost their identity. The division was the family unit; to be transferred out of his division seemed for a time to be a sentence to banishment, in the case of an officer or soldier.

Of the K.O.Y.L.I. battalions the 6th and 7th were broken up; the 10th disappeared in name but was mostly incorporated in its sister battalion, the 9th; the 1/5th joined up with the 2/5th, to be called the 5th Bn. in future, in the 187th Inf. Bde. The headquarters and companies of the 1/5th K.O.Y.L.I. joined the 62nd Div. on January 30th. The other transfers were effected about the same time.

Machine-gun companies were henceforward grouped as battalions. One battalion was formed in each division; the battalion consisted of four companies of four sections each.

Early in the year the British front to be held was extended southwards to relieve French troops; an additional 28 miles were taken over, making a front of 130 miles. This added greatly to the British

Commander-in-Chief's responsibilities at a time when the forces under his control had already been reduced by sending five divisions to Italy, and when he had been forced to diminish the strength of his divisions because the drafts from England were insufficient to replace losses.

By the end of March the American troops in France had a combatant strength of 150,000. These were organised in five divisions, giving the American division twice the strength of a German division. As yet there was only one division which was sufficiently advanced in its training to be initiated in fighting line tactics; the others were undergoing preliminary training behind the lines, it did not seem possible that the presence of the American Army could make its weight felt for some months to come.

A defensive policy was consequently imposed on the Allied commanders for the time, and in the British line all available men were employed in working parties who were busy reconstructing the defence system. The initiative had passed to the side of Germany.

The massing of German troops opposite the British line was fully realised, and it was anticipated that a great blow would be struck in the region where the French and British forces joined hands. By mid-February the enemy had transferred 28 divisions from the east and 6 divisions from the Italian front, and there were others to come. Our aeroplane observers discovered a great increase in the number of ammunition dumps and in the railways and communications generally.

Ludendorff determined to strike two blows against the British line, the one with the German 17th Army of 28 divisions between Croisilles, south-east of Arras, and Mœuvres; the other with the 2nd and 18th Armies, of 22 and 26 divisions respectively, between Villers-Guislain and the Oise south of St. Quentin. The Cambrai (or Flesquières) re-entrant was merely to be "contained" for the time, in the hope that it would become cut off by the operations on both its flanks. The British Armies opposed to these attacks were the Third (Byng), composed of 17 divisions, 10 of which were in the first line and 7 in reserve, and the Fifth (Gough) made up of 11 divisions in the line, with 3 cavalry and 3 infantry divisions in reserve.

When the first great offensive of 1918 was opened by the Germans on March 21st, there was no K.O.Y.L.I. battalion serving in the Third Army, and one only, the 9th, was with the 21st Div. in the Fifth Army. Other battalions of the K.O.Y.L.I. soon became involved, however, when reinforcements were hurried round to support or replace the shattered divisions which had taken part in the first onslaught.

The British forces were disposed in three defence belts, the most advanced line of all being held by a thin outpost screen covering the main positions.

So much for the general dispositions at the commencement of the year. We will now discover how the various battalions of the K.O.Y.L.I. were engaged in the period between the opening of the year and the commencement of the great German offensive.

In Chapter XIII it has been related how the 1/K.O.Y.L.I. spent the long and weary months in camp at Gumus Dere. The Bulgarians opposed to it gave the battalion comparatively little trouble, and inflicted far fewer casualties on it than the relentless enemy, malaria. It was a cruel fate that condemned the senior battalion to a life of inaction and ill-health, while the younger battalions added lustre to the name of the Regiment in the hottest parts of the fighting in France.

THE 1ST BN.

On the other hand the 2/K.O.Y.L.I. was, perhaps, more constantly in action than any other unit of the Regiment and, like other battalions on the western front, when not in action was either in the trenches or preparing for the next battle.

THE 2ND BN.

The last days of the old year were spent by the battalion in a march to Zouafques, the training area, where Christmas was kept on January 3rd with all the customary observances. There were bales of presents awaiting the men, sent out by Gen. Sir Arthur Wynne as Treasurer of the Regimental War Fund. A football match in a snowstorm, in which the officers played the sergeants, ended in a draw. It was the first occasion for twelve months that the military situation permitted the sergeants to assemble in this way for a festive reunion.

News was received that Capt. J. Hassell was awarded the M.C. for the gallant manner in which he led his company during the attack north-west of Passchendaele. Capt. H. S. Howard also received the M.C. for his good work as adjutant of the battalion during the period when it had been engaged in the attack and capture of Ten Tree Alley, the advance from Rouvroy to Nesle, the capture of Savy, occupation of Holnon Wood, the capture of La Fayet, and the defence of Lombartzyde: his C.O. reported that his courage and devotion to duty had been beyond all praise.

Sixteen officers joined with big drafts of other ranks during the month; among the officers were Capt. W. P. Bradley-Williams, Capt. J. Rodgers and Lt. and Qr.-Mr. E. Hodgson.

On January 25th the battalion marched to the Nordhoek area in brigade support, and again on the 27th to the Het Sas area into the front line. While here notification was received that Lce.-Cpl. Swain and Pte. Laverick were to receive the decoration of the Croix de Guerre, granted by the King of the Belgians.

Het Sas was the left sub-sector of the Houthulst Forest sector, which was almost the extreme left of the front held by the Second Army. As the French troops had been withdrawn, the Belgian right now joined the left of the Second (British) Army in the neighbourhood of Houthulst. The forest, which covered an area of over 6,000 acres, was still in the enemy's hands; it clothed the rising ground forming the northern tip of the crescent of high ground which encircles Ypres. The approaches to it from the west and south were over the low-lying swampy country where the mud was deeper and softer than in any part of the line, and where men, floundering by night, were accustomed to wrapping their rifles and Lewis-guns in strips of flannel to save the barrels and sights from becoming choked if they slipped in the mud.

It was just south of Houthulst Forest that there was a certain amount of activity in the middle of February; the Germans were inclined to focus attention on the extreme north as much as possible in order to divert attention from the region of their great efforts which were about to be made further south. The 2/K.O.Y.L.I. was in the midst of this activity, which did not at any time take place on an extensive front. Passchendaele lies about five miles to the south-east.

On the 4th February the battalion relieved the 5/R Scots in Het Sas. The night was moonless and very dark, making the duck-board tracks hard to distinguish. The sub-sector being new to the battalion, every precaution was taken to forearm against surprise. Early morning was spent in getting bearings, patrols were busy by day and throughout the nights which followed. The ground was very wet and pitted with shell-holes; in the hours of darkness the men were at work on improving the position. There were many young officers to be initiated, who gained practical experience in the command of the various "strafing," "listening" and "battle" patrols; the landscape was frequently lit up at night by the enemy's Véry lights, which were followed by bursts of machine-gun fire.

In the night of the 6th one patrol drew fire from a pill-box which it had endeavoured to surprise; in the retirement a fine soldier was killed in the person of Pte. Coleridge, who had been out in France with the battalion for over three years and had earned the M.M. for gallantry in the attack on Ten Tree Alley (Beaumont Hamel) on February 10th, 1917.

On the 8th the battalion went back to brigade support, and on into brigade reserve the following day, but relieved the 16/H.L.I. in the left sector, south of Houthulst Wood, on the 14th. In the night of the 17th special officers' patrols went out to reconnoitre the enemy's position about Surcouff Farm, at the south-west corner of the great forest; it had been decided to raid this position the following night.

The raid was carried out by "B" and "D" Companies, and was of some importance. Orders had been elaborately worked out and were carefully adhered to, with the result that the raid was completely successful. The 2/Border carried out a similar raid at the same time on the right of the K.O.Y.L.I. Congratulatory telegrams were received on the result from all the commands, even from the Commander-in-Chief.

The action of the assaulting companies was as follows:

"D" Company, the right attack, had for its objective three pill-boxes by the farmhouse, while "B" Company, the left attack, was directed on a group of three posts or shelters.

Each company had three platoons in the attack with separate aims in view and one platoon in support.

"Zero" hour was 11 p.m. on February 18th.

Promptly at the hour our artillery bombardment descended on all objectives and the raiders attacked.

The right platoon of the right attack ("D") arrived at its objective in nine minutes. The box was attacked by passing round both its flanks; the box was captured and one prisoner was taken.

The centre platoon of "D" reached its box at about the same time; the defenders came out to fight; five were killed in a bayonet fight, four others were captured with their machine-gun in the building, which was entered and searched.

The left platoon of "D" had advanced with the centre party as far as their objective, and then went on to attack the third box. Lt. A. F. McC. Riggs, in command of this party, rushed up under rifle-fire, and seeing the enemy in the act of pushing a machine-gun into position at a low loophole, he kicked the gun aside and inserted a bomb in the loophole; the bomb destroyed the gun. He then led his men round the box and encountered the enemy at its entrance. Eight surrendered, but others inside the box refused to come out; a bomb was thrown in, to which the defenders replied with another, which exploded and wounded Lt. Riggs on the hand. More bombs followed and the box was taken; ten of the enemy were discovered dead inside.

This company had one officer and six other ranks wounded.

In the left attack the platoons of "B" Company rushed the posts as soon as the barrage lifted, but they were already vacated. All platoons at once pushed forward over some wire to search the area allotted to them, eager to secure prisoners and identifications. Three further posts or shelters were discovered, guarded by a mesh of wire which had to be cut. Parties then streamed through the gaps and rushed the shelters. 2/Lt. E. D. Sewell's party on the left bombed and entered the left shelter; two dead were found and identification was secured. The centre shelter proved a blank. The occupants of the right one refused to surrender and were bombed; when the place was entered six dead were found in it. The platoons then spread out and again pushed forward, but in their eagerness to secure prisoners and beat the record of the company in the right attack, they advanced right into our own barrage and suffered a few casualties. Forty-eight minutes after "Zero" the commander ordered the retirement. A directing tape had been run out for 500 yards to guide men back in the withdrawal. This proved of great value, for the stars were obscured by the smoke from our shell-fire.

There were ten casualties in "B" Company, of whom two other ranks were killed, six wounded and two missing.

The success of the raid was due as much to the capable leadership of the junior officers and section commanders as to the splendid fighting spirit displayed by all ranks. All the men employed had been forward in patrols to reconnoitre the objectives beforehand.

The immediate rewards announced on March 1st included:

M.C. to Capt. C. E. L. Watkins, who had made personal reconnaissance prior to the raid on two successive nights. The excellence of the arrangements in his company were the result of his careful supervision and of his co-ordination of the action of his parties throughout the operation and until withdrawal was complete.

M.C. to Lt. A. F. McCausland Riggs, who continued to superintend his parties after he was wounded, "*displaying the utmost gallantry and dash.*"

M.M.s to Sgt. Ralph Horne, "*absolutely fearless in action,*" who had been on service in France for over three years, and to Lce.-Cpls. George Tanner, James C. Smith, Richard Hunt, Henry Soakell and Clarence McQuillan; also to Ptes. W. Pillsworth, J. Hopkins, and Harry Dilks.

On March 8th, shortly before dawn, after heavy artillery preparation, the enemy delivered a strong local attack on a front of over a mile on this same sector just south of Houthulst Forest. The night had been quiet until 3 a.m., when the barrage opened on the 97th Inf. Bde. line of outposts, where the 10/A. & S.H. were in occupation; the 2/K.O.Y.L.I. was in position as brigade support with Bn. Headquarters at La Chaudière. When the enemy's guns were heard the battalion "stood to," ready for any emergency.

At 7.35 a.m. orders came from the brigade, in consequence of which "A" and "D" Companies moved forward to what was known as the "Corps Line," the second line of defence under the new system. At the same time Bn. Headquarters were shifted to Girdwood Château, near to Bde. Headquarters. At 8.15 the brigade sent news that posts Nos. 13 to 18 were in the enemy's hands and ordered two companies 2/K.O.Y.L.I. ("B" and "C" Companies were detailed) to carry out a counter-attack, drive the enemy from the captured posts, and exploit success as far as our artillery barrage allowed.

As the "Zero" hour for the counter-attack was fixed for 9.20 a.m. there was no time to lose. The C.O. (Maj. Boddington, temporarily), with his Adjutant, Capt. Howard, ran over a mile under artillery fire to issue his verbal orders to the companies. These he detailed with great precision and directed each company to its place in the "jumping-off line," arriving himself at Louvois Farm in that line to establish his headquarters there, at the same time as the companies, which was nine minutes before "Zero" hour.

Maj. Boddington's action, his disregard of fire and his lucid explanations led to success; the men backed up his effort by crossing a mile of shell-torn ground in record time and in the best of spirits.

In the attack which followed, a slight rise of ground, Hill 20, had first to be crossed. Capt. J. Hassell led "B" and Capt. J. Rodgers led "C" Company. For the first 150 yards no great attention was paid to the attackers, but on reaching the rise both companies came under a destructive artillery fire from heavy guns, and on the forward slope a machine-gun barrage opened on them. The Captain of "C" Company, which was on the right, and three N.C.O.s of his Company Headquarters were wounded by one shell (Capt. Rodgers died from his wounds that night). 2/Lt. M. Nicolay assumed command of the company. The companies pressed on and when within 200 yards or so of the captured line of posts could see the enemy leaving them. This proved altogether too much for their stoicism; the companies "accelerated their rate of advance" as their chronicler put it in the diary, and rushed the position "cheering themselves hoarse." About 500 yards of frontage had been wrested from our outpost line by the enemy; the whole of this was recovered and a Lewis-gun, which they had not time to carry off in their precipitate retreat, was retaken and used with effect on the retreating Germans. The enemy at once opened an intense machine-gun fire on the position, but, ignoring this, the companies settled down, using their rifles and Lewis-guns with such effect that the enemy was driven back for a space of over 300 yards beyond our original front line posts. For more than an hour the machine-gun duel was continued until the enemy gave up the fire fight and became comparatively inactive.

The position was maintained throughout the day, and in the early hours of March 9th it was handed over to relieving troops exactly as it had been before the attack, except for one or two posts which had been obliterated by the original heavy gun barrage.

The casualties suffered by the 2/K.O.Y.L.I. included: killed, 2/Lt. W. Hughes and 2 men; died of wounds, Capt. J. Rodgers and 1 man; wounded, 25 men.

The Bde. Commander, Br.-Gen. C. A. Blacklock, sent a message: "*I congratulate Maj. Boddington and all ranks concerned on the gallant attack they made on the morning of the 8th. Nothing could have been finer than the way they tackled an exceedingly difficult situation. It reflects the greatest credit on the efficiency and fighting spirit of the battalion. Well done!*"

Lt.-Col. Lamotte had temporarily been away at a course with the Fourth Army School.

Honours were awarded as follows :—

D.S.O., Lt. (actg. Maj.) H. W. Boddington.

D.S.O. Lt. (actg. Capt.) J. Hassell, "*utterly fearless in action; his men will follow him anywhere.*"

M.C., 2/Lt. M. Nicolay, 2/Lt. H. L. Colley and C.S.M. John Bramley (C.S.M. Bramley was one of the original Expeditionary Force who had already won the D.C.M. at Beaumont Hamel).

D.C.M., Sgt. W. C. Holdway and Lce.-Cpl. J. P. Baxter.

M.M., Pte. G. L. Probert.

On the 12th March Brig.-Gen. Blacklock said farewell to the battalion on his promotion to the command of a division; in an address to the men he said he had "*never seen a better fighting spirit or a more cheery lot of lads in any body of men.*"

It was on the morning of March 13th that C.S.M. Bramley earned his M.C. The battalion was in the front line holding thirteen posts.

At 7-30 a.m. the enemy opened an intense barrage on the line, but specially on Colombo House, a concreted pill-box, and he followed this up with an attempted raid, two parties, each about 60 strong, converging on Colombo House. C.S.M. Bramley, being the officer on duty at No. 1 post, saw the waves of the enemy raiders forming near the pill-box and ordered fire to be opened from his post, though his men were under heavy gun-fire at the time. The enemy lines advanced and were beaten back, but the casualties in No. 1 post from the shell-fire were so numerous that the C.S.M. and one private alone remained unwounded. He then so disposed the men in neighbouring posts that further advances were checked and frustrated. Our barrage came down on the waves of the enemy where they lay, forcing them to rise and scatter. Later No. 1 post became almost surrounded and Colombo House was actually bombed, but the firing from our posts never abated and the enemy was forced to retire. The entrance to Colombo House had become jammed from shell-fire and the occupants were imprisoned, but, thanks to its double casing, the hostile bombs failed to burst inside it.

Our casualties numbered in other ranks, 2 killed, 1 missing and 12 wounded.

A further list of awards was published for this and the previous fighting of March 8th, in which M.M.s were given to Cpl. J. Barley (who had acquired a great reputation for fearlessness and devotion to duty), Lce.-Cpls. G. Palmer, H. Fowler, H. J. Walker, T. Bussey, and Pte. F. Hemmings.

On the 21st, the opening day of the great German offensive, the battalion went back to Baboon Camp on the Yser canal, but only to be transferred to Adinfer, *via* Beaumetz and Ransart, to support the Guards Brigade holding the line in front of Adinfer Wood, a few days later.

The 1/4th Bn.

The first three months of 1918 were spent by the 1/4th Bn. K.O.Y.L.I. in the Ypres sector. During the periods in which the front line trenches were occupied by the battalion it was subject to occasional bursts of heavy gun-fire; for instance, on January 9th, when the area round Hillside Farm was shelled by 5.9's, and casualties resulted, 2/Lts. J. R. Holton and W. A. J. Barnett (King's Own, attd.) and twelve other ranks being wounded, and one man being killed. Lt. A. N. Wills died on March 7th from wounds received three days earlier when in the front line.

While the battalion was temporarily back in its training area at St. Sylvestre Cappel (January 21st), M.M. awards were published, *viz.*, to Sgts. W. Alderson and J. W. Stobie, and Ptes. W. H. Rennison, F. Hill and R. H. Lavender.

A fortnight, commencing from January 26th, was spent in Devonshire Camp at work on the Corps line, the second belt of the new defence line which was being prepared to meet the pressure when the German great attack should develop. Capt. G. H. Brook was awarded the M.C. (Bn. Orders of January 30th).

On the breaking up of the 1/5th Bn. K.O.Y.L.I. on January 29th, the 1/4th Bn. received on its strength the following officers and men: Capt. C. T. W. Etches, Lts. W. Tyler, A. N. Wills and R. B. Nicholson; 2/Lts. F. G. Hobbs, C. James (King's Own, attd.), A. R. Chandler (King's Own, attd), J. Dennett (King's Own, attd.), J. S. Steer (King's Own, attd.), and E. S. Guy (attd.); other ranks, 216; also Hon. Capt. and Qr.-Mr. G. A. McNally, joined from the 62nd Div.

By March 2nd the 1/4th Bn. was back in the front line of the Ypres sector, and continued in this sector till the end of the month, the Bn. diary affording no evidence of unusual activity in this quarter, although the German advance was in full flow further down the line.

The 1/5th Bn.

The 1/5th Bn. K.O.Y.L.I. was in the trenches by Zonnebeke (three miles south-west of Passchendaele) at the opening of the new year, being the right battalion of the left brigade of the 49th Division. On January 4th the battalion moved back to the Anzac area with its headquarters at Anzac House. There was some heavy shelling encountered; a working party on the 7th at Daring Crossing had six other ranks killed and five wounded.

On January 19th there came the first intimation that the battalion was to amalgamate with the 2/5th K.O.Y.L.I. and be absorbed in the 62nd Div.

On the 23rd a party of 124 other ranks, surplus to the requirements for re-posting to other battalions, proceeded to the Fourth Army clearing depôt; with this party went Lt. F. D. Martin, 2/Lts. S. C. Bywater, H. Tomalin and K. H. Doig; Lt. T. E. Clarke and 2/Lt. C. H. Crofts also were not posted. All these officers had been attached.

On the 27th the battalion moved to Brandhoek by train; the party detailed to join the 1/4th K.O.Y.L.I. left on the 29th, and the remainder of the 1/5th Bn. proceeded to join the 187th Inf. Bde., 62nd Div., by train from Poperinghe Station. It left the train at Mont St. Eloi and went to the XIII Corps Reinforcement Camp at Ecoivres.

The battalion was inspected in the camp by Maj.-Gen. W. Braithwaite; it sent a contingent of 9 officers and 212 other ranks under Capt. J. W. Morehouse to join the 2/4th Bn. K.O.Y.L.I. in the same brigade, and, joining with the 2/5th Bn., became known for the future simply as the 5/K.O.Y.L.I.

In the *London Gazette* Lt.-Col. C. C. Moxon (late commanding 1/5th Bn.) was mentioned in dispatches and awarded the D.S.O. (he had previously gained the C.M.G.) R.S.M. J. Helliwell received the D.C.M., and C.S.M. W. Frith was mentioned in dispatches.

Two attached officers of the King's Own, 2/Lts. C. H. Crofts and F. J. Doherty, were awarded gallantry cards for recent services.

The headquarters contingent of the battalion included thirteen officers, *viz.*, Maj. (actg. Lt.-Col.) J. Shearman, Maj. A. E. B. Jackson, Capts. B. A. Beach, P. Bentley, P. F. Farnish, H. Brown, and Capt. and Qr.-Mr. H. Barker, Lts. H. W. Richardson, R. Grigg and R. T. Ebrey (P.W.V. attd.); 2/Lt. F. J. Doherty (King's Own, attd.) and Capt. L. W. Batten (R.A.M.C. attd.).

From February 9th, the 5/K.O.Y.L.I. was commanded by Lt.-Col. O. C. S. Watson, with Maj. Shearman as second in command.

Sgt. H. Wotton and Ptes. H. Smith and R. Hemingway received the Belgian Croix de Guerre (Div. Orders 8/2/18).

Until March 22nd the ordinary routine was pursued in the division, but on March 23rd it became obvious that the division was about to take its part in the fighting. As a preliminary step the 5/K.O.Y.L.I. moved into Arras, and was there billeted in the Communal College.

The 62nd Div. had recently been transferred from the XVII Corps to the XIII, and in the early days of January the division relieved the 56th (London) Div. in the right sector of the XIII Corps front, extending from 500 yards south of Gavrelle to 500 yards north-west of Oppy. On January 6th the 2/4th K.O.Y.L.I. relieved the 4/London in the right (Gavrelle) sub-sector in the front line. The weather was very

THE 2/4TH BN.

bad, with much snow and frost, but it was when a thaw set in that the trenches became abominable, for the sides of the trenches crumbled and fell in. An eye was constantly kept on the wire, Lt. A. Morris being repeatedly mentioned in the Diary in connection with the necessary reconnaissances. The aerial activity on both sides was most pronounced.

On January 24th mention is made of the arrival of two officers of the U.S. Army, to be attached for a course of instruction in the trenches, their names being Lt. Tasker and 2/Lt. Hughes, of the 26th Inf. Regt., the forerunners of a great army.

The 2/4th K.O.Y.L.I. had a little "grouse" of its own when the details of the old 1/5th Bn. arrived in the brigade on February 1st, for the new 5/K.O.Y.L.I. took seniority, and the distinguishing patches worn on the uniform had consequently to be changed; the 2/4th had to resign the blue, and to adopt the red diamond!

After a short spell of work on light railways, tunnelling, etc., at Maroeuil the battalion arrived on March 1st at Ecurie to relieve the 2/I.G., of the 4th Guards Bde., at Brierly Hill. The four company commanders at this time were: ("A") Lt. C. J. McCausland, ("B") Capt. J. W. Morehouse, ("C") Lt. C. Mackenzie, and ("D") Capt. G. L. Hudson.

The occupants of the front line were very much on the alert in these days, listening for such sounds as might be made by the enemy's tractors or by trucks unloading, enduring sudden heavy shelling with various kinds of poison gas, and in ceaseless observation. On the 22nd all leave was stopped "as the German offensive has started."

Mention has been made in Chapter XVI of the disbandment of the 6/K.O.Y.L.I. The month of January, 1918, was spent in training, and in divisional competitions and cross-country runs, at Bray-sur-Somme, and later at Ly Fontaine and Remigny. In these latter billets the men had excellent dug-outs, "bunked, and lighted with electricity." Among the awards published in the *London Gazette* of January 1st, 1918, the D.C.M. was granted to Sgt. G. Donaldson.

THE 6TH BN.

On February 12th the battalion marched under the command of Lt.-Col. W. H. M. Micholls to Crisolles, where it came under the orders of the III Corps Reinforcements Officer.

The 6/K.O.Y.L.I. formed the nucleus upon which was founded the 16th Entrenching Bn. Lt.-Col. Micholls was given the command of the new unit. Capt. A. Barker was appointed actg.-Adjt. and Qr.-Mr. Drafts were added from the K.S.L.I., D.C.L.I., and 10/D.L.I., and the organisation of the battalion proceeded forthwith. This battalion is not to be confounded with the 16th (Garrison) K.O.Y.L.I. which had been serving in the Fifth Army since July, 1916, under the orders of the Provost-Marshal.

One of the last entries in the Diary of the 6/K.O.Y.L.I. records the fact that the officers attended a lecture delivered (at Crisolles) by Lt.-Col. F. T. T. Moore, 3/K.O.Y.L.I.

The 7/K.O.Y.L.I. was engaged in routine work in the Reninghelst area till the 12th February, when it moved to the Wippenhoek area near Poperinghe. Here, on the 15th, the battalion came under the orders of Lt.-Col. W. I. Webb-Brown, O.C. Reinforcements XXII Corps.

The 7th Bn.

Lt.-Col. J. T. Janson, on the 16th, made his farewell speech to the men on the occasion of the departure of the battalion transport to join the 61st Inf. Bde. Maj.-Gen. Douglas Smith, commanding 20th Div., came to pay a farewell visit.

Under the scheme for disbanding and amalgamating battalions the 7/K.O.Y.L.I. constituted No. 14 Entrenching Bn. (Authority, D.A.G. 3rd Echelon, No. S/7074/2 dated 26/1/18).

The 9/ and 10/K.O.Y.L.I. (64th Inf. Bde., 21st Div.) formed part of the VII Corps (Congreve), whose place in the line on the threatened front was that of left Corps of the Fifth Army (Gough). The junction of the Third and Fifth Armies was in the neighbourhood of Gouzeaucourt. The Third Army extended north from that point to the region of Arras, while the Fifth Army covered the ground from Gouzeaucourt southwards to Barisis eight miles south of La Fère, where it met the French line. Of the three divisions which represented the VII Corps the 21st Div., with which we are dealing, was the centre, having the 9th on its left and the 16th on its right. Epéhy was in the front line, Heudicourt and Saulcourt were both behind the front line, Haut Allaines, still further back, was the centre of the divisional reserve.

The 9th and 10th Bns.

Throughout January and February the work was constant, not only in repairing the trenches, which were rotten after the frosts and frequently tumbling in, but in constructing the Green line, or third belt of defences. There is an entry in the 9th Bn. diary of January 17th : "*Enemy very quiet, and apparently in as much trouble over the trenches as we are, as he allows our men to expose themselves without shooting at them.*"

On February 6th 12 officers and 250 other ranks were transferred from the 10th to the 9th Bn., and from that date the 10/K.O.Y.L.I. as a unit ceased to exist.

On February 7th the three-battalion brigade, as newly constituted, was disposed with the 7/Leicesters in front line, the 9/K.O.Y.L.I. in support, and the 9/Leicesters in reserve at Saulcourt.

The 9/K.O.Y.L.I. was back in divisional reserve at Haut Allaines when, on the 28th, there came an order to take up battle positions, and it was promptly conveyed forward to Ambush Camp, Saulcourt, by train. It was clearly foreseen that this part of the line would shortly undergo the ordeal of the attack, and from this date onwards the state of preparedness was intensified.

The story of the German offensive will be told in the next chapter.

The headquarters of the 12/K.O.Y.L.I. were at Ecurie, five miles north of Arras. The sector of the front, for which the 31st Div. was responsible, extended from about 500 yards north-west of Oppy to a point about 800 yards west of Acheville; it contained in its area the Vimy ridge, from which excellent observation was obtained of the enemy's trenches and back areas. Within this area the 12/K.O.Y.L.I. was distributed by companies to the brigades of the division, maintaining trenches, constructing dug-outs, erecting camps and hutting, making tramways and wiring frontages. But besides this routine existence there was the probability that in the near future the battalion would be called upon to cast away the pick and grip the rifle if the enemy achieved success in his offensive. In order to be prepared, all who could be spared, officers and others, were sent to attend schools and courses, for Lewis-gun and bomb, gas and pioneer training.

THE 12TH BN.

A number of honours were published for the work of the past season, among them :

Maj. G. M. Stockings was mentioned in dispatches (Authority L.G. dated 18/12/17); as were Ptes. D. Spink and W. Harrop.

Capt. H. D. Gaunt and 2/Lt. W. Read were awarded the M.C. for continuous good work and for bravery and devotion to duty during the operations about Ypres, July–November, 1917.

Lce.-Cpl. J. W. Garton received the M.M. for gallantry in evacuating wounded men under heavy fire near Ypres.

The Belgian Croix-de-Guerre was bestowed on Maj. Stockings, C.Q.M.S. G. Draper, Cpl. Mallander, Sgt. E. Bedford, actg. C.Q.M.S. H. Brittlebank, C.S.M. A. Hull, and No. 550 Pte. T. Wilson. (Authority D.R.O. 3455).

The battalion was reorganised in three companies to match the reorganisation of the division in three brigades. It moved on the 3rd March to Cambligneul for a rest and to fit itself for a fighting part.

THE GERMAN OFFENSIVE IN THE SPRING OF 1918

AMIENS

XIX

IN the early days of March, 1918, the 9/K.O.Y.L.I. was in divisional reserve (with the rest of the 64th Inf. Bde.) at Guyencourt, under the command of Lt.-Col. A. J. McCulloch. The other two brigades of the division, the 62nd and the 110th, were up in the front line.

The 64th Bde. was at work on the trenches of the Yellow line, which was a chord line forming a support to the salient in the front lines. The lines from front to rear were known by the colours Red (front line), Brown, Green, Yellow. The work was varied, for a considerable amount of time was spent in cable-burying, and on March 12th the battalion started work on its agricultural plot at the transport lines camp, where it had been allotted two acres. Meanwhile in the front lines there was what the diary refers to as a great boom in raids. Some German prisoners who were inclined to talk, had indeed referred to the coming great offensive, and the troops were wild to catch a German who would disclose the date of the attack. On the 18th the 62nd Bde. reported that one of its prisoners gave the 20th as the date.

THE 9TH BN.

On March 19th the battalion moved into new positions in the Brown line, the gardening being postponed *sine die*.

On the 21st the storm broke on the Red line, the two brigades of the 21st Div., the 62nd in the north and the 110th in the south, holding their positions all day in spite of the crushing weight of the bombardment and the attacks by the highly-trained infantry of the enemy. The forward line of machine-gun posts and small redoubts had been penetrated and dominated, mainly owing to the dense fog which on this particular morning rendered futile all the carefully laid preparations to resist the shock. Further to the south, however, the neighbouring division of the same corps, the 16th Div., was exposed to an even greater and more overwhelming violence of attack. Some of its forward battalions were obliterated, and the line was pierced by midday, Lempire and Ronnsoy being entered; again further south Hargicourt fell into the enemy's hands. In consequence, the flank of the VII Corps became exposed, although by the timely assistance of its own reserves it continued to hold the greater part of its own battle positions on the night of the 21st.

The 9/K.O.Y.L.I. in the second line could see nothing of what was taking place in the Red line, but the significance of the tremendous bombardment, which grew in intensity from hour to hour, and the frequency with which the 5.9 shells landed round Guyencourt and Saulcourt, left no room for doubt as to the reality of the arrival of the expected offensive. Early in the afternoon the battalion was withdrawn from its position in the Brown line to occupy trenches south of Guyencourt, but at 4.40 p.m. it was back again in its old position. Lt. T. W. Harrison, commanding "C" Company, and C.S.M. Grimshaw were wounded by an 8-in. shell in the move to the Brown line.

On the 22nd the bombardment of the second line became heavier, a barrage of 8-in. shells descending on "C" Company, but as the company was widely extended there were not more than thirty casualties. It appeared that the Germans were now in possession of Vaucelette Farm as well as of Genin Well copse, and a part of Epéhy. From 2 p.m. German low-flying aeroplanes reconnoitred the Brown line, using machine-gun fire on the occupants of the trenches. By them 2/Lt. J. Hargreaves and two other ranks of "D" Company were wounded. At 3.30 p.m. Germans could be seen advancing from the direction of Peizière along the Peizière-Saulcourt road; they were held up when they reached the Jacqvenne Copse ridge by the fire from the battalion, and a Lewis-gun of "C" Company knocked out a German limber team. Lt.-Col. McCulloch sent the Adjt. back to explain the position to our gunners and a battery opened on the crowded target with excellent results, for the enemy attack was stopped with heavy losses; parties repeatedly attempted to push forward on to the ridge, only to be discovered and forced back. All this time the strain of defending an open flank on the right with dwindling forces was becoming greater, and the time was inevitably coming when the 21st Division would have to move back to straighten the line. A warning was sent from Bde. Headquarters that Villers Faucon, away to the right, was in the enemy's hands, and about 5.20 p.m. a position was indicated to fall back to in the event of the battalion finding itself outflanked. The enemy machine-gun fire was being directed on the Brown line, which showed that the resistance of the first line was disappearing. Signallers now found difficulty in keeping the telephone wires open between companies; the wires were repeatedly cut, but it was essential to preserve communication to the last possible moment. At 5.40 p.m. the battalion observers reported the withdrawal of the E. York Bn. from the Brown line on the right; a running fight was in progress through Saulcourt. Bn. Headquarters warned the right company ("A") of the danger only just in time; the German advance was very rapid and it could not be observed by the company. As it was, one platoon failed to get the order to retire before it was surrounded. Although called upon to surrender it continued to shoot the enemy down and Capt. V. R. Chalk, who was with it, was seen to shoot a German officer with his revolver before the platoon was overrun. Lt. V. R. Gregg carried the messages to "B" and "C" Companies to withdraw, for the wires were now cut.

By 7.50 p.m. the battalion was assembled in the Green line, having accomplished a steady retirement in the face of the advancing enemy and under artillery fire. The losses had been very heavy; about 16 officers and 160 other ranks were now present with Bn. Headquarters. The appointed position was occupied and patrols were sent forward, who found that the enemy was holding a line about 1,000 yards away.

The following morning (March 23rd) there was a thick mist at dawn, under cover of which the Germans launched an attack on the Green line at 6.30 a.m., the infantry being preceded by a line of machine gunners. The attackers came on to within thirty yards of the wire, and were repulsed with considerable losses. The enemy artillery co-operated in the attack, but their range was over-estimated and the shells fell behind the lines.

At 7.30 a.m. a second attack was delivered, still under cover of the mist. This time the fire of the defenders was withheld until the last moment and many Germans dropped right in front of the wire. Again the attack was broken up. Maj. H. Greenwood, with No. 38787 Pte. H. Wright and a Lce.-Cpl. of the 1/E. York., taking advantage of the mist, immediately rushed out to the place where the wire joined the Longavesnes-Péronne road in order to secure two German machine-guns which were lying on the road, and to use them on the retiring enemy. He encountered a heap of dead Germans and an officer and two unwounded soldiers who held up their hands; although unarmed, Maj. Greenwood secured the prisoners, who were marched in. They belonged to the 221st (German) M.G. Company; the officer said that in civil life he was a professor of philosophy. The Adjt., Capt. Hendriks, who had just been wounded, conducted the prisoners to the division. This action on the part of Maj. Greenwood raised the spirits of the men, so much so that, when at 9 p.m. an order was received for a retirement from the position, the idea of retirement was most unpopular; it was hard in the fog to understand the necessity for a move which was becoming vitally urgent owing to the falling back of the main line.

The retirement was carried out under the concentrated fire of machine-guns and rifles. Eight officers and about 100 other ranks were killed or wounded in doing so. Of the officers, Capt. H. N. Teaz and 2/Lt. S. Makin were killed, and Capt. A. E. Day, 2/Lts. J. Magin, F. Slater, V. R. Gregg, C. A. Moon and A. V. Gregory

(King's Own, attd.) were wounded. The enemy had already passed on round the left flank and were holding Templeux la Fosse, which commanded the line of retreat; a détour had to be made southwards instead of heading south-west in the direction of Allaines.

A flank defence with Lewis-guns was organised, which was commanded by 2/Lt. R. K. James. The E. York and D.L.I. battalions suffered in a similar manner.

Bn. Headquarters and the remnant of the 9/K.O.Y.L.I. halted in a position to form a nucleus for resistance when they were clear of the harassing flanking fire from the north. The enemy appeared to be advancing no further than the line Driencourt-Seve Woods for the time.

In the afternoon a further withdrawal was made; later, orders came from a member of the divisional Staff to continue the march to Cléry, where other parties of the battalion were met who had formed up under the instructions issued by the division. Cléry is on the Somme, some three miles west of Péronne.

The retirement of the division was continued on the 24th. On the left of the 9/K.O.Y.L.I. the Lincoln, then the E. York, battalions were withdrawn. The headquarters detachment of the 9/K.O.Y.L.I., now numbering 40, retired to Bois de Hem. Here a stand was made and advancing troops of the enemy were three times checked. To the north-west of this position a very strong German attack could be seen developing with a line of machine gunners moving forward about 600 yards ahead of the infantry. All possible fire was brought to bear on this attack until about 4 p.m., when the British troops on the left were observed to be falling back and the retirement became general. A message came to Lt.-Col. McCulloch to move to Suzanne and to billet there. Suzanne was reached at 8.30 p.m., and remnants of the companies who had become detached in the fighting line now rejoined the Bn. Headquarters. Suzanne is on the north bank of the Somme.

On March 25th the 9/K.O.Y.L.I. moved back to Bray, also on the Somme, in accordance with instructions from the 64th Inf. Bde. Here the commander of the brigade and the G.O.C. 21st Div. visited the Bn. and addressed words of congratulation and encouragement. A composite company, 130 strong, was formed out of all the companies, under the command of Capt. J. P. Shaw, and was sent to join a composite battalion under Maj. Coles, which moved north to take up a defensive line near Carnoy. The 9/K.O.Y.L.I. Headquarters in the meantime went back to Chipilly on the Somme.

On March 26th Lt.-Col. McCulloch was placed in command of a composite force consisting of the nuclei of all the battalions of the division. By 8 a.m. 212 men of the 9/K.O.Y.L.I. under Lt. J. A. Greenshields had joined this force, which took up the line from the river Somme to the Bray-Corbie road. The force numbered 1,200 rifles with two Vickers-guns, and was instructed to conform with the 35th Div. on its left in its retirement. Battalion transport was directed to Baizieux, west of Albert.

This force defended its line till dusk and was then directed to move back to Méricourt, where Brig.-Gen. Headlam met it and directed it to a position between that village and Sailly-le-Sec, where it came under the orders of Brig.-Gen. Cummings. Early in the morning of the 27th, troops of the 3rd Australian Div. passed through and took up a line in advance. The Germans now appeared to have come to a standstill and were seen to be digging in. Our 1st Cavalry Div. was in touch with the enemy and a series of encounters took place.

The 28th was marked by an attack of the Australians, who drove the enemy off the rising ground. On the 29th the valley of the Ancre was heavily shelled by the Germans to prevent reinforcements being sent forward to the fight by Dernancourt. At 9 p.m. Lt.-Col. McCulloch's force was ordered to cross the Ancre to Heilly on the west bank, and by 11.30 p.m. it was in billets there. Next day, at 10.30 p.m., it moved to Frechencourt where it arrived at 1 a.m., and later it marched to Allonville, where all its component battalions were re-constituted, and the 9/K.O.Y.L.I. once more resumed its battalion formation (May 31st).

It must be borne in mind that the 9/K.O.Y.L.I. was fighting in the left corps (VII) of the Fifth Army; this narrative will now have to deal with fighting in the IV Corps of the Third Army, which was north of the Fifth Army. When the German offensive opened on March 21st the 187th Inf. Bde. was in reserve at Bray, the other two brigades of the 62nd Div. meanwhile holding the line in the Acheville and Arleux sectors in front of Vimy, some seven miles north of Arras. Throughout the first day no infantry attack was launched against the 62nd Div. The northern part of the British line was able to hold its positions. Some divisions were immediately detached from the north and were hurried southwards to stem the tide of the German advance. The right of the Third and the whole of the Fifth Armies were being pressed back towards Amiens. The 62nd Div., which included the 5th and 2/4th Bns. K.O.Y.L.I., was taken out of the line and moved through Arras to the neighbourhood of Bucquoy, to come under the orders of the G.O.C. IV Corps (Harper).

The 5th and 2/4th Bns.

The movements of the 5th and 2/4th K.O.Y.L.I. will now be given in more detail.

On March 23rd the 62nd Div. marched southwards on its way to Bucquoy, but the 187th Inf. Bde., which included the two K.O.Y.L.I. battalions, was temporarily detached, to be in reserve to the XVII

Corps and was billeted for the night in the Communal College in Arras. The town was being heavily shelled and bombed by aeroplanes; an attack on the Arras front appeared to be imminent.

On the 24th, the 187th Inf. Bde. at 1.45 p.m. moved forward into a position of readiness in the old British trenches in front of Ronville. The brigade was not called upon to give assistance.

The next day an urgent order came for the brigade to rejoin its division at Bucquoy and the brigade made a forced march by night, arriving at Bucquoy at 3.30 a.m. on the 26th. Marching had been difficult, for the roads were congested with the transport and guns of a retreating army.

March 26th is memorable as the day when the supreme command of the allied forces in France was placed in Gen. Foch's hands; it was the day, too, when our two battalions (the 5th and 2/4th) entered into the historic fight to take their share in holding up the advance of Germany's colossal forces. This night Albert, about 8 miles to the south, was entered by the Germans. The 62nd Inf. Bde. found itself in the Bucquoy-Puisieux line, on the extreme right of the IV Corps. The left flank of the division, where the 185th Inf. Bde. held the trenches, was protected by the 42nd Div., but the right was exposed, for the touch with the V Corps (Fanshawe) had been lost and there was a widening gap which Australian reserves from the south were hurrying to fill.

By 5.30 p.m. the 2/4th Bn. had taken up a defensive flank facing south-east, with a D.W.R. battalion on its left and the 5/K.O.Y.L.I. in support. The position was taken up under the fire of the enemy's machine-guns; Rossignol Wood, lying to the south-east in the undefended gap, was reported to be occupied along its near edge by posts of the enemy with machine-guns. Lt.-Col. B. H. H. Perry commanded the 2/4th K.O.Y.L.I., and the 5th Bn. was commanded by Lt.-Col. O. C. S. Watson. The 2/4th Y. and L. was in brigade reserve.

The night of the 26th passed without incident except for sniping. Patrols were sent out by the 2/4th, but no encounters took place. The order of the companies of the battalion was: on the left "B," centre "A," right "C," and "D" was held in reserve. "C" established visual communication with the 4th Australian Bde. away to the right, but it was not in touch.

At 9 a.m. on the 27th large masses of the enemy were observed to be deploying for attack, and the O.C. "B" Company reported them to be massing in a sunken road to his front. He asked urgently for bombs, but no bombs were available. The position was a network of old trenches up which the usual bombing parties might be expected to attack, and without bombs for countering the attacks the defenders were at a great disadvantage. "B" and "A" Companies were attacked;

the attacks were repeated throughout the day. Twice "B" Company was driven out of the trenches, and twice it recovered them by counter-assault. Heavy casualties were inflicted on the attackers whenever they showed themselves in the open, but when they came bombing up the communication trenches there was no adequate means of opposing them.

At 4 p.m. the position was shelled with 77 mm. and trench-mortar shells, and it was bombed from aeroplanes. An hour later "A" and "B" were driven from their trenches; "D" Company reinforced from reserve and the companies together attempted a counter-attack to restore the situation, but it was too late and a defensive line was formed in rear of the original line. The 5/K.O.Y.L.I. sent up its "B" and "C" Companies to help, and these were utilised in extending the front to the right to reduce the existing gap. An opportunity to retaliate came later with the arrival of four tanks, and with them the two forward companies of the 5th Bn. at 10 p.m. moved out against the enemy in Rossignol Wood. On their return they reported the wood to be clear of the enemy.

During this day's fighting the 2/4th Bn. had suffered many casualties; the losses were estimated at over 160; of the officers, 2/Lt. F. Drake (attd.) were wounded. 2/Lt. Parr died from his wounds on the 29th. Capt. A. E. Pilley, 2/Lts. H. W. Spink and D. O. C. Maggs were missing.

All four companies of the 5/K.O.Y.L.I. were moved into the extreme right of the line during the night, in readiness for a counter-attack to be made on the 28th.

The counter-attack was made with the object of recovering the trenches which had been wrested from the 2/4th K.O.Y.L.I. the previous day. The right flank companies, which consisted of "A," "B" and "C" of the 5/K.O.Y.L.I., and "D" Company, 2/4th K.O.Y.L.I., received a further instruction, *viz.*, to push on to the right and take up a line from the south of Rossignol Wood in a south-westerly direction and to attempt to join hands with the expected Australians. Trusting to the report of the previous reconnaissance in force, Rossignol Wood was thought to be clear of the enemy. The counter-attack was timed to start some hours before daybreak (the Bn. diary of the 2/4th gives the hour as 4.15 a.m.).

The attack was made in three waves; the first wave consisted of "A," "B" and "D" Companies 2/4th K.O.Y.L.I. (from left to right); the second wave of two companies of the 2/4th Y. and L., with one company of the 5/K.O.Y.L.I. on the right; the third wave, of one company 2/4th Y. and L. on the left and two companies of the 5/K.O.Y.L.I.

The old position was retaken. "A," "B," and "C" Companies of the 5/K.O.Y.L.I., and "D" Company, 2/4th K.O.Y.L.I. went on in the darkness (the night was clear and still, with about a quarter moon) to reach their further objective. They very soon came under the fire of machine-guns. Three of these, at least, were taken with a rush, but not before they had done fearful execution among the assaulting companies. Capt. B. A. Beach (5/K.O.Y.L.I.) saw about twenty-five men lying in the open and called on them to come on, but found that they were all dead men. Bombs had been issued in time for this advance and there were bombing fights all down the line. It was obvious that the companies had bumped into a strongly held outpost line.

Before daybreak, on March 28th, the men began to make use of the available cover, for they were in a tangle of old trenches; the officers took stock of their position and judged that they were approximately in the appointed line. Rossignol Wood was on the left (they were facing south-east), and the slope of the ground on which it stood formed the other side of a slight depression, with a road and a light railway lying between. There was higher ground to the front which dominated the position and the ground to the right was dead ground, for the crest of the slope in that direction hid the view. The parapets of the old trenches had long ago fallen in; there was an old traverse here and there, but there was one long stretch of trench dead straight and in the centre of the position. There was a communicating trench which cut into the line from the left rear, and there were also in the front two British tanks which had apparently been abandoned on this ground the night before. There was no sign of the Australian troops who were known to be endeavouring to link up with them. Altogether it would have been hard to discover a more desperate position.

While it was still possible to use a lamp before daylight a message was sent to Bn. Headquarters asking for more bombs and explaining the need of help. The message was received, but of course it was impossible to acknowledge it or to flash an answer which the enemy could not read.

The further story is in the words of a survivor who was taken prisoner when the fight was over.

"*It was not long before we saw the enemy in open order on the skyline to our left front, advancing in strength down the hill. The sun was in our eyes, making it hard to spot targets below the skyline. The enemy were well covered by machine-guns, which harassed us greatly. Soon one gun was enfilading our straight line of trench, making it untenable. 2/Lt. F. C. Lambert spotted this gun and with his Lewis-gun he either silenced it or made it move. Our next trouble was from the tank in front. The Germans were either in it or behind it, and we could not silence it. The position was becoming very unpleasant. I found our left was out of touch, and the portion of front which I could control was split by the length of enfiladed trench; we were suffering heavily, too. I made one or two journeys to get some men from the higher end beyond the straight length, for they were badly bunched in places. On my way back from one of these journeys I noticed that the German machine-gunners had crept closer, and I found that Lt. Lambert and the men round him were dead and their gun damaged.*

"*Shortly after I found that the men on my left were being driven back on me by a bombing party of the enemy; they were attempting to reply with their rifles. Some tried to leave the trench in an endeavour to extricate themselves, but they were immediately shot down. Bombing and machine-gun fighting gradually died down. I found myself left with an officer and about four men, and discovered the enemy right in our rear to be advancing on us by way of the old communicating trench; they were between us and Rossignol Wood. It was obvious that unless we moved quickly we should be hopelessly lost. We were already lost, but could not realise it.*"

The account which is quoted above adds: "*I noticed that the attacking Germans were absolutely fresh, shaved, clean boots, with uniform and equipment in perfect condition. Their open fighting was excellent and outmatched ours, whose only experience had been in trench warfare. During the whole operation only about six shots from our own guns came over us, and we were never fired upon by enemy artillery.*"

It was about 5.30 a.m. when, in answer to the S.O.S. message from his forward companies, Lt.-Col. O. C. S. Watson set out with his sole remaining company ("D") to reinforce his hardly pressed line, but before he could get near to their position he found the way barred impenetrably by the enemy, who had surrounded the forward companies and were now in position across his front. There was no sane course open to him but to retire his company to the original line. As was to be expected, he was himself the last to fall back and he lingered in a communicating trench to shoot down with his revolver the leading men of the advancing enemy, and so to give his men more time. His action was that of a man who has passed through the agony of seeing three of his four sons perish in a blizzard, and who wraps his own cloak, the warm cloak of his knightly achievement, round his last son to protect him.

Lt.-Col. Watson[1] was awarded the V.C. in the *London Gazette* of

[1] *Lt.-Col. Oliver Cyril Spencer Watson, son of William Spencer Watson, M.B., F.R.C.S., was born in London in* 1876. *On passing out of Sandhurst (with Honours) in* 1897 *he was given a commission in the Green Howards and served with that regiment in India. In the Tirah campaign in* 1897 *he was severely wounded while assisting a brother-officer who was mortally wounded. In the Boxer campaign of* 1900 *in China he served as Transport Officer in his battalion. In* 1904 *he was invalided home. After a long illness he left the*

the 8th May, 1918, and the official description of his act of gallantry reads as follows :—

"*Lt.-Col. O. C. S. Watson, D.S.O., 5th Bn., K.O.Y.L.I. At Rossignol Wood, on March 28th, 1918. For most conspicuous bravery, self-sacrificing devotion to duty, and exceptionally gallant leading during a critical period of operations. His command was at a point where continual attacks were made by the Germans in order to pierce the line and an intricate system of old trenches in front, coupled with the fact that his position was under constant rifle and machine-gun fire, rendering the situation still more dangerous. A counter-attack had been made against the enemy position which at first achieved its object, but as the Germans were still holding out in two improvised strong points Lt.-Col. Watson saw that immediate action was necessary, and he led his remaining small reserve to the attack, organising bombing parties and leading attacks under intense rifle and machine-gun fire. Outnumbered, he finally ordered his men to retire, remaining himself in a communication trench to cover the retirement though he faced almost certain death by so doing. The assault he led was at a critical moment and without doubt saved the line. Both in the assault and in covering his men's retirement he held his life as nothing and his splendid bravery inspired all troops in the vicinity to rise to the occasion and save a breach being made in a hardly tried and attenuated line. Lt.-Col. Watson was killed while covering the withdrawal.*"

The remnants of the two K.O.Y.L.I. battalions continued to hold their defensive flank against all attacks, and in the evening the great gap was closed, for the Australians had fought their way northwards until they were able to join hands.

Maj. T. Shearman assumed command of the 5th Bn. Headquarters and "D" Company. The number of casualties in the battalion returned for the day was :—

	Killed.	Wounded.	Missing.
Officers	4	2	10
Other ranks ..	28	80	268

Of the 2/4th Bn. the missing officers were: Capt. G. L. Hudson, 2/Lts. N. Rogerson (attd.) and J. Pownall (attd.) The losses in

Army and took to farming after qualifying at an agricultural college. While living at Wargrave he joined the London Yeomanry (Westminster Hussars). At the outbreak of war he volunteered for foreign service with his Yeomanry regiment and served with it in Egypt. He was promoted Major and accompanied the Hussars to Gallipoli. On returning from Gallipoli he was posted to the 2/5th Bn. K.O.Y.L.I.

Maj. Watson was severely wounded at the battle of Cambrai when in command of his battalion after the death of his gallant namesake. He carried one arm in a sling from that day. As soon as his wounds permitted he returned to his battalion at the front as its Lt.-Col. commanding. One of his own officers wrote of him: "I never met a more modest or gallant gentleman."

other ranks were estimated at 180; the strength of the battalion was reduced to 7 officers and 200 other ranks approximately.

On the 29th the line was heavily shelled but there were no more infantry attacks. Lt.-Col. B. J. Barton returned to command the 2/4th K.O.Y.L.I.; he had been temporarily in command of the brigade.

The two last days of March were not marked by any incident and the enemy in this part of the line had desisted from his attacks. On April 1st the brigade was relieved in the line, the 8/Som. L.I. of the 37th Div. taking over from the 2/4th K.O.Y.L.I., while a battalion of the Lincoln R. relieved the 5/K.O.Y.L.I. Both battalions went back to billets in Authie.

The movements of the 2/K.O.Y.L.I. have been traced up to March 21st, the day before the German offensive started, and we left the battalion in Baboon Camp on the Yser canal. The 97th Inf. Bde. was brought south among the troops that were hurried down to support that all-important point where the right flank of the Third Army was holding up the Germans and bringing the offensive to a standstill.

THE 2ND BN.

By March 27th the 2/K.O.Y.L.I. had reached Lattre St. Quentin, a village seven miles west of Arras, and the same night at 11.45 p.m. it marched *via* Beaumetz and Ransart with orders to support a Guards brigade which was holding the line east of Adinfer Wood and was heavily engaged. Maj. H. W. Boddington was again temporarily in command.

At 5.45 a.m. on the 28th the battalion was ordered into a line of trenches astride the Ransart-Adinfer road, to give it a rest before going into action. At 9 a.m. the new Brig.-Gen. of the 97th Inf. Bde. (J. R. M. Minshull-Ford) rode up and explained the situation ahead, *viz.*, that the enemy was attacking the wood from the east and trying to work round its southern edge.

The battalion in artillery formation advanced for 1,500 yards and entered the wood with "A" and "C" Companies in first line. Patrols were sent forward, and the men dug themselves into a position of support.

In the afternoon, after the enemy attacks had been completely repulsed by the Guards, there was a lull and a relaxation from the tension. The German offensive was, in fact, called off owing to the failure to make further progress.

The 2/K.O.Y.L.I. passed the night in soaking rain in Adinfer Wood. For the next ten days it held the same position, taking its turn in the front trenches.

On the 8th April the Germans bombarded the wood intensely from 3.50 till 8.10 a.m. As was always the case in bombardments of this nature, gas precautions were at once taken, although there was no smell, which was unusual. The enemy were apparently testing a new gas. By noon the casualties from shell-fire were: 1 officer, 57 other ranks. About 2 p.m. many men went sick, a symptom of their complaint being closure of the eyes accompanied by intense pain; by 6 p.m. a large number had to be sent to hospital and many others struggled on at duty in great pain throughout the night.

The shelling was repeated on the 9th for two hours after 6 a.m. The casualties in the battalion were now so numerous that in the night of the 10th it had to be withdrawn to Rabbit Wood to refit. Infected clothes were handed in and exchanged, and men bathed and purified themselves as far as they were able. Of the officers some of the victims who had to go to hospital were: Maj. H. W. Boddington and the Adjt. (Capt. H. S. Howard), Lt. P. A. Franklin, 2/Lts. C. P. Glover, M. Nicolay, J. W. Heritage, E. Morris, and W. Dealtrey.

On the 12th the battalion took over a sector of the front again; it was relieved from the front line on April 25th, and it marched back to billets in La Cauchie.

On May 1st, when at La Cauchie, the Bn. Diary records (with some natural diffidence) that "*The battalion was marched by companies to La Helière, and was put through the Gas Chamber*"!

Maj. J. Hassell became second-in-command (May 19th).

On May 21st one of the forward posts was hit by a shell which killed 2/Lt. N. E. Riley and two other ranks, mortally wounding also 2/Lt. N. Fullard. The enemy was showing great activity and was expected to make an offensive. His front system had been raided at 3 a.m., and it was in retaliation for this that our front system was shelled and attacked by aeroplanes.

In the *London Gazette* of May 24th, actg. Maj. J. Hassell, Capt. G. A. Gamble and Pte. H. Hibbert were mentioned in dispatches.

THE 12TH BN.

Ten miles or so south of Arras the 31st Div. (of which the 12/K.O.Y.L.I. was the Pioneer Battalion) was in readiness to support the divisions of the VI Corps, namely, the 3rd, 34th and 59th Divs., which were in the line on the immediate left of the IV Corps (Harper), some of whose movements we have just been following. The VI Corps (Haldane) was in the Third Army (Byng), and it had the XVII Corps (Fergusson), also of the Third Army, on its left. The German attack on March 21st had met with greater success in the region covered by the 59th Div. than it had on the left of the line of the VI Corps, and part of this division was forced back until Croisilles was uncovered. The 40th Div. was in close support of the divisions in the fighting line and was thrust into the fight on the right of the 34th Div. after the first day's fighting. It had been the German intention to smash a way through the line of the 59th and then to turn northwards; the concentrated effort, though it had dented the line severely, had consequently been only partially successful, due to the magnificent fighting of the 59th Div., whose reserve brigade had frustrated all attempts to break through, and to the prompt assistance afforded by the 40th Div., the proper Corps reserve. The 59th Div. was taken out of the line on the night of the 21st; the 34th Div. also was relieved on the night of the 22nd by the 31st Div. in what constituted the front line of the third system, from the south of Henin to the junction with the St. Leger Switch, and on past the front of Ervillers to the left of the 40th Div.

The 12/K.O.Y.L.I. did not come straight into the fight, for it was constantly employed in its pioneer duties until the 31st Div. had used up its reserves; the story of its entrance on the scene of battle is as follows :—

The battalion, under Lt.-Col. C. B. Charlesworth, received its orders to leave Cambligneul (their camp 10 miles north-west of Arras) on March 22nd by 'bus, and to move to Bellacourt. On the 23rd "B" Company joined the 11/E. York. in the Army line east of Hamelincourt; "C" went to the 11/E. Lan., and "D" to the 10/E. York. These were the battalions of the 92nd Inf. Bde, the reserve brigade of the 31st Div. Later in the day the 92nd Bde. was called up into the line on the exposed flank of the division just north of Ervillers, and the companies of the 12/K.O.Y.L.I. were brought back to Moyenville for work on the Green line. But south of Ervillers the enemy had pushed the line back and were attacking Gommiécourt, so that the right flank of the 31st Div., the 4th Guards Bde. (now belonging to the 31st Div.), was fighting for its very life, and fresh orders to the 12/K.O.Y.L.I. succeeded one another rapidly. The battalion was in great request, digging trenches under the fire of the guns throughout March 24th.

At noon on March 25th the 12/K.O.Y.L.I. was ordered to come up into the line in the neighbourhood of Douchy-les-Ayette; then to dig new lines of trenches in various positions, between the 4/Gren. Gds. on the right and the 92nd T.M. Battery on the left. Capt. W. H. Roberts, Lt. H. R. Skevington and Lt. T. K. Cooper (4th Bn. attd.) were wounded; 3 other ranks were killed and 13 wounded in these operations. The next day passed in the same way. In spite of all attacks the line was being held and the rate of the enemy advance grew slower. On the 27th the battalion was moved to the right of the Gren. Gds. to dig new trenches; Capt. E. Forbes (R.A.M.C. attd.) and Lt. L. F. Phillips were wounded. The company commanders at the time were ("B") Lt. Phillips, ("C") Lt. J. K. Partridge and ("D") Lt. D. E. Oxley.

At 1 p.m. on the 28th the battalion was placed under the orders of the 4th Gds. Bde and was detailed as counter-attack battalion in the event of the enemy breaking through the 3/Coldm. Gds. It was not called upon, however, and during the night of the 29th the battalion was moved back to the sunken road south-east of Douchy-les-Ayette behind the 3/Coldm. Gds., where it was still in position to support the Guards Brigade. There were a few casualties on the 30th; 2/Lt. F. Nobel was wounded; one other rank was killed and seven were wounded. On the 31st the 16/H.L.I. of the 32nd Div. arrived at midnight and relieved the 12/K.O.Y.L.I. which withdrew to Pommier (seven miles west of Ayette).

THE GERMAN OFFENSIVE IN THE SPRING OF 1918

THE NORTHERN ATTACK

XX

ON April 1st the 12/K.O.Y.L.I. marched on to Ivergny, and was transported next by bus to its old quarters in Cambligneul, where it started training in infantry and musketry.

Maj. Stockings returned from leave and took over the command from Capt. G. S. Leach, who had been in command since Lt.-Col. Charlesworth was admitted to hospital.

On April 10th the battalion was moved by 'bus to Vieux Berquin, about 30 miles north, half-way between Caestre and Estaires, in the Bailleul sector. The 31st Div. was here, and it was as a fighting battalion of the line that the 12/K.O.Y.L.I. took up a position next day astride the Caestre-Estaires road, covering the cross-roads in front of La Couronne. A big German attack was in progress; it was coming from a south-easterly direction. The orders to the battalion were to link up with the 92nd Bde. on the left and with the 4th Gds. Bde. on the right. The 92nd Inf. Bde. was not in touch, but the 4/Gren. Gds., of the 4th Gds. Bde., had their left flank south of La Couronne, and the 12/K.O.Y.L.I. aligned itself on the left of the Guards. The position taken up by night was a little too far advanced and in the morning of April 12th the Gds. Bde. Headquarters sent instructions to form a defensive position at La Couronne itself at the cross-roads. With the aid of a company of R.E. of the 50th Div., and some details of a N.F. Bn. of the same division, a line of resistance was hastily constructed. In the afternoon some of the 29th Div. on the left fell back on the same line. About 3 p.m. hostile machine-gun fire opened on the line and increased rapidly in volume; the position was also shelled. The front line troops on the left were steadily falling back. Pivoting on La Couronne the 12/K.O.Y.L.I. found it necessary to throw back its left while its right half still faced east and south-east. The touch with the Gren. Gds. was maintained and on the left the line was now prolonged by a battalion of the S.W.B. In this position the 12/K.O.Y.L.I. dug itself in and passed the night of April 12th.

THE 12TH BN.

About 8.30 a.m. on the 13th the machine-gun fire became intense and an attack developed. The left of the 12/K.O.Y.L.I. successfully beat off four attacks, but at the La Couronne cross-roads the enemy were able to work up the trench which had been constructed ahead the previous day and, covered by trench-mortar fire, dislodged a part of the 12/K.O.Y.L.I., who fell back and formed a new line under heavy fire. This new line faced south-east with its right flank on a stream, and was still in touch with the left portion of its own battalion, which held firm. There was now a gap between the K.O.Y.L.I. and the Gren. Gds. on the right, though by means of runners communication was preserved.

About 1.30 p.m. the right half found itself being enfiladed by machine-guns, and the enemy succeeded, by working down the houses of the village, in breaking the line. The right of the K.O.Y.L.I. was forced back, thus uncovering the right flank of the left half battalion, which became partially surrounded. Under the constant pressure from the enemy the whole battalion gave ground, but rallied on a new line at La Becque farm. After a time this position, too, became untenable owing to a cross machine-gun fire, and the battalion fell back on posts held by Australians of the 1st Austr. Div. in the Rue du Bois. The Australians had just arrived on the scene.

In the early morning of the 14th the battalion was withdrawn from the front line. It had the satisfaction of knowing that at a critical moment, when called upon to take its share in the stern fighting in the front line, it had shown that its brief training was not wasted, and had acquitted itself with honour. The list of awards speaks eloquently to this fact. The battalion fairly earned the title of "Yorkshire Guards," with which it was dubbed that day, but the highest honours were earned by the 4th Gds. Bde., who made a classic stand.

Out of 19 officers and 510 other ranks who went into action the 12th Bn. lost 12 officers and 263 other ranks, the list of officers including all three company commanders and the Adjutant. Lt. J. N. Blenkin and 2/Lt. G. P. Morgan were wounded on the 12th; on the 13th Lt. M. H. Bingham was killed, Lts. J. R. Wilson and L. Forsdike were missing (prisoners of war), and the following were wounded: Capt. F. H. White (died of wounds, April 16th), 2/Lts. C. E. Brierley, C. E. Palmer, P. Atkinson, Capt. V. Mossop and Capt. and Adjt. W. Cooper.

In other ranks 15 were killed, 154 wounded and 94 were missing.

The 12/K.O.Y.L.I. continued until the end of June to act as a fighting unit of the line. The 31st Div. was in the Hazebrouck sector right on from April until the final advance later in the year. The headquarters of the Second Army, in which the division was fighting, were at Staple, five miles north-west of Hazebrouck, and we find the 12/K.O.Y.L.I. taking its turn regularly in the fighting line, in the support lines at Hondeghem and Caestre, or again, as in June from the 1st to the 15th, in the Second Army Reserve, at Staple.

On May 13th the following awards (authority, D.R.O. 3656) were in Bn. orders :—

M.C. Capt. and Adjt. W. Cooper, Capt. G. S. Leach, Capt. V. Mossop, Capt. E. Forbes, R.A.M.C., and Lt. J. N. Blenkin.

Bar to M.M. Cpl. F. Brown.

M.M. Lce.-Cpl. W. Price, Pte. A. R. Mulligan, Cpl. W. Vause, also (May 10th), Sgt. C. Knowles, the M.M.; (May 19th) Pte. T. W. Savile the D.C.M.; and No. 357 Sgt. Ellis was in orders for the M.M. on April 22nd.

Capt. W. Baird, Lt. J. N. Blenkin, Cpl. F. Hemingway and No. 1200 Pte. W. White were mentioned in dispatches (*London Gazette*, 24/5/18).

In the King's Birthday honours list, Capt. W. Cooper was awarded a Bar to his M.C., and Capt. F. H. White (since died of wounds) the M.C.

The explanation for the sudden plunge of the 12/K.O.Y.L.I. for the second time into the mêlée only a fortnight after its first adventure, is to be found in a review of the major operations of the front in Belgium and France. The first great German attack had lasted from March 22nd to the 28th, when it ended strategically in the failure to dislodge the right wing of Gen. Byng's Third Army as we have already seen. The second great effort was made just south of the Oise against the French; the front of the attack reached from Chauny to La Fère and also further south; it commenced on April 6th and was stopped on the 8th when the pace of its achievement was becoming slow. The third great attack was made by Prince Rupprecht's Group of Armies, and opened on April 9th with an attack on the line between Armentières on the north and La Bassée in the south; it was directed on the railway junction of Hazebrouck. Ludendorff had inspected the arrangements for this attack two days before it opened and was satisfied that all was in order, especially in the artillery arm. It was the overwhelming character of the artillery barrages which accounted for the temporary collapse of the resistance of the Portuguese, who held part of the section. For a time the attack went very well for the Germans. The attackers found the fields vacated and the gates left open; streaming through in one part they came upon half a battalion of British troops digging in the open; the British troops in this instance fled, for they were an unarmed party of a labour battalion who had no thoughts at the time of Germans or of the possibility of open gates! Up till noon on April 9th all went well for the attack, but in the afternoon progress was slower. The Germans had reached Estaires—in other words, had penetrated to a depth of 4½ miles; from the south they were threatening Armentières (which they later captured), but were absolutely held up on the other flank at Festubert and Givenchy. During the next two days the progress was slow, but four more miles were gained in the direction of Hazebrouck, and Vieux Berquin was threatened when the 12/K.O.Y.L.I. were among the reinforcements that were rushed into the line on the 11th. The result of this attack, which was a subsidiary to a greater one north, which commenced a day later, was described by Ludendorff as "not satisfactory"; the greater attack achieved the capture of Mount Kemmel, but did not reach the other important heights of its objective, and was brought to a close at the end of April after the arrival of strong French reserves in the allied lines.

THE 1/4TH BN.

Following on the subsidiary offensive made by the Germans against Hazebrouck, in stemming which we have seen the 12/K.O.Y.L.I. to have been engaged, Prince Rupprecht's main attack was made against the Ypres salient and the line down to Armentières. The 49th Div. was taken out of the line of the XXII Corps in front of Ypres and transported south to reinforce the IX, the right Corps of the Second Army (Plumer). Owing to the rapidity of the German advance and to the exigencies of the occasions as they arose, the 49th Div. became quickly split up and the brigades were detached one after another to the assistance of different divisions.

The 1/4th K.O.Y.L.I. was in the Menin sector when, on April 8th, it was relieved in the trenches by the XXII Corps Mounted Regt. to proceed to Scottish Wood camp near Dickebusch.

On April 9th, the day of the German attack north of Armentières, the battalion left Scottish Wood Camp and went by light railway, detraining at Zevecoten Siding; thence by march route to Ontario Camp, Reninghelst, where it rested for the night. At 1 a.m. on the 10th a warning order was received for an early move. At 9 a.m. the battalion left Ontario camp by 'bus under orders to proceed along the Reninghelst-Ouderdom main road to La Clytte near Steynwerck, but owing to the rapid advance made by the enemy the battalion was stopped about one mile west of Neuve Eglise and it bivouacked in fields adjacent to the road. A line of outposts was thrown out and several German stragglers were brought in. Next morning the battalion moved at 1.30 p.m. to hold a line north of Neuve Eglise. 2/Lt. G. W. Barnwell was sent forward with his platoon to reconnoitre, and he reported that after passing through Wulverghem village he found at North Midland farm the advanced headquarters of the 108th Inf. Bde. of the 36th Div. That brigade was taking up a line and the Bde. Commander gave the information that some of the 2/Worc. R. and a company of the R.E. were on his right, and that our troops were falling back from Messines. 2/Lt. Barnwell could find no troops on the left in position, though he met some 300 men of the 25th Div. who were falling back on that flank. In Wulverghem itself he saw an R.E. Company at work preparing the roads for destruction. This company and a machine-gun company also belonged to the 19th Div. At 6.30 p.m. the 2/Worc. R. came back and occupied the right portion of the position, the 1/4th K.O.Y.L.I. edging off a little to the left; "W" and "Z" Companies were in the front line, the other two companies in support. The 1/4th Y. and L. were now in position, prolonging the line to the left. The troops dug themselves in on a new line about 100 yards in advance of the prepared Army line.

Throughout the next day, April 12th, this line, which was now the front line of defence, was persistently shelled. German troops had been observed massing on the right front, and at 4.40 p.m. there was an intense artillery barrage, under cover of which the enemy attacked the right portion of the brigade front. The attack was driven off by machine-gun and rifle-fire. Bn. Headquarters were moved back into cellars in Neuve Eglise at the head of the Kemmel road. 2/Lt. A. R. Chandler was wounded. Lt.-Col. H. C. Fraser rejoined from "B" Echelon with Maj. T. Chadwick.

At 9.30 p.m., under cover of darkness, the enemy attacked, using machine-gun and rifle-fire only. The left half of the sector, including "W" and "Z" Companies, 1/4th K.O.Y.L.I., were driven back into the Army line.

At 7 a.m. on the 13th, in the face of persistent shelling and repeated attacks, the line was forced to fall back and the enemy entered the southern portion of Neuve Eglise as far as the Nieppe road. The headquarters and supports of all three battalions, Worc., Y. and L., and K.O.Y.L.I., combined to deliver a counter-attack, which was successful, and the village was cleared. The K.O.Y.L.I. captured 17 of the enemy in the Y.M.C.A. building. 2/Lts. G. W. Barnwell and A. M. Haigh were killed in this counter-attack; Maj. T. Chadwick, Capt. E. E. Greenough and 2/Lt. J. W. Stroud were wounded.

At 5 p.m. Capt. J. C. Burrows, now in command of "W" and "Z" Companies, sent back for assistance, as he was finding it very difficult to resist the enemy in his attacks and he was slowly having to give ground. "X" Company from the supports was ordered to counter-attack in order to relieve the pressure; they attacked with great spirit and drove the enemy back 150 yards or more.

At 8 p.m. the enemy again penetrated into the southern portion of the village. After turning them out, the Bn. Headquarters details of the Y. and L. and K.O.Y.L.I. formed a right defensive flank, occupying a position on the railway embankment.

On the 14th the battalions were reinforced by the arrival of all details from the "B" Echelon, who dug themselves in to strengthen the new right flank defence. The front line companies were again heavily attacked at 10 a.m. and the enemy penetrated into both flanks of their line. Bombing attacks up the line succeeded at last in ousting the companies, for they had no supply of bombs left to resist them with. "W" and "Z" Companies retired on the reserve line and were directed to dig in behind the "B" Echelon details. The enemy was shelling all positions and the ground behind Neuve Eglise vigorously throughout the day. One shell killed Capt. J. C. Burrows and wounded the Sergt.-Maj. at Bn. Headquarters. Assistance to the hard-pressed line came in the shape of a battalion of the Foresters, who sent a company forward to fill a gap in the line of the K.S.L.I., the next battalion on the left beyond the 148th Inf. Bde.

At 2 p.m. the front line was being so severely handled that Capt. and Adjt. F. W. Mackay was sent back to Bde. Headquarters to ask for a counter-attack to be organised on a large scale, but before any further help arrived the enemy attacked on both sides of Neuve Eglise after a light trench-mortar bombardment, and the line was broken into on both flanks. The Headquarters Company and "Z" Company, 1/4th K.O.Y.L.I., formed a defensive flank and inflicted great loss on the enemy. Lt. F. D. Martin and 2/Lt. W. E. Best were wounded.

At 6 p.m. the position was becoming positively desperate when, to the vast relief of the defenders, it was seen that the enemy was withdrawing to a position about 500 yards to his rear. The severity of the attack was relaxed. Though the village of Neuve Eglise was now in the enemy's hands, the line of the two Yorkshire battalions was again continuous, and during the night that followed both battalions were withdrawn into the reserve. The Foresters relieved the 1/4th K.O.Y.L.I., who went back to the north-east of Mount Kemmel, nominally to re-organise and rest.

The defence of Neuve Eglise soon no doubt became only a memory, as it was immediately succeeded by other exciting and exhausting experiences for the 1/4th K.O.Y.L.I. and their old friends the 4/Y. and L. (the "Hallamshires"), but it is a memory that should never be allowed to fade. In their friendly peace time rivalry of the future these near neighbours will do well to recall occasionally those strenuous days of April, 1918, when shoulder to shoulder they stood in the path of the German steam-roller and helped to check it in its course. It was on April 12th that the Commander-in-Chief, Sir Douglas Haig, issued his memorable message, in which he used the words: "*With our backs to the wall, and believing in the justice of our cause, each one of us must fight to the end.*" Without the added stimulus of that message (for they were at the time it was issued, in the thick of the fight), the two battalions were already acting in its spirit, as their brethren were doing up and down the line.

Not many hours after the 1/4th K.O.Y.L.I. relieved the XXII Corps Mtd. Regt. in a sector of the Kemmel defences. At 12.30 a.m. on April 16th, the battalion received orders to proceed to the

Bde. point of assembly on the Locre-Bailleul road in order to be in readiness to make a counter-attack on the Germans who were driving their attack northwards against the line Wytschaete-Spanbroekmolen-Kemmel. The battalion arrived at the Locre Château at 3 a.m. and found accommodation in the transport sheds. By 10.30 it was in position, holding a line of posts running south-westwards from the château for 800 yards, with Bn. Headquarters at the gamekeeper's cottage. The 1/4th Y. and L. carried the line on to the left, the 1/5th Y. & L. was in brigade reserve, and the 88th Inf. Bde. prolonged the line to the right. Here the battalion remained in position till the following morning, when the brigade was moved southwards to take over a line of posts from the 2/Worc., the 9/H.L.I. and the 9/N.F.; this was a little to the north of Keerseboom, and the taking over was effected by 11.30 a.m. The 1/4th Bns. of the Y. and L. and K.O.Y.L.I. shared Hill Farm as headquarters until an incendiary shell fell on the building and burnt it to the ground. This position was held throughout April 17th and 18th. In the morning of the 19th there was a very unpleasant episode; a field gun opened suddenly at the close range of 500 yards on posts of "W" Company, inflicting casualties to the number of three killed and fifteen wounded. Later the 1/4th K.O.Y.L.I. was relieved by the 3rd Company 1st Bn. 83rd French Inf., and it marched back to Toronto camp, south-east of Poperinghe, for a rest.

On April 22nd a large reinforcement of 186 other ranks was received from the base depôt. The officers with it were: Capt. G. T. Kirk, Lts. O. W. M. Shelton and J. Rodgers, 2/Lts. C. O. Ellison, G. A. Taylor, J. W. Benn, A. J. Nuttall, S. J. Yates, J. Appleton, F. Ashworth and C. A. Arthur.

On April 25th Toronto Camp was shelled. Capt. and Qr.-Mr. G. A. McNally and Lt. E. Massie were wounded, three other ranks were killed and five wounded; the battalion moved to its assembly position south of Ouderdom.

At 12.30 a.m. on the 26th the 148th Inf. Bde. was held in readiness to make a counter-attack, with the 25th Div. on its left and a French Div. on its right. At 4 a.m. the brigade moved forward to the Blue line, but the counter was not delivered and the battalion returned to its original position. There was heavy artillery fire throughout the day and there were many casualties. At 3 p.m. the enemy came on at the double to attack the left of the position, but he was driven back by rifle and Lewis-gun fire; 2/Lt. J. S. Steer was wounded.

On the 27th the position was bombarded with shells of heavy calibre from 3.30 p.m. onwards; the expected infantry attack did not follow. 2/Lt. J. Maxwell was wounded.

At 3 a.m. next morning the brigade relieved a portion of the 21st Div. in the line, and it fell to the lot of the 1/4th K.O.Y.L.I. to take over its line from the 9/K.O.Y.L.I. The 21st Div. had been flung into the fight within a very few days of its desperate experiences on the Amiens front.

On April 29th, after an intense bombardment commencing at five in the morning, the enemy attacked the 148th Inf. Bde. on a wide front. He was repulsed by rifle and Lewis-gun fire, and failed to reach the line at any point. There was a great deal of firing during the day, but there was no serious attack before 5.20 p.m., when our rifles and Lewis-guns were brought to bear on a strong attack which was being launched against part of the line on the right; the attack was broken up; among our casualties, Lt. E. S. Guy was wounded.

Later some of the Australian Lt. Horse came in to strengthen the line; "Y" Company was taken out to make room for them and was transferred to the left as a support to "W" Company.

The next day, April 30th, the 1/4 K.O.Y.L.I. was relieved by the 3/Worc. R., and it proceeded to camp north of Reninghelst. This time the rest was to be a real one.

The losses suffered by the battalion since April 11th numbered: Officers, 3 killed, 13 wounded. Other ranks, 77 killed, 340 wounded, 93 missing.

After a fortnight's training at St. Jan ter Biezen, near St. Omer, and after musketry firing practices at Longueborne, the battalion was moved by train to Proven. Here for some time it found working parties on the rear defences in the XI Corps area.

In due course a number of awards for gallant conduct were published. There were thirty Military Medals given in the 1/4th K.O.Y.L.I.; Lt.-Col. H. C. Fraser received the D.S.O.; Lt. F. E. Massie and 2/Lt. W. E. Boot, the M.C.; Pte F. Chadwick, the D.C.M. (published in Bn. Orders of May 25th and May 27th, 1918).

Gen. Sir Herbert Plumer addressed the officers of the 49th Div. on May 14th and thanked all ranks for the work performed by the division under three separate divisional commanders on the Bailleul-Armentières front.

The 21st Div. was moved from the region of Amiens to the neighbourhood of Ypres at the beginning of April. The remnant of the 9/K.O.Y.L.I. entrained at Amiens for Hopoutre on April 1st, arriving at 1 a.m. on the 2nd, and left in lorries the same day for Kemmel Shelters camp.

THE 9TH BN.

On April 4th the 9/K.O.Y.L.I. went into its new sector just north of Hollebeke, Lt.-Col. McCulloch being in command of the troops in the brigade sector.

After its tour of duty the battalion went back to Locre, where it met a draft of 137 other ranks; a large draft of 264 had already joined at Kemmel. From Locre the battalion moved on the 9th to Maida Camp, two miles south-east of Ypres.

On the 10th the news of the new German offensive became known. For the next few days the 64th Inf. Bde. supported the 9th Div. in front of Wytschaete, where that division was bearing the brunt of a terrific attack. The 9/K.O.Y.L.I., which consisted almost entirely of new drafts, was not engaged, and on April 15th was moved to Ottawa Camp by Zillebeke Lake, and thence to Ouderdom.

On the 16th it moved once more to Maida Camp to work on the G.H.Q. trench line and was here till the 20th.

The Germans had made much headway by this time and our reserves were becoming swallowed up, so that the services of all battalions of the 64th Inf. Bde. were required in the front defences. At 3 a.m. on the 20th the 9/K.O.Y.L.I. carried out a difficult and intricate relief in the line previously held by the 1/E. York and 15/D.L.I. in Onraet Wood of the Wytschaete sector; there were gaps in the line and no communication trenches. There was no infantry attack during the day; after dark, North House was taken over by two platoons of "C" Company from the 2/S. African Bn., which had suffered very heavy losses in the line. During the early hours of the 21st, after the S.O.S. had been sent up, our 18-pounders put down a barrage; unfortunately some of the shells fell too short and caused casualties in our line; 2/Lt. S. Cundall was killed and 2/Lt. H. E. Woods was wounded. On the 23rd the battalion was relieved by the 1/E. York.

The 25th found the battalion again in the trenches; before daylight the enemy bombarded the line with gas shells, but failed to follow up with an infantry attack. When the gas had blown away breakfasts were eaten, but at 6.30 a.m. the gas bombardment was renewed and the area became so impregnated with gas that it was found advisable to move to higher ground where trenches had been dug in readiness. When the attack developed all were suffering more or less from gas. The French troops on the right were pressed back; the enemy came on in great numbers, but the fire from the trenches of the K.O.Y.L.I. did great execution and brought the attack in that sector to a standstill. The enemy was driving in on the right in the direction of La Clytte and Lt.-Col. McCulloch was about to counter-attack with what forces he could muster on the spot when the 15/D.L.I., 240 strong, arrived to reinforce, together with ten Lewis-gun teams from the Tank Corps. With these welcome additions to his strength he re-established the line on his right, joining the right of the 21st Div. to the left of the French 39th Div. From this time till dark the Germans were held off successfully and considerable loss was inflicted on them.

Though he had been wounded in the face by a bullet Lt.-Col. McCulloch carried on, to conduct his battalion in a counter-attack which was arranged for the following morning with the object of re-taking the Vierstraat line. The attack, which started at 4.25 a.m., had to be stopped, for (such was the dislocation and uncertainty in this critical time) the French troops on the right had not received their orders, and the British line on the left was held up by a concentrated machine-gun fire; a promised barrage had not materialised. The K.O.Y.L.I. companies formed the front line of the 64th Bde. in this attack and their position with flanks unsupported became a serious one, until 2/Lt. F. A. Marsden, who commanded "B" Company, with a prompt grasp of the situation, threw back his right to form a defensive flank, and 2/Lt. J. W. Dore, with the centre supporting company, passed across to the left flank and performed a similar service on that flank. The action of these two officers made it possible for Capt. G. F. Ellenberger to withdraw his centre company from the advanced position which he had reached; all the companies suffered severely, and it was thanks to the morning mist that their losses were not even heavier. Capt. Ellenberger then established his companies in a line about 400 yards ahead of the original trenches; his men had secured about 70 prisoners from the enemy's line which they had entered. It was not till noon that the heavy guns of the enemy were brought to bear on the new line in retaliation for the action of the morning; by that time fairly adequate protection had been achieved, for the ground was seamed with old trench lines.

Maj. H. Greenwood took command of the greatly-reduced battalion when the commanding officer at last went back to have his wound dressed.

Two companies of the 5/D.L.I. arrived at about 4 p.m. to strengthen the line; the bombardment was still very heavy.

At 5 p.m. came orders arranging for the relief of the 64th Inf. Bde. by the 148th, and so it came about that the 9/K.O.Y.L.I. handed their trenches over into the keeping of their brethren of the 1/4th K.O.Y.L.I. The relief was completed by 2.30 a.m. on April 28th, under cover of darkness and a dense mist. There had been 262 casualties in other ranks of the 9/K.O.Y.L.I. in the past 24 hours, and the battalion marched back to the Red Horseshoe Camp at Reninghelst about 100 rifles strong. The first grey of dawn was showing in the eastern sky as the last of the Bn. Headquarters party entered the camp after a weary march.

At 2 p.m. that day (April 28th) 5 officers and 155 other ranks of the nucleus party came in, which brought the average strength of the companies up to 70. There were two alarms the following night and the men turned out each time to hold their position of readiness; the enemy's bombardment was so heavy that S.O.S. signals from our infantry's front line, calling for the co-operation of the guns, were visible all along our front.

This great bombardment heralded the closing efforts of the Germans in the great offensive delivered on the Armentières-La Bassée front, sometimes called the Battle of the Lys, though for a further ten days or so they made a tremendous effort to widen the area of their advance by attacking the southern portion of the Ypres salient.

On April 29th the 64th Inf. Bde. was withdrawn to Steenvoorde; next day it marched to Lederzeele, expecting to be accommodated there in billets, but there was no room in Lederzeele, for the whole area was packed with French, American and British troops; the brigade came to rest in a field two miles south of the town; it did not require a very big field for its accommodation.

Some immediate awards were notified to the brigade, of which the following were made to the 9/K.O.Y.L.I. :

Lt.-Col. A. J. McCulloch, D.S.O.
Maj. H. Greenwood, D.S.O.
2/Lt. J. A. Greenshields, M.C.
2/Lt. V. R. Gregg, M.C.

The casualties in the 9/K.O.Y.L.I. during the month of April (according to the "Q" diary, 21st Div.) amounted to :—

	Killed.	Wounded.	Missing.
Officers	2	13	1 (wounded)
Other ranks ..	57	275	107

Of the officers 2/Lt. S. Cundall was killed and 2/Lt. H. E. Woods was wounded on the morning of the 21st; 2/Lt. J. Donovan was killed on the 26th, 2/Lt. P. C. Nicholson was wounded and missing, and the following were wounded, all on April 26th : Lt. (actg. Capt.) V. R. Chalk, 2/Lts. R. F. Halford, C. H. Crowther (5th Bn.), C. Briggs (E. York. attd.), A. Abbott (E. York. attd.), D. Evans, T. Cutler (Green Howards attd.), W. Stabler (E. York. attd.)

Also, Lt.-Col. A. J. McCulloch, wounded (at duty) and the following 2/Lts. wounded : E. S. Parke, J. W. Dore and H. C. Walby (N. Staffs. attd.)

The two German offensives directed against the British had resulted in a considerable loss of ground to the British armies, and had inflicted on them over 300,000 casualties, so that the offensive power of the British was for a short period exhausted. The exhaustion of the German armies which had been engaged in these attacks was at least equally great, and their main objects had not been attained. Ludendorff turned from these uncompleted efforts to deliver his third great effort against the French armies south of the Somme on the Aisne front. This was destined to be the last great effort of the German armies while the initiative lay with them. Even in this zone the K.O.Y.L.I. were represented, for the 21st Div., which included the 9/K.O.Y.L.I., was one of four divisions which, having been badly shattered twice in the months of March and April, were removed from the British line and sent round to the neighbourhood of Rheims to rest and recuperate. It will be seen in the next chapter how much time was allowed to them for rest. Four other British divisions, including the 62nd (with the 5th and 2/4th K.O.Y.L.I.) followed a little later.

THE OFFENSIVE IN CHAMPAGNE AND THE ALLIED COUNTER-ATTACK MAY 27-AUGUST 2, 1918

XXI

BY the end of May, Ludendorff's preparations for his third great effort were complete. Two hundred and seven German divisions, the greatest number ever attained, were present on the "western" front and the initiative still lay with the central powers. The offensive was launched on May 27th, on the Chemin-des-Dames front, threatening Rheims at its eastern limit, pushing southwards beyond Château Thierry in the direction of Paris (40 miles distant), and capturing Soissons on the Aisne. The offensive was stopped on June 6th in the face of the formidable opposition of the French reserves with the addition of the gathering American forces. At Cantigny on May 28th, the 1st American Div. entered into the fighting and gave such a display of its fighting qualities as to establish the reputation of its commanders and soldiers once for all; within a few days the 2nd American Div. in the neighbourhood of Château Thierry increased this reputation and confirmed the opinion of the competence and reliability of the men of the U.S.A. The moral effect of their entrance was very great.

The next effort of the German armies was directed against the French line on either side of Rheims. The colossal artillery and other preparations which were indispensable in connection with each fresh phase of the offensive, required time as well as secrecy to bring them to perfection, and five weeks at this most critical epoch were necessarily consumed before the Germans delivered their attack on July 15th in the Champagne. This attack was broken on the front in four days of tremendous fighting, and it was quickly followed by the victorious counter-offensive which Foch had been preparing against the flanks of the pocket which the German offensive had formed between the Aisne and the Marne. This counter-stroke was the beginning of the great allied offensive which became general, and developed into the uninterrupted march to victory.

The connection of the 9th, and of the 5th and 2/4th Battalions, K.O.Y.L.I., with these events, will now be related.

THE 9TH BN.

We left the sorely reduced 9/K.O.Y.L.I. in company with the other battalions of its brigade, sleeping the sleep of the utterly weary the last night of April in a bare field near Lederzeele. After a cold night the men rose to wash in the ponds near by. Twenty-five tents were delivered to the battalion, and there was a marquee, too, for which the O.C. tossed with the O.C. 15/D.L.I., and won. With the arrival of detachments the average strength of companies reached eighty-five.

Lt.-Gen. Sir A. J. Godley visited the brigade and spoke to it words of great kindness and pride and obvious sincerity; the G.O.C. 21st Div. was not less prompt in expressing his appreciation of the magnificent fighting of the troops, who were promised a long rest.

In the 9/K.O.Y.L.I. a number of names were published in orders as recipients of the M.M., including Sgts. C. Weldon, T. Armstrong and A. Potter; Cpls. G. Morgan, A. J. Harrison, O. Simmonds and C. Martin; Lce.-Cpls. A. Tindall (Bar to M.M.) and M. Davill; Ptes. C. D. Nixon, T. A. Heseltine, S. Fox, J. D. Thompson, H. Wright, J. Dixon, J. Vickers, J. Scales, T. Slater, W. H. Lancashire and W. Laidler.

It was further announced that the division was being sent to a quiet front, where the process of recuperation could be carried out at leisure, so far, that is, as any front could be regarded as a haven of rest.

On May 4th the battalion paraded at 9 a.m. and marched to St. Omer, spending the rest of the day in the train. A halt for tea was made at Noyelle, near Abbeville. Next morning the train was nearing Paris and a stop was made for breakfast at the station of Pontoise. The travellers delighted in the journey through green and fertile country untouched by war, through Paris, and out eastwards to the country of the Champagne. At 11 p.m. the end of the journey was reached and the battalion detrained at Bouleuze, a station about half-way between Fismes and Rheims, and marched on to an excellent French camp at Romigny. The camp was reached at 2.30 a.m., and all the men had beds. For a week they had a real rest, bathing, refitting, route-marching and undergoing a not too strenuous training before occupying a position in a forward area. They were given lessons by French officers in the use of French bombs, and liaison officers lectured them on the subject of their relations with the French army. On May 12th the battalion marched northwards, crossing the river Vesle 10 miles west of Rheims, and heading for the Aisne, into the Pévy area. This proved to be a tiring day in a cold wind and torrents of rain, being a march of 14 miles in full marching order to Prouilly. The next day the 5/299 French Regt. was relieved in the support line near Champignonnières.

The diary describes this as a "very calm and peaceful sector, which seems far removed from the stress and turmoil of the fighting in the north." Acting under the instructions from the French Higher Command, every care was taken to keep the sector a quiet one; the position was about 5 miles south-east of Berry-au-Bac on the river Aisne. On the 21st the 9/K.O.Y.L.I. relieved the 15/D.L.I. in the front trenches. The actual front line was held by day by small sentry groups for observation, which withdrew at night to a line of resistance 400 to 500 yards in rear.

In the night of the 24th-25th the Leicester brigade on the left made a raid, but found the German trenches heavily wired and impenetrable; there was no retaliation to our barrage, but a rather ominous silence.

At 9.30 p.m. on the 26th 2/Lt. F. A. Marsden, who commanded the right company, sent in a message to Bn. Headquarters to say that the French on his right had warned him of an impending German attack. This had been suspected for the past two or three days, for new dumps had appeared, wire had been cleared and the movements of troops on the roads in the rear of the German trenches had been detected. Listening sets had confirmed the existence of unusual telephone activity, and that Germans were speaking "in clear" of barrages, trenches and troops. A little later the brigade sent warning that a prisoner said the German barrage was to commence at 1 a.m. on the 27th. As a precaution the bridges across the Aisne-Vesle canal in the front of our position were ordered to be destroyed.

True to the warning a terrific and accurate bombardment of gas and H.E. shells opened at 1 a.m. The trenches and the country behind them were enveloped in the fog of violent explosions and saturated in gas. It was not till 5 a.m. that the first news reached Bn. Headquarters from the forward lines. Then Lt. J. P. Shaw and 2/Lt. L. M. Holmes, who had been captured but had escaped, came in. They had been with "D" Company, the only company whose trenches were on the north side of the canal. The enemy infantry had attacked about 3 a.m. and had been held off for considerably more than an hour, thanks in particular to our Lewis-gun fire. A hand-grenade fight had developed, all posts had been surrounded and the personnel killed or captured with the exception of these two officers and five or six other ranks; Lt. R. K. James, who had commanded the company, was killed.

"C" Company continued to hold out in its fort of Wattignies for some hours, and at 7 a.m. Lt.-Col. McCulloch determined on a counter-attack to relieve the pressure on Wattignies; meanwhile bombers had worked up to the Bn. Headquarters, which had to be shifted to Ouvrage de la Meule. At 7-30 a.m. two platoons of the 15/D.L.I. joined in to assist to form a left flank defensive line, seeing that the Leicester line had been forced back and the enemy were working round on that flank.

At about 7.30 "A" Company in Jemmapes bastion was attacked in earnest. 2/Lt. J. A. Greenshields was seriously wounded by a shell and sent back. The company made a stout resistance and countered twice. At 9.30 the Germans attacked once more and got into the main position, destroying all except thirty-eight men under 2/Lt.

J. Hurley, who, finding themselves cut off from their own headquarters, fell back in a south-easterly direction and joined the 1/E. York.

At 10.30 a.m. "A" Company in Jemmapes and "B" Company in Redoute Mousquetaires were still gallantly holding out though the enemy were all round them. At 11 a.m. the Bn. Headquarters were attacked from the north by grenadiers and were forced to move back to the Cauroy line, where by noon they were established just south of the 15/D.L.I. Headquarters. At 2 p.m. it was an accepted fact that all sound of firing and grenades from the direction of Jemmapes and Mousquetaires had ceased and that their resistance was over.

There were now about thirty men and 2/Lt. Holmes with the Bn. Headquarters. At 3.30 p.m. the O.C. moved his detachment to a better position half-a-mile south of Cauroy where, with the aid of some of the D.L.I., he formed a line which gained touch with the 3/Zouaves on his right. The position was a good one and the enemy grenade attacks were held off till dark. The enemy were within 30 or 40 yards all night. The orders for a further retirement in the night had failed to reach the detachment, which found itself in an isolated position at dawn; however, it opened fire on the enemy advancing through Cauroy at 5.30 a.m. before it retired fighting to take up a position along the Trigny heights. About 6 a.m. Lt.-Col. McCulloch was wounded in the side by a bullet. The detachment was now under Lt. H. C. Walby's command. On arrival in the new position north of Trigny a Lewis-gun team from the nucleus party arrived upon the scene.

At 3 a.m. on May 29th the Trigny heights were abandoned, so the detachment fell back in a southerly direction across the Vesle viâ Muizon and joined the remainder of the brigade there. The bridges over the river were now destroyed and a position south of the river was occupied; a second Lewis-gun team from the nucleus party came in and was attached temporarily to the 1/E. York. The line of resistance was being stiffened by the accession of several battalions of French infantry, and later the 64th Inf. Bde. received orders to move back to a position on the hills between Rosnay and Germigny.

In the night at 1 a.m. on the 30th, as large reinforcements of French troops had arrived in the line, the 64th Inf. Bde. was taken out and moved south to Marfaux, a distance of 7 miles or so. Here detachments from the companies, who had been fighting their way back mixed up with other units, found their Bn. Headquarters; also in the case of the 9/K.O.Y.L.I. 2 officers with 45 men and the Band had already joined the battalion transport, and thus the strength of the battalion was brought up to 217.

At midday the brigade with its transport moved southwards towards the Forêt d'Epernay and crossed the Marne at Damery at 6 p.m. It bivouacked for the night in a clearing of the forest 1½ miles south of Vauciennes. A small draft made the numbers of the 9/K.O.Y.L.I. up to 236.

May 31st was spent in a march to Chaltrait (which was reached by 1.15 p.m.), and in washing and cleaning up; the men were hot, tired and a little footsore. Next day a company was made up to join a new composite battalion, named the 64th Independent, for duty with the 21st Independent Bde. Motor 'buses carried the 3 officers and 107 other ranks of the K.O.Y.L.I. to the front. The remainder of the battalion left for Congy on June 3rd to be billeted in houses in the village. A further draft of 40 men went to the Independent battalion and 2/Lt. E. S. Parke went also in command of a mounted patrol.

The following immediate honours were published:—

Bar to D.S.O. Lt.-Col. A. J. McCulloch.
Bar to M.C. Capt. G. F. Ellenberger, 2/Lt. J. W. Dore.
M.C. Lt. H. C. Walby.

Lt.-Col. McCulloch, who had recovered from his wound, returned to duty on June 8th; on the 9th the battalion moved to Essart, and on the 14th by 'bus to Fère Champenoise, where it entrained for Pont Remy, arriving at 6.45 p.m., June 15th, and marching to Bainest on the main Rouen road. On the 18th it again moved by 'bus to Beauchamp-le-Vieux, where it was billeted in the town and met with a most kind reception by the Mayor and townsfolk. It was joined on the 20th by the details of the Independent Bn., by some small drafts, and by 16 new 2/Lieutenants.

It came as a great shock when an order was received on the 24th reducing the battalion to the status of a Cadre battalion, but mercifully, though farewell inspections and valedictory addresses were recorded, the order was reconsidered and nothing more was heard of it. Many honours were conferred on all ranks of the battalion on the following dates:—

June 28th: a/R.S.M. O. Maltby, granted a commission and taken on the strength of officers, also awarded a Bar to his D.C.M. for the recent fighting. M.M.'s awarded to Lce.-Cpl. J. T. Poole; Ptes. H. Green, R. Bullock and J. Jones.

July 4th: D.C.M., Pte. W. H. Barber. M.S.M., Lce.-Cpl. W. H. Richardson. M.M., Sgt. H. J. Routledge, Lce.-Cpl. E. Cooke, Ptes. C. E. Maude, H. E. Ogley, (a/Cpl.) G. H. Horsfield, W. Wainwright, Lce.-Cpl. T. Wilbor. (Authority, IX Corps H.R./561 dated 30/6/18.)

July 11th: Bar to M.C., t/Capt. L. D. Spicer, Bde. Maj. 64th Inf. Bde.; Lt. H. C. Walby. M.C., 2/Lt. T. Hindle, Qr.-Mr. and Hon. Capt. W. K. Pethed, t/Capt. G. de H. Dawson, R.A.M.C. attd., a/Capt. J. Hurley.

The 21st Div. moved to camp at Puchevillers on July 4th, and by July 25th it was ready for action again, for on that date the 9/K.O.Y.L.I. marched to position in reserve trenches by Mailly, east

K.O.Y.L.I. man in the Château de Commetreuil Wood. 20 July, 1918

To face page 961.

of Mailly Maillet. Here Brig.-Gen. H. R. Headlam said farewell to his brigade before taking up his appointment as an Inspector of training, and he was succeeded in the command of the 64th Inf. Bde. by Lt.-Col. A. J. McCulloch.

Maj. H. Greenwood was appointed to command the 9/K.O.Y.L.I.

We must return to the story of the German offensive in the Champagne and take up the thread of the 62nd Div. previous to its entrance into that theatre of operations.

THE 5TH AND 2/4TH BNS.

We left the two territorial battalions, the 5th and the 2/4th K.O.Y.L.I., on April 1st at Authie, in divisional reserve of the 62nd Div., which was taking up the active defence of the Bucquoy sector. April was a comparatively quiet month for this sector, for the heavy fighting was transferred further north. The battalions had an opportunity, especially when in divisional reserve at Authie, to absorb and train the new drafts which were pouring in to fill the gaps made in their ranks during the glorious defence of Bucquoy in March.

Maj. F. H. Peter, R.W.F., arrived (April 3rd) to command the 5/K.O.Y.L.I.

The following honours were published, in addition to Lt.-Col. Watson's V.C., in the same battalion:

Capt. and Adjt. P. Bentley, Bar to M.C. 2/Lts. W. G. Pretsell and F. J. Doherty, M.C. C.S.M.'s Fletcher and C. Cooper, D.C.M. Sgt. E. Raywood, Bar to M.M. Sgts. W. Robinson and J. Wright, M.M. Cpls. J. Machin and J. Macnamara, Lce.-Cpl. J. Bell, Lce-Cpl. F. G. Ayre, Ptes. H. Bower, F. Brompton, T. Spicer and H. Womersley, M.M.

The casualties reported in the 62nd divisional diary for the period March 25th–1st April included:

	Killed.		Wounded.		Missing.	
	Offrs.	O.R.	Offrs.	O.R.	Offrs.	O.R.
5/K.O.Y.L.I. ..	4	28	1	106	10	246
2/4th K.O.Y.L.I.	1	15	2	82	6	218

On April 13th 2/Lt. F. J. Doherty (King's Own, attd.) was wounded and on April 14th 2/Lt. A. H. Fehr was missing, both of the 5th Bn. In other ranks on these same days, 17 were killed, 27 wounded and 1 man was missing.

By the end of April the strength of the 2/4th Bn. had been made up to 39 officers (including attached) and 790 other ranks; there were 24 Lewis-guns in the possession of the battalion.

The month of May was spent in the same sector; the artillery on both sides was very active. In June, too, there was constant activity and both battalions took part in raids.

The 5th Bn. had Capt. W. G. James wounded (May 18th) in making a reconnaissance; also 2/Lt. C. H. Crofts (May 26th), 2/Lt. W. G.

Houghton (June 1st), and 2/Lts. F. Bottomley and W. Donnelly (June 23rd), all wounded. On June 2nd C.S.M. Fletcher, a fine soldier who had won the D.C.M. and the M.M., was killed by shell-fire during a relief.

Brig.-Gen. A. J. Reddie, comdg. the 187th Inf. Bde., held inspections of both battalions towards the end of June.

Lt.-Col. C. A. Chaytor (K.O.Y.L.I.) arrived at Couin and assumed command of the 2/4th Bn. on June 27th.

C.S.M. J. C. Simnett and Lce.-Sgt. France were awarded the D.C.M.; R.Q.M.S. J. W. Roughton and Pte. J. Maher received the M.S.M. in June. They were all in the 5th Bn.

It has been told earlier in this chapter that the Germans attacked in the Champagne east and west of Rheims on July 15th, and that after four days of strenuous fighting their offensive was held up and had made little, if any, progress; also that Gen. Foch was waiting for a favourable opportunity to deliver a mighty counterstroke on both flanks of the salient in the German line between Rheims and Compiègne (on the river Oise). The 62nd Div. was sent round via Paris just in time to take part in the opening phase of that counterstroke and the story of its entrance into the fight, which involved the 5th and 2/4th K.O.Y.L.I. battalions, will now be described.

On July 14th both battalions marched from their camp at Couin in the Bucquoy area to Doullens, and left by train "for an unknown destination." A stop was made at Beauvais the following morning for breakfast; the train then took them on the P.L.M. railway through Paris to St. Florentine which was reached at 12.30 a.m. on July 16th; proceeding through Arcis to Sommesous, the battalions detrained there and were transported via Chalons by 'bus to Aulnay on the Marne. From Aulnay they marched to Bisseuil on the 17th, where the morning of the 18th was spent mostly in the river in splendid weather. Bisseuil is on the Marne about 5 miles east of Epernay. Sudden orders were received and the battalions left Bisseuil at 10.30 p.m., marching all night and arriving at 5.30 a.m. at the Bois de Pourcy, where they were in the neighbourhood of their battle stations for a great attack on the following morning (July 20th). While the remainder of the battalion rested during the day the officers and leading N.C.O.s were deeply engaged in studying maps and routes and reconnoitring the forward area, preliminary to taking up battle positions. The scene may readily be imagined. The summer conditions, grand country, the corn standing ripe in the valleys, the men resting under the shade of forest trees, glad to loosen their packs after a long night march, the eager study of the maps, those indispensable attendants on leadership, and withal the indescribable sense of a great event impending. What could not have been appreciated, for the future could not be foreseen, was that they were on the eve of commencing the final act of the great drama, and that from the morrow would date the wresting of the all-important initiative from the German High Command by the joint action of French, American and British troops on the Champagne front.

The salient made by the German forces when they pushed southwards, six weeks back, over the Chemin des Dames, over the Aisne, and on to the river Marne itself between Château Thierry and Epernay, became a source of danger to the Germans when they failed to widen it in July. Foch's counterstroke was in two wings, one directed at either flank of the salient south of the Aisne. The 62nd Div. with the 51st Div. composed the (British) XXII Corps, and it was this corps which was brought in to reinforce the Fifth (French) Army in the region of Rheims against the eastern flank of the German salient. The two British divisions were directed to operate down the valley of the river Ardre, which runs north-westwards to join the river Vesle at Fismes, the 51st Div. being on the left, the 62nd Div. on the right, of the river.

The K.O.Y.L.I. battalions received their orders for the attack of the following morning at a little after 8 p.m. on July 19th. They were in their assembly positions by 3 a.m. on the 20th, the 187th Inf. Bde. being disposed with the 5/K.O.Y.L.I. on the right, the 2/4th Y. & L. on the left, and the 2/4th K.O.Y.L.I. in support; the 185th Inf. Bde. fought on the left of the 187th, between it and the Ardre, and the 2/4th Y. & L. (Hallams) had on its immediate left the 8/W. York, the battalion which, for its action a week later, received the crowning honour of the French Croix de Guerre.

The barrage opened at 8 a.m. In a densely wooded country the 5/K.O.Y.L.I. advanced under cover of the barrage to work through the woods, which were thickly studded with machine-gun posts. The objective was a line on which the Château of Commetreuil stood, but between the line of departure and the château itself 2,500 yards of the Commetreuil wood, the left or western portion of which was known as the Bois-du-petit-champ, had to be traversed in the teeth of the determined opposition of numerous machine-gunners. The fire from the château drive and from a clearing in the south-west corner of the wood held up the centre company, which lost all its officers, three of whom were killed, while almost the entire company was laid low. The left company fought its way through the Bois-du-petit-champ which faced it, arriving at a higher level of the wooded hills before it was in its turn held up; this company also suffered severely and the whole of its contact party was shot down, which occasioned a loss of touch with the 8/W. York on its left. But the 185th Bde. away to the left was as yet quite unable to overcome the tremendous resistance it was meeting with from the villages of Marfaux in the valley and Cuitron on the higher level.

CORRECTION

Page 963. Lines 21-24 should read:—

"...... 5/K.O.Y.L.I. on the *left*, the 2/4th Y. and L. (*Hallams*) on the *right*, and the 2/4th K.O.Y.L.I. in support; the 185th Inf. Bde. fought on the left of the 187th,

The left company of the 5/K.O.Y.L.I. pushed on till its numbers were so reduced that without support it could not hold its ground; it had to withdraw to the edge of the wood again, where all that remained came under the orders of the officer commanding the reserve company.

The right company fared better; the two platoons on the left were stopped at the south-east corner of the Château wood, but the two platoons on the right reached the wood to the west of Courmas, the village which was the objective of the 2/4th Y. & L. Expecting to find this wood occupied by the Y. & L., 2/Lt. P. Moore (W. York. attd.), who now commanded these two platoons, advanced with a small party but came under a close fire, losing his orderly by his side; he then organised an attack with ten men, of whom five were killed and four wounded, but he had forced the enemy to leave the little wood, except a party who held on to the last corner; 2/Lt. Moore rushed the party, and killed one machine-gunner; he also took two prisoners and captured a machine-gun. Turning the gun on some of the enemy who were retreating by a forest track, he cut off the last of them, capturing two more prisoners and another gun. He then turned the gun on a path which led north-west and worked it with effect until the gun went out of order; being unfamiliar with its mechanism he was unable to put it right, so he set about collecting all the men in his vicinity and advanced in the direction of Bouilly. His force was too slender for him to attempt the capture of the village by a *coup-de-main*, and he withdrew and consolidated a position along the north-east bank of the château lake.

With his reserve company Capt. J. A. H. Oliphant, after collecting the remnants of the left company, moved up to stiffen the attack on the château. He reached the junction of the carriage drives and extended his men along the south-east edge of the wood, but there he came under such a destructive fire of machine-guns from the château itself and from a clearing in the wood on his left front, that he was forced to withdraw a little to a less exposed position where he remained in close support.

This day (July 20th) the 2/4th K.O.Y.L.I. had arrived in its support position, six cross roads, by 4 a.m., and for 1½ hours had been under shell-fire, when Lt. A. Woodger (E. York. attd.) was wounded.

The battalion was ordered to follow the 2/4th Y. & L. at a distance of 500 yards. All the time it was advancing through the wood a heavy enemy barrage was bursting over it. 2/Lt. R. Macbeth, who was in command of "B" Company, was wounded, his place being taken by 2/Lt. A. Maylor.

The 2/4th Y. & L. became heavily engaged in the advance on Courmas and the 2/4th K.O.Y.L.I. was brought into action on its left, "C" Company being near the right flank of the 5/K.O Y.L.I.

and "A" Company between "C" and the left of the 2/4th Y. & L. "B" Company was in support and "D" in reserve.

After leaving the cover of the wood, "C" Company worked its way forward by section rushes until it was in line with the first wave of the 5/K.O.Y.L.I. In crawling through a cornfield west of Courmas the casualties were very heavy, for machine-gun nests were concealed in the corn and at any moment men came suddenly under their fire. Four of the officers were hit, 2/Lt. S. T. Swaby (W. York. attd.) being left in command.

"A" Company advanced in artillery formation from the wood and extended on the ridge south-east of Courmas. On coming under machine-gun fire from the left flank, the men were disposed along the Courmas-Onrézy road, after capturing a machine-gun. Here the company was in prolongation of the line of the 2/4th Y. & L., which was held up for a time. A machine-gun which was enfilading the 2/4th Y. & L. was captured by the K.O.Y.L.I. men, the crew being killed, but a captain who was with them was captured. An attempt was made to advance in the direction of Bovilly, but the machine-gun fire, which enfiladed the advance, proved too intense.

"B" Company, from support, seeing the gaps that were being made in the line ahead of it, filled in an interval and then proceeded to rush a nest of machine-guns, capturing four of them.

Meanwhile French troops on the right of the 187th Bde. were making steady progress, and all positions won on July 20th were held. During the night that followed some slight improvement of positions was arrived at, and the three forward companies of the 2/4th K.O.Y.L.I. held a line on the Courmas-Bovilly road from Courmas itself to the cross-roads at the north corner of Château wood, facing the building.

July 21st was spent chiefly by the brigade in reorganising for further action; owing to the density of the wood in which the 5/K.O.Y.L.I. was fighting it was very difficult to ascertain its exact line and to straighten it where necessary. The line ran generally south-east from Courmas.

On the 22nd the 9/D.L.I. went through and attacked on the right of the 2/4th K.O.Y.L.I., and that battalion co-operated to protect the left flank of the attackers. When the attack was brought to a standstill the K.O.Y.L.I. men dug in on the line they had reached. The 186th Bde., on the left of the 187th, made considerable headway in clearing the Bois-du-petit-champ; the heroes of the day were the 5/D.W.R., who captured 41 machine-guns and over 200 prisoners in a hard and bitter day's fighting.

On the 23rd the villages of Cuitron and Marfaux, which for three days had successfully resisted all attempts to take them, fell to the final onslaught of the 186th Inf. Bde. Thus the left flank of the

5/K.O.Y.L.I., which battalion had been reorganised in two companies, was relieved from the active resistance it had hitherto met with and was able to push forward in touch with the brigade on its left. During the day the 77th French Div. attacked with tanks, occupying Bovilly with its left troops; the village was taken over in the evening by sixty men of "D" Company 2/4th K.O.Y.L.I., under Maj. E. G. L. Whiteaway.

On July 24th both battalions were withdrawn for a rest into bivouac in the Bois-de-Contagnon, with headquarters in Nogent, but on the 27th they were up in the line again in an attack which started at 6.50 a.m. on the enemy positions from Marfaux to Espilly. The 51st Div. was attacking too; the 187th Inf. Bde. was sandwiched between two brigades of the 51st Div. The three battalions of the 187th Bde. attacked in line, the 5/K.O.Y.L.I. on the right and the 2/4th on the left. The first objectives were soon reached and the attack continued. By 2.5 p.m. the 5/K.O.Y.L.I. had occupied Chamuzy, and the line was consolidated finally about half-a-mile ahead of the village. Next day the line was carried forward to Bligny, and on the 29th the French troops operating on the right met with a vigorous resistance which forced them back slightly and checked the whole line. The Germans were fighting desperately for time to effect their retirement from the salient.

On the 30th the 187th Inf. Bde. was relieved in the Bligny sector and the 79th French Infantry Regt. took over the positions held by the K.O.Y.L.I., both the battalions moving back to bivouac in the Ferme-de-Contagnon. Next day the brigade moved to Germaine, and the splendid effort of the 62nd Div. was brought to a close.

The XXII Corps (51st and 62nd Divisions) left the Marne and was moved back by train behind the British line between Ypres and Amiens. The services rendered by the two divisions could not better be epitomised than in the Order of the Day, No. 63, issued by the G.O.C. the French Fifth Army, of which the following is a translation:—

"*Headquarters, Fifth Army*, 30/7/18.

"*Now that the XXII British Corps is on the point of leaving the Fifth Army, the Army Commander expresses to it all the thanks and admiration due on account of the great deeds which it has just accomplished.*

"*The very day of its arrival, eager to have the honour of sharing in the victorious counter-attack which had just held up the enemy's furious onslaught on the Marne, and was commencing to throw him back in disorder to the North, the XXII Corps, making forced marches, and allowing the minimum time for reconnaissance, flung itself with spirit into the battle. In unremitting efforts, harassing the enemy with constant pressure, it fought for ten successive days until it made the valley of the Ardre, so freely watered with its blood, its own.*

Fighting in Champagne. Outposts on duty in shell hole on the edge of a wood, 2 August, 1918

To face page 966.

"Thanks to the heroic courage and to the proverbial tenacity of the sons of Great Britain, the unceasing and repeated efforts of this brave Corps have not been in vain; 21 officers and more than 1,300 other ranks taken prisoners, 140 machine-guns and 40 guns captured from the enemy, four of whose divisions have successively been rough-handled and repulsed; the upper valley of the Ardre reconquered, with the heights which dominate it north and south; such is the summary of the British share in the operations of the Fifth Army.

"Scottish Highlanders of General Carter-Campbell's 51st Division! Yorkshire lads of General Braithwaite's 62nd Division! New Zealand and Australian Mounted Troops! All the officers and soldiers of the XXII Corps, so ably commanded by General Sir A. Godley, you have just added a glorious page to your history.

"Marfaux, Chaumuzy, Montaigne de Bligny—those magic names will be inscribed in letters of gold in the annals of your regiments.

"Your French allies will remember with emotion your brilliant gallantry and your perfect comradeship in the fight.

(signed) Berthelot,

General Commanding Fifth Army."

The casualties for this period on the Marne in the two K.O.Y.L.I. battalions were :—

5/K.O.Y.L.I. : Officers, 4 killed, 6 wounded; other ranks, 57 killed, 283 wounded, 14 missing, 60 gassed, etc.

2/4th K.O.Y.L.I. : Officers, 2 killed, 12 wounded; other ranks, 29 killed, 313 wounded, 61 missing, 45 gassed, etc.

The officers of the 5/K.O.Y.L.I. were :—

Killed.—Lt. (a/Capt.) W. Short, 2/Lt. C. H. Crofts (King's Own, attd.), Lt. A. E. Burnell, all on July 20th; 2/Lt. W. G. Pretsell on the 21st.

Wounded.—Lt. J. Ingle (July 22nd), 2/Lt. A. Marr (W. York. attd.), 2/Lts. F. R. Corson (W. York. attd.), J. Wagstaffe (W. York. attd.), G. R. Maskell (D.W.R. attd.), and Lt. B. C. Orme (62nd Bn. M.G. Corps), all on July 20th.

The officers of the 2/4th K.O.Y.L.I. were :—

Killed.—2/Lt. R. N. Milburn (July 20th), 2/Lt. J. McCormick (July 28th).

Wounded.—Lt. (a/Capt.) J. H. Wellington (E. York. attd.), Lt. A. Woodger (E. York. attd.), 2/Lts. P. G. Russell, F. Cocker, J. Blackstock, R. Macbeth, C. V. Smith, J. W. Baldock, and C. E. Inchcliffe (missing), all on July 20th; 2/Lt. E. Nicholson (W. York. attd.) (July 23rd); also 2/Lts. C. Hirst and T. C. Hunter (W. York. attd.) on the 27th.

By August 5th both battalions were once more in Minden camp at Couin, from which they had marched on July 14th.

THE BATTLES OF AMIENS AND BAPAUME, 1918

XXII

WHILE General Foch was delivering his victorious counter-stroke which drove the Germans back from the Marne, Sir Douglas Haig's plan for the offensive to be delivered by the British armies was maturing. The region in which the offensive was to start was chosen by Sir Douglas Haig, and in his choice Foch concurred, stipulating that the French First Army (Debeney) should attack side by side with the British Fourth Army (Rawlinson), both to be under the direct orders of the British commander-in-chief. The part of the line selected was that immediately east of Amiens, including both banks of the Somme.

Gen. Sir Henry Rawlinson had perfected his plan for the attack. During the past three months the Australian Corps, forming part of his Fourth Army, had so harassed the enemy opposed to it that it had gained a complete ascendancy over him. On July 4th a preliminary operation, skilfully conceived and finely carried out by six Australian battalions and sixty tanks, together with four companies of the American 33rd Div., who were attached for initiation, was the means of acquiring the high ground between Hamel and Villers-Brétoneux, which greatly assisted the preparation for the next move.

The Canadian Corps, to which the 32nd Div. was attached (including the 2/K.O.Y.L.I.) had been kept out of the more recent fighting behind the line in the neighbourhood of Arras. The Canadian Corps was to be added to the Fourth Army for the offensive and the problem which had to be dealt with by the Headquarters Staff was that of the introduction of the Canadian Corps on the right of the Australian Corps without the cognizance of the enemy; the appearance of the Canadians in their renewed vigour in any section of the front was bound to create alarm and suspicion in the minds of the opposing staff. The reinforcements which arrived to the Fourth Army in the first week of August (apart from the cavalry, ninety-six whippet tanks and part of the artillery, which went by road), were brought up in some 290 special trains. This was a difficult movement to camouflage, yet secrecy was an essential feature to secure success, and the success of this offensive near Amiens was triumphant.

With this short account of the preliminary considerations the movements of the 2/K.O.Y.L.I. prior to coming into the Fourth Army area of operations will, it is hoped, be more readily understood and appreciated.

Throughout June and until July 6th the 2/K.O.Y.L.I. was employed in and out of the front line about Ransart, some six miles south of Arras. There was a raid on June 1st which is worthy of mention, as having been well-organised and successful in achieving its object. The raiding party was under 2/Lt. G. H. Taylor, and the covering party was commanded by Lt. E. Keel. An enemy post was raided, which resisted. 2/Lt. Taylor, assisted by Pte. J. S. Storey, dashed in while the post was being cleared, and dragged out an unwounded German. The whole affair was over, and the covering party was back in the line, fifteen minutes after "Zero" time, and there were no casualties on our side. 2/Lt. Taylor received the M.C., and Sgt. J. Lounds and Pte. Storey the M.M.

THE 2ND BN.

On July 6th the battalion was relieved in the line by the 1/Scots Guards and the period of its service in the sector was complete. It marched to a point north of Ransart, where all ranks were entertained with a hot tea meal before entraining in two trains. The battalion experienced a very hearty send-off, the Divisional Band playing popular airs.

The battalion detrained at Bavincourt and marched to billets in Sombrin. Here for the next twelve days it was being re-equipped and trained under very comfortable conditions. On July 18th it was conveyed by 'bus and train to Proven, west of Ypres, where it underwent further training in School camp. In an order for the parade of the battalion in battle order on July 23rd the battalion band is mentioned for the first time. It is significant to note in all the diaries of this period, in all battalions, the spirit of optimism which prevailed in spite of the recent prodigious attacks of the Germans; there was a general feeling that the enemy had played his trump cards and had failed to win the game. So we find that on August 1st the battalion was given over to the celebration of Minden Day, with battalion sports at which the band of the 1/5th Border Regt. attended to add to the attractions and show good fellowship.

A display had been made of Canadian troops in this area to give the impression of a concentration with the immediate object of re-taking Mount Kemmel. The 32nd Div. was still attached to the Canadian Corps and it was destined to follow the fortunes of that Corps in the battle of Amiens, and to be severed from it only when the Canadian Corps was quietly taken out of the line of the Fourth Army about August 20th.

On August 7th, the diary records that "We move to another Army area." The battalion entrained that day, arriving at Longpré next morning, whence it was taken by 'bus to Domart, on the river Luce (which runs into the Somme in front of Amiens). Domart lies south-east of Amiens about ten miles. On the 9th the battalion marched from the Bois-de-Gentelles, where its bivouac had been, to near Beaucourt just north of the Amiens-Roye road. The great attack had already started with the Canadian as right Corps of the British line (the First French Army operated on its right), the Australian Corps in the middle, and the III Corps extended from the Somme to the Ancre. The Canadian Corps had attacked with three divisions in line, another Canadian Div. in support, and the 32nd Div. in reserve; in its first day's fighting it captured over 5,000 prisoners and 161 guns.

On the morning of the 10th Lt.-Col. Lamotte received operation orders at 4 a.m. and the 2/K.O.Y.L.I. marched on about five miles to a position of deployment about 1,000 yards to the east of Beaufort. The battalion moved forward in support, the other two battalions of the 97th Inf. Bde. being in action ahead of it; at dusk the battalion took up a defensive position with both its flanks thrown back and sections of Vickers guns on either extreme flank.

On the morning of August 11th the battalion came into the line; it deployed for action on a frontage of 800 yards at 8 a.m. The action of the 11th was more or less tentative. The extreme objective of the Corps had not been reached, *i.e.*, the town of Roye, but the Le Quesnoy-Lihons position was firmly occupied, and against the stiffening resistance and strong counter-attacks of the enemy it was not intended to incur disproportionate loss for the sake of some very little gains of ground.

The battalion was deployed twenty-five minutes before "Zero"; the attack duly went forward at "Zero," and direction was well maintained, but the enemy's positions were found to be strongly guarded with machine-guns and numerous lines of wire, forming an objective such as artillery and tanks would be expected to deal with, and no progress could be made. It was disappointing to arrive at the orchard and find that all the apples had been picked. It was "according to plan" that the battalion remained in the position it had reached and withdrew to Beaufort about midnight.

From the 11th onward Gen. Rawlinson rested his troops. The battle of Amiens was complete. Altogether the French and British armies had taken 40,000 prisoners and 600 guns, and had pierced the German line on a front of nearly 50 miles to a depth of from 6 to 13 miles.

The 2/K.O.Y.L.I. went back to Berteaucourt, by Domart, on the north bank of the Luce on August 14th, and was there visited by the Divisional General, who congratulated the men on their good work of the past few days. Bathing and cleaning became the order of the day.

The casualties on August 10th and 11th amounted to 1 officer killed and 4 wounded, 27 other ranks killed and 79 wounded.

In order to bring the 2/K.O.Y.L.I. into line with other battalions of the regiment in the march to victory it will be useful to carry its story forward a few days now to the end of August. The 32nd Div. was being detached from the Canadian Corps and put into the line on the right of the Australians.

On August 17th the battalion was moved by 'bus to near Harbonnières, four miles north of the Luce, into a country which had been the scene of the Australians' advance in the recent battle. Here the 17th Bn. A.I.F. was relieved in the reserve line. By 1 a.m. on the 19th a portion of the front line was taken over from the 22nd Bn. A.I.F. A hostile counter-attack was imminent, for the enemy had been forced back during the past twenty-four hours, and there was a new and unfinished line left for the two forward companies to occupy. The line was just east of Framerville and south of Herleville; the enemy's line ran through a Crucifix cross-roads ahead. There was a bombardment at 10.15 a.m., followed by an attack on two of our posts just west of the Crucifix. Both posts were carried, but Capts. B. V. Pring and E. V. H. Bradley, the commanders of the two companies concerned, independently organised counter-attacks and, with the help of 2/Lts. R. Powell, R. Martin and V. E. Butters, reoccupied the posts. On the 20th the posts were attacked again, when 2/Lt. R. Powell and Sgt. Beavis were killed. On the 21st there were a dozen casualties, among whom 2/Lt. F. Calvert (1/5th Border, attd.) was wounded. The 22nd was passed in preparations for battle operations. 2/Lt. V. E. Butters received the immediate reward of the M.C. for his extreme gallantry when re-taking the post on the 19th. He showed great skill and initiative and recaptured the Lewis-gun.

At 2 a.m. on August 23rd the battalion formed on tape lines on a frontage of 650 yards. An attack was to be made in connection with the main attack of the Third Army, which was altogether on a front of 33 miles. The men were very cheerful and full of confidence. "Zero" hour was 4.45 a.m. The enemy put down a counter-preparation barrage at 2.30 and again at 4 a.m. with gas. It was bright moonlight. Just before "Zero" there was an intense quiet, broken by the noise of the tanks coming up behind the battalion. Our barrage was concentrated and most accurate, striking about 300 yards ahead of the tape. The men went forward eagerly, almost overtaking the barrage, and followed by the tanks.

The right company, "C," went straight for its objective, just north of the Crucifix, killing and capturing many of the enemy on the way; "B" Company in close support mopped up and took many machine-guns and one field-gun. The left company, "D," also advanced straight to its objective, passing through the village of Herleville and leaving many trophies there to be collected, but driving out all the enemy on its way; "A" Company, the left support, collected many machine-guns, two heavy and two light trench-mortars. The reserve platoons of "A" and "B" Companies established themselves in the reserve line west of the village. By 90 minutes from "Zero" hour all companies were in position and had rendered maps of their dispositions to Bn. Headquarters.

About 7 a.m. the Divisional Commander met the C.O. in the position of the right platoon of "A" Company; a great patch of wood between the battalion on the left of the 2/K.O.Y.L.I. and the Australians was still in the enemy's hands and a counter-attack from that direction appeared to be threatening. Flank defences were arranged and the attack did not materialise, but the enemy was active with bombing attacks throughout the day. At dusk by a concerted movement the front line companies of this and neighbouring battalions pushed forward suddenly and seized a better line 400 yards ahead, which they immediately consolidated.

This had been a busy day in the dressing-stations. All the day the wounded and prisoners poured in. For two hours our men, the prisoners, the wounded and the dressers, were forced to wear box-respirators at the Quarry station; the area was also heavily bombarded in the evening and again after dark by the enemy airmen.

On August 24th the battalion was relieved by the 15/H.L.I. and marched back to Harbonnières, where it had an opportunity to check casualties and stores.

The casualties suffered in the capture of Herleville were: killed, 2/Lt. H. Hargreaves and 14 other ranks; wounded, 2/Lts. F. K. Black, G. Musgrove and A. G. E. Alexander; other ranks, 81.

Immediate awards of the M.C. were made to three officers to whose skill and leadership was greatly due the complete success at Herleville, *viz.*, to Capts. E. E. E. Cass and H. J. Knight, and 2/Lt. W. Butler.

The line was advancing; the 2/K.O.Y.L.I. went forward to the Quarry again on the 27th, and the next day through Vermandovillers to Deniécourt; it took over a section of the outpost line on the 29th from the 2/Manch., where the Bn. Headquarters were in a large hut on the left bank of the Somme near Misery. There was a conference in the hut, attended by the Brig.-Gen. The latter had just left the hut at 11 p.m. with Maj. J. Hassell, who was temporarily in command of the battalion., when the enemy shelled it. The first shell fell in the officers' mess with disastrous results; Capt. and a/Adjt. D. F. Hutchinson and three other ranks were killed; also the French liaison officer; Capt. G. R. Thomas and Lt. R. E. Wellington and seven other ranks were wounded.

The duties of Actg. Adjt. were taken over by Lt. A. Pontefract.

North of the Somme the III Corps in its advance from August 21st–23rd captured Albert, giving that name to the battle which was fought on this part of the front.

Immediately to the left of the III Corps, which, as we have seen, was attacking just north of the Somme, came the V Corps (Shute), being the right corps of the Third Army (Byng), which had the IV Corps (Harper) next in line and the VI Corps (Haldane) on the left or north. The left portion of the V Corps front was now occupied by the 21st Div. (Campbell) which, like the phœnix, was already rising again in renewed youth after its very recent self-sacrifice in the Champagne. The 9/K.O.Y.L.I., still in the 64th Inf. Bde., was about to enter upon the last, and by no means the least, glorious period of its famous record.

THE 9TH BN.

No sooner had the right flank of the Third Army been made secure by the gain of ground by the III Corps (in which the 2/K.O.Y.L.I. had achieved its task at Herleville), than Gen. Byng's Third Army began to move. On August 14th, in consequence of signs of intended withdrawal being noticeable in the enemy's lines, preliminary steps were already being taken. The 9/K.O.Y.L.I., north of the river Ancre, made a tentative advance, and found that, east of Beaumont Hamel, the enemy held a position along the Beaucourt road. Again on the 15th the enemy position was tested and the battalion met with a heavy gun fire by which all companies suffered some casualties. After "A" Company had rushed a German post which was holding up the advance, the whole line pushed forward to a position in and about Artillery Lane.

On August 23rd the battalion moved up from support in order to take part in an attack due to start about midnight. At dusk the battalion was moved round *via* Beaucourt to the south side of the Ancre, which had been formed by the enemy into a formidable obstacle by damming and artificial obstructions.

In the attack the 1/E. York was left of the brigade with its left on the river bank, the 9/K.O.Y.L.I. on the right, and the 15/D.L.I. was in support. Each of the leading battalions advanced, with three companies in front line, in line of platoons. The barrage opened at 11.15 p.m. The line of advance for the battalion, which was led by Lt.-Col. Greenwood, was due east. After passing through outposts of a battalion of the N.F. the attackers encountered strongly-held machine-gun positions; these were rushed and prisoners were sent back. On arrival at Battery Valley some dug-outs and strong posts were cleared and a 4.2 gun, also one machine-gun, were captured; undaunted by heavy machine-gun fire the battalion continued to advance towards the Grandcourt-Thiepval road. It was when on the way there that several shells from our heavies fell short, for the battalion was in advance of its expected line, and there were several casualties. Lt.-Col. Greenwood was blown off his feet and thrown against a post, receiving internal injuries, but he was still able to lead his battalion against the objective. The latter was reached, the companies were re-organised, and the men, who were eager to get on, worked forward and dug in about 400 yards ahead of the objective line. The 15/D.L.I. came forward to form a defensive flank when it was seen that the right flank was in the air.

At 3 a.m. the companies commenced a further advance of about 2,500 yards, showing exceptional dash and courage; the machine-gun fire from flanks and front was very heavy, but there was no wavering and the machine-gun posts were taken with a rush; Grandcourt road and Boom ravine were crossed; at 4 a.m. the objective was reached and the men soon established a position in a line of shell holes. The whole advance had been a very remarkable one and it had been led by daring leaders. Brig-Gen. McCulloch and Lt.-Col. Greenwood, of course, were old associates in the 9/K.O.Y.L.I., and the other battalion commanders made up a worthy confederacy. It was a long advance to make in the teeth of the enemy by night and across country pitted with old shell holes. Early in the morning the Brigadier was wounded and the command of the brigade devolved on Lt.-Col. Holroyd-Smith, commanding the 15/D.L.I. When day dawned the brigade was found to be unsupported, firmly fixed in the German line, with the K.O.Y.L.I. the front line. The enemy attacked constantly with rifles and bombs. Every inch of ground was held; a succession of attacks made by the enemy reserves was repulsed before noon when, tired of his attempts to dislodge the attackers, the enemy retired; his losses must have been considerable, for 130 of his dead were counted as they lay in front of the line held by the 9/K.O.Y.L.I.

The wounded brigadier was the first to explain to Div. Headquarters the predicament of his brigade: about 10.30 a.m. Capt. L. D. Spicer (9/K.O.Y.L.I.), who was Bde.-Maj., succeeded in getting back to make his report also; there was nothing that could be done to help the forward battalions during the day except by sending heartening messages which were dropped by aeroplane. In the evening troops were advanced on either flank, and the survivors were rescued from a situation which had been desperate while the enemy was making his counter-attacks.

At 7 p.m. the brigade withdrew into divisional reserve, and the 9/K.O.Y.L.I. spent the night in Boom ravine.

After a day of refitting the battalion was again up in line at 6 a.m., August 26th, prepared to continue the advance eastwards. Our advanced troops at the time were holding the line of the blue 'cut.' The battalion passed through this line to seize certain positions held by the enemy near the Ligny Tilloy-Luisenhof Farm road. The advance was over open country which was swept by rifle and machine-gun fire. The left flank became exposed when the next battalion was held up, and after crossing the yellow 'cut' the casualties were so heavy that cover had to be found in the shell holes. Maj. T. A. Walsh (Som. L.I. attd.) advanced the right company to within 300 yards of the objective, but was forced, after holding his position for some hours, to withdraw, as the troops on his right had already done.

After dark the battalion was mustered in the yellow 'cut,' and was organised as a single company, for its losses had been very heavy. A line of posts was established 300 yards in front of the 'cut' and patrols went out 800 yards further. So the position was held during the night and the following day. At 8.30 p.m., the 27th, the battalion was relieved in the line by the N.F., but it continued to move forward, occupying trenches in the blue 'cut' again on the 29th, as the enemy was falling back. Here Lt.-Col. Greenwood, owing to wounds and sickness, was forced to hand over the command to Maj. Walsh and to repair to the dressing station. The battalion underwent a brief refitting, and was occupied in salvage work for two or three days.

The summary of the casualties for August is as follows :—

Officers, killed 3, wounded 13. Other ranks, killed 52, wounded 237, missing 23.

This is a heavy summary for three or four days' fighting, and it proves not only the obstinacy of the Germans in their withdrawal from their hardly-won positions, but also the wonderful spirit with which this battalion was imbued. Time after time the 9/K.O.Y.L.I. came out of action reduced to the strength of one company or less; it was given just long enough to absorb, but (one would have thought) no time to assimilate, its waiting drafts, when it was hurled back into the battle. And it always went back with the one idea of doing its utmost in the most direct manner possible.

Divisional *esprit de corps* no doubt had a good deal to do with it; regimental pride still more, perhaps, for no new draft was many hours in its ranks before it was instructed in, and made thoroughly familiar with, the record of the Regiment in general, and the 9th Bn. in particular. Those drafts knew what was expected of them and they were not found wanting.

It was this battalion that had started its career at Halton Park so inauspiciously in October, 1914. Horrified at the want of magnitude of the army bacon rasher at the first breakfast in camp, the battalion was conspicuous by its absence from the next parade; worse than that, it, or a great part of it, set off to trudge to the station, grousing on the way about its "rights"! It was in this battalion, too, some weeks later (after it had learnt discipline!) that "A" Company faced "B" Company one night in two trenches in which they passed the night to practice service conditions. There was an extensive No Man's Land; the companies were deadly foes, at any rate that night; after some terrible patrol affairs, the companies entered wholeheartedly into a quite unofficial battle in which the weapons used were over-ripe tomatoes, eggs, home-made stink bombs, sticks, fists, pepper, squibs and bad language. It was said, so infectious was the madness, that the spirit of reprisal was communicated even to an officer's patrol. However, even from its earliest days the battalion had the good fortune to be commanded by officers who were not only wise and capable, but human, and, having passed through the stage of infantile ailments unscathed, it rapidly developed as a blood brother in the family of the K.O.Y.L.I.

To quote an officer of the 9/K.O.Y.L.I., who was writing after the war, the battalion "*from July to November*, 1918, *was in practically continuous first-class engagements in the front line two days out of three, in common with the rest of the B.E.F., when the war really was a Great War.*"

We have seen that the 9/K.O.Y.L.I., as a part of the V Corps, entered into the battle of Bapaume in the southern portion of the Third Army line. We shall deal now with the 5th and 2/4th Bns. K.O.Y.L.I., which entered the battle line on the northern side in the VI Corps.

THE 5TH AND 2/4TH BNS. IN THE BATTLE OF BAPAUME.

The 62nd Div. enjoyed a very brief spell of re-fitting and reorganising. On August 19th the division was transferred to the VI Corps, entailing a march to Authie in the case of the two K.O.Y.L.I. battalions. On August 23rd the division was again on the move, and these two battalions were moved by 'bus to Adinfer and marched thence to a position of concentration near Courcelles. The 187th Inf. Bde. was at once brought up into close support, and on the 24th relieved a part of the 2nd Div.

The offensive of the Third Army (Byng) had commenced on August 23rd. During the 24th, the 6th and the 99th Inf. Bdes. of the 2nd Div. had attacked in the direction of Mory, a village which lies 3½ miles to the north of Bapaume. Mory itself had not been taken, but the 6th Inf Bde. had fought its way to a line east of Ervillers, a village one mile short of Mory, while the 99th Inf. Bde. had pushed on further and had taken Mory copse, 1,000 yards or so north of Mory and more than half-a-mile in advance of the left of the 6th Inf. Bde. The two brigades were connected by a defensive flank line facing south, in which troops from both brigades were freely mingled. To the north of Mory copse a Guards brigade was next in line.

The task of the 5/K.O.Y.L.I., which was ordered to relieve the 2/S. Staffords and the 17/R.F. of the 6th Bde., was a difficult one. It was eventually accomplished, and the 2/4th Y. & L. took over the line from the left of the 5/K.O.Y.L.I. to Mory copse. The 2/4th K.O.Y.L.I. was in brigade reserve west of Ervillers.

An attack was ordered to commence on the morning of the 25th at 9 a.m., but owing to the impossibility of completing the necessary arrangements by that hour satisfactorily, an attempt was made to postpone the hour till 10.30 a.m. Telephonic communications had been greatly interfered with by the enemy's gun-fire; the order for the postponement reached the 5/K.O.Y.L.I. and the Guards Bde. on the left, but it arrived at Bn. Headquarters of the 2/4th Y. & L. too late.

The objective was the high ground east and south-east of Mory. The village itself was in the path of the 5/K.O.Y.L.I.; the battalion was directed to push patrols through Mory; to the north Mory was already threatened owing to the previous day's advance; the 5/K.O.Y.L.I. probably forced the enemy to abandon the village by throwing the weight of its attack on its southern flank; it definitely came into our hands after the advance of the 27th. The 5/K.O.Y.L.I. diary states that the brigade attacked and occupied Mory and the valley running south of Mory. 2/Lts. H. E. Butterfield and P. Moore (W. York., attd.) were wounded in the advance.

Meanwhile the 2/4th Y. & L., the left battalion of the brigade, had started to attack alone at the time originally arranged, 9 a.m. It met with severe opposition, especially from machine-guns posted on the high ground to the south-east. Advancing eastwards with its left covering Mory copse, it worked forward about 350 yards, where advantage was taken of any cover that could be found, including a sunken road. The 2/4th K.O.Y.L.I. was ordered up from behind Ervillers to support the Y. & L. Three companies, "A," "B" and "C," moved up into the position between Mory and Mory copse, from which the 2/4th Y. & L. had set out, and the fourth was in support. The advance of the battalion was made by Lt.-Col. Chaytor in widely extended artillery formation, as it was broad daylight and the country was very open.

The orders issued to the 2/4th K.O.Y.L.I. were, as soon as the Y. & L. had pressed home their attack, to move forward and attack in a southerly direction and secure the high ground west of the old Third Army line. They were fighting over familiar country. However, as we have seen, the Y. & L. were completely held up and no further move could be made until the situation on the left was cleared, for the copse was now not held, and beyond the copse were the enemy.

The enemy's low-flying aeroplanes soon located the 2/4th K.O.Y.L.I. in its unprotected position and the shelling increased. The companies were moved forward by driblets into a sunken road beyond the crest line of the slope on which they lay.

By 3.30 p.m. the enemy shell-fire had increased into a regular barrage. It was directed first on the Y. & L. in advance in the neighbourhood of the light railway track, and it gradually came forward up the slope to the sunken road. Shrapnel and various kinds of poison-gas shells were used; great clouds of gas were drifting westwards, accounted for by the explosion by our guns of a large dump of gas projector shells left behind during the retreat in March.

By 5 p.m. the S.O.S. was being sent to Bn. Headquarters both by visual signal and runners. The headquarters moved out to take up a defensive position, suffering heavily from the gun-fire also. Suddenly Capt. G. E. Spencer heard heavy machine-gun fire close in front; he jumped on to the bank of the sunken road to get a better view, then went forward a little and discovered that the forward posts of the Y. & L. had been driven in and that the enemy were advancing to the attack. He called up a section of Lewis-gunners who promptly got into action, and then called upon his company to follow him and charged the oncoming enemy. Lt. H. L. Hollard, who commanded "B" Company, led his men over on the left and was soon up in line with "A," while Lt. J. L. Rodger followed with "C" Company in support. The remnants of the 2/4th Y. & L. also joined in. The counter-attack was completely successful, the enemy were driven back with heavy casualties, demoralised, and they came immediately under our barrage which had been promptly and skilfully put in. Almost simultaneously Capt. G. Skirrow, in command of "D" Company in support, noticed that the enemy were working round the left flank and were in possession of Mory copse; taking two platoons with him he rushed for the copse; attacking the crew of a machine-gun with his revolver he accounted for them all and, getting into touch with the Guards who were now coming in from the north, drove the enemy out and cleared the copse. A considerable number of prisoners were collected, and by the action of the front line companies all lost ground was regained. The battered 2/4th Y. & L. was withdrawn and the 2/4th K.O.Y.L.I. consolidated the line throughout the night, getting in water, recovering wounded, etc., in spite of the difficulty of movement occasioned by the enemy machine-gun fire.

During the 26th there was no change in position for the 2/4th Bn., but the 5/K.O.Y.L.I. continued its advance and captured the high ground south-east of Mory, establishing themselves in the old Third Army (blue) line.

On the 27th the advance continued, the 5/K.O.Y.L.I. on the right and the 2/4th on the left; the Guards were on the left of the 187th Bde. The 5/K.O.Y.L.I. attacked towards the sugar factory west of Vraucourt; "D" Company attacked with "B" in support and the other companies in reserve. The battalions captured 7 officers and 108 men of the German 5th Grenadier R. 2/Lt. Logan with his C.S.M. and one runner, with great coolness and promptitude took the surrender of the prisoners, being the headquarters of a battalion in dug-outs.

The 2/4th Bn. had "C" and "D" Companies in front line, who advanced steadily in two waves until they reached the old Third Army trenches. "D" Company on the left had to overcome a deal of machine-gun opposition, and lost its gallant commander, who was killed; the company was led by 2/Lt. J. H. Fisher after this.

That night the 1/5th Devon relieved the 5/K.O.Y.L.I. in the line, and the 8/W. York. took over from the 2/4th. Both battalions went back to the neighbourhood of Courcelles.

The 5/K.O.Y.L.I. had two officers wounded on the 27th August, *viz.*, 2/Lts. E. Callear (W. York., attd.), and R. F. Tee. The casualties in other ranks during the three days' fighting amounted to: killed 26, wounded 111, missing 16, gassed 13.

In the 2/4th K.O.Y.L.I. on August 25th, 2/Lts. J. T. Porter and R. T. Fox were killed; Lt. H. L. Hollard (A.S.C., attd.) and 2/Lts. G. Hall, A. Maylor, and S. Wiggins (5/K.O.Y.L.I.) were wounded.

On the 27th Lt. (a/Capt.) G. Skirrow (W. York., attd.) was killed and 2/Lts. J. L. Rodger, S. T. Swaby (W. York., attd.) wounded; also 2/Lt. R. B. Johnston was gassed.

The casualties in other ranks of the 2/4th numbered 199.

Maj.-Gen. Sir Walter Braithwaite relinquished command of the 62nd Div. on August 27th, on promotion to the command of a Corps; he was succeeded by Maj-Gen. Sir R. D. Whigham. The division was indeed fortunate in its commanders. All ranks cherished a sense of personal attachment to the commander they were parting with, who had proved himself so able and considerate.

BATTALIONS OF THE K.O.Y.L.I. IN VARIOUS ARMIES, 1918

XXIII

FOLLOWING on the advances of the Fourth and Third Armies the First Army (Horne) commenced its forward move, protecting the left flank of the Third Army, on August 26th, 1918.

As there were no battalions of the K.O.Y.L.I. involved in its advance, the fortunes of the First Army will not be followed, but the growing importance of the offensive made by the First Army, followed by that of the newly-constituted Fifth Army (Birdwood), which came in to the line still further to the north, completed the front of the advancing British line into one continuous whole and must not be lost sight of.

In this chapter a glance will be taken at the remaining battalions of the K.O.Y.L.I. which were, up to the end of August, outside the area of the armies more immediately concerned in the great advance.

It took the battalions from Macedonia fully two-and-a-half months to recover strength and tone, and to expel the malaria from their systems. Measures for their recovery had been adopted on the journey to France from the first, and quinine was a daily ration. Immediately after being posted to the 151st Inf. Bde. of the 50th Div., Gen. Sir Henry Rawlinson, to whose Army (the Fourth), the 50th Div. belonged, made his inspection, and the men and officers were forthwith sent to England on leave in batches. During the month of August 451 other ranks of the 1/K.O.Y.L.I. proceeded on leave to the U.K., the best tonic that could have been devised.

THE 1ST BN.

On July 14th the battalion took part in the French National celebrations (storming of the Bastille), at Dieppe. On August 1st the regimental holiday (Minden Day) was observed with sports, football and a concert.

Throughout August and September the 50th Div. underwent a steady training. On September 15th the 1/K.O.Y.L.I. marched from camp at Martin Eglise to Dieppe, where it entrained for Sus St. Leger, in the Third Army area. After training here for ten days it finally moved by 'bus to Rainneville in the Fourth Army area, where the 50th Div. was concentrated before entering into the line of the great advance.

Lt.-Col. H. Mallinson was in command, Capt. A. E. Starling was Adjutant, and Maj. G. de Hoghton was appointed 2nd-in-command.

In battalion orders of September 28th Lt. C. H. Hastings, C.Q.M.S.

F. Ibbeson and Pte. T. E. Chesterman were "mentioned in dispatches" for gallant conduct during the period 21/9/17 to 28/2/18.

Following on its great efforts in March and April, 1918, the 1/4th K.O.Y.L.I. (in the 49th Div.) was granted a long period in which to recover and refit before again taking part in important fighting. The division was relegated to the Flanders front, no longer the arena for pitched battles, but now the quietest front, where young formations could be initiated and convalescents could regain their nimbleness.

THE 1/4TH BN.

However, quiet as the Ypres front may have been in comparison to the line further south, it was not without its excitements; below Ypres the ground which had been taken by the Germans in April was wrested from them piece by piece in a long series of minor engagements, and the troops right away up the line, the British Second Army, the French and the Belgians, were all filled with eagerness to harass their foes and join in the hunt.

On June 2nd, when the 1/4th K.O.Y.L.I. was in brigade reserve in front of Ypres by the Menin Gate the enemy covered all adjacent roads and communications with a harassing fire of (Yellow Cross) gas shells; this continued from 9.30 p.m. till 1.15 next morning. The battalion suffered 44 casualties in wounded or gassed, including Lts. G. S. Day and J. Rodgers.

For the fighting in April the following names appeared in the "mentions" in the King's Birthday honours list:—

Capt. (a/Lt.-Col.) H. C. Fraser, Capt. C. T. W. Etches, Sgt. E. J. Preece, C.S.M. F. Jones and R.Q.M.S. H. Milner, the two latter receiving the D.C.M.

In June, after a successful raid, 4 M.M.'s were awarded to Sgt. F. Clarke, Ptes. Crelly, Arundel and Langford respectively. After another, Capt. C. A. Stiebel (19/L.F., attd.) and 2/Lt. J. Burkinshaw were granted M.C.'s and Cpl. T. Mackenzie received the D.C.M.

On July 30th a raid on the enemy position was carried out with the help of an artillery barrage. Four German prisoners were taken and important identifications were made. The raiding party was commanded by Lt. J. W. Lamb, who had with him 2/Lts. T. Bentley and J. Battiland, the former of whom was wounded; there were also 17 casualties in other ranks. Lt. Lamb received the M.C., and Sgt. E. J. Preece the D.C.M.

Early in August "B" Bn., 118th American Inf. Bde., did a tour of duty in the front line.

On August 15th M.M.'s were awarded to Cpl. J. Hustwaite, Lce-Cpls. W. E. Dixon, T. Gowland and W. Oldroyd, and Pte. A. Todd in connection with Lt. Lamb's raid.

On August 12th Lt. L. G. S. Ludlow was missing and five other ranks were wounded.

On the 22nd the 1/4th K.O.Y.L.I. proceeded via Proven to Herzeele for training, and on for battalion training to Framecourt. It left Framecourt for Blangy, east of Arras, on September 2nd, and finally went into the front line as right battalion of left brigade in the divisional front.

Raids were frequent; in one on the night of September 17th, made under cover of a barrage, the enemy's post was entered, but 2/Lt. D. H. Siddall and one private soldier were killed, and three other ranks were wounded. Another raid on the 21st was more costly; Capt. C. A. Stiebel was in charge; the required information was obtained, but at the cost of two other ranks killed, eleven wounded, and 2/Lt. H. H. Spelman and seven other ranks missing.

On the night of the 22nd "Z" Company, under Capt. W. J. Hindle, attacked the same post with success; one prisoner was brought in, also a machine-gun, and the remainder of the detachment were killed. Lt. R. A. Hargreaves and 2/Lt. W. N. Dawson were wounded; twelve other ranks were also wounded. Pte. A. Campbell was awarded the M.M. This is the last incident mentioned in the diary for September; the first week in October was spent in training at Marœuil, four miles north-west of Arras.

THE 8TH BN. IN ITALY.

Throughout January, February and the first fortnight of March the 8/K.O.Y.L.I. (70th Inf. Bde., 23rd Div.) occupied the same sector of the line on the Piave river, which it had originally taken over. Back behind the line in billets at Biadene for training, then forward to Venegazzu as reserve battalion to the 70th Inf. Bde., and again into the trenches facing the Piave, the battalion passed through an uneventful period, while the mighty preparations were being made by the German armies for the offensive on the western front in France. In order to concentrate their forces for this great offensive, the German divisions on the Italian front were withdrawn in the early spring, leaving the Austro-Hungarian armies to fight out their battles without German help on the Italian front. Gen. Plumer also, commander of the British forces in Italy, was withdrawn to re-assume command of his army in northern France. His place was taken by Gen. Lord Cavan, a worthy successor.

Apart from occasional crossing of the Piave by patrols to bomb an enemy post or gather information, there were few exciting incidents to record. 2/Lt. J. W. Butterworth took a patrol of eight men across to bomb a post on January 19th.

In the new year's honours list Lt.-Col. D. Quirk, Capt. E. A. Martin and Sgt. W. Hopper were 'mentioned,' also Capt. and Adjt. E. B. B. Speed received the M.C.

The battalion came out of its trenches on the Piave for the last time on March 14th before marching to a fresh sector of the front.

The new sector was back west of the river Brenta, facing north, up on the Asiago plateau a little distance to the south of the town of that name. The first march, on the 16th, was to S. Pietre, where the battalion remained a week; Povolaro was reached on the 25th, and Thiene on the 26th. On the 27th it was carried on in lorries to Granezza.

Granezza was the headquarters of the division. The road passing northwards through Granezza to Asiago, about five miles distant, was the boundary line, separating the 23rd Div. on the west side from a French division to the east. Pria dell Acqua, 70th Inf. Bde. Headquarters, was on the same road about half-way between Granezza and the front trench line.

April was a very quiet month. 2/Lt. T. M. Meikle earned the M.C., Lce.-Cpl. H. Darrell a Bar to his M.M., and Lce.-Sgt. E. Oliver and Pte. G. Milson the M.M., during the month for good work on night patrol duty.

May was a month of routine work. So far there had been no casualties in this sector.

Maj. G. L. Pyman took over the command of the 8/K.O.Y.L.I. when Lt.-Col. Quirk proceeded on leave to the U.K. on June 2nd.

An attack by the Austrians had long been expected. It was delivered in great force on June 15th. Two army groups, those of Generals Conrad and Boroevic, attacked simultaneously; Conrad, who had twenty-seven divisions at his disposal, attacked the Asiago positions from the north or Trentino side; Boroevic, with twenty-three, attacked from east to west against the Piave trenches. Conrad's attack on the Asiago upland was a complete failure; the eastern offensive was partially successful for two days, but the Austrians were finally forced back across the river. The Austrian losses totalled 96,000 men, while the Italians had lost heavily also, 40,000 men in killed and wounded alone.

On the morning of the attack the 8/K.O.Y.L.I. was in brigade reserve behind the right battalion. At 12.30 p.m. "A" Company, which was at Pria dell Acqua, received orders from the Bde. Headquarters to move up at once to the S. Sisto ridge and reinforce the 11/Foresters in the front line. The company reached the Foresters' Headquarters at 1.15, and at once moved on towards the front line. The commander, Capt. B. H. Horsley, took two of his platoons forward to the right flank of the Foresters, leaving the other two in rear; on arrival he found that a considerable portion of the line on the right of the Foresters was already in the hands of the enemy, a party of whom, numbering fifteen, had passed over the trenches and was in the open about one hundred yards south of them. The enemy were also in strength just beyond the front wire, and there were some of them working forward by way of a communicating trench to join the party of fifteen.

Capt. Horsley directed 2/Lt. T. M. Meikle with the leading platoon to start clearing the trench from the left, while he himself kept down the enemy fire with the other; he sent back word to 2/Lt. H. G. Houchin to reinforce with the other half-company and to hold back any attack from the front. Capt. Horsley then joined 2/Lt. Meikle in the forward trench, where he found an encounter with the Austrians in the trench in progress. Choosing two or three specially good bombers the two officers led an attack with such determination that the enemy soon began to surrender and progress became quicker. Dug-outs were bombed one after another, some of the enemy surrendering and others fighting. Meanwhile along the front our wires were being cut and the enemy were dribbling through the gaps, and still there were the fifteen in the open to be dealt with, as well as the men in the communicating trench. Sgt. J. M. Campbell was posted with a captured machine-gun in a position to fire down the communicating trench, and Cpl. H. Bennett with a Lewis-gun close by assisted by turning its fire on the party of fifteen. Cpl. Bennett shot down five men, and the remaining ten surrendered. Capt. Horsley was then able to make progress down the main trench and he cleared it of the enemy for about 300 yards, eventually joining the French troops beyond.

In this operation Capt. Horsley took six officers and over one hundred men prisoners, capturing also six machine-guns, three of which were quickly brought into action against the enemy. A very large number of dead were in the front trench and in and beyond the front wire. Subsequently, as a result of sending patrols into No Man's Land further prisoners and material were added, including 20,000 rounds of ammunition for the machine-guns.

Capt. Horsley was supported by "C" Company, which also came into action.

Everywhere else the line in the Asiago sector was held.

The casualties in the 8/K.O.Y.L.I. included 2/Lt. L. R. Wagstaff gassed, five other ranks killed, thirty-one wounded, and one gassed.

The battalion was relieved on the 17th by the 8/Green Howards and until the end of October, when the Italians launched their great final offensive which shattered the Austro-Hungarian armies, there was little fighting on any Italian front. The offensive power of the Austrians was broken when the June offensive failed so signally.

After the June dispatches the following honours and awards to members of the 8/K.O.Y.L.I. were published:—

Maj. G. L. Pyman (already D.S.O.) was awarded the M.C.; Capt. B. H. Horsley the D.S.O., Capt. J. E. F. Mann the M.C.; 2/Lt. T. M. Meikle, Bar to M.C.; 2/Lt. H. G. Houchin the M.C.

Sgts. Wilkie and Campbell and Cpl. Bennett received the D.C.M.; Sgt. Greenbury received the M.S.M.

Lt.-Col. D. Quirk, Maj. K. E. Poyser, Capt. E. B. B. Speed, 2/Lt J. H. Cater, R.S.M. Geddess, Sgt. Woodcock and Sgt. Slater were all 'mentioned.'

Later No. 38518 Sgt. Wilkie received the Croix-de-Guerre (Fr.).

The 8/K.O.Y.L.I. was at Montecchio Maggiore when Minden Day was celebrated, and for some days was working on heavy battery positions at Cima del Fonte. On August 21st, when at Magna Boschi in the left brigade of the divisional front, the line came under a heavy shelling. There were many casualties in the battalion, seven other ranks being killed, twenty-eight wounded and one shell-shocked.

Early in September the battalion marched to Serona camp for training, returning to the front line on September 15th. There was a certain amount of activity and Capt. C. F. Barrett was mortally wounded on the 22nd, 2/Lt. J. Reid also being wounded.

Lt.-Col. D. Quirk returned from sick leave on October 5th. The battalion was at that time training at Cornedo; it went on from there by train on October 14th to Treviso, a city ten or twelve miles from the Piave and only twenty-five miles by train from Venice. Treviso was now the centre of activity for the troops, Italian and British, which were to operate under Lord Cavan in the impending great advance. Lord Cavan's front extended from Selettuol to Palazzon, behind the Piave.

The great offensive began on the night of October 26th. The 8/K.O.Y.L.I. was in reserve to the 68th Inf. Bde. on the 27th in its attack. One company crossed the Piave in the morning of the 28th, the remainder of the battalion crossing at 10.30 p.m. The XIV British Corps attacked with the 23rd Div. on the left and the 7th Div. on the right. The attacking forces reached the line of the river Monticano, the whole of Lord Cavan's force reaching the line of the river by the 29th.

At 5 a.m. on the 30th, the 8/K.O.Y.L.I., now re-transferred to the 70th Inf Bde., resumed the advance, crossed the Monticano, and took up a position on the southern bank of the Meschio. The Austrians had been skilfully manœuvred out of their last line of defence, and from now onwards their armies were in headlong retreat. At 9 a.m. on the 31st the 8/K.O.Y.L.I. resumed its advance to Pestarole. This day the whole of the Asiago plateau, too, had been recaptured and the Austro-Hungarian troops on the whole front were routed. On November 2nd the 8/K.O.Y.L.I. went into billets in Mai. An armistice was signed on the 3rd and the cessation of hostilities was declared on the Italian front at 3 p.m. on the 4th.

The battalion rested at Mai till the 8th, and moved back to the Piave on the 9th; thence to Vascon next day, and on to Cendon on the 11th, where the great news was received of the cessation of hostilities with Germany.

It was not till December 23rd that the first demobilisation draft left the 8/K.O.Y.L.I. for the United Kingdom.

In the last advance from the Piave, to be known to history as the battle of Vittorio Veneto, 300,000 prisoners and 5,000 guns were taken by the Italians and their allies.

On June 10th, 1918, the Headquarters nucleus of a new battalion, which was at first called the 10/Garrison Bn., was assembled at Etaples. From Etaples it was sent by train the same day to Watten, and it marched to Buysscheure, where the battalion was to be organised. The men of this nucleus formation, with few exceptions, belonged to categories B1 and B2; they marched the six miles most creditably carrying full packs, ground sheets and blankets, in spite of the fact that B2 men are certified as medically unfit to march more than five miles.

THE 15TH BN.

On arrival in their new camp they found the name of the battalion had been changed to 15/K.O.Y.L.I. (Garrison).

The officers originally with the Bn. Headquarters were : C.O., Lt.-Col. F. C. McCordick; 2nd-in-C., Maj. J. Ralston Bock; Adjt., Capt. L. M. Sandison; Asst. Adjt., Lt. J. W. Swanson; Transport Officer, Capt. A. Lindemere; Qr.-Mr., Lt. F. Nunley; M.O., Capt. C. H. Carroll, R.A.M.C.

On the 11th, about 700 other ranks arrived from various Labour battalions to complete the strength; they were all B1 and B2 men. The new battalion was posted to the 120th Inf. Bde. of the 40th Div. Maj.-Gen. J. Ponsonby, commanding the division, inspected the battalion on the 15th. The division was part of the XV Corps (De Lisle), of the Second, or northernmost (British) Army. The division was holding that part of the line which was west of Armentières, to which the British troops had been pushed back in April. This was now the quietest part of the front, a training area for convalescents. On the 23rd the 15/K.O.Y.L.I. left for La Belle Hotesse for training. It was here assigned a sector of the West Hazebrouck trench line, after being inspected by Brig.-Gen. C. J. Hobkirk, commanding the 120th Inf. Bde. Three Labour Companies, the 84th, 92nd and 110th, were attached to the battalion as reserves.

The battalion was inspected by H.R.H. the Duke of Connaught on July 2nd, and on the 9th by Maj.-Gen. J. Paton, the new G.O.C., 40th Div.

On July 16th the title "Garrison" was dropped and the battalion became plain 15/K.O.Y.L.I.

Lt.-Col. T. W. T. Isaac succeeded Lt.-Col. McCordick in the command, the latter leaving for Canada on duty.

After performing a musketry course at Lumbres in the first week of August the battalion moved up, first to Aval Wood in support, and then into front line in relief of the 11/E. Lanc., being for the time attached to the 92nd Inf. Bde. In carrying out the relief a sergeant was killed and ten other ranks were wounded, and the following day (August 14th) a Lewis-gun team of two corporals and two privates was killed by a T.M. shell. The line was becoming more active; it was expected that the Germans would shortly make a new offensive in this northern field; in fact there is little doubt this would have been done, had not the success of the Third Army settled that question once for all and diverted to itself the concentrated attention of the enemy. In the meanwhile the XV Corps was not idle, but with a succession of lesser attacks was employed in recovering, yard by yard, the ground lost in April.

The 15/K.O.Y.L.I. was engaged in such an operation on August 23rd. "A" and "C" Companies attacked a portion of the enemy trench line between Cochin corner and Pont Rondin. "C" Company on the left, under Capt. W. E. Garrod, advanced about 700 yards and made several prisoners; 2/Lt. S. Scarr with his runner captured a machine-gun after killing or making prisoners of the crew.

In the night of the 27th also a further raid resulted in the capture of a dozen prisoners and a machine-gun.

Ptes. Ward and Carter of "B" Company received the M.M. for gallant conduct on the 14th and 15th of the month.

On September 11th the battalion was moved in lorries to reserve, south-west of Steenwerck, and on the following day into the support line in Nieppe Switch, before taking over the front line on the 16th from the 10/K.O.S.B. It moved back to reserve again on the 19th, and to Nieppe on October 1st.

The general advance of the Second Army, together with the Belgians and French, had commenced on September 28th.

When the Third Army had broken the Hindenburg Line, and the combined offensive of the Belgians, French and British Second Army began to make progress in the north, the Germans in front of the Fifth Army, which was sandwiched between the British Second and Third Armies, were forced to go too. The whole line was shortly pressing forward in one great sweep from the sea to the right flank of the American armies east of Rheims.

The 15/K.O.Y.L.I. in the right flank of the Second Army, though this part of the front was the region of least resistance, still could claim a place in the march to victory.

Leaving Armentières behind on October 5th, where it had been temporarily in support, it went on into the front line. On October 8th the battalion was heavily shelled with gas and suffered fifty-two casualties, mostly in "B" Company. The 11/Camerons relieved it on the 9th, Capt. Groves being wounded by shell-fire during the process. The battalion went back to Erquinghem, south-west of

Armentières, where a draft of sixty men arrived from England who were posted to "B" Company.

On the 16th, in consequence of the retirement of the enemy, the battalion was ordered forward to Rue Marle, south of Armentières, and on to Champreuille next day, and to Wambrechies on the 18th (nine miles east of Armentières); here it met French civilians pouring in from the liberated country where, since 1914, they had been in the enemy's hands.

On the 19th the 120th Inf. Bde. was concentrated at St. Andre, five miles south of Wambrechies, to be employed for the next few days on improving the roads and communications. The whole brigade was billeted in the monastery.

The brigade moved east to Lannoy (eleven miles) on the 28th, where it remained in reserve till November 6th, when it moved on three or four miles to Nechin, where the battalion was in divisional support.

On November 10th the battalion moved across the river Scheldt to Herinnes, where the news reached it on the 11th that hostilities were to cease at 11 a.m.

A concert was organised for the evening to celebrate the Peace.

The battalion remained in the district in billets at Toufflers until it was demobilised. The G.O.C. Div. presented medals to the undermentioned on the square at Lannoy on December 8th :—

Bar to M.C., Capt. W. E. E. Garrod. M.C., 2/Lt. S. Scarr. M.M. and Bar, a/C.S.M. Roberts. M.M., Sgt. R. W. Shaw, Ptes. B. Broadley and J. Brazier. Croix de Guerre with silver star, Sgt. L. Hanson.

2/Lt. F. T. Thewlis received the M.C. for conspicuous work as Transport Officer.

THE LAST PHASE, 1918, TO THE CAPTURE OF THE HINDENBURG LINE

XXIV

THE evacuation of the Lys salient by the Germans in the face of the Second and Fifth British Armies was effected by the end of the first week in September. By the end of the second week, at the southern end of the western front, General Pershing completed the preliminary operations of the allies by recovering the St. Mihiel salient, employing nine (out of twenty-five) of the American divisions which were in readiness to take the field. "*Success had fired the Allied troops with enthusiasm, while the Americans were fresh and inspired with the zeal of crusaders.*" From this time forward Belgians, British, French and Americans went steadily forward in the advance to final victory, not by any means chasing a runaway foe, but attacking, and again attacking, an enemy who contested every inch of the ground; here breaking down opposition with the help of masses of tanks and utilising the friendly natural fog or artificial clouds, there out-manœuvring the German machine-gunners, who gallantly covered their infantry and gave time to the artillery to take up fresh positions of resistance.

The Hindenburg Line was a system of trenches covering St. Quentin in the south, extending northwards to Mœuvres, and north-westwards to Quéant; from Quéant it was prolonged northwards again to Drocourt. Every effort had been made by the enemy to render the line impregnable. The attack on the Drocourt-Quéant system commenced on September 2nd, when the First Army smashed and captured the northern portion and, pushing on through the gap it had created, rendered the rest of that section untenable. The Germans were forced to fall back on the line of the Canal du Nord–Havrincourt–Epéhy–Vermand. Thus they lost the Drocourt-Quéant line together with the northern part of the Hindenburg Line between Quéant and Havrincourt.

The greater part of September was devoted by the British armies to preparations for the assault on the enemy's second positions. South of Havrincourt he held strong trench lines in front of the Hindenburg Line; they were in reality part of the Hindenburg or "Siegfried" system; they had to be taken before the main Hindenburg Line itself could be assaulted. The Third and Fourth Armies both experienced hard fighting in the capture of these obstacles. All was ready, however, for the assault by September 27th, when the Third and First Armies attacked in the direction of Cambrai, and captured the line of the Canal du Nord; they continued their victorious advance on the 28th, and on the 29th the Fourth Army also advanced to the attack, covered by an enormous artillery barrage. Between Holnon, three miles west of St. Quentin, and Bellenglise the 1st and 46th Divs. of the IX Corps (Braithwaite) captured the line and pierced it to a depth of three miles, the 32nd Div. passing through the 46th and completing the capture of the Hindenburg Reserve Line. The rest of the Hindenburg Line was rapidly reduced after the two ends had been pierced; with the loss of the line the enemy lost the last of his main lines of defence on this sector of his front, and henceforward had to rely on the natural features of the country.

In following the fortunes of the K.O.Y.L.I. battalions in this period the story will be taken in order from the right.

THE 2ND BN.

After the capture of Herleville (August 23rd) the 2/K.O.Y.L.I. went on in support till the evening of September 3rd, when it took over an outpost line in front of Misery from the 10/A. & S.H. Officers' patrols were constantly engaged in watching the river Somme and the canal banks, but were all the time exposed to machine-gun fire from the posts on the opposite bank, from St. Christ on the left, and from the marsh on the far side of the river Somme. The bridge at St. Christ was badly damaged and covered by machine-guns; at Cizancourt to the right of Misery there was no means of crossing.

At 11 a.m. on September 5th came orders to the battalion to cross the Somme by foot-bridges which had been constructed at St. Christ by the Royal Engineers. The operation was a general one; the French were operating on the right, the 1/5th Border was the next battalion on the left. The crossing was opposed by rifle-, machine-gun- and field-gun-fire. A quarry in St. Christ was strongly held; our 6-in. mortars fired some rounds into it and, at about 3 p.m., a platoon of "B" Company under 2/Lt. F. Woollerton managed to get across at St. Christ. At the same time at Cizancourt a crossing was effected by "A" Company, under Capt. E. V. H. Bradley, by a very skilful and dashing movement. It gave the signal to the enemy to clear out, and he did this at the double. The crossing was now simplified; a large number of prisoners were taken. Companies then pushed on over the high ground to the east of the Somme valley towards Ennemain, meeting with slight opposition. Ennemain was entered and before nightfall our front line was established on the ridge 1,500 yards east of the village, that is, two and a half miles beyond the river.

The prisoners captured in the crossing numbered 4 officers and 101 other ranks. Our casualties were only 6 wounded.

On the 6th an advance was made to a line east of Monchy-Lagache and Douvieux, part of which was an old enemy trench system; the weather was very hot.

The French had gained Lanchy on our right. The Australian Light Horse went through and reported that there were none of the enemy within 2 or 3,000 yards.

On September 7th the advance started at 7 a.m.; the objectives were 6,500 yards ahead. In this advance our 18-pounder field guns followed up very closely and gave great assistance by engaging and silencing all opposition. The enemy did not wait in his trenches; by 1 p.m. the objective line was reached and occupied. Villerque was in the captured line and battalion headquarters were established there. By night the 10/A. & S.H. relieved the 2/K.O.Y.L.I., which went back as battalion in support. The casualties had been 3 other ranks killed, 35 wounded.

From the 8th to the 11th it remained in support, and on the 12th the division was relieved in the front. The 97th Inf. Bde. was conveyed by 'bus to Villers Bretonneux, ten miles east of Amiens, where it immediately commenced a course of musketry and other training and was joined by several officers to fill the gaps. The 2/K.O.Y.L.I. moved up at 9 p.m. on September 22nd by 'bus again to Vraignes, east of the Somme, just north of the straight main road from Amiens to St. Quentin. Here it remained training till the 28th, the eve of the great attack on the Hindenburg Line, when it moved forward to Le Verguier.

On September 29th the 46th Div. (Boyd), of which the 32nd (Lambert) was in support, attacked the Hindenburg Line at dawn; our guns had been pounding the position for two days, and the barrage under which the 46th Div. attacked was intense. There were other divisions attacking on either flank. The Hindenburg Line was pierced by the 46th Div., the troops of which had forced the passage of the St. Quentin Canal, and at 11 a.m. orders came to the 2/K.O.Y.L.I. to move forward to the Hindenburg support trench system 1,000 yards east of the canal. Later in the afternoon a further forward move was made to pass through the 46th Div., which had gained its objective east of Magny.

The companies pushed forward rapidly in the face of heavy artillery and machine-gun fire to spurs which commanded the village of Levergies. Capt. E. E. E. Cass discovered an enemy battery in the act of withdrawing its guns; working a Lewis gun himself he directed a concentrated fire on the battery and shot down the detachments and teams, although under direct fire of another battery 2,000 yards away, which was covering the withdrawal of the first one. He led two platoons forward and seized the hostile battery which consisted of four H.V. and one 8-in. howitzer. Capt. B. V. Pring established his company on a spur overlooking Levergies also;

with great dash the company gained the high ground to the right of the village, and by a swift stroke captured a battery of four guns and several machine guns. Thus the enemy was forced to abandon his forward positions and fall back to the village.

Preparations for an attack were made on the 30th and careful reconnaissances were made of the approaches to the village; in the afternoon in conjunction with other units (the 14th Inf. Bde. was co-operating on the right), Capt. Pring advanced some 500 yards, being in advance of the troops on both his flanks; under fire from three sides he established the Lewis guns of his company for all-round defence and placed his wounded in a nearby trench. The company was enabled to establish itself in its exposed position and it caused the enemy to withdraw many of his posts to the village itself. The subsequent attack on the village in the evening under artillery bombardment was greatly facilitated.

The village was rushed under cover of the growing darkness. Capt. Cass led his company, in spite of artillery and machine-gun fire, into the village, and right through it, fighting on the way and securing thirty prisoners, while Capt. Pring led his own and other companies on the right until they established themselves on the exposed flank beyond it. The capture of Levergies was a very brilliant affair, and the success of the operation was largely due to the dash and initiative of these two company commanders, both of whom subsequently received the D.S.O. By daybreak the battalion was established in line east of Levergies.

2/Lt. H. Hutchinson was killed in this attack, and Lt. O. H. Cooke, 2/Lts. G. Musgrove, H. Gunn and F. Hilton were wounded.

Of other ranks 7 were killed and 52 wounded. In addition to the howitzer and 8 field guns, between 30 and 40 machine guns were taken.

Sgt. R. D. Leng won the D.C.M. for the splendid pluck he displayed on the 30th. He had temporarily to withdraw his section to a trench 100 yards in rear before the assault; finding that two of his men were missing he twice went forward to the exposed position and brought away the two men in turn, whom he found wounded; this was in the face of machine-gun fire and of a battery firing over open sights.

We left the 9/K.O.Y.L.I. at the end of August a few miles south-west of Bapaume in the neighbourhood of Le Sars. On September 2nd the battalion was in support to the 2/E. York., which made an attack on Lubda copse near Villers au Flos. That night the 21st Div. was taken into corps reserve; reinforcements met the battalion consisting of 11 officers and 237 other ranks.

THE 9TH BN.

Two days later the division was taken out of corps reserve and ordered into a new area south-eastwards.

The 9/K.O.Y.L.I. marched on September 5th *via* Beaulencourt and Le Transloy to Sailly Saillisel and then moved in the evening to a reserve position south of Le Mesnil en Arrouaise; the 64th Inf. Bde. was in divisional reserve.

On the 7th a move was made to trenches near Equancourt, the Canal du Nord being crossed by a new bridge built by the R.E. On the morning of the 9th an attack was delivered by the 64th Inf. Bde. against positions on Lowland ridge and Chapel hill. The 9/K.O.Y.L.I. was ordered to take Lowland support and Lowland trench. The move from Equancourt was made at midnight. The battalion marched *via* Fins and Heudicourt to the starting point. "B" and "D" Companies were in the first line, "C" in support and "A" in reserve. The programme was carried out; Lowland support was taken and occupied, but the enemy in the second trench resisted stoutly and there was hard fighting; the battalion found itself in advance of its neighbours, so the second objective had to be abandoned and the Lowland support line was occupied. At 5 p.m. the attack on Lowland trench was repeated; many casualties were occasioned in retaking it, but again the flanks were quite exposed and the trench had to be abandoned a second time.

In the early morning of September 10th the 2/E. York. passed through to attack the trench once again; this battalion also lost heavily and the trench could not be held. That night the 9/K.O.Y.L.I. was relieved by the 1/Wilts., and it marched back to Equancourt for a longer rest and refitting.

On September 12th the enemy aeroplanes were very busy round Equancourt and carried out a raid, two of the machines being brought down.

After rehearsing an attack on Vaucelette farm on the 16th and 17th the battalion moved forward in the early morning of the 18th, marching in single file to its starting point. At 5.30 a.m. it advanced to the Yellow line, previously occupied by the 62nd Inf. Bde., which had attacked the first objective; the advance was resumed by the 62nd Bde. followed by the 9/K.O.Y.L.I. close up behind the barrage, until the railway was reached. Here the barrage halted for forty-five minutes, giving time to reorganise before the next advance. At 9.45 the battalion went through the 62nd Inf. Bde. and advanced with little opposition until arriving at Beet trench, the final objective. Sharp fighting then ensued, but the enemy was driven out and the trench occupied. Half an hour after midnight the enemy made a counter-attack on the trenches left of the K.O.Y.L.I. and drove the occupants back some hundreds of yards, leaving the flank open. Maj. T. A. Walsh rushed up a platoon of "A" Company with the headquarters details to fill the gap; the retiring troops joined in to retake their line; this was done and the enemy was severely punished.

Maj. Walsh was wounded and handed over the command of the battalion to Capt. A. F. Ennals.

The remainder of "A" Company was sent to the left to reinforce while a battalion of the 62nd Inf. Bde. was hurried up to support the line. The pressure, which was severe, was further relieved during the night by an attack which our troops were making further north.

During this operation the 64th Inf. Bde. took about 400 prisoners, a large number of machine guns and several field guns. One battery, consisting of two 77 mm. and two 105 mm. guns was captured complete with personnel and teams.

The 64th Bde. was relieved by the 98th Bde., 33rd Div., and moved back a few miles to the area east of Etricourt.

Maj. H. W. H. Tyler arrived to command the 9/K.O.Y.L.I.

Preparations were in progress all along the line for the great attack on the Hindenburg Line; it was, however, decided not to deliver an infantry attack on this section of the front, although on the 26th commanding officers were engaged in a conference at which the details of a projected attack on Gonnelieu were discussed. Gonnelieu, three miles west of the Escaut river, formed a strong advanced position covering the Hindenburg line. While the guns were thundering a few miles ahead the battalions of the 64th Inf. Bde., who had received large drafts early in the month, were able to seize a fleeting opportunity to train them.

The men were extraordinarily fit and in excellent spirits; there was practically no sickness.

On October 4th Maj. W. C. Ratcliffe joined as second-in-command. On the 6th a move was made; the brigade crossed the Escaut river at Honnecourt; the enemy had evacuated the line.

The casualties in the 9/K.O.Y.L.I. during September were as follows: (taken from the "Q" lists of the 21st Div.)

Officers: 5 killed, 9 wounded.

Other ranks: 21 killed, 148 wounded, 48 missing.

A special order issued by Headquarters 21st Div., of Friday, September 20th, 1918, reads as follows:—

"*The successes gained by this division in the recent fighting, which culminated in the magnificent and successful attack carried out on September 19th, will probably never be surpassed by any division in the British army. That any division, after suffering the heavy casualties this division suffered while breaking up the almost overwhelming attacks of the enemy, should be capable, with practically no respite, of passing to the offensive and, during a month's hard and continuous fighting, of carrying out one brilliant attack after another, would hitherto have been considered totally impossible.*

"*It has, however, been accomplished by this division in no uncertain manner.*

"It has only been accomplished because of the splendid 'esprit de corps' which animated all ranks, and the 'will to win' which every officer, N.C.O. and man throughout the division has so clearly shown.

"You have set yourselves a tremendous standard and you now have to live up to that standard. This will require the best that every man can give.

That you will succeed in doing so I have no doubt at all.

(signed) David G. M. Campbell, Maj-Gen.,
comdg. 21st Division."

The 62nd Div. attacked from Vaulx-Vraucourt towards Morchies, with the 3rd Div. on its left and the 5th on its right on September 2nd.

THE 5TH AND 2/4TH BNS.

The German line south of Quéant at this time ran west of Lagnicourt, between Bois de Vaulx and Bois de Maricourt and through Haplincourt down to Peronne. Our interest will be centred on the Bois de Vaulx.

All three battalions of the 187th Inf. Bde. took part in the assault, the 2/4th K.O.Y.L.I. on the right, the 5/K.O.Y.L.I. in the centre, and the 2/4th Y. & L. on the left; the 9/D.L.I. was allotted to the brigade as a reserve for the day. "Zero" hour was 5.30 a.m. The advance was started under a heavy enemy barrage. The men were only too anxious to get away from the enemy barrage and get under the protection of our own. On the brigade's right flank the 2/4th K.O.Y.L.I. had "A" and "B" Companies in the first wave, whose duties were to capture the first and second objectives; the two other companies passed through the leaders in the second position, after it had been taken, and went on to assault the third or final objective. The operation had obviously been expected and the leading lines came at once under machine-gun fire. The attack made excellent progress; many of the enemy were killed, and the capture of prisoners and machine guns was considerable.

Further to the left all went splendidly with the 5/K.O.Y.L.I. till 7 a.m. Vaulx wood was passed and the troops were heading for Maricourt wood when it was found that the 2/4th Y. & L. on the left was meeting with serious resistance and was getting on but slowly, for the brigade on its left was making no headway at all. Both the K.O.Y.L.I. battalions were suffering from enfilade fire from the left and the enemy were working round the left flank to re-occupy Vaulx wood, which was now in the left rear. Lt.-Col. Peter sent orders to "A" Company, the support, to occupy the Vaulx-Lagnicourt and Vaulx-Morchies roads at all costs and do its utmost to prevent the enemy from seizing Vaulx wood. The troops in the front wave were soon almost surrounded, but the survivors held the line they had reached with great gallantry till night came. The 9/D.L.I. came into action in the afternoon and cleared Vaulx wood.

When this was accomplished the situation in the front became less critical. The line was established along the high ground which the front troops had held on to so tenaciously.

Like August 27th, September 2nd had been a critical day which called for the best qualities of courage, dash and determination on the part of company officers and men.

In the night the enemy shelled the area very heavily for a time. It was concluded that this was a parting demonstration and that he was going, which proved to be the case.

The captures by both the K.O.Y.L.I. battalions during the day were numerous; the 5th Bn. alone took over 200 prisoners and a quantity of material, including three field guns, four trench mortars and fifty machine guns; the 2/4th had taken its share, but it had no field guns to its credit.

In the 5th Bn. Maj. T. Shearman was second-in-command, and Capt. P. Bentley (who eventually finished the war with three Bars to his M.C.) was Adjutant. The casualties in the battalion amounted to about 200; of the officers, the killed and wounded on September 2nd were: killed, 2/Lts. F. Bottomley, W. C. Neilson (E. York., attd.) and J. Billing (E. York., attd.); wounded, Capt. A. C. Lynn, Lt. R. A. Houghton, 2/Lts. J. S. Bowden and C. P. Howells (Green Howards, attd.).

In the 2/4th Bn. there were fourteen other ranks killed and 137 wounded; of the officers 2/Lt. A. E. Martin was killed and the wounded included Capt. R. Townend, Lt. J. F. Sutherland (R.A.S.C., attd.), 2/Lts. J. H. Fisher (W. York., attd.), L. W. Johnson, and G. E. W. Pollard. 2/Lts. J. H. Fisher and G. E. W. Pollard died of their wounds.

The Hindenburg Line ran eastwards from Quéant through Prouville to Mœuvres, and then southwards, the front system of resistance passing through Havrincourt and Gouzeaucourt to Epéhy, and on past Holnon, west of St. Quentin.

On September 2nd Quéant fell into British hands. South of Quéant the Germans were pushed steadily back behind their main line, but before the great attack on the southern portion of the Hindenburg Line, which was not due till the end of the month, every preparation for the assault was made by depriving the enemy of his forward system of protection.

From the 3rd to the 10th September the 187th Inf. Bde. was re-organising and training at Behagnies, where on the 11th it received orders for an attack to be made on Havrincourt.

The same evening it left its billets in Velu wood to take up its attack positions north of Havrincourt wood. The 5/K.O.Y.L.I. was in the front line and was directed on the village of Havrincourt. The attack was launched at 5.25 a.m. on the 12th. The first objective was the western part of the village; the 2/4th K.O.Y.L.I. supported the 5th Bn. "B" and "C" Companies of the 5th Bn. were in the first line; "C" Company under Capt. T. A. H. Oliphant had for its objective the triangular south-west corner of the village; "B" Company under Lt. E. S. French, who was killed during the advance, was allotted Putney Avenue and a further trench line; "D" under Lt. C. M. Wilson moved in rear of "C," with a further objective in the village; while "A" under Capt. W. Crow followed "B," having an additional objective also. Early in the advance "B" Company lost all its officers and for a time became disorganised; realising this Capt. Crow pushed on past the flank of "B," captured his own objective, which was to the left of that of "B," and then made good the objective of "B." The whole of the objectives were gained without great loss. This was greatly due to the splendid action of Sgt. L. Calvert, of "C" Company, who rushed forward and put two machine guns and their crews out of action, single-handed, at a critical moment: he bayoneted three men and shot four, capturing both the guns in Bogart's Hole. For this conspicuous act of bravery he was awarded the V.C., a distinction which reflected honour on both the Territorial battalions.

The 2/4th K.O.Y.L.I. came up and took over Putney trench, the first objective, while the 5th Bn. went on to Clarges avenue. The latter company was bombed out of its new position once, as it was without bombs at the time; after replenishing, it went forward again and stormed the enemy out. The position was then consolidated.

Throughout the 13th and 14th the battalions fought to maintain their positions with success. The enemy bombardment on the latter day was terrific and the aeroplanes were busy dropping bombs on the forward lines. Considering that the British troops were holding on to a portion of the Siegfried line, which they had penetrated, the activity of the enemy is hardly to be wondered at. The valour and determination displayed by officers and men were beyond all praise, exceeding that displayed in any of their victorious attacks of recent days.

The 5th Bn. captured 4 field guns, 4 trench mortars, 17 heavy and 23 light machine guns, with 120 prisoners. The casualties in the battalion included 1 officer killed and 3 wounded; 17 other ranks killed, 159 wounded, and 11 missing. The officers were: Lt. E. S. French, killed; 2/Lts. F. J. F. Clarke, J. S. Fernie and E. Morton, wounded.

In the 2/4th Bn. 2/Lts. A. Kilner, A. T. Pitman, and F. Wilkinson were wounded on the 12th, and 2/Lt. J. W. Baty was wounded on September 13th.

The division was relieved by the 3rd Div. in the night of September 15th–16th, and the 187th Inf. Bde. went back to Behagnies, where it was engaged in refitting and training.

On September 25th the 187th Bde. moved up from Behagnies to Frémicourt, and the following night found the two K.O.Y.L.I. battalions in assembly positions east of Hermies ready to attack. The 62nd Div. was, possibly designedly, advancing over familiar ground, for it had fought in this country in 1917. The 2/4th Y. & L. and the 2/4th K.O.Y.L.I. were in first line and were followed by the 5/K.O.Y.L.I. in support. The Canal du Nord was crossed by a newly made bridge.

The troops of the 3rd Div. were ahead of the 187th Inf. Bde. and they were attacking the first objective in the Hindenburg support line south of Flesquières and east of Ribécourt; the 62nd Div. was ordered to follow up their attack and pass through the 3rd Div. in the first objective.

At 5.20 a.m. on September 27th the attack started with the 2/4th K.O.Y.L.I. on the right, following closely behind the 9th Inf. Bde. of the 3rd Div.; it assisted it in the capture of Ribécourt after severe fighting, in which Capt. G. E. Spencer, commanding "A" Company, rendered conspicuous service. No further advance could be made until the high ground south of Ribécourt had been taken by the 42nd Div. on the right. The 5/K.O.Y.L.I. came up and occupied a defensive position facing south-east. During the remainder of the day the situation remained unchanged; a re-distribution of companies was made in battalions and the position was consolidated.

At 4.30 a.m. on the 28th the attack was continued with battalions in the same order as the day before. The 5/K.O.Y.L.I. was assigned the task of securing the crossings of the river Escaut (Scheldt), which at this point is still referred to as the St. Quentin canal; these were the crossings south-east of Marcoing; those opposite Marcoing were allotted to the 186th Inf. Bde.

The attack of the 2/4th K.O.Y.L.I. was at first attended with great success and the first objective in the Hindenburg support was carried, together with a large number of prisoners who seemed to have been taken completely by surprise. This success was due in a large measure to Capt. Spencer, who was in command of the supporting companies; he realised that the leading companies had failed to get their orders and with great presence of mind and initiative pushed forward his own command and assumed the rôle of the leaders.

"A" Company (Capt. G. E. Spencer) now was in front on the right, "B" Company on the left; the advance was continued with "C" Company behind "A" and "D" Company in support of "B." A stubborn resistance was encountered. There were two field guns in the way of "B" Company, firing point blank, and four more opposed "A." The detachments were shot down by our Lewis-gunners and the men rushed to the guns, which were captured; the men were not to be stopped by any obstacle; they were helped, too, by a most effective creeping barrage and by an enveloping fog. There was a thrilling moment when a party of the enemy under an officer was discovered to be breaking through between "A" and "B"; "B" was engaged in throwing back its flank at the moment, to cover our people beyond them on the left, who were falling back under pressure from a counter-attack; however, the officer was killed and his party was dispersed.

"B" then advanced again; "A," which was now very weak owing to losses at Ribécourt, was reinforced by two platoons of "C," and the line went forward and captured a further trench and a sunken road. As they neared the objective the supports pushed up into line, "D" Company coming in on the left of "B"; the company was rewarded by coming upon a 9-in. gun with three horses attached; the horses were sent back to the rear.

The 5/K.O.Y.L.I. attempted to pass through to its objective, but was met by such a heavy fire from Welsh ridge and Marcoing copse that the effort had to be postponed till 6.30 p.m. when artillery support was arranged for. The attack was then made with complete success, and several more guns, machine guns and prisoners were added to the list of captures.

So all objectives were taken, with from 300 to 350 prisoners by the 2/4th K.O.Y.L.I. alone, 121 of whom were taken in the sunken road.

The attack was resumed on September 29th at 7.30 a.m., in a dense fog under a creeping barrage, the 2/4th K.O.Y.L.I. on the right and the 5/K.O.Y.L.I. on the left assisted by one company 2/Y. & L. By 1 p.m. the brigade had fought its way to its final objective which included Masnières (where over 300 prisoners were taken) and Les Rues Vertes, together with the trench system immediately east of those places. Masnières village was taken by the 5/K.O.Y.L.I., the Y. & L. Company acting as "moppers up"; the men were sorely disappointed at the smallness of the "bag" in Masnières, a paltry 300, whereas false rumour had led them to expect that, hidden in "the catacombs," they would take at least 3,000! At any rate there were many men in the battalion who were familiar with Masnières and its possibilities, for the place had been in British hands in the Cambrai battle of November, 1917.

While the 5/K.O.Y.L.I. was dealing with Masnières the 2/4th K.O.Y.L.I. was similarly engaged with Les Rues Vertes. In the fog a party was early discovered on the right flank of "B" Company; it was skilfully rounded up and yielded fifty prisoners; in another spot twenty-nine men were taken and three 5.9 guns with their barrels hot from firing; close by the battery twenty-one men of its complement were surprised at breakfast. "D" Company took fifty prisoners and a number of machine guns in Les Rues Vertes itself.

The 9th Div. relieved the 62nd on September 30th.

The 5/K.O.Y.L.I. had the following casualties among officers: 2/Lt. W. C. H. Stott, killed (September 27th); 2/Lt. G. F. Spence (W. York., attd.), wounded (September 27th); 2/Lt. A. Wood, killed (September 29th), Lt. C. H. Wilson, died of wounds (September 29th); and 2/Lt. C. P. Howells (King's Own, attd.), killed (September 30th). In other ranks 7 were killed, 56 wounded and 14 missing.

The 2/4th K.O.Y.L.I. had 2/Lt. (a/Capt.) C. Hirst wounded (September 27th), and a/Capt. G. E. Spencer wounded (September 30th).

In the 5th Bn. diary for October, in addition to Sgt. Laurence Calvert's V.C., mention of which has been made previously, a number of honours for the September operations are mentioned:—

D.S.O., Capt. (a/Lt.-Col.) F. H. Peter and Capt. (a/Maj.) T. Shearman. Third Bar to M.C., Capt. and Adjt. P. Bentley.

Bar to M.C., Capt. T. H. H. Oliphant, Lt. C. E. Townend and 2/Lt. H. Tomalin (Green Howards, attd.).

M.C., Capt. W. L. Crawford, 2/Lt. (a/Capt.) W. Crow, Lt. C. E. Townend, 2/Lt. H. Tomalin and 2/Lt. G. Trigg.

D.C.M., Sgt. H. V. Ward, Lce.-Sgt. H. Tordoff, Ptes. G. H. Bevans and A. E. Allen.

The 2/4th Bn. diary does not mention the honours gained for this period, but among them were:—

D.S.O., Lt.-Col. C. A. Chaytor and Capt. G. E. Spencer. Bar to M.C., Maj. G. Beaumont, Capt. and Adjt. A. E. Earle. M.C., Capt. J. T. E. Clarke and Capt. C. Hirst [authority, *187th Inf. Bde. in France*, 1917 *and* 1918].

The last mention of the 12/K.O.Y.L.I. was dated June 15th, when the 31st Div. moved forward from Second Army reserve at Staple into position in the line; the 12/K.O.Y.L.I. was temporarily brigaded in the 94th Inf. Bde.

THE 12TH BN.

In the King's Birthday honours list (dated June 3rd) three D.C.M.'s were bestowed on the battalion, *viz.*, to C.S.M. C. Featherstone, C.S.M. G. S. Parker (since killed in action) and Pte. S. Holmes.

From this time onwards until the final advance small portions of the German line were constantly being recovered in surprise attacks. The 31st Div. made such an attack on June 28th, when the companies of the 12/K.O.Y.L.I. wired the posts in the new front captured by the division in the early morning. About 1,100 yards of wire entanglement had to be erected before daylight. One company was told off to each infantry brigade for this work.

July was spent chiefly on works near Hazebrouck in a new line of resistance. Among the casualties Lts. L. Forsdike and J. R. Wilson were both reported to have been captured by the enemy.

On August 9th the 31st Div. re-took Vieux Berquin.

From August 26th onwards the battalion was employed in the Bailleul sector on construction and repairing works, opening up the roads leading into Bailleul after the enemy had been forced to retire. When the 31st Div. was relieved by the 29th on September 1st, the 12/K.O.Y.L.I. continued in the line following up the infantry in the advance. 2/Lt. J. B. Clarke had been reported missing, but was now declared to have been wounded and a prisoner-of-war.

On September 28th the 31st Div. attacked Ploegsteert wood and Warneton. The 12th Bn. stood by for any necessary work, being employed throughout the following night on road repairs.

On October 10th Lt.-Col. C. B. Charlesworth rejoined to take command of the battalion. The month was spent close up behind the advancing line, for the enemy were steadily retiring. On the 16th the battalion was near Warneton, on the 18th at Quesnoy, and by the 22nd at Nechin. On the 27th the 31st Div. relieved the 29th as reserve division of the II Corps and the 12/K.O.Y.L.I. moved to a new area, marching from Lannoy to Mouscron, and from there to Staceghem on October 29th.

On November 1st the battalion followed up and assisted the attack on Audenarde, marching on the 3rd to billets in Halluin and on the 7th to Marcke. On the 9th it assisted the R.E. in making the approaches to bridges over the river Escaut (Scheldt) which had just been abandoned by the Germans. Moving from Orroir to Renaix on the 11th it found billets there in houses and schools.

The news of the signing of the armistice was received in the morning.

The battalion was notified on the 13th that the 31st Div. would not proceed to Germany.

By November 27th, after a series of marches, the battalion returned *via* Ypres to Staple with an effective strength of 41 officers and 843 other ranks. It had not long to wait before the process of disbanding began to affect it, for the first parties for demobilisation left for England on December 12th.

THE LAST PHASE, EAST OF THE HINDENBURG LINE, 1918

XXV

IN the slight sketch of the sequence of events with which the more recent narrative of the K.O.Y.L.I. battalions has been embroidered, the collapse of the German forces on the western front has been foreshadowed. The issues were moving rapidly to a climax. Following the shattering of the Hindenburg Line the outlying states of the Central Powers collapsed one after another, Bulgaria before the Allies under the leadership of Gen. Guillaumat, the Turks before Gen. Allenby, and the Austrians under the shock of Gen. Diaz' offensive.

Undoubtedly the tanks had played an outstanding part in many of the battles in the advance to victory. To escape the weight of their onslaught the Germans had made the most of the great waterways where tanks could not be brought into action, but by the end of September the last of the great reinforced protective lines was overcome and the pace of the retreat was daily accelerated. Yet the retreat never developed into a rout on the western front as it did, for instance, on the front in Italy.

In the final stage of the British advance the K.O.Y.L.I. was worthily represented. Both regular battalions, three territorial (1/4th, 5th, and 2/4th), and three service (9th, 12th and 15th) were taking part.

It remains only to describe the actions of six of these in the last forty days of the war, and they will be taken in the order in which they occupied positions in the line from right to left.

On October 3rd a combined attack of the 32nd Div. (on the right) and the 46th (on the left) was commenced at 6.5 a.m. The 2/K.O.Y.L.I. was right battalion of left brigade, and it attacked just north of Sequehart. The troops were preceded by a very strong barrage and objectives were reached in the face of concentrated field- and machine-gun fire. A great number of German dead were lying near Sequehart, where the enemy had defended the village and the Fonsommes line. On the eastern side of the hill the new positions were exposed and our troops suffered a number of casualties from artillery fire.

THE 2ND BN.

The night was uneventful as was the following day. The 97th Inf. Bde. was relieved in the night of October 4th, and went back to gun-pits and dug-outs near Levergies cemetery. The next three days were occupied in marching back to Catelet, where the

2/K.O.Y.L.I. remained till October 18th refitting. There is a rather quaint entry in the diary for the 10th, when two officers are named as "taking French leave"! As they were both back at duty a few days later (without a Court Martial) it is reasonable to conclude that the expression was used in this case without the sinister significance which is generally ascribed to it.

A preliminary attempt to oust the enemy from Sequehart had been made on the 2nd, when the battalion had four killed and eighty-three wounded in other ranks, and 2/Lt. A. G. E. Alexander wounded. 2/Lt. L. Parker was killed on October 1st.

On the 3rd, when Sequehart was taken, the casualties were: 2/Lts. F. S. Maud and L. Woollerton killed; Lt. E. Keel, 2/Lts. E. D. Sewell and L. Ashton wounded; other ranks, killed sixteen, wounded eighty-three.

By October 21st the battalion was back in Sequehart, where it was billeted in the houses. The K.O.Y.L.I. men felt that they had a proprietary interest in the village, which they had recovered for the inhabitants at a cost of 200 of their killed and wounded. Life was becoming vastly interesting in these days, especially to those members of the 2/K.O.Y.L.I. who found themselves fighting their way over ground which they had once before traversed in the retreat from Le Cateau in 1914. The Adjutant (Capt. H. S. Howard), three warrant officers (R.S.M. J. Bramley, C.S.M. J. Turner, and R.Q.M.S. A. W. Beeching), and thirty-one N.C.O.s and men had come to France with the battalion in August, 1914, and were serving in it on the day of the cessation of hostilities. What a contrast to these men to be welcomed as liberators by the people whom, four years previously, they had been forced to abandon to their fate!

The battalion moved on a little two days later to the neighbourhood of Bohain, seven miles west of the Oise; here it was engaged in training before its next entry into the line for a tour of duty.

Bohain is a small town. On Sunday, October 27th, there was a Thanksgiving service in the church for the town's liberation by British troops, which was attended by the troops and by a distinguished gathering of French and British officers and local inhabitants. The band of the 2/K.O.Y.L.I. supplied the musical portion of the service; the church, a large one, was crowded. The service was opened with an impressive rendering of the *Marseillaise;* there was not a dry eye among the civil portion of the congregation; even among the soldiers (so one soldier has recorded) there was a noticeable swallowing of lumps in the throat. The town priest preached a vigorous sermon amid the sobs of the women and children, and the service ended with "God Save the King."

On October 31st the 2/K.O.Y.L.I. left Bohain in full marching order for St. Souplet, only four miles south of Le Cateau. Here the 97th Bde. was in divisional reserve, the 32nd Div. having relieved the 6th Div.

On November 3rd two companies, "A" and "C," were detached in aid of the 96th Inf. Bde. at Happegarbes, west of Landrécies. The enemy occupied the line of the Sambre canal with defences on the west bank. Our two companies were assigned a position in the line of attack the next day, accompanying the 15/Lan. Fus. "C" Company acted as centre company of the Fusiliers' line, with "A" in support. Offensive operations opened with a tremendous barrage at 5.45 a.m. Unfortunately the K.O.Y.L.I. caught the fringe of this barrage and suffered 30 casualties. In a dense fog the companies moved forward across open country, through hedgerows, dykes and railway cuttings, and across a marsh to the canal bank. The enemy barrage came down with great intensity and caused many more casualties. In spite of obstacles, moving in quick time, the two companies went on their way and gained their objectives, ahead of the companies on their right and left, who were worn out by their splendid exertions of the previous days and were unable to keep up with the fresh ones. They were the only companies to cross the Sambre in the first assault. Throughout the day they held on tenaciously to the position they had gained, missing no opportunity of harassing the foe; towards evening the hostile resistance weakened. The 96th Inf. Bde. crossed the canal through Landrécies and occupied the objective positions to the east, having been greatly helped by the presence of the Yorkshiremen on the far bank.

The officers with the companies were: ("A") Capt. H. J. Knight, 2/Lts. H. L. Colley and J. P. Frazer; ("C") Capt. B. V. Pring, 2/Lts. W. Butler, G. Coombs, G. Platts and H. Robinson. Of these 2/Lt. Colley was killed and 2/Lt. G. Platts was wounded.

In other ranks five were killed, eighty wounded and twenty-four missing.

In the meantime Bn. Headquarters and other companies paraded in battle order at 9.15 a.m. and at 4.20 p.m. crossed the Sambre-Oise canal by a bridge at Ors to take up a position three-quarters of a mile east of the canal and one mile north of Catillon. Enemy H.E. shell-fire caused about twenty casualties in the crossing.

November 5th was occupied by the brigade in making a short advance to a line between Maroilles and Prisches. On reaching Le Grand Fayt at 1.30 p.m. on the 6th the 2/K.O.Y.L.I., which now was complete, went through the 1/5th Border and 10/A. & S.H. and became assaulting battalion, and so advanced for four miles to its objective on the Marbaix-Avesnes road. Lt.-Col. Lamotte, who had been on (sick) leave in France, rejoined at night. Capt. A. E. Kemble had led the battalion in his absence, and had made all the preparations for the advance on Avesnes.

The advance was continued at 7.45 a.m. on November 7th. The 2/K.O.Y.L.I. went forward in artillery formation, with "B" and "D" leading. The town of Avesnes was the objective. At 9 a.m., when one and a quarter miles west of the town, the opposition from machine-gunners began to cause delay, but it did not prevent the troops from seizing their objective line one mile west of the town. At 12.15 p.m. a regular attack was launched in the direction of the enemy defences, which were strongly held with machine guns and artillery. Without unduly exposing themselves the attackers used every possible means of harassing the defenders; the K.O.Y.L.I. Lewis guns were assisted by the guns of a company of the Div. M.G. Bn., and by the 161st Battery R.F.A., together with an armoured car and a squadron of the 20th Hussars. Night descended on the attackers but the pressure was kept up throughout the hours of darkness, and daylight again found the position appreciably improved. From dawn onwards the companies worked forward by the process of dribbling; although advances were minute their effect on the enemy was unmistakable. At 2 p.m. they showed signs of breaking, the signal for intense activity. One after another the defences were rushed until finally the companies rose and swept forward through the defences, through the town, and finally to seize a position one mile or so east of the town. The men were on the heels of the Germans and a number of prisoners and machine guns were secured. The battalion was determined, as there were rumours of an armistice in the air, that, if this was to be its last fight, it should be a good one

Capt. A. E. Kemble who, as second-in-command, was with the leading companies, deserves a great share of the credit for the manner in which the final success was achieved. The following is an extract from the Order in which he was awarded the D.S.O.: "*His initiative, skill and pluck were remarkable. He . . . . was continually with the companies in advance; he personally led some companies who were losing direction, under fire, to their objective . . . . It was he who animated their relentless pressure culminating in the taking of Avesnes. After passing through the town he reorganised his company on the eastern edge, and led it forward to the final objective line two kilometres beyond. While engaged in this task and just five minutes before darkness he was hit in the right leg by a sniper's bullet which caused a most dangerous wound and subsequent amputation of the leg. With great devotion he urged his men forward and was afterwards found lying helpless on the battlefield.*"

At dawn on the 9th patrols reconnoitring a mile to the front discovered no sign of the enemy. The 1/5th Border passed through and took up the pursuit, while the 2/K.O.Y.L.I. withdrew to billets in Avesnes in the course of the afternoon.

The following officers had taken part in the fight:—

Bn. Headquarters: Lt.-Col. L. Lamotte, Capt. A. E. Kemble, Capt. H. S. Howard and Lt. J. G. Kennedy.

"A" Company: Capt. H. J. Knight, 2/Lt. J. P. Frazer.

"B" Company: Capt. E. E. E. Cass, 2/Lts. R. Martin and H. Wilkinson.

"C" Company: Capt. B. V. Pring, 2/Lts. W. Butler and G. Coombs.

"D" Company: 2/Lts. B. A. Lewis (comdg.), W. C. Holdway, A. H. Leak and W. Southwick.

T.O., Lt. C. P. Halliday. Bde. Liaison Officer, Lt. N. R. Gray.

2/Lt. B. A. Lewis was killed; Capt. A. E. Kemble, 2/Lts. R. Martin and H. Robinson were wounded.

In other ranks sixteen were killed and 145 wounded.

On November 10th the battalion moved to billets in Hautlieu, where on the 11th the news of the armistice arrived. "The news was received quietly by the men." Brig.-Gen. G. A. Armitage, commanding the 97th Inf. Bde., went round the companies and spoke to the men, thanking them for their gallant fighting in the recent operations.

That night Lt.-Col. C. R. Ingham Brooke arrived to command the battalion *vice* Lt.-Col. Lamotte, who for nearly a year had directed it and shared in its strenuous work of achievement.

In addition to the honours already referred to as having been bestowed on members of the 2/K.O.Y.L.I. for services in the last phase, the following were from time to time notified in battalion orders:—

For conspicuous services on October 3rd:—

M.C., 2/Lt. W. Mustard and 2/Lt. A. G. E. Alexander.

D.C.M., Sgt. E. Taylor.

November 4th:—

M.C., 2/Lt. G. H. Platts and 2/Lt. J. P. Frazer.

M.M., Sgt. F. Richardson, Sgt. R. D. Leng, D.C.M., Cpl. E. Hayes, Lce.-Cpl. O. Cliffe, Pte. J. Easter, Cpl. G. Moodie, Pte. C. W. Major.

November 7th:—

M.C., 2/Lt. R. Martin.

D.C.M., Pte. J. Boyle, Cpl. G. Moodie.

M.C., Rev. B. H. Smith, C.F. "*In the attack on Avesnes (November 7th) when the house occupied by Bn. Headquarters at a crossroads was bombarded by 5.9 calibre shells and the first shell wounded six of our men, there being no medical officer present, he rushed out into the open and carried the men in, bandaged them all during the bombardment, encouraging them all the time the shells were bursting. He continually kept close to the firing line, seeking opportunities to care for and comfort the wounded, regardless of his personal safety.*"

The 2/K.O.Y.L.I. moved by easy stages through Ramousies and Montbliart to Rance in Belgium, where the British front line had halted on November 11th. Here the Colours of the battalion arrived from England, having been brought by Lt. K. J. Box, Sgt. W. Tinsley and Sgt. F. Stevens, the escorting party.

On December 12th the battalion marched to Senzeille, and by the 15th had reached Dorinne. In passing over the Meuse this day, to commemorate the crossing of the river by the 1st Bn. in its glorious march to Minden in 1759, the colours of the 2nd Bn. were uncased. At midday with colours flying and the band and buglers playing a combined march, the bridge was crossed amid the greetings of the wondering inhabitants of Yvoir.

On December 18th a move was made to better billets in Spontin, whose splendid old castle, the home of an old crusading family, became the headquarters of the battalion.

Here we must take leave of the 2/K.O.Y.L.I., busy with ceremonial drill and recovering the pre-war conditions. A meeting of the battalion branch of the Regimental Association was held in the château the day after its arrival.

The 1/K.O.Y.L.I. now belonged to the XIII Corps (in Rawlinson's Fourth Army), which came into the line towards the end of September in the III Corps area and relieved that corps at the critical time of the breaking of the Hindenburg Line. The XIII Corps (Morland) had the V Corps of the Third Army on its left, and the Australians on its right. The Australians were shortly after relieved by the II American Corps and they retired for a rest after their heroic exertions.

THE 1ST BN.

It is interesting to note how the battalions of the K.O.Y.L.I. were fighting side by side in October, though probably quite unaware of their proximity, and were converging on Le Cateau, the scene of the destruction of the 2nd Bn. in 1914. For instance, on October 31st the 1/K.O.Y.L.I. was resting in billets in Le Cateau; on the same day the 2/K.O.Y.L.I. halted for the night in St. Souplet in its march from Bohain back to its place in the fighting line; St. Souplet is only four miles south-west of Le Cateau.

The 1/K.O.Y.L.I. marched to Epehy on October 1st. The following day it moved in support of the 149th Inf. Bde in the Hindenburg Line and relieved the remnants of the 37th and 39th Bns. Australian I.F. The enemy were shelling the road from Lempire to Bony and inflicted some casualties on the relieving battalion.

Lt.-Col. H. Mallinson was temporarily left out to command the divisional battle reserves. Maj. G. de Hoghton took the battalion into action on the 3rd; Capt. A. E. Starling was Adjutant.

The attack of October 3rd was made at daybreak on the villages of Le Catelet and Gouy beyond; they lie in a basin on the east side of the St. Quentin canal; the rising ground behind was known as Prospect hill. The 151st Inf. Bde. was right brigade of the 50th Div.

in the attack, the 149th was the left; the 1/K.O.Y.L.I. supported the 149th.

The attack was started in a thick mist. The 6/Inniskg., behind which the 1/K.O.Y.L.I. was advancing, had Prospect hill for its objective, but in the fog this battalion was drawn by the firing from Gouy out of its true course, and became involved in the assault on this strongly held position. This was Maj. de Hoghton's opportunity; realising the situation, he carried on past the right flank of the Fusiliers and attacked the hill defences. In spite of a heavy barrage of the enemy 5.9 guns the battalion hurried on to gain the advantage of our own artillery barrage; the assault was made with great dash; it was the first chance the battalion had of showing its mettle since shaking off the worst of the malaria of Macedonia, and the men were eager to make the most of it. By 10 a.m. the hill was in their hands and the position was rapidly consolidated. The villages had also been secured. The losses in some of the battalions of the 50th Bde. had been heavy, but all objectives had been secured and 300 prisoners had been captured. The enemy made vigorous counter-attacks all through the rest of the day, but any parts of the new line which were temporarily lost were recovered before night.

The casualties in the 1/K.O.Y.L.I. were: killed, Lt. J. G. V. Ewinge, 2/Lt. P. J. Hill and forty-two other ranks; wounded, Maj. G. de Hoghton, Capt. R. Meadows (Warwick, attd.), Lt. D. Shires, 2/Lts. W. Brown, F. J. Highman, J. G. Hudson, L. Botterill, and 143 other ranks; missing, three other ranks.

The battalion captured three officers and 206 other ranks of the enemy. It was relieved at midnight by the 7/Wilts. and went south into the Hindenburg Line below Bony.

Capt. Starling was in command on the 4th, when the battalion was engaged in supporting the 2/Munster Fusiliers and 4/K.R.R.C. at Guillamont farm; it then moved to the region of Vendhuile, and to Gouy on the 7th. In the early morning of the 8th it attacked Villers farm, starting at 1 a.m., supported by a section of the 50th M.G. Company. The farm was strongly held by machine gunners, but the objective was gained by 2.45 a.m. Lt. P. C. Scott was killed and seven other ranks; Lt. K. Paterson and twenty-four other ranks were wounded. Four light trench mortars and a number of machine guns, one German officer and nine other ranks were captured. Lt.-Col. Mallinson resumed command on the 9th.

The battalion was in billets in Maretz till October 16th, when it marched to Escaufort, where it bivouacked for the night before delivering an attack on the enemy positions on the banks of the river Selle. The assembly position for the attack on the 17th was about 800 yards north of St. Souplet and the objective was on the Wassigny–Le Cateau road.

The barrage opened at 5.30 a.m.; three minutes later it lifted to the railway line. Some difficulty was experienced at the river; some small portable bridges were used for the crossing, which was fortunately covered by a dense fog. It was here that C.S.M. Christopher Brady distinguished himself and won a well-merited D.C.M. Under cover of the fog, but in the face of heavy hostile machine gun fire, he went forward alone and "mopped up" some machine gun emplacements, killing three of the enemy and capturing twenty. This fine act of courage at a critical moment in the fight materially helped the successful issue of the battle.

There was another incident of the crossing of the Selle. Lt.-Col. Mallinson and his R.S.M., G. Miller, fell into the river. Both could swim, but in the case of the commanding officer an attack of malaria was the result of the immersion.

After the crossing the companies advanced towards the railway line, "A" on the right, "B" on the left, "C" in support and "D" in reserve. "D" had the task of "mopping up" the enemy detraining point. The advance met with strong resistance from machine gunners and bombers. The railway embankment position was captured by 6.15 a.m. Companies then moved along the eastern side of the railway towards their next objective. At this stage touch was being kept with both the 4/K.R.R.C. and the 6/Inniskg., but later, owing to the mist and casualties, the touch with the latter battalion was lost.

At about 10 a.m. the objective in the Wassigny–Le Cateau road was reached. Patrols now ascertained that there was a long gap in the line owing to the fact that the 6/Inniskg. was held up near the detraining point. "C" Company was thrown back to form a defensive flank, while the remaining companies were being counter-attacked. At last, having expended all their ammunition, the companies were forced to fall back to the railway line, though "C" Company held on all day to its advanced position aided by a section of Vickers guns; at about 4 p.m. the 2/Dub. Fus. moved up and filled the gap.

About 7 p.m. three battalions, the 2/Dub. Fus., the 2/Munster Fus., and the 1/K.O.Y.L.I., were placed under Lt.-Col. Mallinson's orders to re-take the objective on the higher ground. This operation was successfully carried out during the night and the new position was consolidated.

On the 18th a further advance was made to a line east of Basuel, which was occupied in two hours after some fighting. At 9-30 a brigade of the 25th Div. passed through, and continued to press the retiring enemy. At 7 p.m. the 1/K.O.Y.L.I. withdrew to the position of the morning, and went back to billets in Avelu next day.

The casualties since the 16th had been:—

Killed: Lt. F. S. Scott, Lt. O. Tuke (E. York., attd.), and Lt. C. A. R. Bromham (Devon, attd.).

Wounded: Lt. L. Franklin, Lt. F. Roebuck, 2/Lt. C. W. Gale. Capt. T. F. J. Upton was wounded but remained at duty. Lt. W. Harrold was gassed.

In other ranks 14 were killed, 123 wounded, 40 missing and 3 gassed. Approximately 200 prisoners were captured.

In Avelu large drafts of officers and other ranks joined to fill the gaps. The battalion was inspected by Brig.-Gen. Sugden and by Maj.-Gen. H. C. Jackson, commanding 50th Div. It marched to Maurois on the 29th, and to Le Cateau on October 30th, where it remained some days in billets. While at Le Cateau Sgts. W. Hooley and F. G. Smith were in orders to receive the M.M. for gallant conduct at Prospect hill, but Sgt. Smith had since been killed in action.

The wastage in October had amounted to:—

Officers: killed, 6; wounded, 12; gassed, 1; sick, 1.

Other ranks: killed, 57; wounded, 274; gassed, 3; sick, 68; missing, 40; died, 1.

Reinforcements numbered, officers 5, other ranks 419.

The battalion moved to Bousies, five miles north-east of Le Cateau, on November 3rd to take up its place in the line of advance through the forest of Mormal. At 7.45 a.m. next morning it started to march *via* Fontaine-au-bois; after passing through the 150th Inf. Bde., which had gained its objective in the forest, it pushed on through the forest in the face of considerable opposition. The enemy continued to retire before the advancing line until nightfall, when the battalion bivouacked for the night. At 4 a.m. on the 5th it was ready to resume the advance, but the battalion now changed its place in the 151st Bde. from left flank battalion to right.

An attack was made on Hachette farm, which was reached by 10 a.m., after which the 149th Bde. passed through and took up the pursuit. The 1/K.O.Y.L.I. was billeted in Noyelles the night of November 6th and went on through the 149th Bde. to attack towards Dourlers. Next morning it met with very severe opposition and sustained many casualties; the objective was not reached till 9.30 a.m. on the 8th, the battalion reaching the Avesnes-Dourlers road, some five miles north of Avesnes. The new position was held under heavy shell-fire until 3.15 p.m., when the Scottish Horse passed through just after a heavy counter-attack had been successfully dealt with. The battalion then withdrew to Monceau where it was billeted in farms and rested for the next few days.

At Monceau the news of the armistice was received.

The following were in the list of honours published at the end of November:—

D.S.O., a/Maj. G. de Hoghton.

M.C., a/Capts. A. E. Starling, H. W. Lyne and H. W. Mottley, Lts. B. Pontefract, L. Franklin and H. W. Moon, 2/Lt. S. G. Whiting.

AT BAVAI

The 1st Battalion saluting the Colours on their arrival from England

To face page 1011

D.C.M., C.S.M. C. Brady and C.S.M. F. C. Thorley.

Bar to M.M., Sgt. W. Hooley.

M.M., 18, including Sgt. S. Freeman and Lce.-Cpl. Allport.

Bar to D.C.M., R.S.M. G. Miller.

The casualties in November had been:—

Officers: killed, Capt. T. F. J. Upton, Lt. C. W. Telfer and Lt. G. H. Neligan (all near Semousies on November 8th); wounded, Capt. H. W. Lyne, Lts. J. L. St. Leger Bunnett, H. B. Judge and 2/Lt. A. Brook.

Other ranks: killed, 26; wounded, 132; missing, 4; gassed, 3.

The 1/K.O.Y.L.I. remained in Monceau till the end of the year. As in the 2nd Bn. a meeting to reconstruct the branch of the Regimental Association was held on December 15th, at which the flourishing condition of the Association was explained, with the advantages of membership; for under successive commanding officers at the depôt and the fostering care of the Hon. Sec., Maj. W. G. Judge, who had formerly been Qr.-Mr. of the 2nd Bn. and was, during the war, acting in that capacity at the depôt, the funds had increased by leaps and bounds.

H.M. The King visited the troops at Monceau on December 3rd.

We now come to the line of advance of the 9/K.O.Y.L.I., only some four miles to the north of that of the 1/K.O.Y.L.I. For a few days the 9th Bn. had been out of the front line a little south-east of Heudecourt. This battalion, which in its colt days had been high-spirited, like many other good young thoroughbreds, and had required judicious and careful handling, had long since developed into the perfect chaser and was now (on October 5th) moving collectedly to negotiate the biggest water jump, the Escaut river, which lay ahead of it, the last great fence before coming to the straight in the race for victory. It so happened that there was no need for the battalion to extend itself; it was reported by the airmen that the Hindenburg line was evacuated; the battalion crossed the river at Honnecourt by a wooden bridge. This was not taken by the battalion or by any part of the 21st Div. as a signal to slacken its efforts; far from it, "that hard-bitten old scrapper," as Conan Doyle appositely, if somewhat irreverently, describes the 21st Div., merely saved its wind for the final gallop.

THE 9TH BN.

Behind the Escaut there was still a strongly entrenched position, that of Masnières-Beaurevoir, which was the support trench system of the Hindenburg line. The 64th Inf. Bde. moved forward to attack a portion of this system on the morning of October 6th. The 9/K.O.Y.L.I. was in support to the 1/E. York. and the 15/D.L.I. The programme of the day was altogether too ambitious, for a second objective was given in the village of Walincourt on the high ground behind. No progress could be made without longer preparation. The attack was resumed at midnight on the Beaurevoir line. The 9/K.O.Y.L.I. came up into the first line, having "A" Company supported by "B" on the right, and "C" supported by "D" on the left. "Zero" hour was 1 a.m. The barrage opened punctually and the troops followed close behind. The Beaurevoir line was carried with a rush. By 2.30 a.m. all objectives were gained at very little cost. The enemy counter-barrage had fortunately fallen behind the assaulting troops. Later on other troops passed through and developed this successful offensive.

On the 8th the 9/K.O.Y.L.I. moved to Hout farm, where it rested on the 9th; it moved into the village of Walincourt on October 10th. Here the men were comfortably billeted and in the evening the battalion band played in the village bandstand. A draft of ten 2/Lts. and ninety other ranks was made welcome. The battalion was paraded on the 12th to give Brig.-Gen. Edwards an opportunity of communicating the divisional commander's message (quoted in the previous chapter).

Lt.-Col. H. Greenwood rejoined the battalion from the sick list on October 15th.

On the 22nd the battalion moved forward through Inchy to an attack assembly position east of Neuvilly. On the morning of the 23rd an attack was duly launched by the 64th Inf. Bde. and one objective after another was taken right up to Vendegies, which was reached by 9 a.m.

The advance had been obstinately contested all the way and the volume of the enemy artillery and machine-gun fire had been very considerable; the losses would have been much greater if the line had not been checked from time to time to give time for machine-gun nests to be dealt with. In the case of one of these posts which was encountered west of Ovillers, half-way between Neuville and Vendegies, there had been casualties from the machine-gun fire. Lt.-Col. Greenwood, a firm believer in "leading" where there was any freedom of movement as was the case in open warfare such as this, and being always to be found at the point where difficulty was being encountered, managed to outwit the machine-gun post and rushed it single-handed, killing or capturing the occupants. Again at the entrance to Ovillers, accompanied by two of the battalion runners, he outmanœuvred another post, treating it in the same way as the former one. Later the leading line of the battalion was facing Duke's wood, having achieved one of its objectives, and found the enemy were almost surrounding the position with machine guns and some artillery; the enemy at once proceeded to counter-attack. The attack was repulsed, whereupon Col. Greenwood at once followed up the retreating enemy whose position he stormed (it was the final battalion objective for that day), and captured it with 150 prisoners, eight machine guns and one field gun.

The 62nd Inf. Bde. then passed through and established itself in the next position ahead, but not without a stiff fight.

On the 24th the two brigades together carried the line further to Poix-du-Nord, having attacked one position at 4 a.m. and a further one at 4 p.m.

In the morning attack again Col. Greenwood rushed a machine-gun post and handled his command conspicuously well in face of heavy opposition. The battalion objective, which was south of the village, was occupied and the hill was held in spite of heavy casualties. During the day the enemy appeared to be strengthening his position, and it was of vital importance to keep him on the move; the attack in the evening was a bold one and the enemy position was skilfully captured with important consequences, for the flank of the division was thereby safeguarded. It was obvious that Col. Greenwood had the entire confidence of his men, who would have followed him anywhere.

At 8 p.m. on the 25th the 64th Bde. was relieved by the 51st and moved to billets in Vendegies; it moved back the next day to the little town of Inchy on the Le Cateau-Cambrai road, only four miles north-west of Le Cateau. A draft had arrived for the battalion and was addressed by the C.O. on parade.

As October 27th was a Sunday, the battalion band played in one of the squares of the town. The diary refers to a spirit of elation among the men who found themselves in close neighbourhood of Le Cateau.

On the 29th the battalion moved back to Vendegies, where for six days the brigade busied itself in an intensive training to bring battalions up to their normal state of efficiency in case of further employment. One can be certain that those drafts were duly thrilled and impressed!

Special attention was paid to the training and drilling of Lewis-gunners.

A congratulatory message was received when at Vendegies from the Commander-in-Chief thanking the division and the brigades for the "noble part" they had played in the recent fighting; the message referred to their "unflinching resolution."

On November 4th the 21st Div. was back in the line, and the 64th Inf. Bde. once again advanced due east to capture a new line by Futoy, the 9/K.O.Y.L.I. being support battalion. It was now on the verge of the great forest of Mormal, and the country was reminiscent of some quiet English countryside with its hedgerows and small enclosed fields and orchards, heavy foliage and detached cottages.

On the 5th progress was continued through the great forest; progress was necessarily rather slow and laborious; a halt for the night was made at a hamlet, La-grande-carrière.

The whole of the Fourth, Third and First Armies were involved in the advance; the passage of the Sambre was the immediate object; troops were ordered not to confine their energies to the objectives, but to push on as far as they could; beyond the Sambre the Avesnes-Maubeuge road was the goal. The Limont-fontaine and Eclaibes villages on the near side of the road stood in the path of the 64th Inf. Bde.

At nightfall on November 5th most of the 21st Div. had reached the west bank of the Sambre. During the night light bridges were thrown across the river and the infantry in the right of the division forced a crossing which enabled the remainder further north to do the same.

Throughout November 6th the advance was continued relentlessly. Though the transport was hindered by the desperate condition of the roads through the forest, the infantry pushed ahead enthusiastically. The 110th Inf. Bde. was leading this day, and on the morning of the 7th it went ahead to seize the first objective of the day. The 64th Bde. then extended for attack and passed through.

In spite of excellent formation and good leading on the part of the company officers, the morning advance was held up by the intense fire of guns and machine guns. A fresh attack was organised in the afternoon on the villages about Limont-fontaine. The 9/K.O.Y.L.I. was in the front line. Ably led, the battalion this time made splendid progress and carried all before it by sheer determination. The villages were stoutly held and fierce fighting took place in the streets both of Limont and Eclaibes; the men fought regardless of casualties and simply refused to be denied the victory they had set out to gain. Both these villages were captured and cleared of the enemy, many of whom were taken prisoner.

The 17th Div. went through at midday on the 8th and the 21st retired from the front line for a rest. The 9/K.O.Y.L.I. withdrew to Bachant, and on to Berlaimont. On November 11th it was on the march to Limont again (the battalion's "own" village by right of capture) when the news of the armistice reached the men on the march. There was no outward demonstration, but inwardly no doubt there was a supreme feeling of satisfaction.

No statistics and no names are to be gleaned of casualties, trophies or honours for this last period from the diaries; there were so many other more urgent matters to be dealt with, especially in the case of a service battalion, which was bound to be one of the earliest to be broken up. But there is one exception:

December 18th proved to be a day of supreme gratification in the history of the 9/K.O.Y.L.I. The battalion was notified that the

V.C., the blue riband of the fighting forces, was conferred on Lt.-Col. Harry Greenwood in recognition of his services on November 23rd and 24th. Every officer and man of the battalion was intensely proud to learn that their leader had been so signally rewarded, and all had a right to feel that beyond the personal recognition the honour was intended to apply to all ranks of this famous fighting battalion.

And now we have to bid farewell for all time to the Service battalions. From the 6th and 7th, at the end of their strenuous and distinguished period of existence, we have already parted; the 10th, brilliant twin-brother, became united to the 9th Battalion and shares its glory; the 8th, with fresh laurels won in Italy, passes from our view; the 12th, indispensable whether with pick or rifle, shared the fortunes of the 31st Div. to the very last; the 15th and 16th gallantly played out their honourable, if less spectacular, parts; to the 9th seems due this special word:

You, embodiment as you were of the Service Battalion spirit, survived to see the finish of the war in the foremost fighting line in France. As centre of the K.O.Y.L.I. battalions that contended near Le Cateau to expel the invaders from the soil of France, you brooked no defeat and your spirit never flagged while you helped to force the enemy to leave defeated by the very road on which the 2nd Battalion had once striven to stem the oncoming tide.

In the company of the most notable of the fighting forces of the allied nations, you achieved for yourself distinguished recognition.

The King's Own Yorkshire Light Infantry is proud of your record, and heartily recognises that its reputation was secure in your hands and those of the other Service battalions. Farewell!

The scheme for the demobilisation of the 9/K.O.Y.L.I commenced to be put in force from December 1st, when the first batch of miners left for Cambrai *en route* for England.

The 187th Inf. Bde. was withdrawn from the front line and was training and refitting in the area of Ribécourt, west of the Escaut river, during the first part of October. From October 9th onwards the brigade moved leisurely forwards, following up the advance of the fighting line which had been making headway. The first halt was at Masnières on the Escaut. On the 10th it reached Estourmel where it was in billets; the village had suffered little from shell-fire, and for three days the men were occupied in training and bathing. Other billets were found in Catteniėres (October 13th to 18th), Bevillers (October 19th), and Quiėvy (till October 24th).

THE 5TH AND 2/4TH BNS.

The brigade was in divisional reserve; the division had captured Solesmes and progress was being made towards Romeries. On the 31st the 187th Bde. was billeted at Romeries, which is only three miles north-west of Vendegies, where the 64th Inf. Bde., including the 9/K.O.Y.L.I., was resting in billets at the time.

Within a narrow sector of the advancing line, having Le Cateau for its centre, the tale of the K.O.Y.L.I. battalions is thus complete. It is a curious fact that they stood in line in parade order of seniority of denomination, that is, the regular battalions on the right flank, the territorials on the left flank, and the Service battalion in the centre. The 1/4th, the 12th and the 15th battalions, though still in the picture, belong to more distant sectors.

On November 2nd the two territorial battalions, the 5th and the 2/4th, moved once again into the line in support at Ruesnes. On the 4th both were in the attacking line.

The attack was directed on Orsinval and Frasnoy. The first objective was allotted to the 5/K.O.Y.L.I.; the 2/4th K.O.Y.L.I. then passed through and attacked the second; after that was taken the 2/4th Y. & L. passed on to take the third. The "Zero" hour was 5.30 a.m.

The 5th Bn. met with its first big obstacle at La Folie farm. A heavy mist arose when the attack was starting, which made it difficult to maintain direction, but it also aided the attackers by covering their manœuvre to turn the flank of the defence and by 5 a.m. the farm was captured. Then came the Rhonelle river; the two leading companies crossed by wading, the others by improvised bridges (planks and tree-trunks). The fighting at Orsinval was severe round the mill and also in the north end of the village, but the troops were in a spirit to take no denial, and the village was occupied by 7 a.m.

Over 200 prisoners were taken by the 5/K.O.Y.L.I. Later, when the other troops had passed through, the battalion was withdrawn to billets in Orsinval for the night.

At Frasnoy also the 2/4th K.O.Y.L.I. encountered a deal of machine-gun fire. Owing greatly to the way our Lewis guns were handled the machine-gun fire was silenced and the troops entered the outskirts of the village, mopping up the nearer houses and taking machine guns and prisoners. However there was a better field of fire to be had behind the village, and this line was occupied for the time being. It was 9.25 a.m. when the 2/4th Y. & L. passed on to attack the next objective.

The 2/4th K.O.Y.L.I. had lost 2/Lt. W. Campbell (Y. & L., attd.) killed, and 71 other ranks killed and wounded.

The companies of the 2/4th had been commanded in the action by Capt. Clarke ("B"), Capt. A. Fox ("C"), Capt. C. Fox ("D") and Capt. P. D. Rooke ("A") in support. The battalion finally moved back to Frasnoy for the night, and remained in support during the next three days while the line was advancing to the further side of Mecquignies.

Meanwhile the 5/K.O.Y.L.I. went on in the morning of the 5th, being attached to the 185th Inf. Bde. for further operations.

Following up the 2/20th London the battalion went through when the latter halted on the line it had won, and attacked Le Trenchon. By 4 p.m. the companies had fought their way into line with the 186th Bde. (right) and the Guards (left). In the night the Londoners again went on and took up the chase, leaving the 5/K.O.Y.L.I. to return to the 187th Bde.

The 187th Inf. Bde. was now facing the southern part of Maubeuge with fort De Grevaux in its left front. The Guards on the left were pushing on rapidly against the fortress itself. There was the river Sambre to be crossed, with Louvroil and Sous-le-bois to be attacked beyond. The high ground protecting the approaches to the river had first to be gained.

On the morning of November 7th the 187th Bde. attacked with the 2/4th Y. & L. on the left, the 2/4th K.O.Y.L.I. in the centre, and the 1/10th Manch. on the right; the 5/K.O.Y.L.I. was in support. The advance proceeded successfully to a point, and the first objective was in the hands of the troops by 8 a.m. From that time onwards the enemy shelled with guns of all calibres very heavily, and there was intense machine-gun fire coming from the high ground. The 5/K.O.Y.L.I. had kept close up, and when the leading battalions were held up by the firing the battalion deployed for attack at 2 p.m. By 4.15 the whole of the high ground from which the obnoxious machine-gun fire had come was cleared by the battalion.

During the night that followed the 5/K.O.Y.L.I. received orders to exploit its previous day's success by attacking the De Grevaux fort next day. It was a very formidable strong point bristling with machine guns; the first attack was made at midday, and a second one followed the same evening after dark, but neither met with success, unless viewed as reconnaissances made in order to gather better information. At 4.30 a.m. on the 9th a third assault was delivered and the fort was captured. Simultaneously with the final assault the right reserve company of the 5/K.O.Y.L.I. pushed some parties over the Sambre who established posts on the farther bank, and thus greatly assisted the advance of the other battalions of the 187th Inf. Bde.

Of the other battalions of the brigade, the 2/4th Y. & L. on the left had Sous-le-bois for its objective while the 2/4th K.O.Y.L.I. was ordered to march against Louvroil. The latter advanced on a one-company front, "C" Company (Capt. A. Fox) leading.

At 6.30 a.m. the battalion crossed the Sambre by a foot-bridge and at once formed for attack; there was no opposition, however, for the enemy had abandoned Maubeuge, which was occupied by the Guards at midday, and the whole line was in retreat. The two battalions pushed forward to slightly elevated ground, where they threw out a line of outposts on the bank of a stream, a tributary of the Sambre. A quantity of stores of all kinds fell into their hands.

The 187th Bde. was concentrated in Sous-le-bois the next day (November 10th).

A message was received at 8.30 a.m. on the 11th to say that hostilities would cease at 11 a.m.

In this last advance the Guards Div. and the 62nd had taken great numbers of prisoners and guns of all calibres; the 5/K.O.Y.L.I. in its attack had captured 220 men and from 40 to 50 machine guns. The casualties in the battalion had been:

Officers: died of wounds, 2/Lt. T. R. Allott; wounded, Capt. H. Brown, Lt. C. Evers (York. Dgns., attd.), Lt. S. C. Bywater, and 2/Lt. H. S. Phillips.

Other ranks: killed, 21; wounded, 151; missing, 3; gassed, 16.

During November there was a further list of honours granted to members of the 5/K.O.Y.L.I. for the operations in October. It included: Bar to M.C., Capt. W. Crow. M.C., 2/Lt. J. Stansfield. 2nd Bar to M.M., Pte. S. H. Smith. Bars to M.M. to Sgt. E. Boughey, Sgt. G. Hamilton, Lce.-Cpl. F. Porter and Pte. T. Robinson. Nineteen M.M.'s, including one to Sgt. H. Tordoff, who already had the D.C.M. and M.S.M. Médaille militaire (Fr.), to Sgt. H. V. Ward.

The 2/4th K.O.Y.L.I. casualties on November 8th were:

Officers: 2/Lt. F. Cotterill (Y. & L., attd.), died of wounds; wounded, Capt. P. D. Rooke.

Other ranks, killed and wounded, fourteen.

A week later the 62nd Div. started on its march into Germany. The German frontier was crossed on December 17th. Battalions had sent escorting parties to England for their colours, and these were received at Elsenborn on the 20th on the line of march. The destination of the 5/K.O.Y.L.I. in the army of occupation was Embken, which was reached on Christmas Eve; the 2/4th K.O.Y.L.I. at the same time went into billets at Vlatten, near by.

The 1/4th Bn.

Under the command of Lt.-Col. S. C. Brierly the 1/4th K.O.Y.L.I. had been training at Marœuil early in October. On October 8th the battalion proceeded by 'bus to the front, the 148th Inf. Bde. being temporarily in the First Army reserve in the Drocourt-Quéant trench system. The 49th Div. had relieved the 11th Div. in the line. On the 10th the Bde. proceeded by route march to Faubourg St. Remy, on the outskirts of Cambrai. By the 13th the 1/4th K.O.Y.L.I. was up in brigade reserve at Avesnes-le-sec, some eight miles north-east of Cambrai and three miles east of the Escaut river. That day the 148th

Inf. Bde. delivered an attack east of Avesnes-le-sec, and in the evening the 1/4th K.O.Y.L.I. took over the front line which the other battalions had won. For the next three days the same line was held in the face of counter-attacks and determined opposition. During the period 2/Lt. N. Clayton and three other ranks were killed, Capt. F. W. Mackay, 2/Lt. C. A. Cummings, 2/Lt. W. L. Burkinshaw and twenty-four other ranks were wounded, 2/Lt. G. H. Turner and two other ranks were reported missing. The 1/4th K.O.Y.L.I. was relieved by the 1/Hants on the 17th and marched back to the neighbourhood of Cambrai on the 18th, eleven other ranks being gassed on the way. The remainder of October was spent in training.

On November 1st the battalion moved up to a position in support, south of Maing, and at 3 p.m. it moved up further to a covered position west of Famars. At 10 p.m. the same day it side-stepped to a part of the line in front of La Villette, in preparation for an attack, having the 4/Y. & L. on its left and the 7/D.W.R. on its right. The headquarters of the battalion were in Aulnoy. The XXII Corps (Godley), with its 4th Div. on the right and 49th Div. on the left, was advancing to force the passage of the Rhonelle.

At 5.30 a.m. on November 2nd, part of the 148th Inf. Bde., including the 1/4th K.O.Y.L.I., together with the 147th Bde., attacked under cover of a heavy barrage in order to re-establish the line along the Marly-Preseau road; this had been lost in a counter-attack on the previous afternoon. The operation was successful and the ground was recovered with about 100 prisoners. At 9 a.m. the centre company, "Y," pushed forward and established section posts along the road. At 3 p.m. the same company, together with "W," attacked alongside the 4/Y. & L. (Hallams) under a barrage and successfully established the line 200 yards forward. They took seventeen prisoners and two machine guns. This sector of the line, just south of Valenciennes, was stubbornly defended and the front line was heavily bombarded with 5.9 shells in the evening.

The casualties in the 1/4th K.O.Y.L.I. were:

Officers wounded: 2/Lts. C. Ansley, F. R. Oxley, S. J. Yates and C. E. Sewell.

Other ranks: seven killed, sixty-eight wounded.

The evening bombardment, as was suspected, was the prelude to a retirement on the part of the enemy, and on the 3rd at 11 a.m. the whole of the line, including the Canadians (left) and the 56th Div. (right), made a general advance. The 56th Div. was marching in a north-easterly direction; it gradually joined forces with the Canadians, until the brigades of the 49th Div. could be taken out of the line a little before reaching Estreux.

The 1/4th K.O.Y.L.I. formed up on the La Villette-La Flac road facing east, and awaited orders. Billets were occupied in Haulchin that night.

On November 5th the 148th Inf. Bde., which had been preceded by its transport, was withdrawn in lorries twenty-five miles to Auby, north of the Scarpe; the 1/4th K.O.Y.L.I. marched two miles further north to Le Forest to be billeted there in and near the château. At Le Forest the news of the armistice was received on the 11th by the battalion, which had already realised that its campaigning days were drawing to an end.

The names of twenty-one recipients of the M.M., and three recipients of Bars for services in October and November, were published in orders.

The battalion spent Christmas in Le Forest. The first of the parties of miners left for home on December 26th.

So ended the Great War. The soldiers at last had won Peace.

Photo by Catcheside, York.

MEMORIAL CHAPEL IN YORK MINSTER

The side screens of Ironwork

To face page 1021.

MEMORIALS

THUCYDIDES has recorded the noble words of Pericles spoken more than two thousand three hundred years ago as a funeral oration over the Athenian warriors who fell in the campaign of B.C. 431. The words still ring true and are equally applicable to our honoured dead, our regimental fathers, whose campaigns are commemorated in York Minster and elsewhere:—

"Our ancestors dwelt in this land from time immemorial and by their valour handed it down to us through successive generations so that we found it free. But if they are worthy of praise still more worthy are our fathers, who in addition to their own inheritance bequeathed to us this vast Empire of ours which they acquired after many struggles. Of their deeds in the field, by which the various parts of the Empire were gained, of the vigour with which our fathers protected that Empire from the invader, I will say nothing, since you know the story. So they died. It was a death worthy of a warrior. And we who are left must yet determine to fight with no less daring than they. By giving their lives for the common good they won for themselves glory which is ever young and the most honourable of all sepulchres; not that in which they are buried, but that in which their glory survives, to be called to remembrance on every fitting occasion whether in word or deed. For the whole world is the sepulchre of famous men. They are not commemorated merely by the writing on stones in their own country, but in foreign countries, too, the unwritten memorial of them lives on, carried not in stone records, but carved in the hearts of men. Let them be our pattern."

Surely it is meet and right also, when we enumerate the fighting memorials of our Regiment, to remember those impressive words from Ecclesiasticus:—

"Let us now praise famous men and our fathers that begat us. All these were honoured in their generations and were the glory of their times. There be of them some that have left a name behind them that their praises might be reported. And some there be which have no memorial, who are perished as though they had never been, and are become as though they had never been born and their children after them. But these were merciful men whose righteousness hath not been forgotten. Their seed standeth fast and their children for their sakes. Their seed shall remain forever and their glory shall not be blotted out. Their bodies are buried in peace but their name liveth for evermore."

The memorial chapel of The King's Own Yorkshire Light Infantry in the north transept of York Minster was dedicated and opened for use on Saturday, May 9th, 1925, by His Grace The Archbishop of York and General Sir Arthur Singleton Wynne, G.C.B., Colonel of the Regiment.

"The Minster is the home of the deepest and most abiding memories of all that has been highest and best in the life of Yorkshire for long centuries. Into this great treasure house of memories these men of The King's Own Yorkshire Light Infantry are now gathered."

These words constituted the key-note of the dedicatory address by the Archbishop, and it is a fact worthy of record that a sum exceeding five thousand pounds sterling has been contributed by members of The King's Own Yorkshire Light Infantry for the beautification of York Minster to the glory of God and in proud remembrance of all those who have laid down their lives for God and Sovereign and country during seven reigns, while doing their duty in The Regiment. "*Dulce et decorum est pro patria mori.*"

Special services are held in the regimental memorial chapel on eight anniversaries of special regimental interest, *viz.*:—

January 16	Battle of Corunna	1809
January 29	Action at Shin Kamar ..	1898
April 24	Second Battle of Ypres ..	1915
June 18	Battle of Waterloo	1815
July 1	Battle of the Somme ..	1916
August 1	Battle of Minden	1759
August 26	Battle of Le Cateau	1914
Nov. 27	Battle of Modder River ..	1899

A short description follows of the memorials now enclosed within The King's Own Yorkshire Light Infantry Memorial Chapel in York Minster, the Cathedral Church of Saint Peter, the Mother Church of the Province of York, founded in A.D. 627.

(1) The Peninsular Memorial of The King's Own Yorkshire Light Infantry to the memory of 18 officers, 24 sergeants and 610 rank and file was unveiled in York Minster in the North Transept, on Monday, March 31st, 1913.

The Memorial consists of a tablet in marble bearing the inscription in gold lettering.

The tablet is supported by two marble shafts of floriated design, on which are bars of bronze bearing the names of Peninsular Battles, *i.e.*, on the left Corunna, Salamanca, Pyrenees, Nivelle; and on the right, Fuentes d'onor, Vittoria, San Sebastian, Orthes. These are the eight clasps to "The Peninsula Medal" earned by The 51st Light Infantry.

At the base of the tablet is a bronze die of decorated work containing a glass case, in the centre of which is enclosed a Peninsular Medal (not awarded till 1847) with eight clasps. These are the same as the eight battle honours awarded to The King's Own Yorkshire Light Infantry except that "Peninsula" replaces "San Sebastian" on the Regimental Colour.

The centre of the Memorial is occupied by the large marble tablet. At the top, over the centre of the tablet, is a medallion of Sir John Moore, who served in the 51st as Ensign and Major, and as Lieut.-Col. in command from 1790 to 1795; he was killed in action at Corunna on January 16th, 1809, exactly thirty-two years after he had joined The 51st Regiment as an Ensign in Minorca.

The inscription cut beneath reads:—

"This memorial was erected in 1913 by The King's Own Yorkshire Light Infantry to the following officers and non-commissioned officers of The 51st Light Infantry who lost their lives for their country in the Wars of 1808–1814." The names are:—

LT.-GENERAL SIR JOHN MOORE, K.B. (Corunna, 16 Jan., 1809).
MAJOR FREDERICK SPARKS (Spain, 13 November, 1811).
CAPTAIN CHARLES WILKINSON MERCER (died Walcheren, 29 August, 1809).
CAPTAIN THOMAS HENRY BLOOMFIELD (died Walcheren, 1809).
CAPTAIN JOHN MCCABE (San Munos, 17 November, 1812).
CAPTAIN CHARLES AYTOYNE DOUGLAS (Lezaca, 31 August, 1813).
LIEUT. & ADJUTANT J. JENNINGS (died Walcheren, 13 Sept., 1809).
LIEUT. WILLIAM EDWARD WHITE (Spain, 1809).
LIEUT. THOMAS KEPPE CHAMLEY (Spain, 1809).
LIEUT. RALPH WESTROPP (Badajos, 11 June, 1811).
LIEUT. RICHARD WILSON (Burgos, 28 October, 1812).
LIEUT. JOHN SAMUEL PERCY (Vittoria, 21 June, 1813).
LIEUT. ROBERT DODD (after Lezaca, 14 Sept., 1813).
LIEUT. MAURICE STEPHENS (Nivelle, 10 Nov., 1813).
LIEUT. JOHN D. TAYLOR (Nivelle, 10 Nov., 1813).
LIEUT. J. H. DREW (Lugo, 6 Jan., 1809).
LIEUT. HENRY HONEY (Lugo, 4 Jan., 1809).
LIEUT. & QR.-MR. J. MILLS (Valladolid, 11 Oct., 1812).
SERGEANT REES WELLS (killed in Spain, 13 Jan., 1808).
SERGEANT OWEN MCCARTHY (died Hospital, 26 June, 1811).
SERGEANT JOHN FITTON (died Hospital, 11 Oct., 1811).
SERGEANT THOMAS BUTCHER (died Hospital, 9 Jan., 1812).
SERGENAT JAMES DOWNES (died 21 January, 1812).
SERGEANT DANIEL LANE (died Hospital, 2 January, 1813).
SERGEANT THOMAS DOYLE (died Hospital, 17 May, 1811).
SERGEANT JOHN MINSHULL (died Hospital, 29 June, 1811).
SERGEANT JOHN BRAUND (died Hospital, 25 Nov., 1811).
SERGEANT JAMES BALL or BALE (died Hospital, 20 Jan., 1812).
SERGEANT SAMUEL UTTING (died Hospital, 21 Feb., 1812).
SERGEANT JOHN HANGER (died Hospital, 22 Jan., 1813).

SERGEANT JOSEPH BEECHAM (killed, 21 June, 1813).
SERGEANT WILLIAM SORRELL (killed, 31 July, 1813).
SERGEANT RICHARD FORRESTER (killed 31 Aug., 1813).
SERGEANT ROBERT ROCHE (died Hospital, 16 Oct., 1813).
SERGEANT ANDREW CURZON (killed, 10 Nov., 1813).
SERGEANT HUGH PERCY (taken prisoner 17 Nov., 1812, died later).
SERGEANT JAMES STOTHERS (killed 21 June, 1813).
SERGEANT WILLIAM HANKS (died of wounds, 5 Aug., 1813).
SERGEANT RICHARD TREVELLAN (died of wounds, 6 Aug., 1813).
SERGEANT HENRY MARSHBANK (or MARSLAND) (died of wounds, 15 Nov., 1813).
SERGEANT THOMAS WEBSTER (killed 10 Nov., 1813).
SERGEANT MICHAEL SMITH (died 28th Oct., 1813).

"Also to six hundred and ten rank and file of The Regiment whose names, inscribed on a parchment roll, are deposited with the Minster Authorities."

The names of the 610 rank and file of 51st Light Infantry, inscribed on the parchment, are preserved in an oaken casket which bears a silver medallion in the form of a square surmounted by a "Minden" wreath of bay and laurel, and is now deposited in the walnut cabinet in the chapel.

The service for the dedication of the memorial to the 652 officers, non-commissioned officers and private men of The 51st Light Infantry who fell in The Peninsula, 1808–1814, was held in York Minster, and it began at 3.0 p.m., Monday, March 31st, 1913, with the *Dead March* in *Saul*, followed by eight verses of the Rev. Charles Wolfe's *The Burial of Sir John Moore*.

The memorial was then unveiled by General Sir Arthur S. Wynne, G.C.B., Colonel of The King's Own Yorkshire Light Infantry, and was received by the Dean of York, the Very Reverend A. P. Purey-Cust, D.D.

Prayers were then said, followed by a hymn; the *Last Post* was sounded by Buglers from the 51st Regimental Depôt, Pontefract, and lastly *God Save the King* was played.

In the course of his speech when unveiling the Peninsular Memorial, General Wynne said :—

"We are assembled here in York Minster by kind permission of the Dean and Chapter to do honour to and perpetuate the memory of General Sir John Moore and 18 officers, 24 sergeants and 610 rank and file of The 51st Light Regiment who were killed in action or died of wounds or disease contracted on service in the Peninsular War from the year 1808 to 1814, inclusive. The King's Own Yorkshire Light Infantry have already in this Minster memorials to those who fell in Burma, in India, and in South Africa, as well as to 288 men, women and children who died of cholera in India at Mean Meer in the short space of seven weeks in 1861. It is only fitting, therefore, that those who gave their lives for their Sovereign and their Country during a period which contributed so much to England's greatness and added eight battle honours to the Colours of The Regiment should also be commemorated. As no memorial has previously been erected, the centenary of the death of Sir John Moore was rightly considered a most appropriate occasion for taking the matter in hand. This illustrious and distinguished soldier performed the greater part of his Regimental service in The 51st Regiment, now The King's Own Yorkshire Light Infantry; he learned his first military lessons as an Ensign in The 51st Regiment, and, although he was promoted into another Regiment, he rejoined the 51st as Major and commanded it for five years as Lieutenant-Colonel and trained it to the highest state of perfection. He was so proud of the efficiency of the 51st for service, that, to use his own words, in 1793, he wrote: 'I have got the machine into as good order as I can and I wish to have it used; to go with the 51st upon service is the object next my heart.'

"Sir John Moore's centenary was duly celebrated in the Second Battalion, The King's Own Yorkshire Light Infantry, at Mandora Barracks, Aldershot, in 1909; and this memorial is the result of a resolution passed by the officers at that time.

"Mr. Dean: In the name of The King's Own Yorkshire Light Infantry, I present to you this memorial and casualty roll and testimony to the heroism and self-sacrifice of the dead to be an incentive to valour and patriotism in the living and to add to the adornment of this ancient and sacred edifice."

(2). In January, 1855, Lt.-Col. W. H. Elliott, K.H., and officers of The 51st King's Own Light Infantry placed a Monument of pure Carrara marble in York Minster in memory of those of The Regiment who fell during the Second Burmese War, or Pegu Campaign, in 1852–1853.

Underneath the statue is engraved:—

"This Monument is erected by the surviving officers of the Fifty-First or King's Own Light Infantry (The Second Regiment of the West Riding of Yorkshire) to the memory of MAJOR W. H. HARE, CAPTAINS E. L. WALLEY and W. BLUNDELL, LIEUTENANTS J. W. BATEMAN and R. PILMER, ENSIGNS A. N. ARMSTRONG and J. CLARKE and three hundred and three non-comissioned officers and private men, who fell at Burma in and during the war of 1852–3."

Beneath was placed a scroll truss on which were inscribed the names of the non-commissioned officers and men.

In the autumn of 1899 this memorial was removed to the North Transept to join the other memorials of The King's Own Yorkshire Light Infantry in York Minister. In the new position there was not sufficient space to place the scroll below the memorial, so the names were cut afresh on two new slabs of marble and placed on the two sides of the memorial; the list is headed by the name of Sgt.-Maj. T. F. Mills.

(3). In 1861 Lt.-Col. A. C. Errington and the officers and soldiers of The 51st King's Own Light Infantry placed a memorial in York Minster in memory of Lt.-Col. A. H. Irby, 256 soldiers, 16 women and 16 children of The Regiment, who died of Cholera in India at Mean Meer in August and September, 1861. The 2nd Bn. The Connaught Rangers, known then as the 94th Regiment (green facings), who had suffered from the same outbreak of cholera and at that time had no county connexion, joined with the 51st in the erection of a single memorial. The sum of £400 was contributed (*viz.*, £170 from the 94th and £230 from the 51st) by the surviving officers, warrant officers, non-commissioned officers and private men. A series of four windows on the west side of the north transept was selected for the memorial. They are four of the six windows of The King's Own Yorkshire Light Infantry memorial chapel. These four windows, each four feet wide and seventeen feet six inches high, are sister lights of beautiful early detail, and fine proportions. The designs on the memorial glass inserted in these windows represent incidents from the lives of Joshua, Gideon, Caleb and David.

The inscription on a brass tablet at the foot of the windows reads as follows:—

> "The above four windows were erected in memory of the Officers, Non-Commissioned Officers, Rank and File, Woman and Children, of the 51st and 94th Regiments who died of Cholera in India. A.D. 1861."

(4). In 1888 a brass tablet, size 17 inches by 28 inches, was placed on the west wall of the North Transept, by the 1st Bn. The King's Own Yorkshire Light Infantry on return home from the last (Third) Burmah War, bearing the following inscription:—

> "To the memory of three Officers and 298 Non-Commissioned Officers and Men of the (51st) 1st Battalion King's Own Yorkshire Light Infantry who fell in India from A.D. 1872 to 1887, including the campaigns Jowaki, 1877; Afghanistan, 1878–1880; Burma, 1886–1887."

The inscription is preceded by the words: Minden, Corunna, Fuentes d'onor, Salamanca, Vittoria, Pyrenees, Nivelle, and followed by the words: Orthes, Peninsula, Waterloo, Pegu, Ali Musjid, Afghanistan. At the top is I.H.S., surmounted by a sacred crown, and at the bottom, in the centre, the Bugle horn with "51" within.

The officers include Lt. B. S. Thurlow (March 22nd, 1880) and Lt. A. A. R. Balfour (Nov. 10th, 1886), killed on active service in Afghanistan and Burmah respectively.

(5). On Friday, October 13th, 1899, consequent on the outbreak of The War in South Africa, three sets of old Colours of the First Battalion were laid up in the Minster above the Memorials, *viz.:* (*a*) The Waterloo Colours, 1814 to 1838; (*b*) Colours carried 1838 to 1855; (*c*) Colours carried 1855 to 1897.

At the end of this ceremony two memorial brasses were unveiled on the west wall, *viz.*, The Shin Kamar Memorial and a Memorial to two officers of The Regiment who were accidentally killed in 1894, namely Lt.-Col. H. C. Symons (July 18th, 1894), commanding 2nd Bn., and Capt. W. H. M. Burke (April 20th, 1894), Adjutant 1st Bn.

The Shin Kamar brass is surmounted by the regimental bugle horn badge, with the white rose in the centre, the Tudor crown above it, and a Minden wreath of bay and laurel leaves on each side of the brass.

The inscription reads:—

> "To the Glory of God and sacred to the memory of the Officers, Non-Commissioned Officers and Privates, Second Battalion, King's Own Yorkshire Light Infantry, who were killed in the action on Shin Kamar Pass, Tirah, North-West Frontier, 29 January, 1898. Lieutenants T. P. Dowdall, M. R. Walker, E. St. G. Hughes, Colour Sergeant W. Guest, Lance-Sergt. W. E. Axleby, Corporals W. Johnson, G. Dawes, Lance-Corporals A. Whiteley, R. Cantrill, J. Sawyer, Privates J. C. J. Turner, J. Amery, H. Corbridge, W. Deakin, A. H. Ashby, J. Bailey, J. Dolophin, W. Dutton, J. Moran, G. H. Tite, W. Hill, J. Kerins, A. Beeley, I. Maddison, D. Beattie, W. Corrigan, W. Dixon, A. Warner, W. Harris. S. Bend died 30th Jan. A. Rivett, died 10 Feb. 1898. Erected by the Officers, Non-Commissioned Officers and Privates, past and present, of the First and Second Battalions."

On Friday, October 13th, 1899, after the three sets of Colours of the 1st Bn. had been laid up, Maj.-Gen. Sir Richard Westmacott, K.C.B., D.S.O., spoke as follows, when unveiling the above mentioned memorial brasses:—

> "The name of Colonel Symons is to be remembered in The King's Own Yorkshire Light Infantry with honour, respect and affection. The magnificent discipline and perfect steadiness of the men in the Shin Kamar Pass under the most trying circumstances reflects back upon every one who has commanded The Regiment and not least upon my old friend, Colonel Symons. If I mentioned all who distinguished themselves that day I should have to mention every officer and man in The Regiment. On that day there was man's work to be done and it was done by men.

They set a glorious example of what could be done and showed once again what British officers and men can do when the time comes. Who would not rather fall fighting for his Queen and Country, as those gallant fellows did, giving their lives for their wounded comrades, than drivel out a long old age to die struggling in bed, a nuisance to themselves and all belonging to them. Speaking for myself, a feeling of pride comes over me when I look back on that day and realise I can claim comradeship with those brave men as a soldier and an Englishman."

(6). The South African Memorial of The King's Own Yorkshire Light Infantry in York Minster, is placed on the east wall of the west aisle of the north transept. The Colours of the Second Battalion, which were in use from 1868 to 1905, having been laid up on June 20th, 1906, hang above it.

On Tuesday, June 23rd, 1903, at noon, General Wynne unveiled this memorial to all those of The King's Own Yorkshire Light Infantry who fell during the South African War, 1899 to 1902, and handed it over to the custody of the Dean of York Minster (The Very Reverend A. P. Purey-Cust, D.D.) in the presence of a large gathering of distinguished officers of The Regiment, including Col. G. P. F. Byng, Col. C. St. L. Barter, C.B., Col. Sir Henry Johnson, Bart., Lt.-Col. H. N. C. Heath and Col. J. F. Mayman, V.D.

The Band of the 1st Bn. and a Guard of Honour came up from Barossa Barracks, Aldershot, to attend the ceremony. A large number of warrant officers, non-commissioned officers and men of The Regiment, including many who were no longer serving, were present at the Minster.

The South African Memorial is a beautiful tablet in white alabaster of Gothic design with the figures of St. Michael, St. George, Gideon and Joshua in brass in high relief, with three brass panels on which are inscribed the names of those who died.

The inscription reads:—

"Roll of Officers, Warrant Officers, Non-Commissioned Officers and men of The King's Own Yorkshire Light Infantry, who have been killed in action or who have died from wounds or disease in South Africa during the South African Campaign, 1899–1902."

Major P. W. A. A. Milton.
Major A. R. Power.
Captain F. T. Thorold.
Lieut. E. V. I. Brooke.
Lieut. C. F. B. Powell.
2/Lieut. L. W. Long.
Lieut. R. E. Shepherd.
Lieut. A. W. Wallace.
2/Lieut. L. H. Marten.

2/Lieut. F. Conway.
Sergt.-Major J. Casson.
Colour-Sergt. H. Lawton.
Sergt. W. Bedford.
Sergt. H. Williams.
Sergt. J. H. Wallace.
Sergt. E. Lockwood, also 124 Rank and File.

The grand total is 140 of all ranks, *viz.*, ten officers, one warrant officer, five sergeants, 124 rank and file, including eight privates of the "Volunteer" Companies furnished by the Unit now known as 4th Bn. K.O.Y.L.I. (T.A.); their names are Privates W. Hardwick, T. Colley, T. Whitaker, S. Cook, G. J. W. Stamp, E. Halliday, T. P. Tomlinson, L. Senior.

A Memorial has also been erected in South Africa at Modder River, as narrated elsewhere in this chapter.

(7). The Memorial of The King's Own Yorkshire Light Infantry for The Great War was unveiled by General Sir A. S. Wynne, G.C.B., Colonel of The Regiment, on Minden Day, 1922, and handed over to the Dean (The Very Reverend W. Foxley Norris, D.D.) who, together with Chancellor George Austen, M.A., conducted the dedicatory service. The inscription on the Memorial reads:—

"Remember before God the 9,447 of all ranks of The King's Own Yorkshire Light Infantry who gave their lives in The Great War, 1914–1919, whose names are inscribed in the Book of Remembrance laid up in this Minster. Cede Nullis."

The memorial, which is fixed in one of the arcades of the west aisle of the north transept, is a beautiful piece of work and is composed of an upper and a lower tablet separated by the string course of the arcading.

The lower tablet is 4 ft. 5 in. in height and 2 ft. 11 in. in width; it contains the inscription and is of bronze with an inlaid border of mother-of-pearl. It is fixed to the wall by bronze bolts in its four corners, the bolts being concealed by Tudor roses in high relief of polished tin, the leaves behind the roses being of green enamel with gold outline and the seeds in the centre of bronze entirely gilt. In the upper part of the lower tablet is the bugle horn with the white rose of York in the centre, which forms the regimental badge. The bugle horn is of cast and chased bronze and entirely gilt, but the rose is white enamel. The bugle is surmounted by the royal Tudor crown in cast and chased bronze entirely gilt. The crown is embellished with glass jewels representing two rubies and two emeralds with a large sapphire in the centre. The crown links the lower and upper tablets together.

The upper tablet, 2 ft. 4 in. in height and 2 ft. 11 in. in width, follows the outline of the trefoil arch of the arcading, and is composed of a groundwork of lapis-lazuli on a bronze background. The border has a narrow strip of mother-of-pearl incised and a wider strip of dark bronze outside it. The upper tablet is secured to the stone work by bronze bolts concealed by three Tudor roses in high relief of polished tin with gilded seeds similar to those in the lower tablet. In the centre of the lapis-lazuli ground is a representation of the pelican in its piety, the pelican and its young being of translucent gold enamel and the drops from the breast in red enamel.

The whole of the gilding is "mercurial," an ancient process of applying pure gold to metal in a solution of mercury and subjecting the solution to heat; this gilding is said to be practically imperishable.

The "Book of Remembrance" which accompanies the memorial is 11 in. by 8 in., and contains 94 pages of vellum on which the 9,447 names are beautifully inscribed. It is richly bound in light infantry green levant morocco leather. The regimental badge is in oxidised silver and beneath it is the inscription in gilt letters, the whole being surrounded by a panel of K.O.Y.L.I. ribbon, namely, sea-green and blue separated by a narrow buff stripe. The inscription reads:—

> "Book of Remembrance containing names of 9,447 of all ranks of The King's Own Yorkshire Light Infantry who gave their lives during the Great War, 1914–1918, referred to in the memorial in the north transept of York Minster."

Mention should also be made of the very beautiful memorial of the 6th (Service) Bn. K.O.Y.L.I., which is placed on one of the pillars which bound the east side of the memorial chapel. It was erected by the 6th Bn. to the memory of all who were killed in action or died during the period 1914 to 1918 while serving in that battalion.

The service included the hymn "O Valiant Hearts" (Arkwright), the 126th Psalm and the "Nunc Dimittis."

After unveiling the memorial to the glory of God and to the sacred memory of the nine thousand four hundred and forty-seven of all ranks, General Wynne, in the course of his address, said that the north transept of York Minster had frequently been the scene of such a ceremony in connection with The King's Own Yorkshire Light Infantry, but never before to commemorate a loss to The Regiment on such a huge scale or to pay homage to so many of their comrades. The First of August was chosen for the Memorial Service because it was the anniversary of the battle fought on the plains of Minden in 1759 where the Fifty-first Regiment, more than one hundred and sixty years ago, shared in the glory of that great victory and won immortal fame. At the outbreak of The Great War in 1914, Yorkshire was foremost in the offer of the flower of her manhood to help fill the ranks of the military forces of the Crown. Nineteen battalions were added to the peace establishment of The King's Own Yorkshire Light Infantry, originally raised in the West Riding in 1755. By their splendid services during 1914 to 1919, these men not only upheld but enhanced the grand reputation for which The Regiment had always been famous.

The Book of Remembrance is preserved in the walnut cabinet in the Chapel.

(8). Special chairs have been placed in the Memorial Chapel to commemorate the eight soldiers of the First Battalion who died on active service in Mesopotamia during the operations in Iraq in the winter of 1920-1921.

(9). There hang in the north transept of York Minster, within the Chapel and above the Regimental memorials described above, no less than five stand of Colours of the First and Second Battalions The King's Own Yorkshire Light Infantry, *viz.:*—

1st Bn. K.O.Y.L.I. (*a*) Waterloo Colours, 1814 to 1838; (*b*) 1838 to 1855; (*c*) 1855 to 1897; 2nd Bn. K.O.Y.L.I., (*d*) 1842 to 1868; (*e*) 1868 to 1905.

The single Colours issued in The Great War to seven "Service" Battalions K.O.Y.L.I., *viz.:* 6th, 7th, 8th, 9th, 10th, 15th and 16th Service Battalions, were also lodged alongside on June 25th, 1920. They are miniature "King's Colours" and consist of The Great Union.

Note.—The laying up of Colours in York Minster on various dates is fully described in the two volumes of *The History of The King's Own Yorkshire Light Infantry,* 1755 *to* 1914, by Colonel H. C. Wylly, C.B., and particularly in Volume 2 on pages 597 to 610.

(10). The Memorial Chapel of The King's Own Yorkshire Light Infantry in York Minster was dedicated and opened on Saturday, May 9th, 1925, by His Grace The Archbishop of York (The Right Honourable and Most Reverend Cosmo Gordon Lang, D.D.) and General Sir A. S. Wynne, G.C.B., Colonel The King's Own Yorkshire Light Infantry.

The Chapel railings enclose the west end of the north transept of the Minster, where are lodged the old Colours of The 51st Light Infantry, of The 105th Light Infantry and of the "Service" battalions of The King's Own Yorkshire Light Infantry which were raised during the Great War 1914 to 1918. On the walls are installed the memorials, already described, to those of The Regiment who have given their lives during seven reigns for God and Sovereign and Country from 1755 to 1925, and their names are inscribed in the rolls and Book of Remembrance now preserved in the walnut cabinet within the Chapel. On the floor of the Chapel are emplaced special chairs bearing the Regimental Crest, including eight which record the names of the soldiers of the first battalion who met their deaths during the operations in Mesopotamia in 1920.

The new railings which enclose the east side of the Chapel and face the Colours are impaled with the sixteen regimental battle honours, while the ten battle honours of The Great War selected out of fifty-nine awarded, to be borne on The King's Colour of The King's Own Yorkshire Light Infantry, are inscribed on the ancient iron railings which close the south end of the Chapel.

In formally presenting the Chapel to the Dean of The Minster, General Wynne spoke as follows:—

"Remember before God all ranks of The King's Own Yorkshire Light Infantry whose names are recorded on the memorials and rolls of honour assembled in this Chapel and who died whilst serving their Sovereign and their Country."

The lesson was from Ecclesiasticus, Chapter 44, verses 1 to 15, and the hymn, "O Valiant Hearts" (Arkwright).

The Archbishop in his address said:—

"It is well that we should make remembrance now and thus enable those who come after us to make remembrance for all time of those who have died for their Regiment and their Country. We who remain may have changed and may have proved unworthy of their sacrifice, but those men cannot change. The Mother Church will watch and guard their memories in the unchanging silences which remain here through the drift of generations. Knowing that their lives were marked by The Cross, the Mother Church will lay that sacrifice at the feet of God and in the silence of her unceasing prayer will commend their souls to Him. This Chapel will always be a most sacred place to The Regiment, for it will preserve the records of the men who gave it lustre; and the successors of those men will come here to recall their sacrifice and to recall them in their prayers. But we owe them something deeper and more exacting than remembrance or prayers. We owe them fidelity to the trust which they have bequeathed to us, the trust to make the manhood of this Country, in ideals, in service, and in love of God, worthy of the sacrifice which they have offered.

After the Blessing, the "Last Post" and the "Reveille" were sounded by the buglers of the First Battalion, The King's Own Yorkshire Light Infantry, from Gravesend, and the service concluded with the National Anthem played by the Band.

God Save The King.

A brief recapitulation may now be made of memorials of The King's Own Yorkshire Light Infantry erected at places other than York Minster.

(*a*) Meerut. This monument was erected by the officers, N.C.O.s and men of The 105th Light Infantry in memory of the 105 soldiers of the Regiment, including R.S.M. Cornelius Sullivan, whose names are engraved on it, and of the 15 women and 17 children who died at Meerut between December 25th, 1868, and November 5th, 1872.

(*b*) Subathu. Memorial to the soldiers and families of The 51st King's Own Light Infantry who died at Subathu during the period 1878 to 1880. Erected by all ranks of 2nd Bn. K.O.Y.L.I. in the Subathu Garrison Church and dedicated on October 31st, 1926. The 29 names are carved on beautiful panels of shesham wood, the whole designed and executed by Lt. C. Huxley and Pioneer-Sgt. P. Jowett, 2nd Bn. K.O.Y.L.I.

(*c*) Poona. A memorial of design similar to that at Meerut. Erected by the officers, N.C.O.s and men of the 2nd Bn. The King's Own Yorkshire Light Infantry to the memory of their comrades who died in Poona from 1893 to 1895. The 42 names are carved on the faces of the octagonal column and include Lt.-Col. H. C. Symons (July 18th, 1894), Capt. B. C. Holt (July 22nd, 1893), and No. 1218 Sgt. T. Lewis (March 1st, 1893).

(*d*) Ahmednagar. A brass memorial tablet in the Garrison Church in memory of twelve N.C.O.s and men of 2nd Bn. The King's Own Yorkshire Light Infantry who died while stationed at Ahmednagar and Satara, 1898 to 1899, and includes Colour-Sgt. F. Wigley (October 27th, 1898), who won the D.C.M. at Shinkamar.

(*e*) Modder River. The K.O.Y.L.I. Memorial erected at Modder River, South Africa, to the memory of 140 of all ranks of The Regiment who fell during the South African War, 1899 to 1902, is placed about half a mile west-south-west of the railway bridge over the Modder River and is visible from the train. It consists of a stone cross at the top of a lofty granite column with the inscription cut on the base; the whole is surrounded by an iron fence.

(*f*) Crete and Weymouth. Memorial tablets to soldiers of The Regiment who lost their lives drowned at sea were placed in the cemetery at Melcombe Regis, Weymouth, by 51st K.O.L.I. when stationed at Weymouth and Portland, 1868 to 1870, and in the churchyard of the Garrison Church at Candia by 2nd Bn. K.O.Y.L.I. when stationed in Crete, 1903-1904.

(*g*) Biarritz. In 1882, in St. Andrew's Church at Biarritz, a memorial porch was dedicated to the memory of British officers who were killed in action in the south-west of France from October, 1813, to April, 1814. It includes the names of two officers of 51st Light Infantry killed at Nivelle on November 10th, 1813, *viz.*, Lt. Maurice Stephens and Lt. John D. Taylor.

(*h*) Pontefract. On September 27th, 1923, a memorial to all the men of Pontefract who fell in The Great War was unveiled at Town End, Pontefract, by Brig.-Gen. C. R. I. Brooke, C.M.G., D.S.O., M.P. The memorial includes the regimental badges of The King's

Own Yorkshire Light Infantry and of The York and Lancaster Regiment.

(*k*) Sandhurst. A marble slab panel has been placed in the Chapel of the Royal Military College at Sandhurst to the memory of the 33 officers of The King's Own Yorkshire Light Infantry killed in The Great War who had previously been Gentlemen Cadets at the R.M.C.

(*l*) Japan. In St. Andrew's Church, Shiba, Tokyo, on April 14th, 1922, H.R.H. The Prince of Wales, K.G., unveiled a memorial tablet in honoured memory of nine British officers who formerly served in Japan and laid down their lives for King and Country in The Great War, 1914-1919. It includes the names of two officers of the K.O.Y.L.I., *viz.*, Major C. A. L. Yate, V.C. (September 20th, 1914), and Captain (Temp. Lt.-Col.) H. F. G. Carter, M.C. (February 28th, 1919).

(*m*) Shorncliffe. A statue and garrison hall with library, erected at Shorncliffe Camp to the memory of Lieutenant-General Sir John Moore, K.B., were unveiled and opened by Field-Marshall H.R.H. The Duke of Connaught, K.G., on July 5th, 1923. A stained-glass window was placed in the hall by the officers of The King's Own Yorkshire Light Infantry. The design includes an approximate reproduction of the cross-belt badges worn by the officers of The Regiment in 1790 and in 1854.

(*n*) Guildhall at York. Finally, mention must be made of the large silver bell presented to the Lord Mayor and Corporation of the City of York in 1855 by The 51st K.O.Y.L.I. at the conclusion of the Second Burmese War as a memorial of The Regiment in the Pegu Campaign.

On Tuesday, July 3rd, 1855, in the Guildhall at York, Captain A. H. Irby, on behalf of Lieutenant-Colonel A. C. Errington and all ranks of The 51st King's Own Light Infantry (Second Yorkshire West Riding Regiment) presented to The Lord Mayor and Corporation of the City of York a large silver Burmese bell which had been captured in Burmah on active service during 1852.

This bell is of beautiful design and weighs six hundredweights. It is two feet in height and one foot nine inches in breadth at the mouth. The metal is two and a half inches thick and the bell is suspended by a chain of large links. Both bell and chain are of silver and the bell is covered with Burmese characters. The inscription on the tablet in the Guildhall placed below the bell, reads as follows:—"The Bell suspended above this tablet was captured from the Great Pagoda of Rangoon at the storming of that City by Her Majesty's Forces on the 14th April, 1852. It was presented to the

City of York by the officers, non-commissioned officers, and soldiers of The 51st Light Infantry or Yorkshire West Riding Regiment, and was placed in this ancient hall as a trophy of the distinguished services of that gallant Regiment on that and other occasions during the Burmese War. George Wilson Esquire, Lord Mayor, July, 1855."

We have now enumerated those memorials of the dead which have been fixed permanently in York Minster and elsewhere; but the standing memorials earned for The King's Own Yorkshire Light Infantry by those who sacrificed their lives doing their duty are displayed on The Colours on which are borne the Battle Honours won.

The Battle Honours for "The Great War" awarded to The Regiment are fifty-nine in number, and testify to the variety and importance of the services rendered by 26 battalions, beginning with the action of the Second Battalion at Mons on 23rd August, 1914, and ending with the action of the First Battalion in pursuit of the Germans on November 11th, 1918.

The fifty-nine are as follows:—

"Mons," "Le Cateau," "Retreat from Mons," "Marne, 1914, '18," "Aisne, 1914, '18," "La Bassee, 1914," "Messines, 1914, '17, '18," "Ypres, 1914, '15, '17, '18," "Hill 60," "Gravenstafel," "St. Julien," "Frezenberg," "Bellewaarde," "Hooge, 1915," "Loos," "Somme, 1916, '18," "Albert, 1916, '18," "Bazentin," "Ancre, 1916," "Arras, 1917, '18," "Scarpe, 1917," "Delville Wood," "Pozieres," "Guillemont," "Flers-Courcellette," "Morval," "Le Transloy," "Langemarck, 1917," "Menin Road," "Polygon Wood," "Broodseinde," "Poelcappelle," "Passchendaele," "Cambrai, 1917, '18," "St. Quentin," "Bapaume, 1918," "Lys," "Hazebrouck," "Bailleul," "Kemmel," "Scherpenberg," "Tardenois," "Amiens," "Hindenburg Line," "Havrincourt," "Epehy," "Canal du Nord," "St. Quintin Canal," "Beaurevoir," "Selle," "Valenciennes," "Sambre," "France and Flanders, 1914-18," "Piave," "Vittoria Vaneto," "Italy, 1917-18," "Struma," "Macedonia, 1915-17," "Egypt, 1915-16."

The Victoria Cross was awarded to Major C. A. L. Yate, Lance-Corporal F. W. Holmes, Private H. Waller, Sergeant J. W. Ormsby, M.M., Private W. Edwards, Lieut.-Colonel O. C. S. Watson, D.S.O., Sergeant L. Calvert, M.M., and Lieut.-Colonel H. Greenwood, D.S.O., M.C., during the Great War.

On The King's Colour are emblazoned ten for the Great War selected out of the 59 honours granted, while on The Regimental Colour are inscribed the sixteen honours awarded during the period 1755 to 1914, *viz.*:—

BATTLE HONOURS ON THE REGIMENTAL COLOUR K.O.Y.L.I.

Battle Honour.	*Date of Action*	*Honour awarded by Order dated.*
1. Minden ..	1 August, 1759 ..	1 January, 1801.
2. Corunna ..	16 January, 1809 ..	9 August, 1834
3. Fuentes D'Onor	5 May, 1811 ..	9 December, 1871
4. Salamanca ..	22 July, 1812 ..	9 August, 1834
5. Vittoria	21 June, 1813 ..	24 December, 1816
6. Pyrenees ..	28 July— 2 August, 1813 ..	9 August, 1834.
7. Nivelle	10 November, 1813	24 December, 1816
8. Orthes	27 February, 1814 ..	9 August, 1834
9. Peninsula ..		6 April, 1815.
10. Waterloo ..	18 June, 1815 ..	8 December, 1815.
11. Pegu	**See note*	11 October, 1855.
12. Ali Masjid ..	21 November, 1878	7 June, 1881.
13. Afghanistan ..	1878-80	7 June, 1881.
14. Burma	1885-87	1 August, 1887 and 1 December, 1890.
15. Modder River ..	28 November, 1899	21 December, 1904
16. South Africa ..	1899-1902	21 December, 1904

*"Pegu"—The Second Burmese War, 1852-1853;
The Capture of White House Stockade, 12 April, 1852.

The significance of The Colours was emphasised by The King very recently, for on July 5th, 1926, His Majesty King George V. presented Colours at Buckingham Palace, London, to 1st Bn., The King's Own Yorkshire Light Infantry, to replace the Colours which had been presented to 1st Bn. The King's Own Yorkshire Light Infantry in Dublin on August 27th, 1897, by H.R.H. The Duchess of York, who was accompanied by H.R.H. The Duke of York, K.G. (now Their Majesties King George V. and Queen Mary).

On this occasion (July 5th, 1926) His Majesty made the following address:—

"Colonel Thorp, Officers, Non-Commissioned Officers and Men of the 1st Battalion The King's Own Yorkshire Light Infantry. Your Battalion received the Colours to which you bid farewell to-day nearly thirty years ago in Dublin from the Queen, then Duchess of York, and that happy memory increases my pleasure in presenting to you these new Colours. I regret that it was not possible for the whole of the 1st Battalion to be on parade to-day.

"Life in every age has centred round a Flag, and Colours still are the link uniting all ranks—the sacred symbol of their allegiance to God, their Sovereign and Country.

"The King's Own Yorkshire Light Infantry has a record extending over 170 years. Minden Day is celebrated annually to commemorate the first engagement of the 51st, one of the six Regiments of British Infantry who 'Charged the enemy cavalry ranked in order of battle and tumbled them to ruin.'

"In 1809 you were created a Light Infantry Corps in memory of General Sir John Moore, who served in the 51st from Ensign to Commanding Officer.

"Your Colours show distinguished service in the Peninsula, at Waterloo, in Burma, Afghanistan, and in South Africa.

"In the Great War you added fresh lustre to the good name of the Regiment, and I am proud to think that these achievements will be emblazoned on my Colour and handed down to posterity.

"In giving you these Colours I am confident that, both at home and abroad, in peace and in war, you and those who come after you will ever maintain the grand traditions of the Regiment."

The Battle Honours inscribed on the Colours are as follows:—

THE KING'S COLOUR (10).

Le Cateau; Marne, 1914-18; Messines, 1914-17-18; Ypres, 1914–15–17–18; Somme, 1916–18; Cambrai, 1917–18; Havrincourt; Sambre; Italy, 1917–18; Macedonia, 1915–17.

THE REGIMENTAL COLOUR (16).

Minden; Corunna; Fuentes D'Onor; Salamanca; Vittoria; Pyrenees; Nivelle; Orthes; Peninsula; Waterloo; Pegu; Ali Masjid; Afghanistan, 1878–80; Burma, 1885–87; Modder River; South Africa, 1899–1902.

This account may well be concluded by adapting and repeating in slightly altered form the memorable words written in 1870 by Mr. William Wheater, who compiled the first printed record of The Regiment:—

"More than a century and a half have elapsed since The King's Own Yorkshire Light Infantry was raised in 1755 in the West Riding of Yorkshire, yet from the very first period of its existence down to the present time it has possessed one of the highest reputations in the British Service. Its celebrity began at Minden, and has continued on the Indian Frontier, in the Peninsula, Burma, and South Africa with a lustre that has never paled; and should England again call for its services on the Field of battle The Regiment will be worthy of its traditions so long as its members recollect that they are called by the spirit of those grim warriors of the Great War of 1914–1918, who, few in numbers but of giant heart, faced Britain's foes on the plains of Flanders with the majestic confidence of invincibility to perpetuate the glory which had been entrusted to their keeping and descended to them from generations of soldiers for whom the world could produce no match."

THE REGIMENT HAS NOT FORGOT THAT IT SHARED IN THE GLORY OF MINDEN.

Inspection Report, dated April 18*th*, 1775.

INDEX

A

B

INDEX

C

D

E

F

G

H

I

J

K

L

M

N

O

P

Q

R

S

T

U

V

W

Y

Z

Percy Lund, Humphries & Co. Ltd.
3 Amen Corner, London, E.C.4
And at Bradford

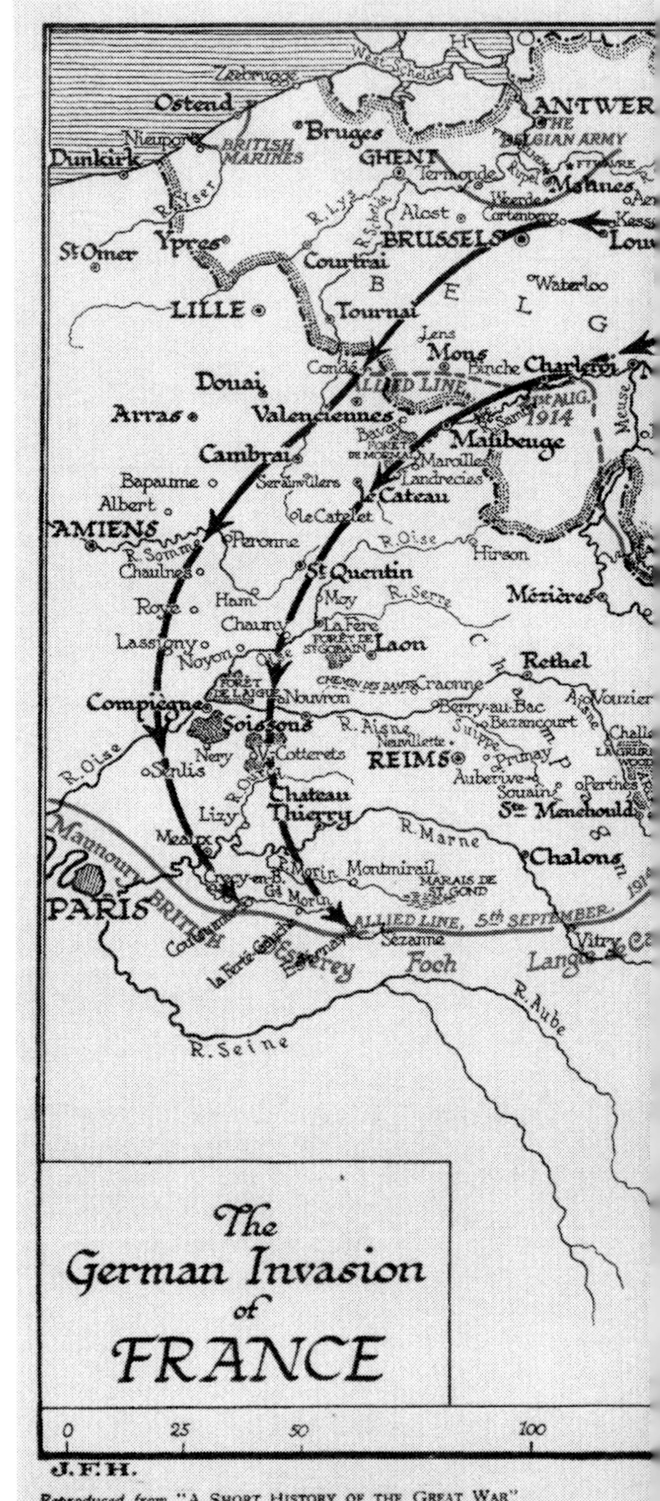

Reproduced from "A Short History of the Great War"
by Prof. A. F. Pollard
By kind permission of G. Methuen & Co. Ltd.

COLOGNE
Maastricht
Aix-la-Chapelle
Visé
LIÉGE
Verviers
Limburg
The march of the German right wing under Von Kluck
Rhine
COBLENZ
LUXEMBURG
R. Moselle
R. Semoise
Montmédy
Longwy
Spincourt
Étain
R. Saar
METZ
Verdun
Eparges
St. Mihiel
Pont-a-Mousson
Saarburg
Toul
NANCY
Blamont
STRASSBURG
MT. DONON
Lunéville
R. Moselle
Meuse
Mirecourt
St. Dié
Epinal
Colmar
Munster
Metzeral
Neu Breisach
Steinbach
Mulhouse
Belfort
Altkirch
SWITZERLAND
150
200
Miles
250

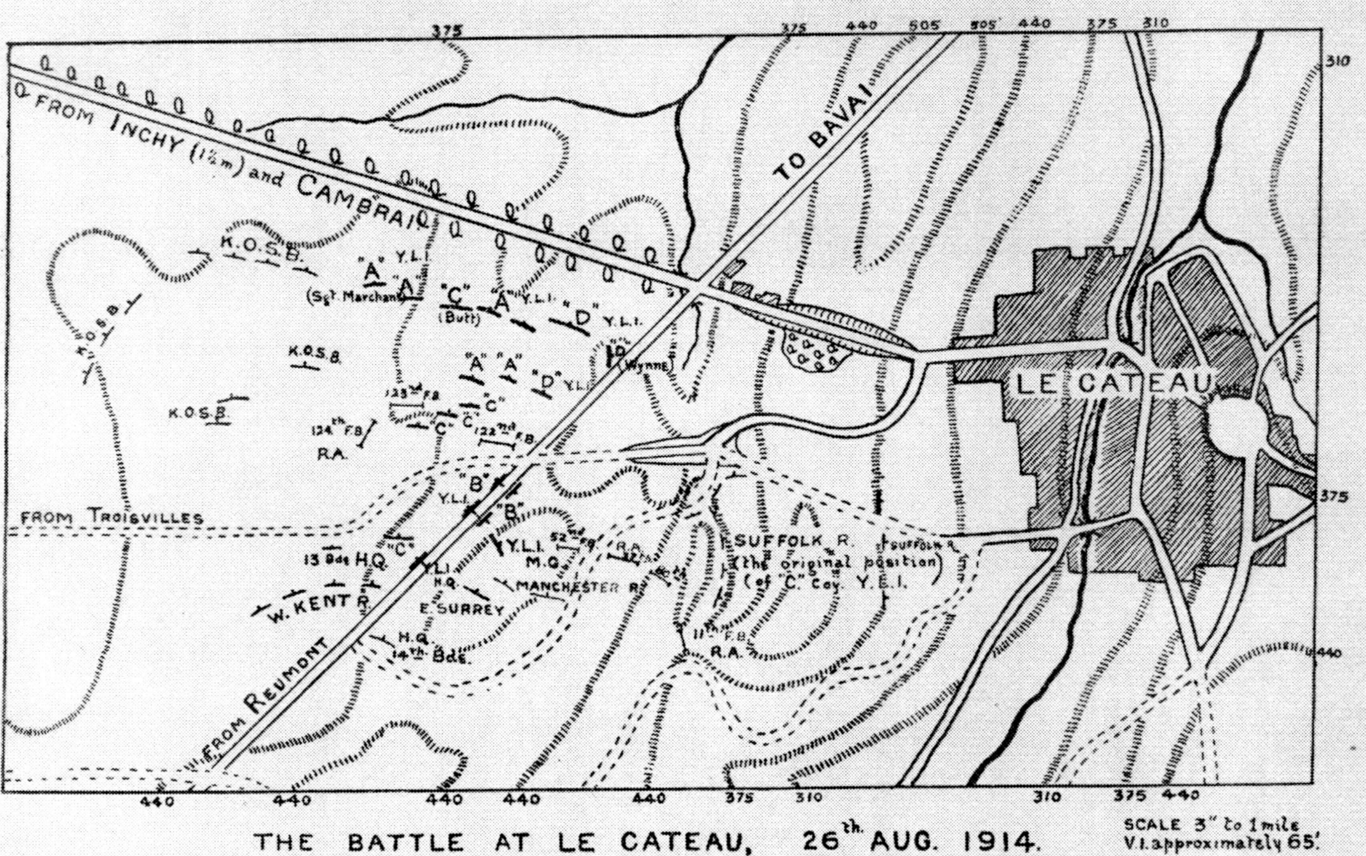

THE BATTLE AT LE CATEAU, 26th AUG. 1914.

Reproduced from "The Bugle"

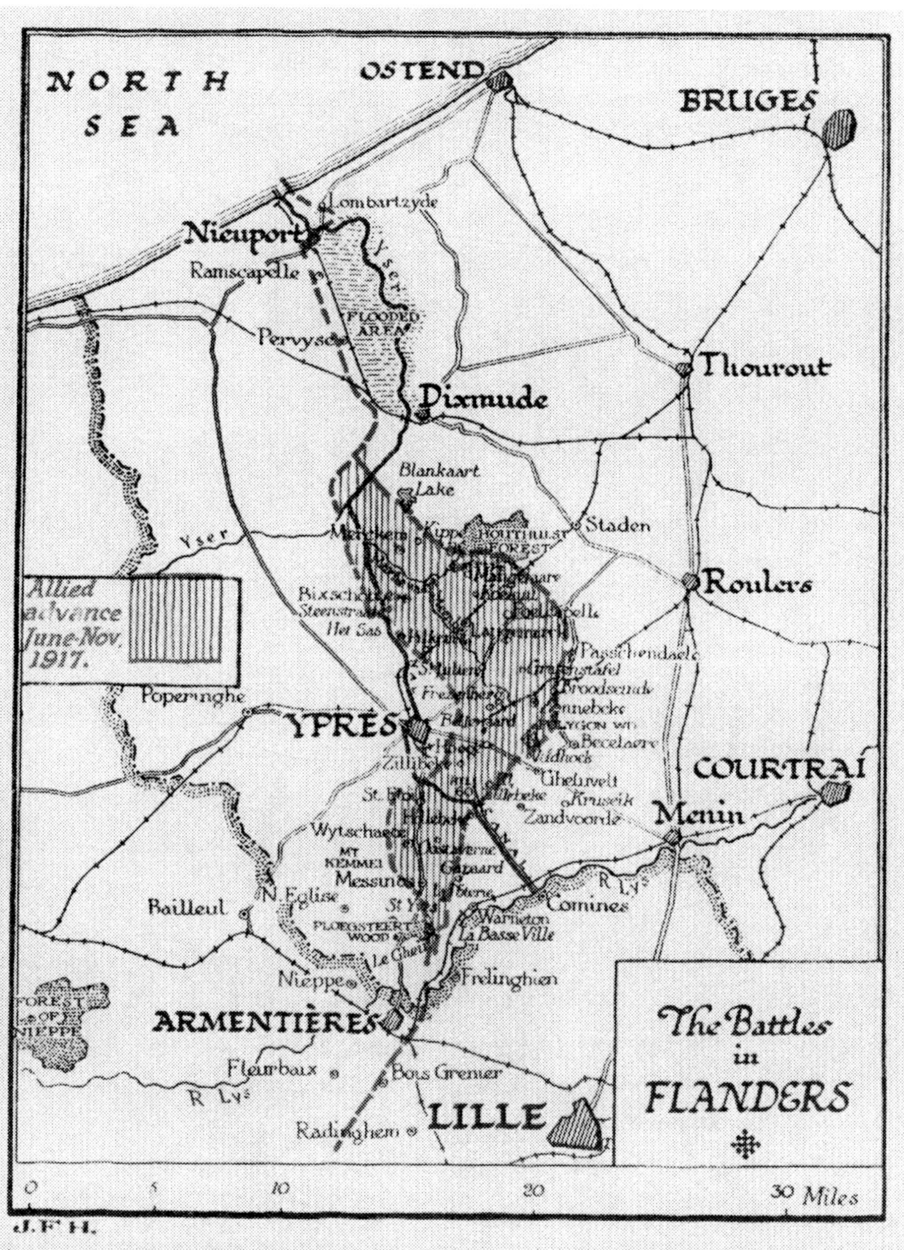

J.F.H.

Reproduced from "A Short History of the Great War"
by Prof. A. F. Pollard
By kind permission of G. Methuen & Co. Ltd.

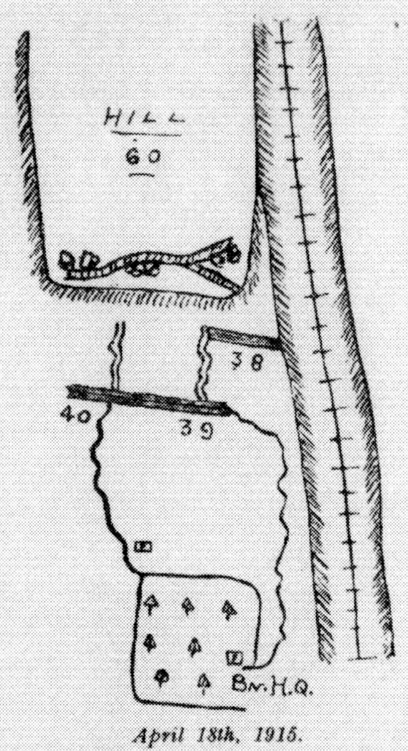

April 18th, 1915.

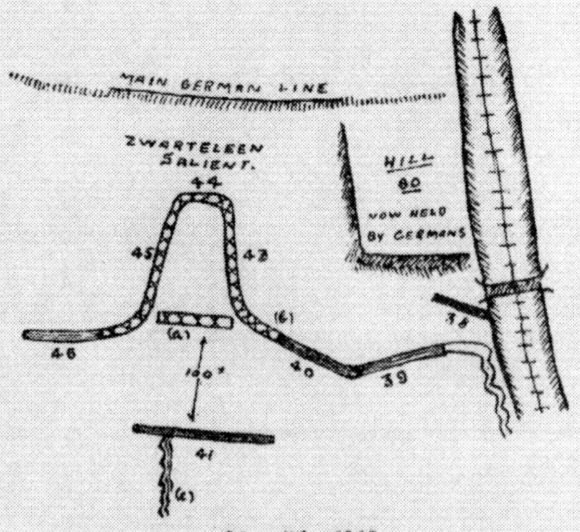

May 7th, 1915.

Reproduced from "THE BUGLE"

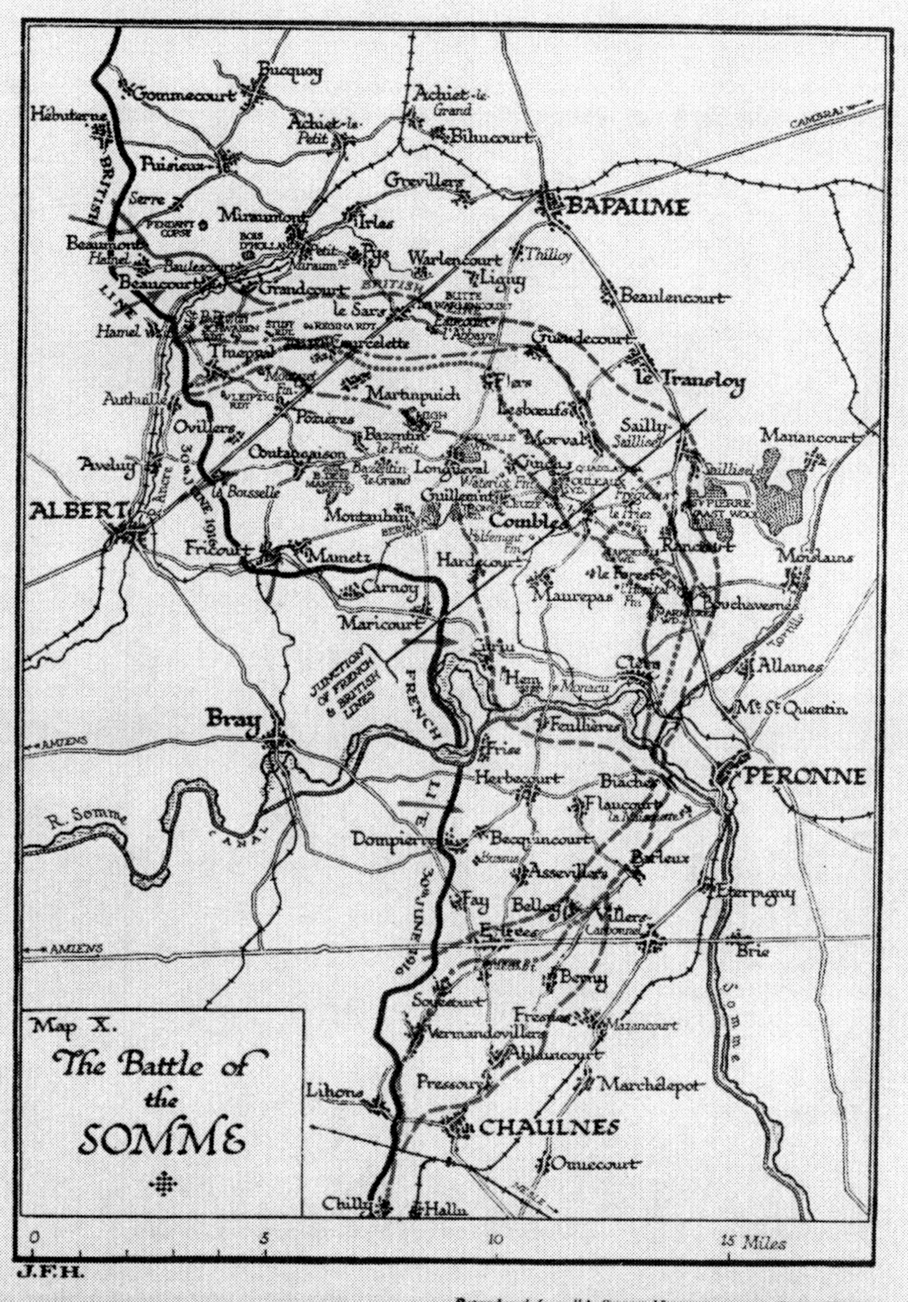

Reproduced from "A SHORT HISTORY OF THE GREAT WAR"
by Prof. A. F. Pollard
By kind permission of G. Methuen & Co. Ltd.

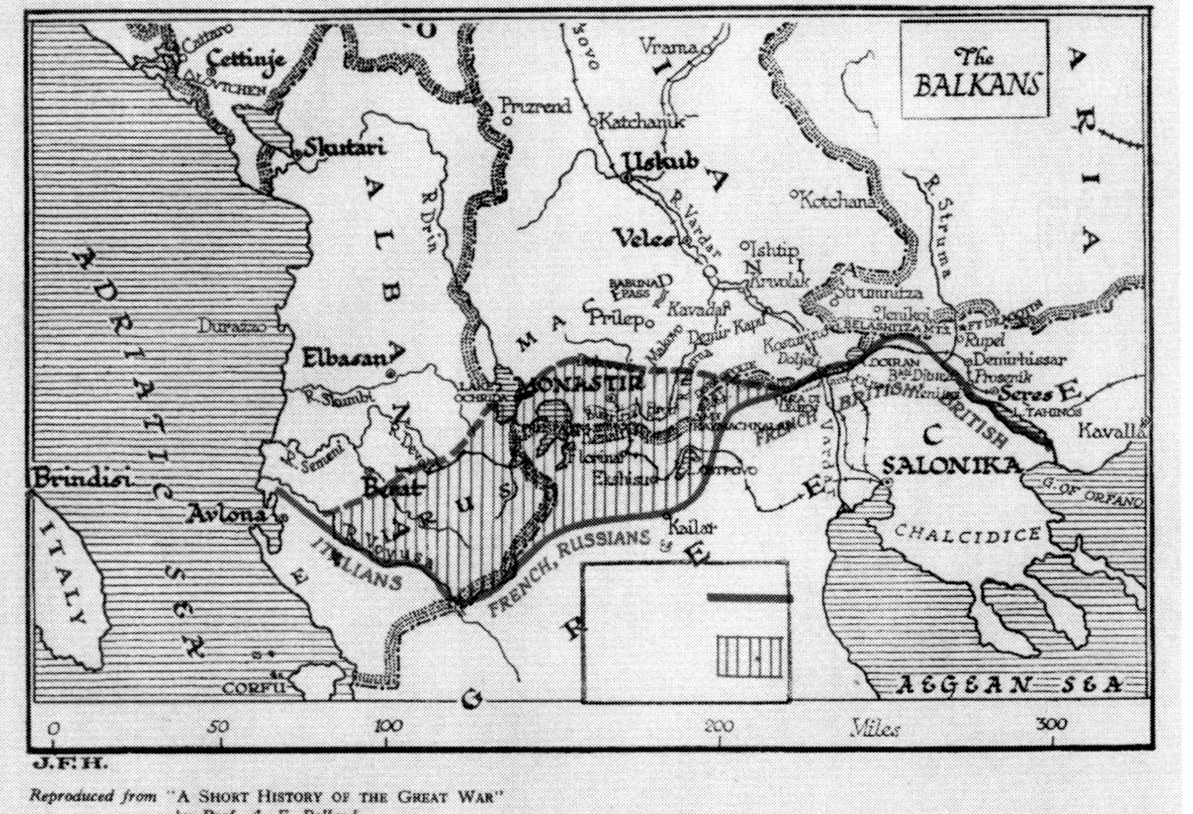

Reproduced from "A SHORT HISTORY OF THE GREAT WAR"
by Prof. A. F. Pollard
By kind permission of G. Methuen & Co. Ltd.

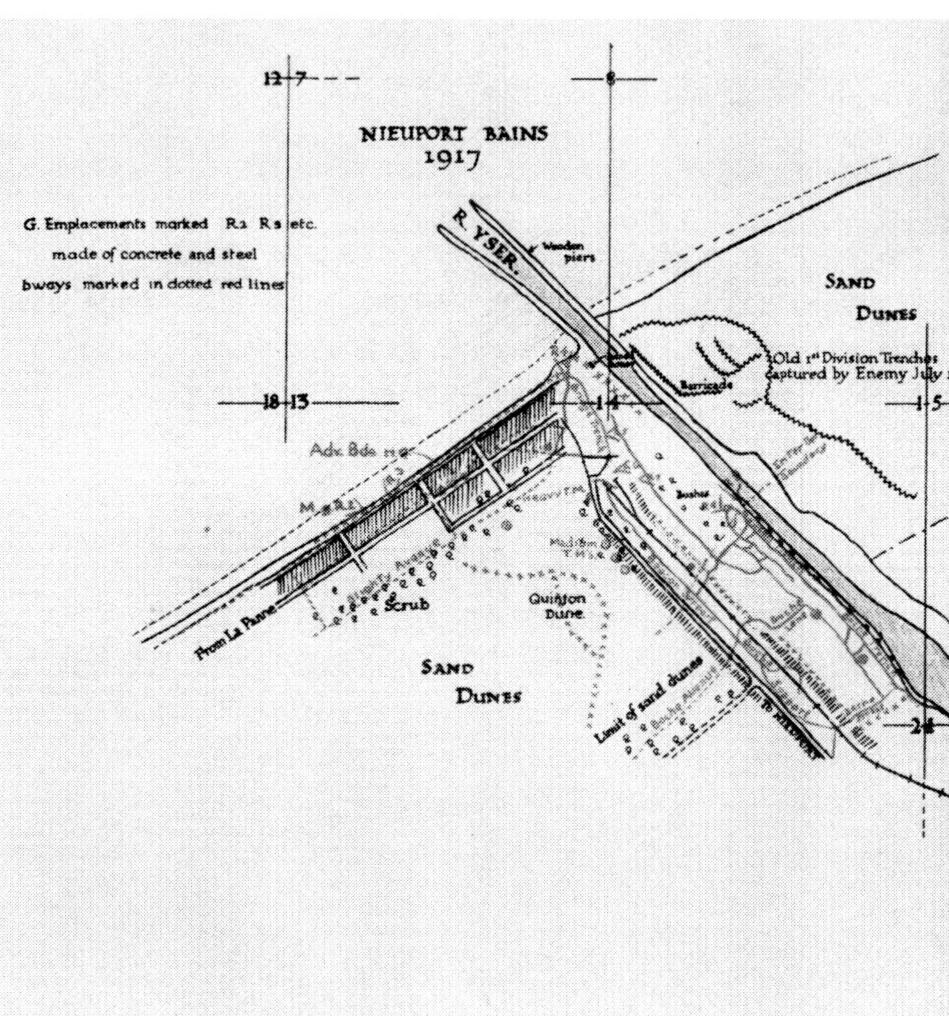

NIEUPORT BAINS
1917
G. Emplacements marked R2 R3 etc.
made of concrete and steel
bways marked in dotted red lines
R. YSER.
Wooden piers
SAND
DUNES
Old 1st Division Trenches
captured by Enemy July 1
Barricade
Scrub
From La Panne
Quinton Dune
SAND
DUNES
Limit of sand dunes

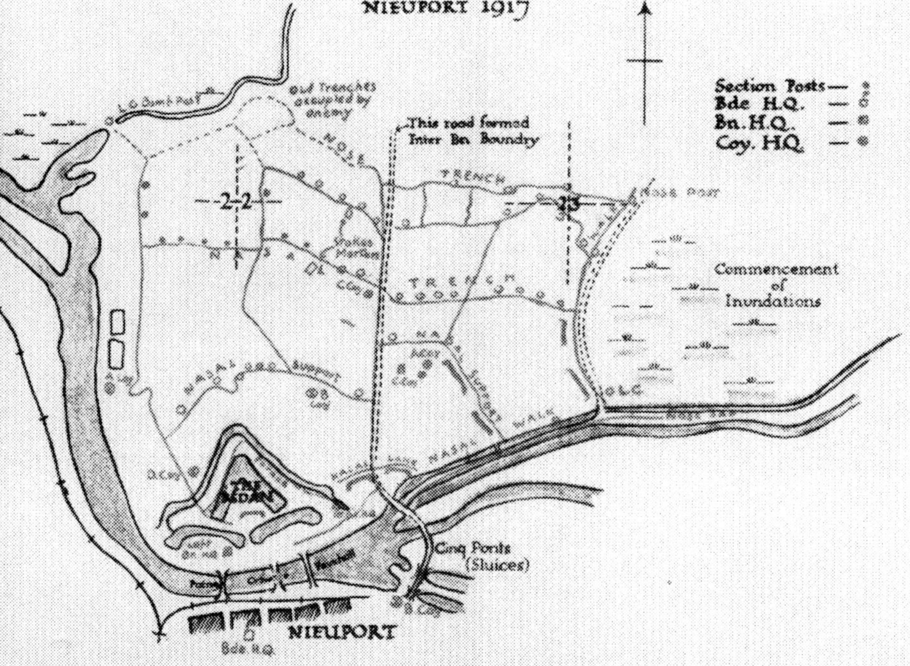

From a map drawing by Captain R. L. Bond, D.S.O., M.C., R.E.

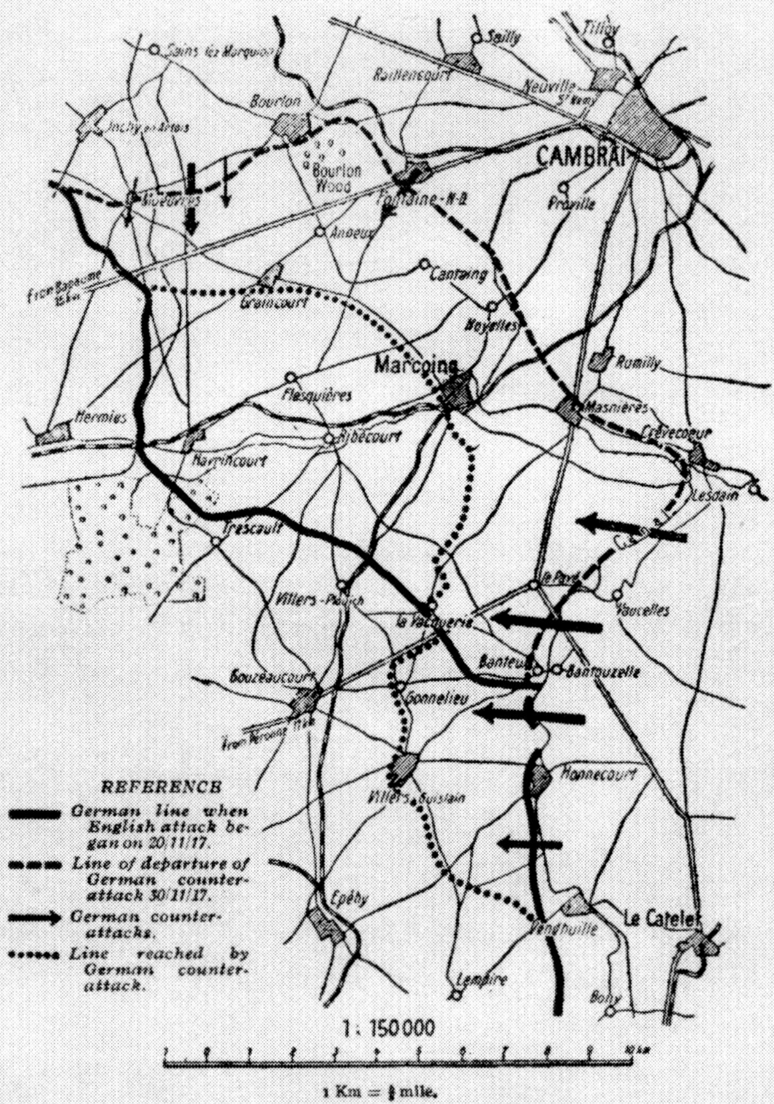

Reproduced from "My War Memories"
by Gen. Ludendorff
By kind permission of Hutchinson & Co.

THE MAIN BATTLE LINES OF THE

WESTERN FRONT

Reproduced from "HARMSWORTH NEW ATLAS"
By kind permission of G. Harmsworth & Co. Ltd.

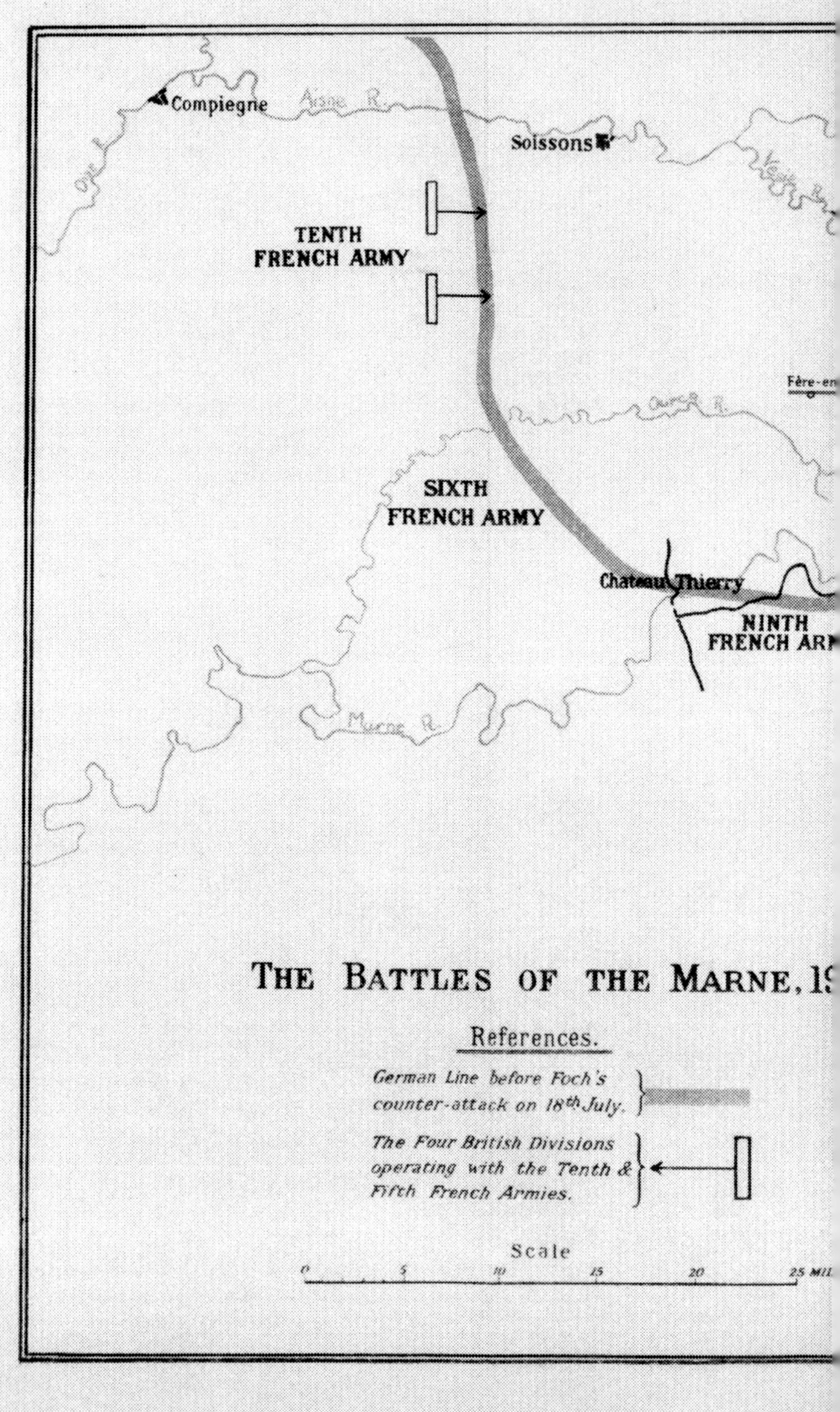
Compiegne
Aisne R.
Soissons
Oise R.
Vesle R.
TENTH
FRENCH ARMY
Ourcq R.
SIXTH
FRENCH ARMY
Chateau Thierry
NINTH
Marne R.
THE BATTLES OF THE MARNE, 19
References.
German Line before Foch's counter-attack on 18th July.
The Four British Divisions operating with the Tenth & Fifth French Armies.
Scale
0
5
10
15
20
25

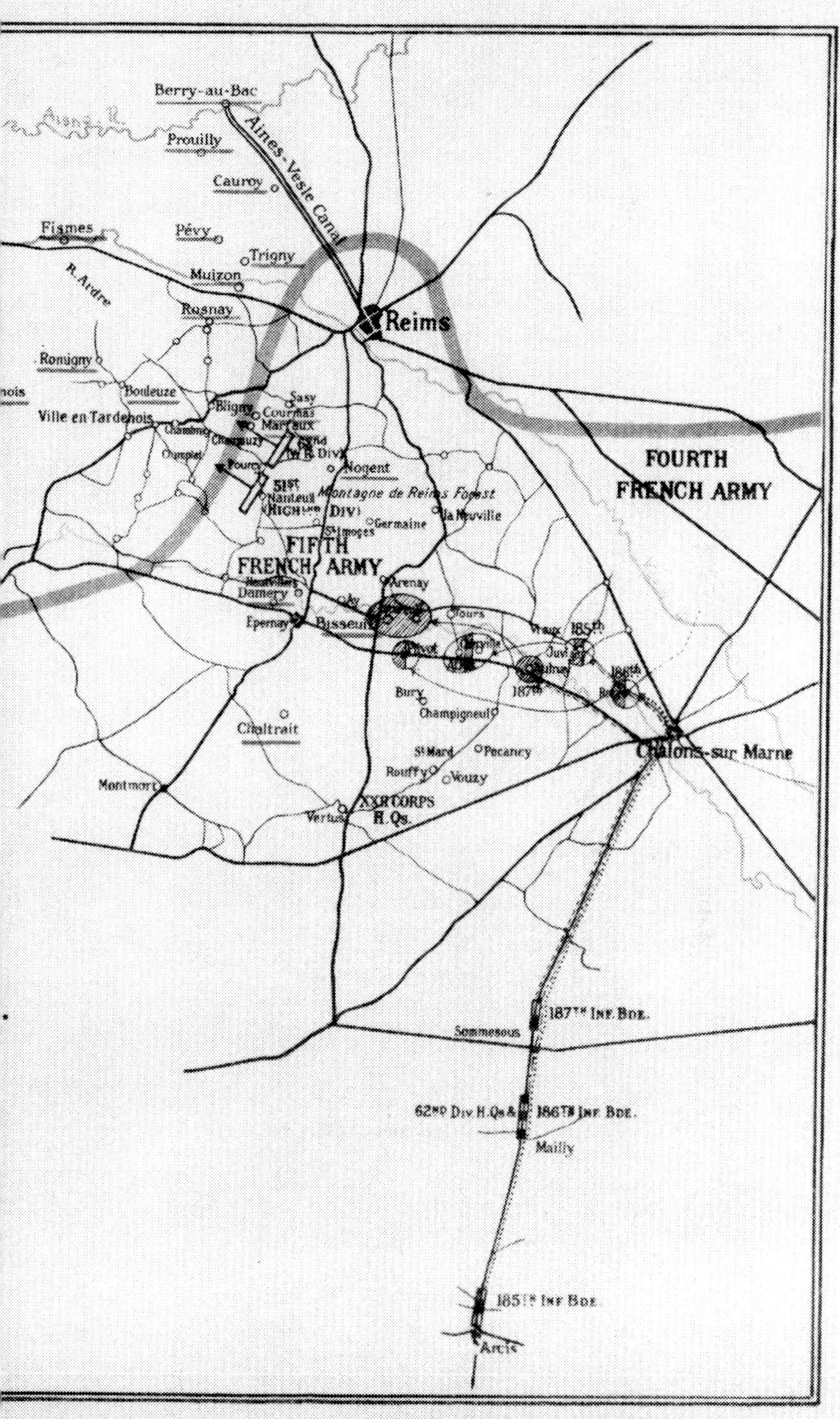

Reproduced from "THE WEST YORKSHIRE REGIMENT IN THE WAR" *Vol. I*
by Everard Wyrall
By kind permission of John Lane, Bodley Head Ltd.

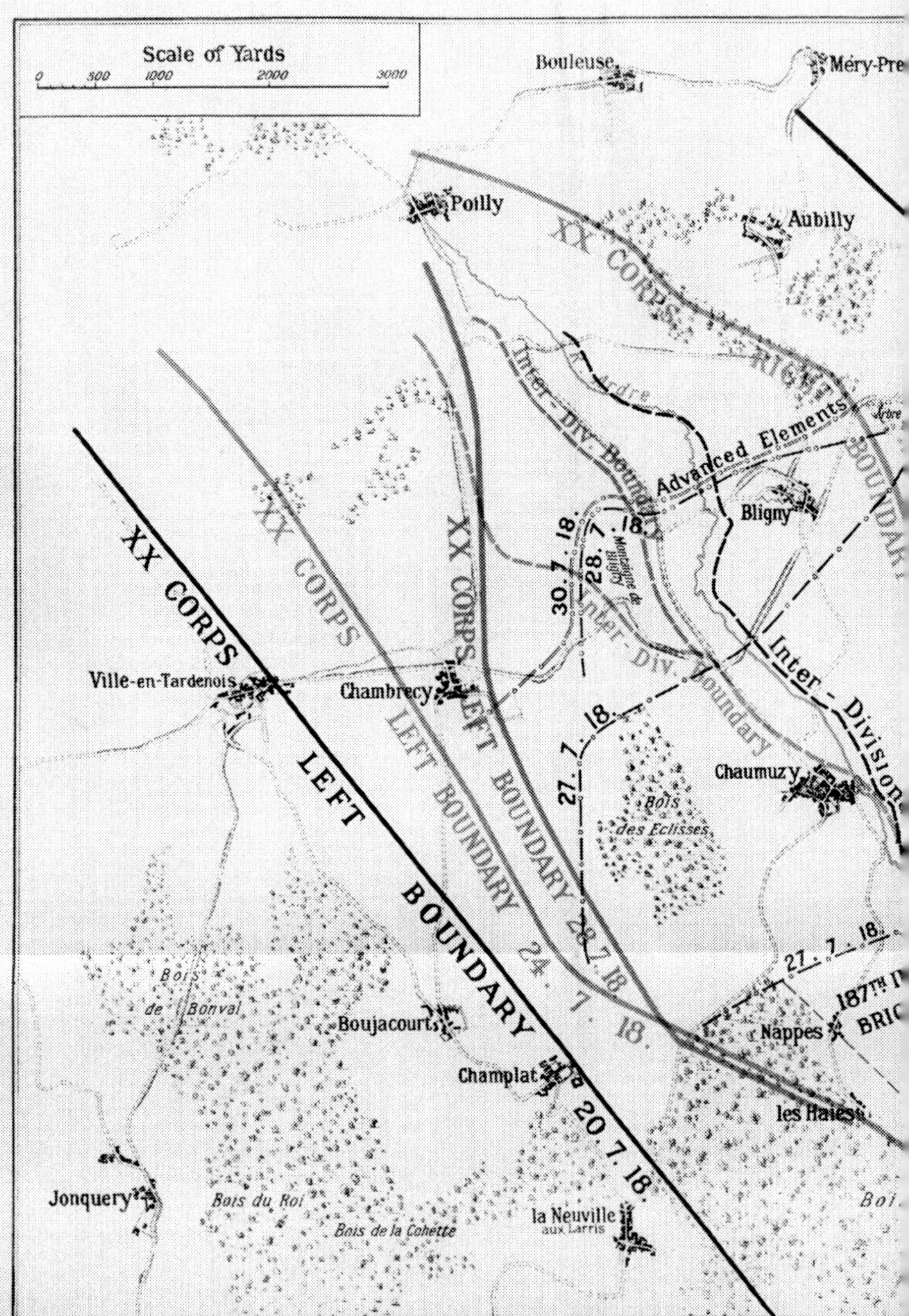
Scale of Yards
0
500
1000
2000
3000
Bouleuse
Méry-Pre
Poilly
Aubilly
XX CORPS RIGHT BOUNDARY
Inter - Div. Boundary
R. Ardre
Advanced Elements
Ardre
Bligny
30. 7. 18.
28. 7. 18.
XX CORPS
XX CORPS
XX CORPS
LEFT BOUNDARY
Inter - Div. Boundary
Inter - Division
Ville-en-Tardenois
Chambrecy
LEFT BOUNDARY
LEFT BOUNDARY
27. 7. 18.
Chaumuzy
Bois des Eclisses
BOUNDARY
24. 7. 18.
28. 7. 18.
27. 7. 18.
187TH
BRIG
Bois de Bonval
Boujacourt
Nappes
Champlat
20. 7. 18.
les Haies
Jonquery
Bois du Roi
Bois de la Cohette
la Neuville aux Larris
Boi

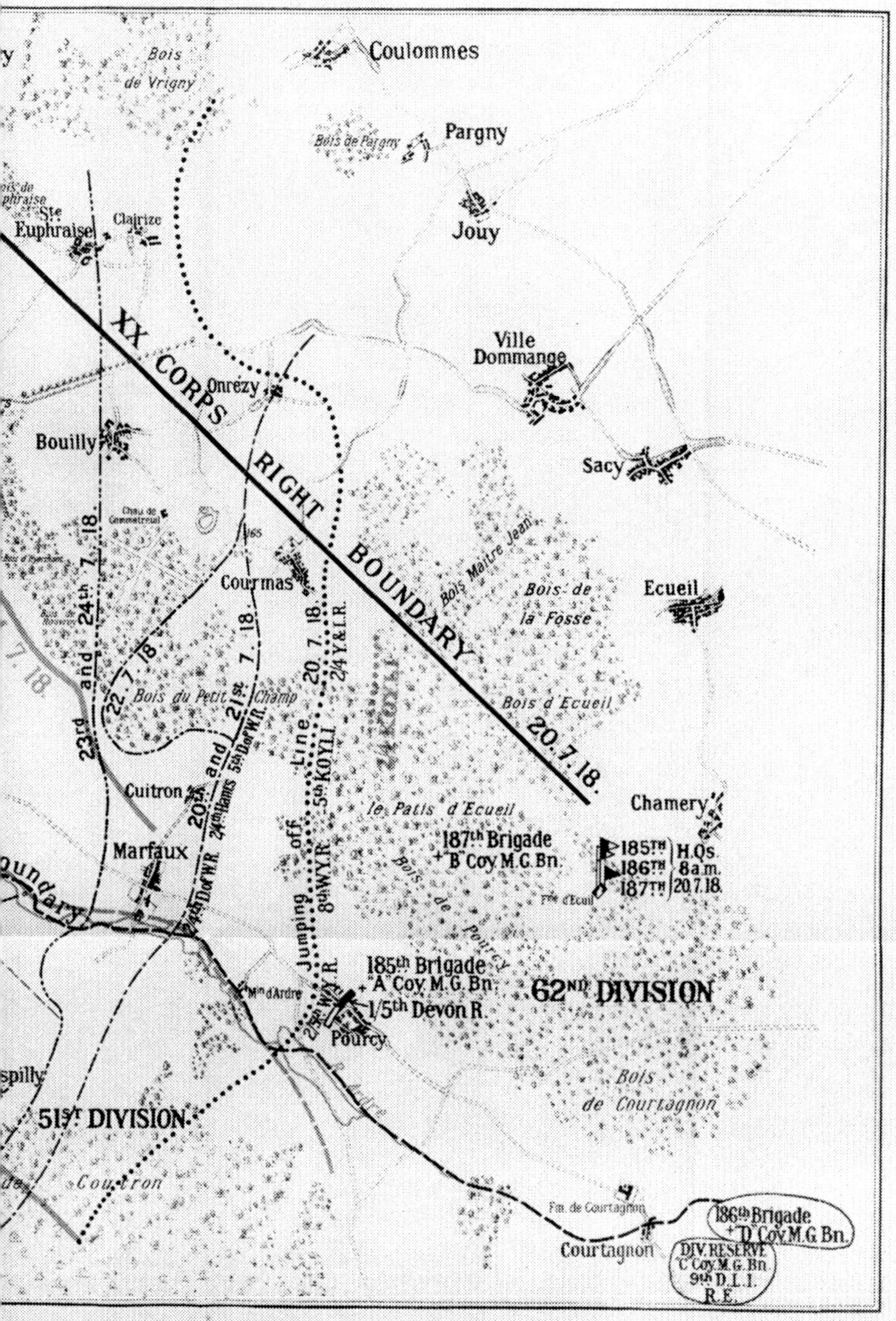

Capture of Marfaux.

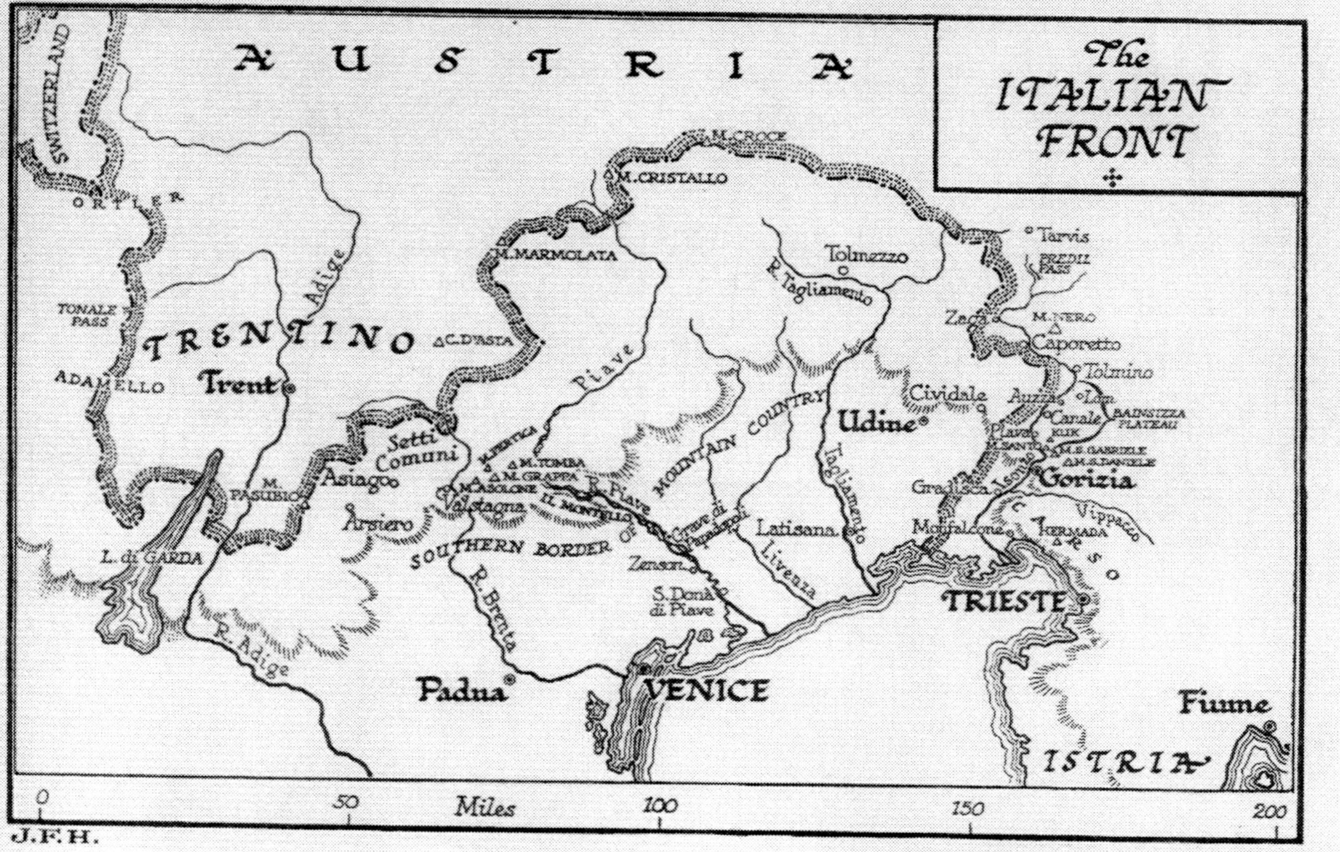

Reproduced from "A Short History of the Great War"
by Prof. A. F. Pollard
By kind permission of G. Methuen & Co. Ltd.

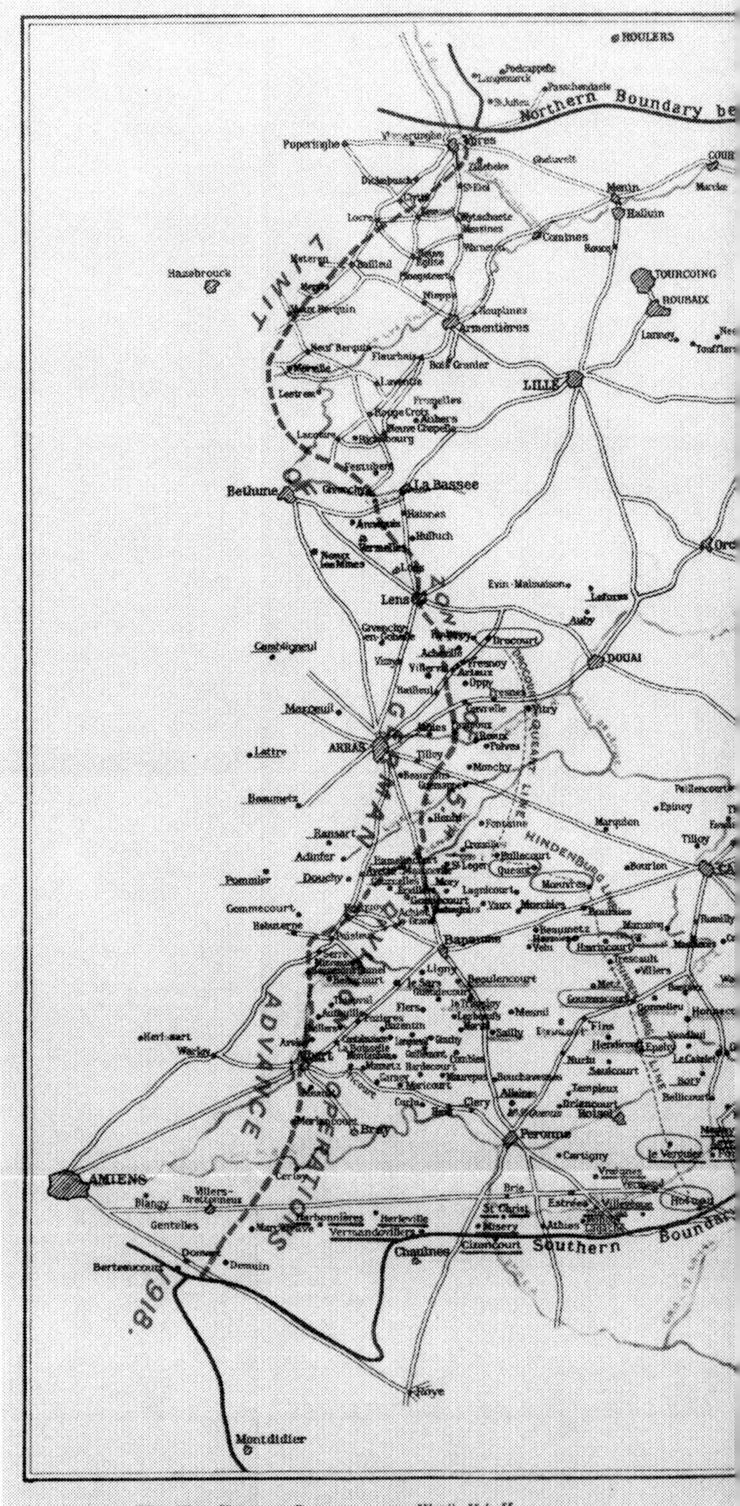

Reproduced from "The West Yorkshire Regiment in the War" *Vol. II*
by Everard Wyrall
By kind permission of John Lane, Bodley Head Ltd.

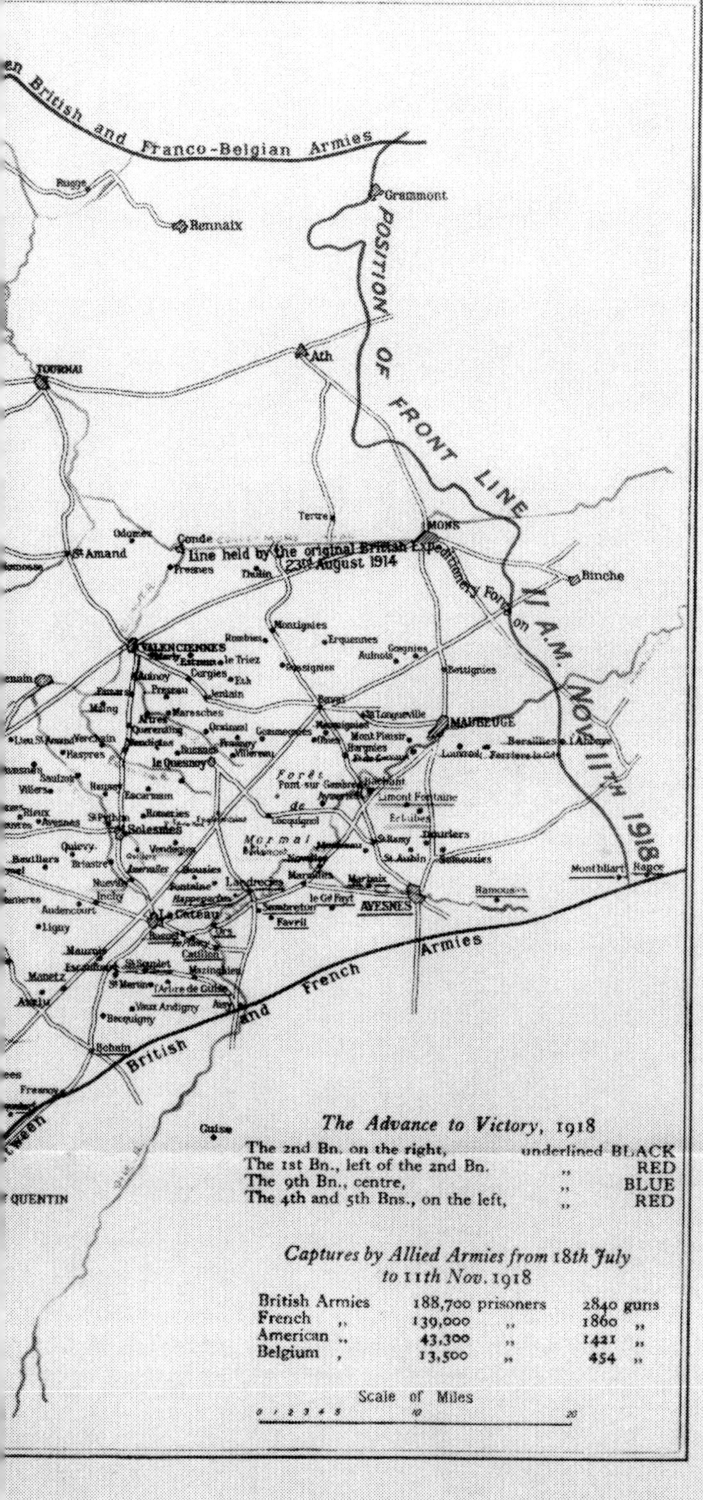
British and Franco-Belgian Armies
Grammont
Renaix
POSITION OF FRONT LINE 11 A.M. NOV 11TH 1918
Ath
TOURNAI
MONS
Binche
Conde
St Amand
Line held by the original British Expeditionary Force on 23rd August 1914
Fresnes
VALENCIENNES
Montignies
Le Quesnoy
MAUBEUGE
Forêt de Mormal
Solesmes
Landrecies
AVESNES
Favril
Le Cateau
Catillon
Mazinghien
Vaux Andigny
Becquigny
Bohain
Guise
QUENTIN
British and French Armies
The Advance to Victory, 1918
The 2nd Bn. on the right, underlined BLACK
The 1st Bn., left of the 2nd Bn. ,, RED
The 9th Bn., centre, ,, BLUE
The 4th and 5th Bns., on the left, ,, RED
Captures by Allied Armies from 18th July to 11th Nov. 1918
British Armies 188,700 prisoners 2840 guns
French ,, 139,000 ,, 1860 ,,
American ,, 43,300 ,, 1421 ,,
Belgium , 13,500 ,, 454 ,,
Scale of Miles
0 1 2 3 4 5 10 20

Lightning Source UK Ltd.
Milton Keynes UK

173203UK00001B/146/A

9 781843 427636

»Ich verstehe«, entgegnete der Kardinal. »Ihr seht Euch als Brutus. Das macht mich zum Caesar, also sollte ich mich geschmeichelt fühlen. Aber Eure unehrenhafte Tat bestand aus etwas mehr als ein paar Dolchstichen, de Thou.«

Mehr und mehr war der Sarkasmus in seinem Tonfall Kälte gewichen. De Thou hatte gehört, daß der Kardinal gelegentlich zu erschreckenden Wutausbrüchen imstande war, doch da er ihn immer nur in Ausübung von Staatsfunktionen erlebt hatte und ihm eher zu wenig als zu viel Gefühl zutraute, hatte er es nicht geglaubt. Jetzt konnte er nicht verhindern, daß seine Haut sich unwillkürlich zusammenzog, als die schneidende, zornige Stimme fortfuhr:

»Ihr wäret bereit gewesen, eine spanische Armee ins Land zu holen und ihnen halb Frankreich in den Rachen zu werfen! Das ist nicht mehr jugendliche Torheit, das ist Verrat der schlimmsten Sorte, Monsieur. Wißt Ihr, was man in Spanien dafür mit Euch tun würde? Man würde Euch Euren adligen Rang aberkennen und Euch vierteilen lassen, aber nicht, ohne Euch vorher gefoltert zu haben.«

De Thou glaubte zu begreifen. »Ich werde auch unter der Folter nicht mehr sagen.«

Der Kardinal musterte ihn noch einen Moment lang, dann bedeutete er seinen Wachen, die Tür wieder zu öffnen. »Es scheint, ich habe Euch überschätzt. Ich hoffe, die Aussicht, heroisch zu sterben, ist Euch ein gebührender Trost, de Thou.«

Er hätte es nicht für möglich gehalten, doch aus irgendeinem Grund hatte de Thou das Gefühl, bei diesem Gespräch den kürzeren gezogen zu haben, ganz abgesehen davon, daß ihn der Vorwurf des Verrates stärker traf, als er erkennen ließ.

»Monseigneur«, rief er dem Kardinal nach, um den schlechten Geschmack der Niederlage aus seinem Mund zu vertreiben, »ich hoffe doch, Ihr habt Euren Handlanger, der uns ans Messer geliefert hat, gebührend belohnt?«

Der Kardinal drehte sich noch einmal um. Sein Gesicht wurde durch den Schatten, den die geöffnete Tür warf, scharf in zwei Hälften geteilt.

»Ich weiß nicht, wen Ihr meint«, sagte er langsam. »Aber falls Ihr Euch auf den Musketier beziehen solltet, der so zuvorkommend war, mir das Leben zu retten, dann wäre ich Euch für nähere Auskünfte dankbar. Der Mann scheint den Dienst Seiner Majestät nämlich quittiert zu haben, ohne Wert auf eine Belohnung zu legen.«

»Ihr wißt genau, daß ich Euch nichts sagen werde, was man als Geständnis auslegen kann.«

»De Thou«, erwiderte der Kardinal, und Auguste de Thou meinte, leise Belustigung herauszuhören, »Ihr habt mir schon längst alles gestanden, was ich wissen wollte.«